Science in the Kitchen

A Scientific Treatise On Food Substances and Their Dietetic Properties, Together with a Practical Explanation of the Principles of Healthful Cookery, and a Large Number of Original, Palatable, and Wholesome Recipes

BY

Ella Eaton Kellogg

Foods

The purposes of food are to promote growth, to supply force and heat, and to furnish material to repair the waste which is constantly taking place in the body. Every breath, every thought, every motion, wears out some portion of the delicate and wonderful house in which we live. Various vital processes remove these worn and useless particles; and to keep the body in health, their loss must be made good by constantly renewed supplies of material properly adapted to replenish the worn and impaired tissues. This renovating material must be supplied through the medium of food and drink, and the best food is that by which the desired end may be most readily and perfectly attained. The great diversity in character of the several tissues of the body, makes it necessary that food should contain a variety of elements, in order that each part may be properly nourished and replenished.

The Food Elements.—The various elements found in food are the following: Starch, sugar, fats, albumen, mineral substances, indigestible substances.

The digestible food elements are often grouped, according to their chemical composition, into three classes; *vis.*, carbonaceous, nitrogenous, and inorganic. The carbonaceous class includes starch, sugar, and fats; the nitrogenous, all albuminous elements; and the inorganic comprises the mineral elements.

Starch is only found in vegetable foods; all grains, most vegetables, and some fruits, contain starch in abundance. Several kinds of *sugar* are made in nature's laboratory; *cane*, *grape*, *fruit*, and *milk* sugar. The first is obtained from the sugar-cane, the sap of maple trees, and from the beet root. Grape and fruit sugars are found in most fruits and in honey. Milk sugar is one of the constituents of milk. Glucose, an artificial sugar resembling grape sugar, is now largely manufactured by subjecting the starch of corn or potatoes to a chemical process; but it lacks the sweetness of natural sugars, and is by no means a proper substitute for them. *Albumen* is found in its purest, uncombined state in the white of an egg, which is almost wholly composed of albumen. It exists, combined with other food elements, in many other foods, both animal and vegetable. It is found abundant in oatmeal, and to some extent in the other grains, and in the juices of vegetables. All natural foods contain elements which in many respects resemble *albumen*, and are so closely allied to it that for convenience they are usually classified under the general name of "albumen." The chief of these is *gluten*, which is found in wheat, rye, and barley. *Casein*, found in peas, beans, and milk, and the *fibrin* of flesh, are elements of this class.

Fats are found in both animal and vegetable foods. Of animal fats, butter and suet are common examples. In vegetable form, fat is abundant in nuts, peas, beans, in various of the grains, and in a few fruits, as the olive. As furnished by nature in nuts, legumes, grains, fruits, and milk, this element is always found in a state of fine subdivision, which condition is the one best adapted to its digestion. As most commonly used, in the form of free fats, as butter, lard, etc., it is not only difficult of digestion itself, but often interferes with the digestion of the other food elements which are mixed with it. It was doubtless never intended that fats should be so modified from their natural condition and separated from other food elements as to be used as a separate article of food. The same may be said of the other carbonaceous elements, sugar and starch, neither of which, when used alone, is capable of sustaining life, although when combined in a proper and natural manner with other food elements, they perform a most important part in the nutrition of the body. Most foods contain a percentage of the *mineral* elements. Grains and milk furnish these elements in abundance. The cellulose, or woody tissue, of vegetables, and the bran of wheat, are examples of *indigestible* elements, which although they cannot be converted into blood in tissue, serve an important purpose by giving bulk to the food.

With the exception of gluten, none of the food elements, when used alone, are capable of supporting life. A true food substance contains some of all the food elements, the amount of each varying in different foods.

Uses of the Food Elements.—Concerning the purpose which these different elements serve, it has been demonstrated by the experiments of eminent physiologists that the carbonaceous elements, which in general comprise the greater bulk of the food, serve three purposes in the body;

1. They furnish material for the production of heat;

2. They are a source of force when taken in connection with other food elements;

3. They replenish the fatty tissues of the body. Of the carbonaceous elements,—starch, sugar, and fats,—fats produce the greatest amount of heat in proportion to quantity; that is, more heat is developed from a pound of fat than from an equal weight of sugar or starch; but this apparent advantage is more than counterbalanced by the fact that fats are much more difficult of digestion than are the other carbonaceous elements, and if relied upon to furnish adequate material for bodily heat, would be productive of much mischief in overtaxing and producing disease of the digestive organs. The fact that nature has made a much more ample provision of starch and sugars than of fats in man's natural diet, would seem to indicate that they were intended to be the chief source of carbonaceous food; nevertheless, fats, when taken in such proportion as nature supplies them, are necessary and important food elements.

The nitrogenous food elements especially nourish the brain, nerves, muscles, and all the more highly vitalized and active tissues of the body, and also serve as a stimulus to tissue change. Hence it may be said that a food deficient in these elements is a particularly poor food.

The inorganic elements, chief of which are the phosphates, in the carbonates of potash, soda, and lime, aid in furnishing the requisite building material for bones and nerves.

Proper Combinations of Foods.—While it is important that our food should contain some of all the various food elements, experiments upon both animals and human beings show it is necessary that these elements, especially the nitrogenous and carbonaceous, be used in certain definite proportions, as the system is only able to appropriate a certain amount of each; and all excess, especially of nitrogenous elements, is not only useless, but even injurious, since to rid the system of the surplus imposes an additional task upon the digestive and excretory organs. The relative proportion of these elements necessary to constitute a food which perfectly meets the requirements of the system, is six of carbonaceous to one of nitrogenous. Scientists have devoted much careful study and experimentation to the determination of the quantities of each of the food elements required for the daily nourishment of individuals under the varying conditions of life, and it has come to be commonly accepted that of the nitrogenous material which should constitute one sixth of the nutrients taken, about *three ounces* is all that can be made use of in twenty-four hours, by a healthy adult of average weight, doing a moderate amount of work. Many articles of food are, however, deficient in one or the other of these elements, and need to be supplemented by other articles containing the deficient element in superabundance, since to employ a dietary in which any one of the nutritive elements is lacking, although in bulk it may be all the digestive organs can manage, is really starvation, and will in time occasion serious results.

It is thus apparent that much care should be exercised in the selection and combination of food materials. The table on page 484, showing the nutritive values of various foods, should be carefully studied. Such knowledge is of first importance in the education of cooks and housekeepers, since to them falls the selection of the food for the daily needs of the household; and they should not only understand what foods are best suited to supply these needs, but how to combine them in accordance with physiological laws.

Condiments.—By condiments are commonly meant such substances as are added to season food, to give it "a relish" or to stimulate appetite, but which in themselves possess no real food value. To this category belong mustard, ginger, pepper, pepper sauce, Worcestershire sauce, cloves, spices, and other similar substances. That anything is needed to disguise or improve the natural flavor of food, would seem to imply either that the article used was not a proper alimentary substance, or that it did not answer the purpose for which the Creator designed it. True condiments, such as pepper, pepper sauce, ginger, spice, mustard, cinnamon, cloves, etc., are all strong irritants. This may be readily demonstrated by their application to a raw surface. The intense smarting and burning occasioned are ample evidence of the irritating character. Pepper and mustard are capable of producing powerfully irritating effects, even when applied to the healthy skin where wholly intact. It is surprising that it does not occur to the mother who applies a mustard plaster to the feet of her child, to relieve congestion of the brain, that an article which is capable of producing a blister upon the external covering of the body, is quite as capable of producing similar effects when applied to the more sensitive tissues within the body. The irritating effects of these substances upon the stomach are not readily recognized, simply because the stomach is supplied with very few nerves of sensation. That condiments induce an intense degree of irritation of the mucous membrane of the stomach, was abundantly demonstrated by the experiments of Dr. Beaumont upon the unfortunate Alexis St. Martin. Dr. Beaumont records that when St. Martin took mustard, pepper, and similar condiments with his food, the mucous membrane of his stomach became intensely red and congested, appearing very much like an inflamed eye. It is this irritating effect of condiments which gives occasion for their extended use. They create an artificial appetite, similar to the incessant craving of the chronic dyspeptic, whose irritable stomach is seldom satisfied. This fact with regard to condiments is a sufficient argument against their use, being one of the greatest causes of gluttony, since they remove the sense of satiety by which Nature says, "Enough."

To a thoroughly normal and unperverted taste, irritating condiments of all sorts are very obnoxious. It is true that Nature accommodates herself to their use with food to such a degree that they may be employed for years without apparently producing very grave results; but this very condition is a source of injury, since it is nothing more nor less than the going to sleep of the sentinels which nature has posted at the portal of the body, forthe purpose of giving warning of danger. The nerves of sensibility have become benumbed to such a degree that they no longer offer remonstrance against irritating substances, and allow the enemy to enter into the citadel of life. The mischievous work is thus insidiously carried on year after year until by and by the individual breaks down with some chronic disorder of the liver, kidneys, or some other important internal organ. Physicians have long observed that in tropical countries where curry powder and other condiments are very extensively used, diseases of the liver, especially acute congestion and inflammation, are exceedingly common, much more so that in countries and among nations where condiments are less freely used. A traveler in Mexico, some time ago, described a favorite Mexican dish as composed of layers of the following ingredients: "Pepper, mustard, ginger, pepper, potato, ginger; mustard, pepper, potato, mustard, ginger, pepper." The common use of such a dish is sufficient cause for the great frequency of diseases of the liver among the Mexicans, noted by physicians traveling in that country. That the use of condiments is wholly a matter of habit is evident from the fact that different nations employ as condiments articles which would be in the highest degree obnoxious to people of other countries. For example, the garlic so freely used in Russian cookery, would be considered by Americans no addition to the natural flavors of food; and still more distasteful would be the asafetida frequently used as a seasoning in the cuisine of Persia and other Asiatic countries.

The use of condiments is unquestionably a strong auxiliary to the formation of a habit of using intoxicating drinks. Persons addicted to the use of intoxicating liquors are, as a rule, fond of stimulating and highly seasoned foods; and although the converse is not always true, yet it is apparent to every thoughtful person, that the use of a diet composed of highly seasoned and irritating food, institutes the conditions necessary for the acquirement of a taste for intoxicating liquors. The false appetite aroused by the use of food that "burns and stings," craves something less insipid than pure cold water to keep up the fever the food has excited. Again, condiments, like all other stimulants, must be continually increased in quantity, or their effect becomes diminished; and this leads directly to a demand for stronger stimulants, both in eating and drinking, until the probable tendency is toward the dram-shop.

A more serious reason why high seasonings leads to intemperance, is in the perversion of the use of the sense of taste. Certain senses are given us to add to our pleasure as well as for the practical, almost indispensable, use they are to us. For instance, the sense of sight is not only useful, but enables us to drink in beauty, if among beautiful surroundings, without doing us any harm. The same of music and other harmonics which may come to us through the sense of hearing. But the sense of taste and was given us to distinguish between wholesome and unwholesome foods, and cannot be used for merely sensuous gratification, without debasing and making of it a gross thing. An education which demands special enjoyment or pleasure through the sense of taste, is wholly artificial; it is coming down to the animal plane, or below it rather; for the instinct of the brute creation teaches it merely to eat to live.

Yet how wide-spread is this habit of sensuous gratification through the sense of taste! If one calls upon a neighbor, he is at once offered refreshments of some kind, as though the greatest blessing of life came from indulging the appetite. This evil is largely due to wrong education, which begins with childhood. When Johnnie sits down to the table, the mother says, "Johnnie, what would you like?" instead of putting plain, wholesome food before the child, and taking it as a matter of course that he will eat it and be satisfied. The child grows to think that he must have what he likes, whether it is good for him or not. It is not strange that an appetite thus pampered in childhood becomes uncontrollable at maturity; for the step from gormandizing to intoxication is much shorter than most people imagine. The natural, unperverted taste of a child will lead him to eat that which is good for him. But how can we expect the children to reform when the parents continually set them bad examples in the matter of eating and drinking?

The cultivation of a taste for spices is a degradation of the sense of taste. Nature never designed that pleasure should be divorced from use. The effects of gratifying the sense of taste differ materially from those of gratifying the higher senses of sight and hearing. What we see is gone; nothing remains but the memory, and the same is true of the sweetest sounds which may reach us through the ears. But what we taste is taken into the stomach and what has thus given us brief pleasure through the gratification of the palate, must make work in the alimentary canal for fourteen hours before it is disposed of.

Variety in Food.—Simplicity of diet should be a point of first consideration with all persons upon whom falls the responsibility of providing the family bills of fare, since the simplest foods are, as a rule, the most healthful. Variety is needed; that is, a judicious mingling of fruits, grains, and vegetables; but the general tendency is to supply our tables with too many kinds and to prepare each dish in the most elaborate manner, until, in many households, the cooking of food has come to be almost the chief end of life. While the preparation of food should be looked upon as of so much importance as to demand the most careful consideration and thought as to its suitability, wholesomeness, nutritive qualities, and digestibility, it should by no means be made to usurp the larger share of one's time, when simpler foods and less labor would afford the partakers equal nourishment and strength.

A great variety of foods at one meal exerts a potent influence in creating a love of eating, and is likewise a constant temptation to overeat. Let us have well-cooked, nutritious, and palatable food, and plenty of it; variety from day to day, but not too great a variety at each meal.

The prevalent custom of loading the table with a great number of viands, upon occasions when guests are to be entertained in our homes, is one to be deplored, since it is neither conducive to good health nor necessary to good cheer, but on the contrary is still laborious and expensive a practice that many are debarred from social intercourse because they cannot afford to entertain after the fashion of their neighbors. Upon this subject a well-known writer has aptly said: "Simplify cookery, thus reducing the cost of living, and how many longing individuals would therebybe enabled to afford themselves the pleasure of culture and social intercourse! When the barbarous practice of stuffing one's guests shall have been abolished, a social gathering will not then imply, as it does now, hard labor, expensive outlay, and dyspepsia. Perhaps when that time arise, we shall be sufficiently civilized to demand pleasures of a higher sort. True, the entertainments will then, in one sense, be more costly, as culture is harder to come by than cake. The profusion of viands now heaped upon the table, betrays poverty of the worst sort. Having nothing better to offer, we offer victuals; and this we do with something of that complacent, satisfied air with which some more northern tribes present their tidbits of whale and walrus."

TABLE TOPICS.

"Let appetite wear reason's golden chain,
and find in due restrain its luxury."

A man's food, when he has the means and opportunity of selecting it, suggests his moral nature. Many a Christian is trying to do by prayer that which cannot be done except through corrected diet. —*Talmage.*

Our pious ancestors enacted a law that suicides should be buried where four roads meet, and that a cart-load of stones should be thrown upon the body. Yet, when gentlemen or ladies commit suicide, not by cord or steel, but by turtle soup or lobster salad, they may be buried on consecrated ground, and the public are not ashamed to read an epitaph upon their tombstones false enough to make the marble blush.—*Horace Mann.*

It is related by a gentleman who had an appointment to breakfast with the late A.T. Stewart, that the butler placed before them both an elaborate bill of fare; the visitor selected a list of rare dishes, and was quite abashed when Mr. Stewart said, "Bring me my usual breakfast,—oatmeal and boiled eggs." He then explained to his friend that he found simple food a necessity to him, otherwise he could not think clearly. That unobscured brain applied to nobler ends would have won higher results, but the principle remains the same.—*Sel.*

Study simplicity in the number of dishes, and a variety in the character of the meals.—*Sel.*

I have come to the conclusion that more than half the disease which embitters life is due to avoidable errors in diet, ... and that more mischief, in the form of actual disease, of impaired vigor, and of shortened life, accrues to civilized man from erroneous habits of eating than from the habitual use of alcoholic drink, considerable as I know that evil to be.—*Sir Henry Thompson.*

The ancient Gauls, who were a very brave, strong, and hearty race, lived very abstemiously. Their food was milk, berries, and herbs. They made bread of nuts. They had a very peculiar fashion of wearing a metal ring around the body, the size of which was regulated by act of Parliament. Any man who outgrew in circumference his metal ring was looked upon as a lazy glutton, and consequently was disgraced.

To keep in health this rule is wise:
Eat only when you need, and relish food,
chew thoroughly that it may do you good,
have it well cooked, unspiced, and undisguised.—*Leonardo da Vinci!*

THE DIGESTION OF FOODS.

It is important that the housekeeper not only understand the nature and composition of foods, but she should also know something of their digestive properties, since food, to be serviceable, must be not only nutritious, but easily digested. Digestion is the process by which food rendered soluble, and capable of being absorbed for use in carrying on the various vital processes.

The digestive apparatus consists of a long and tortuous tube called the alimentary canal, varying in length from twenty-five to thirty feet, along which are arranged the various digestive organs,—the mouth, the stomach, the liver, and the pancreas,—each of which, together with the intestines, has an important function to perform. In these various organs nature manufactures five wonderful fluids for changing and dissolving the several food elements. The mouth supplies the saliva; in the walls of the stomach are little glands which produce the gastric juice; the pancreatic juice is made by the pancreas; the liver secretes bile; while scattered along the small intestines are minute glands which make the intestinal juice. Each of these fluids has a particular work to do in transforming some part of the food into suitable material for use in the body. The saliva acts upon the starch of the food, changing it into sugar; the gastric juice digests albumen and other nitrogenous elements; the bile digests fat, and aids in the absorption of other food elements after they are digested; the pancreatic juice is not confined in its action to a single element, but digests starch, fats, and the albuminous elements after they have been acted upon by the gastric juice; the intestinal juice is capable of acting upon all digestible food elements.

The Digestion of a Mouthful of Bread—A mouthful of bread represents all, or nearly all, the elements of nutrition. Taking a mouthful of bread as a representative of food in general, it may be said that its digestion begins the moment that it enters the mouth, and continues the entire length of the alimentary canal, or until the digestible portion of the food has been completely digested and absorbed. We quote the following brief description of the digestive process from Dr. J.H. Kellogg's Second Book in Physiology[A]:—

[A]

Good Health Pub. Co., Battle Creek, Mich.

"*Mastication.*—The first act of the digestive process is mastication, or chewing the food, the purpose of which is to crush the food and divide it into small particles, so that the various digestive fluids may easily and promptly come into contact with every part of it.

"*Salivary Digestion.*—During the mastication of the food, the salivary glands are actively pouring out the saliva, which mingles with the food, and by softening it, aids in its division and prepares it for the action of the other digestive fluids. It also acts upon the starch, converting a portion of it into grape-sugar.

"*Stomach Digestion.*—After receiving the food, the stomach soon begins to pour out the gastric juices, which first makes its appearance in little drops, like beads of sweat upon the face when the perspiration starts.

As the quantity increases, the drops run together, trickle down the side of the stomach, and mingle with the food. The muscular walls of the stomach contract upon the food, moving it about with a sort of crushing action, thoroughly mixing the gastric juice with the food. During this process both the openings of the stomach are closed tightly. The gastric juice softens the food, digests albumen, and coagulates milk. The saliva continues its action upon starch for sometime after the food reaches the stomach.

"After the food has remained in the stomach from one to three hours, or even longer, if the digestion is slow, or indigestible foods have been eaten, the contractions of the stomach become so vigorous that the more fluid portions of the food are squeezed out through the pylorus, the lower orifice of the stomach, thus escaping into the intestine. The pylorus does not exercise any sort of intelligence in the selection of food, as was once supposed. The increasing acidity of the contents of the stomach causes its muscular walls to contract with increasing vigor, until finally those portions of the food which may be less perfectly broken up, but which the stomach has been unable to digest, are forced through the pylorus.

"*Intestinal Digestion.*—As it leaves the stomach, the partially digested mass of food is intensely acid, from the large quantity of gastric juices which it contains. Intestinal digestion cannot begin until the food becomes alkaline. The alkaline bile neutralizes the gastric juice, and renders the digesting mass slightly alkaline. The bile also acts upon the fatty elements of the food, converting them into an emulsion. The pancreatic juice converts the starch into grape-sugar, even acting upon raw starch. It also digest fats and albumen. The intestinal juice continues the work begun by the other digestive fluids, and, in addition, digests cane-sugar, converting it into grape-sugar.

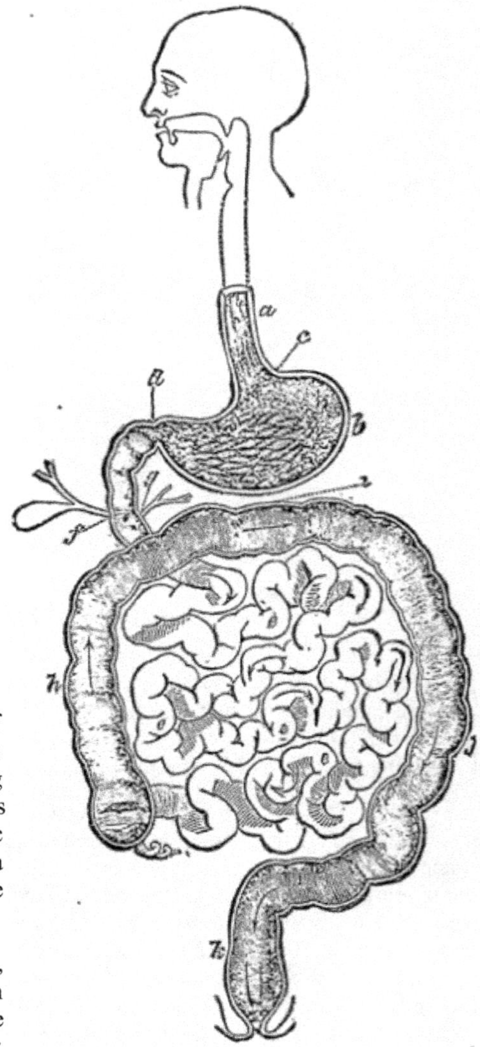

The Alimentary Canal

- a. Esophagus;
- b. Stomach;
- c. Cardiac Orifice;
- d. Pylorus;
- e. Small Intestine;
- f. Bile Duct;
- g. Pancreatic Duct;
- h. Ascending Colon;
- i. Transverse Colon;
- j. Descending Colon;
- k. Rectum.

"*Other Uses of the Digestive Fluids.*—In addition to the uses which we have already stated, several of the digestive fluids possess other interesting properties. The saliva aids the stomach by stimulating its glands to make gastric juice. The gastric juice and the bile are excellent antiseptics, by which the food is preserved from fermentation while undergoing digestion. The bile also stimulates the movements of the intestines by which the food is moved along, and aids absorption. It is remarkable and interesting that a fluid so useful as the bile should be at the same time composed of waste matters which are being removed from the body. This is an illustration of the wonderful economy shown by nature in her operations.

"The food is moved along the alimentary canal, from the stomach downward, by successive contractions of the muscular walls of the intestines, known as peristaltic movements, which occur with great regularity during digestion.

"*Absorption.*—The absorption of the food begins as soon as any portion has been digested. Even in the mouth and the esophagus a small amount is absorbed. The entire mucous membrane lining the digestive canal is furnished with a rich supply of blood-vessels, by which the greater part of the digestive food is absorbed.

"*Liver Digestion.*—The liver as well as the stomach is a digestive organ, and in a double sense. It not only secretes a digestive fluid, the bile, but it acts upon the food brought to it by the portal vein, and regulates the supply of digested food to the general system. It converts a large share of the grape-sugar and partially digested starch brought to it into a kind of liver starch, termed glycogen, which it stores up in its tissues. During the interval between the meals, the liver gradually redigests the glycogen, reconverting it into sugar, and thus supplying it to the blood in small quantities, instead of allowing the entire amount formed in digestion to enter the circulation at once. If too large an amount of sugar entered the system at once, it would be unable to use it all, and would be compelled to get rid of a considerable portion through the kidneys. The liver also completes the digestion of albumen and other food elements."

Time Required for Digestion.—The length of time required for stomach digestion varies with different food substances. The following table shows the time necessary for the stomach digestion of some of the more commonly used foods:—

	hrs	min
Rice	1	00
Sago	1	45
Tapioca	2	00
Barley	2	00
Beans, pod, boiled	2	30
Bread, wheaten	3	30
Bread, corn	3	15
Apples, sour and raw	2	00
Apples, sweet and raw	1	30
Parsnips, boiled	2	30
Beets, boiled	3	45
Potatoes, Irish, boiled	3	30
Potatoes, Irish, baked	2	30
Cabbage, raw	2	30
Cabbage, boiled	4	30
Milk, boiled	2	00
Milk, raw	2	15
Eggs, hard boiled	3	30
Eggs, soft boiled	3	00
Eggs, fried	3	30
Eggs, raw	2	00
Eggs, whipped	1	30
Salmon, salted, boiled	4	00
Oysters, raw	2	55
Oysters, stewed	3	30
Beef, lean, rare roasted	3	00
Beefsteak, boiled	3	00
Beef, lean, fried	4	00
Beef, salted, boiled	4	15
Pork, roasted	5	15
Pork, salted, fried	4	15
Mutton, roasted	3	15
Mutton, broiled	3	00
Veal, broiled	4	00
Veal, fried	4	30
Fowls, boiled	4	00

Duck, roasted	4	30
Butter, melted	3	30
Cheese	3	30
Soup, marrowbone	4	15
Soup, bean	3	00
Soup, mutton	3	30
Chicken, boiled	3	00

The time required for the digestion of food also depends upon the condition under which the food is eaten. Healthy stomach digestion requires at least five hours for its completion, and the stomach should have an hour for rest before another meal. If fresh food is taken before that which preceded it is digested, the portion of food remaining in the stomach is likely to undergo fermentation, thus rendering the whole mass of food unfit for the nutrition of the body, besides fostering various disturbances of digestion. It has been shown by recent observations that the length of time required for food to pass through the entire digestive process to which it is subjected in the mouth, stomach, and small intestines, is from twelve to fourteen hours.

Hygiene of Digestion.—With the stomach and other digestive organs in a state of perfect health, one is entirely unconscious of their existence, save when of feeling of hunger calls attention to the fact that food is required, or satiety warns us that a sufficient amount or too much has been eaten. Perfect digestion can only be maintained by careful observance of the rules of health in regard to habits of eating.

On the subject of Hygiene of Digestion, we again quote a few paragraphs from Dr. Kellogg's work on Physiology, in which is given a concise summary of the more important points relating to this:—

"The hygiene of digestion has to do with the quality and quantity of food eaten, in the manner of eating it.

"*Hasty Eating.*—If the food is eaten too rapidly, it will not be properly divided, and when swallowed in coarse lumps, the digestive fluids cannot readily act upon it. On account of the insufficient mastication, the saliva will be deficient in quantity, and, as a consequence, the starch will not be well digested, and the stomach will not secrete a sufficient amount of gastric juice. It is not well to eat only soft or liquid food, as we are likely to swallow it without proper chewing. A considerable proportion of hard food, which requires thorough mastication, should be eaten at every meal.

"*Drinking Freely at Meals* is harmful, as it not only encourages hasty eating, but dilutes the gastric juice, and thus lessens its activity. The food should be chewed until sufficiently moistened by saliva to allow it to be swallowed. When large quantities of fluid are taken into the stomach, digestion does not begin until a considerable portion of the fluid has been absorbed. If cold foods or drinks are taken with the meal, such as ice-cream, ice-water, iced milk or tea, the stomach is chilled, and a long delay in the digestive process is occasioned.

"The Indians of Brazil carefully abstain from drinking when eating, and the same custom prevails among many other savage tribes.

"*Eating between Meals.*—The habit of eating apples, nuts, fruits, confectionery, etc., between meals is exceedingly harmful, and certain to produce loss of appetite and indigestion. The stomach as well as the muscles and other organs of the body requires rest. The frequency with which meals should be taken depends somewhat upon the age and occupation of an individual. Infants take their food at short intervals, and owing to its simple character, are able to digest it very quickly. Adults should not take food oftener than three times a day; and persons whose employment is sedentary say, in many cases at least, adopt with advantage the plan of the ancient Greeks, who ate but twice a day. The latter custom is quite general among the higher classes in France and Spain, and in several South American countries.

"*Simplicity in Diet.*—Taking too many kinds of food at a meal is a common fault which is often a cause of disease of the digestive-organs. Those nations are the most hardy and enduring whose dietary is most simple. The Scotch peasantry live chiefly upon oatmeal, the Irish upon potatoes, milk, and oatmeal, the Italian upon peas, beans, macaroni, and chestnuts; yet all these are noted for remarkable health and endurance. The natives of the Canary Islands, an exceedingly well-developed and vigorous race, subsist almost chiefly upon a food which they call gofio, consisting of parched grain, coarsely ground in a mortar and mixed with water.

"*Eating when Tired.*—It is not well to eat when exhausted by violent exercise, as the system is not prepared to do the work of digestion well. Sleeping immediately after eating is also a harmful practice. The process of digestion cannot well be performed during sleep, and sleep is disturbed by the ineffective efforts of the digestive organs. Hence the well-known evil effects of late suppers.

"*Eating too Much.*—Hasty eating is the greatest cause of over-eating. When one eats too rapidly, the food is crowded into the stomach so fast that nature has no time to cry, 'Enough,' by taking away the appetite before too much has been eaten. When an excess of food is taken, it is likely to ferment or sour before it can be digested. One who eats too much usually feels dull after eating.

"*How Much Food is Enough?*—The proper quantity for each person to take is what he is able to digest and utilize. This amount of various with each individual, at different times. The amount needed will vary with the amount of work done, mental or muscular; with the weather or the season of the year, more food being required in cold than in warm weather: with the age of an individual, very old and very young persons requiring less food than those of middle age. An unperverted appetite, not artificially stimulated, is a safe guide. Drowsiness, dullness, and heaviness at the stomach are indications of an excess of eating, and naturally suggest a lessening of the quantity of food, unless the symptoms are known to arise from some other cause.

"*Excess of Certain Food Elements.*—When sugar is too freely used, either with food or in the form of sweetmeats or candies, indigestion, and even more serious disease, is likely to result. Fats, when freely used, give rise to indigestion and 'biliousness.' An excess of albumen from the too free use of meat is harmful. Only a limited amount of this element can be used; an excess is treated as waste matter, and must be removed from the system by the liver and the kidneys. The majority of persons would enjoy better health by using meat more moderately than is customary in this country.

"*Deficiency of Certain Food Elements.*—A diet deficient in any important food element is even more detrimental to health than a diet in which certain elements are in excess.

"The popular notion that beef-tea and meat extracts contain the nourishing elements of meat in a concentrated form, is a dangerous error. Undoubtedly many sick persons have been starved by being fed exclusively upon these articles, which are almost wholly composed of waste substances. Prof. Paule Bernard, of Paris, found that dogs fed upon meat extracts died sooner than those which received only water."

Food combinations.—Some persons, especially those of weak digestive powers, often experience inconvenience in the use of certain foods, owing to their improper combinations with other articles. Many foods which are digested easily when partaken of alone or in harmonious combinations, create much disturbance when eaten at the same meal with several different articles of food, or with some particular article with which they are especially incompatible. The following food combinations are among the best, the relative excellence of each being indicated by the order in which they are named: Milk and grains; grains and eggs; grains and vegetables or meats; grains and fruits.

Persons with sound stomachs and vigorous digestion will seldom experience inconvenience in making use of other and more varied combinations, but dyspeptics and persons troubled with slow digestion will find it to their advantage to select from the bill of fare such articles as best accord with each other, and to avoid such combinations as fruits and vegetables, milk and vegetables, milk and meats, sugar and milk, meat or vegetables, fats with fruits, meats, or vegetables, or cooked with grains.

TABLE TOPICS.

Now good digestion waits on appetite, and health on both—*Shakespeare.*

We live not upon what we eat, but upon what we digest.—*Abernethy.*

If we consider the amount of ill temper, despondency, and general unhappiness which arises from want of proper digestion and assimilation of our food, it seems obviously well worth while to put forth every effort, and undergo any sacrifice, for the purpose of avoiding indigestion, with its resulting bodily ills; and yet year after year, from the cradle to the grave, we go on violating the plainest and simplest laws of health at the temptation of Cooks, caterers, and confectioners, whose share in shortening the average term of human life is probably nearly equal to that of the combined armies and navies of the world.—*Richardson.*

Almost every human malady is connected, either by highway or byway, with the stomach.—*Sir Francis Head.*

It is a well-established fact that a leg of mutton caused a revolution in the affairs of Europe. Just before the battle of Leipsic, Napoleon the Great insisted on dining on boiled mutton, although his physicians warned him that it would disagree with him. The emperor's brain resented the liberty taken with its colleague, the stomach; the monarch's equilibrium was overturned, the battle lost, and a new page opened in history.—*Sel.*

Galloping consumption at the dinner table is one of the national disorders.—*Sel.*

The kitchen (that is, your stomach) being out of order, the garret (the head) cannot be right, and every room in the house becomes affected. Remedy the evil in the kitchen, and all will be right in parlor and chamber. If you put improper food into the stomach, you play the mischief with it, and with the whole machine besides.—*Abernethy.*

Cattle know when to go home from grazing, but a foolish man never knows his stomachs measures.—*Scandinavian proverb.*

Enough is as good as a feast.

Simplicity of diet is the characteristic of the dwellers in the Orient. According to Niebuhr, the sheik of the desert wants only a dish of pillau, or boiled rice, which he eats without fork or spoon. Notwithstanding their frugal fare, these sons of the desert are among the most hearty and enduring of all members of the human family. A traveler tells of seeing one of them run up to the top of the tallest pyramid and back in six minutes.

One fourth of what we eat keeps us, and the other three fourths we keep at the peril of our lives. —*Abernethy.*

COOKERY.

It is not enough that good and proper food material be provided; it must have such preparation as will increase and not diminish its alimentary value. The unwholesomeness of food is quite as often due to bad cookery as to improper selection of material. Proper cookery renders good food material more digestible. When scientifically done, cooking changes each of the food elements, with the exception of fats, in much the same manner as do the digestive juices, and at the same time it breaks up the food by dissolving the soluble portions, so that its elements are more readily acted upon by the digestive fluids. Cookery, however, often fails to attain the desired end; and the best material is rendered useless and unwholesome by a improper preparation.

It is rare to find a table, some portion of the food upon which is not rendered unwholesome either by improper preparatory treatment, or by the addition of some deleterious substance. This is doubtless due to the fact that the preparation of food being such a commonplace matter, its important relations to health, mind, and body have been overlooked, and it has been regarded as a menial service which might be undertaken with little or no preparation, and without attention to matters other than those which relate to the pleasure of the eye and the palate. With taste only as a criterion, it is so easy to disguise the results of careless and improper cookery of food by the use of flavors and condiments, as well as to palm off upon the digestive organs all sorts of inferior material, that poor cookery has come to be the rule rather than the exception.

Another reason for this prevalence of bad cookery, is to be found in the fact that in so many homes the cooking is intrusted to an ignorant class of persons having no knowledge whatever of the scientific principles involved in this most important and practical of arts. An ethical problem which we have been unable to solve is the fact that women who would never think of trusting the care of their fine china and bric-a-brac to unskilled hands, unhesitatingly intrust to persons who are almost wholly untrained, the preparation of their daily food. There is no department of life where superior intelligence is more needed than in the selection and preparation of food, upon which so largely depend the health and physical welfare of the family circle.

The evils of bad cookery and ill-selected food are manifold, so many, in fact, that it has been calculated that they far exceed the mischief arising from the use of strong drink; indeed, one of the evils of unwholesome food is its decided tendency to create a craving for intoxicants. Bad cookery causes indigestion, indigestion causes thirst, and thirst perpetuates drunkenness. Any one who has suffered from a fit of indigestion, and can recollect the accompanying headache and the lowness of spirits, varying in degree from dejection or ill-humor to the most extreme melancholy, until the intellectual faculties seemed dazed, and the moral feelings blunted, will hardly wonder that when such a condition becomes chronic, as is often the case from the use of improperly prepared food, the victim is easily led to resort to stimulants to drown depression and enliven the spirits.

A thorough practical knowledge of simple, wholesome cookery ought to form a part of the education of every young woman, whatever her station in life. No position in life is more responsible than that of the person who arranges the bills of fare and selects the food for the household; and what higher mission can one conceive than to intelligently prepare the wherewithal to make shoulders strong to bear life's burdens and heads clear to solve its intricate problems? what worthier work than to help in the building up of bodies into pure temples fit for guests of noble thoughts and high purposes? Surely, no one should undertake such important work without a knowledge of the principles involved.

THE PRINCIPLES OF SCIENTIFIC COOKERY.

Cookery is the art of preparing food for the table by dressing, or by the application of heat in some manner.

Fuels.—Artificial heat is commonly produced by combustion, caused by the chemical action of the oxygen of the air upon the hydrogen and carbon found in fuel. The different fuels in common use for cooking purposes are hard wood, soft wood, charcoal, anthracite coal, bituminous coal, coke, lignite, kerosene oil, gasoline, and gas. As to their respective values, much depends upon the purpose for which they are to be used. Wood charcoal produces a greater amount of heat than an equal weight of any other fuel. Soft wood burns quicker and gives a more intense heat than hard wood, and hence is best for a quick fire. Hard wood burns slowly, produces a larger mass of coals, and is best where long-continued heat is desired. Anthracite coal kindles slowly, and burns with little flame or smoke, but its vapor is sulphurous, and on that account it should never be burned in an open stove, nor in one with an imperfect draft. Its heat is steady and intense. Bituminous coal ignites readily, burns with considerable flame and smoke, and gives a much less intense heat than anthracite, Lignite, or brown coal, is much less valuable as fuel. Coke is useful when a short, quick fire is needed. Kerosene and gas are convenient and economical fuels.

Making Fires.—If coal is the fuel to be used, first clean out the stove by shaking the grate and removing all ashes and cinders. Remove the stove covers, and brush the soot and ashes out of all the flues and draft holes into the fire-box. Place a large handful of shavings or loosely twisted or crumpled papers upon the grate, over which lay some fine pieces of dry kindling-wood, arranged crosswise to permit a free draft, then a few sticks of hard wood, so placed as to allow plenty of air spaces. Be sure that the wood extends out to both ends of the fire-box. Replace the covers, and if the stove needs blacking, mix the polish, and apply it, rubbing with a dry brush until nearly dry, then light the fuel, as a little heat will facilitate the polishing. When the wood is burning briskly, place a shovelful or two of rather small pieces of coal upon the wood, and, as they ignite, gradually add more, until there is a clear, bright body of fire, remembering, however, never to fill the stove above the fire bricks; then partly close the direct draft. When wood or soft coal is used, the fuel may be added at the same time with the kindling.

Care of Fires.—Much fuel is wasted through the loss of heat from too much draft. Only just enough air should be supplied to promote combustion. A coal fire, when well kindled, needs only air enough to keep it burning. When the coal becomes red all through, it has parted with the most of its heat, and the fire will soon die unless replenished. To keep a steady fire, add but a small amount of fuel at a time, and repeat often enough to prevent any sensible decrease of the degree of heat. Rake the fire from the bottom, and keep it clear of ashes and cinders. If a very hot fire is needed, open the drafts; at other times, keep them closed, or partially so, and not waste fuel. There is no economy in allowing a fire to get low before fuel is added; for the fresh fuel cools the fire to a temperature so low that it is not useful, and thus occasions a direct waste of all fuel necessary to again raise the heat to the proper degree, to say nothing of the waste of time and patience. The addition of small quantities of fuel at short intervals so long as continuous heat is needed, is far better than to let the fuel burn nearly out, and then add a larger quantity. The improper management of the drafts and dampers has also much to do with waste of fuel. As stoves are generally constructed, it is necessary for the heat to pass over the top, down the back, and under the bottom of the oven before escaping into the flue, in order to properly heat the oven for baking. In order to force the heat to make this circuit, the direct draft of the stove needs to be closed. With this precaution observed, a quick fire from a small amount of fuel, used before its force is spent, will produce better results than a fire-box full under other circumstances.

An item of economy for those who are large users of coal, is the careful sifting of the cinders from the ashes. They can be used to good advantage to put first upon the kindlings, when building the fire, as they ignite more readily than fresh coal, and give a greater, quicker heat, although much less enduring.

Methods of Cooking.—A proper source of heat having been secured, the next step is to apply it to the food in some manner. The principal methods commonly employed are roasting, broiling, baking, boiling, stewing, simmering, steaming, and frying.

Roasting is cooking food in its own juices before an open fire. A clear fire with intense heat is necessary.

Broiling, or *grilling*, is cooking by radiant heat over glowing coals. This method is only adapted to thin pieces of food with a considerable amount of surface. Larger and more compact foods should be roasted or baked. Roasting and broiling are allied in principle. In both, the work is chiefly done by the radiation of heat directly upon the surface of the food, although some heat is communicated by the hot air surrounding the food. The intense heat applied to the food soon sears its outer surfaces, and thus prevents the escape of its juices. If care be taken frequently to turn the food so that its entire surface will be thus acted upon, the interior of the mass is cooked by its own juices.

Baking is the cooking of food by dry heat in a closed oven. Only foods containing a considerable degree of moisture are adapted for cooking by this method. The hot, dry air which fills the oven is always thirsting for moisture, and will take from every moist substance to which it has access a quantity of water proportionate to its degree of heat. Foods containing but a small amount of moisture, unless protected in some manner from the action of the heated air, or in some way supplied with moisture during the cooking process, come from the oven dry, hard, and unpalatable.

Proper cooking by this method depends greatly upon the facility with which the heat of the oven can be regulated. When oil or gas is the fuel used, it is an easy matter to secure and maintain almost any degree of heat desirable, but with a wood or coal stove, especial care and painstaking are necessary.

It is of the first importance that the mechanism of the oven to be used, be thoroughly understood by the cook, and she should test its heating capacity under various conditions, with a light, quick fire and with a more steady one; she should carefully note the kind and amount of fuel requisite to produce a certain degree of heat; in short, she should thoroughly know her "machine" and its capabilities before attempting to use it for the cooking of food. An oven thermometer is of the utmost value for testing the heat, but unfortunately, such thermometers are not common. They are obtainable in England, although quite expensive. It is also possible at the present time to obtain ranges with a very reliable thermometer attachment to the oven door.

An Oven Thermometer

A cook of good judgment by careful observation and comparison of results, can soon learn to form quite a correct idea of the heat of her oven by the length of time she can hold her hand inside it without discomfort, but since much depends upon the construction of stoves and the kind of fuel used, and since the degree of heat bearable will vary with every hand that tries it, each person who depends upon this test must make her own standard. When the heat of the oven is found to be too great, it may be lessened by placing in it a dish of cold water.

Boiling is the cooking of food in a boiling liquid. Water is the usual medium employed for this purpose. When water is heated, as its temperature is increased, minute bubbles of air which have been dissolved by it are given off. As the temperature rises, bubbles of steam will begin to form at the bottom of the vessel. At first these will be condensed as they rise into the cooler water above, causing a simmering sound; but as the heat increases, the bubbles will rise higher and higher before collapsing, and in a short time will pass entirely through the water, escaping from its surface, causing more or less agitation, according to the rapidity with which they are formed. Water boils when the bubbles thus rise to the surface, and steam is thrown off. If the temperature is now tested, it will be found to be about 212° F. When water begins to boil, it is impossible to increase its temperature, as the steam carries off the heat as rapidly as it is communicated to the water. The only way in which the temperature can be raised, is by the confinement of the steam; but owing to its enormous expansive force, this is not practicable with ordinary cooking utensils. The mechanical action of the water is increased by rapid bubbling, but not the heat; and to boil anything violently does not expedite the cooking process, save that by the mechanical action of the water the food is broken into smaller pieces, which are for this reason more readily softened. But violent boiling occasions an enormous waste of fuel, and by driving away in the steam the volatile and savory elements of the food, renders it much less palatable, if not altogether tasteless. The solvent properties of water are so increased by heat that it permeates the food, rendering its hard and tough constituents soft and easy of digestion.

The liquids mostly employed in the cooking of foods are water and milk. Water is best suited for the cooking of most foods, but for such farinaceous foods as rice, macaroni, and farina, milk, or at least part milk, is preferable, as it adds to their nutritive value. In using milk for cooking purposes, it should be remembered that being more dense than water, when heated, less steam escapes, and consequently it boils sooner than does water. Then, too, milk being more dense, when it is used alone for cooking, a little larger quantity of fluid will be required than when water is used.

The boiling point for water at the sea level is 212°. At all points above the sea level, water boils at a temperature below 212°, the exact temperature depending upon the altitude. At the top of Mt. Blanc, an altitude of 15,000 feet, water boils at 185°. The boiling point is lowered one degree for every 600 feet increase in altitude. The boiling point may be increased by adding soluble substances to the water. A saturated solution of common baking soda boils at 220°. A saturated solution of chloride of sodium boils at 227°. A similar solution of sal-ammoniac boils at 238°. Of course such solutions cannot be used advantageously, except as a means of cooking articles placed in hermetically sealed vessels and immersed in the liquid.

Different effects upon food are produced by the use of hard and soft water. Peas and beans boiled in hard water containing lime or gypsum, will not become tender, because these chemical substances harden vegetable casein, of which element peas and beans are largely composed. For extracting the juices of meat and the soluble parts of other foods, soft water is best, as it more readily penetrates the tissue; but when it is desired to preserve the articles whole, and retain their juices and flavors, hard water is preferable.

Foods should be put to cook in cold or boiling water, in accordance with the object to be attained in their cooking. Foods from which it is desirable to extract the nutrient properties, as for broths, extracts, etc., should be put to cook in cold water. Foods to be kept intact as nearly as may be, should be put to cook in boiling water.

Hot and cold water act differently upon the different food elements. Starch is but slightly acted upon by coldwater. When starch is added to several times its bulk of hot water, all the starch granules burst on approaching the boiling point, and swell to such a degree as to occupy nearly the whole volume of the water, forming a pasty mess. Sugar is dissolved readily in the either hot or cold water. Cold water extracts albumen. Hot water coagulates it.

Steaming, as its name implies, is the cooking of food by the use of steam. There are several ways of steaming, the most common of which is by placing the food in a perforated dish over a vessel of boiling water. For foods not needing the solvent powers of water, or which already contain a large amount of moisture, this method is preferable to boiling. Another form of cooking, which is usually termed steaming, is that of placing the food, with or without water, as needed, in a closed vessel which is placed inside another vessel containing boiling water. Such an apparatus is termed a double boiler. Food cooked in its own juices in a covered dish in a hot oven, is sometimes spoken of as being *steamed* or *smothered*.

Stewing is the prolonged cooking of food in a small quantity of liquid, the temperature of which is just below the boiling point. Stewing should not be confounded with simmering, which is slow, steady boiling. The proper temperature for stewing is most easily secured by the use of the double boiler. The water in the outer vessel boils, while that in the inner vessel does not, being kept a little below the temperature of the water from which its heat is obtained, by the constant evaporation at a temperature a little below the boiling point.

Frying, which is the cooking of food in hot fat, is a method not to be recommended—Unlike all the other food elements, fat is rendered less digestible by cooking. Doubtless it is for this reason that nature has provided those foods which require the most prolonged cooking to fit them for use with only a small proportion of fat, and it would seem to indicate that any food to be subjected to a high degree of heat should not be mixed and compounded largely of fats. The ordinary way of frying, which the French call *sauteing*, is by the use of only a little fat in a shallow pan, into which the food is put and cooked first on one side and then the other. Scarcely anything could be more unwholesome than food prepared in this manner. A morsel of food encrusted with fat remains undigested in the stomach because fat is not acted upon by the gastric juice, and its combination with the other food elements of which the morsel is composed interferes with their digestion also. If such foods are habitually used, digestion soon becomes slow and the gastric juice so deficient in quantity that fermentation and putrefactive changes are occasioned, resulting in serious disturbance of health. In the process of frying, the action of the heat partially decomposes the fat; in consequence, various poisonous substances are formed, highly detrimental to the digestion of the partaker of the food.

Adding Foods to Boiling Liquids.—Much of the soddenness of improperly cooked foods might be avoided, if the following facts were kept in mind:—

When vegetables, or other foods of ordinary temperature, are put into boiling water, the temperature of the water is lowered in proportion to the quantity and the temperature of the food thus introduced, and will not again boil until the mass of food shall have absorbed more heat from the fire. The result of this is that the food is apt to become more or less water-soaked before the process of cooking begins. This difficulty may be avoided by introducing but small quantities of the food at one time, so as not to greatly lower the temperature of the liquid, and then allowing the latter to boil between the introduction of each fresh supply, or by heating the food before adding it to the liquid.

Evaporation is another principle often overlooked in the cooking of food, and many a sauce or gravy is spoiled because the liquid, heated in a shallow pan, from which evaporation is rapid, loses so much in bulk that the amount of thickening requisite for the given quantity of fluid, and which, had less evaporation occurred, would have made it of the proper consistency, makes the sauce thick and unpalatable. Evaporation is much less, in slow boiling, than in more rapid cooking.

Measuring.—One of the most important principles to be observed in the preparation of food for cooking, is accuracy in measuring. Many an excellent recipe proves a failure simply from lack of care in this respect. Measures are generally more convenient than weights, and are more commonly used. The common kitchen cup, which holds a half pint, is the one usually taken as the standard; if any other size is used, the ingredients for the entire recipe should be measured by the same. The following points should be observed in measuring:—

1. The teaspoons and tablespoons to be used in measuring, are the silver spoons in general use.

2. Any material like flour, sugar, salt, that has been packed, should either be sifted or stirred up lightlybefore measuring.

3. A cupful of dry material is measured level with the top of the cup, without being packed down.

4. A cupful of liquid is all the cup will contain without running over. Hold the cup in a saucer while measuring, to

prevent spilling the liquid upon the floor or table.

Comparative Table of Weights and Measures.—The following comparative table of weights and measurements will aid in estimating different materials:—

One heaping tablespoonful of sugar weighs one ounce.

Two round tablespoonfuls of flour weigh one ounce.

Two cupfuls of granulated sugar weigh one pound.

Two cupfuls of meal weigh one pound.

Four cupfuls of sifted flour weigh one pound.

One pint of oatmeal, cracked wheat, or other coarse grains, weighs about one pound.

One pint of liquid weighs one pound.

One pint of meat chopped and packed solid weighs one pound.

Seven heaping tablespoonfuls of sugar = one cupful.

Five heaping tablespoonfuls of flour = one cupful.

Two cupfuls of liquid or dry material = one pint

Four cupfuls of liquid or dry material = one quart.

Mixing Materials.—In the compounding of recipes, various modes are employed for mingling together the different ingredients, chief of which are *stirring*, *beating*, and *kneading*.

By *stirring* is meant a continuous motion round and round with a spoon, without lifting it from the mixture, except to scrape occasionally from the sides of the dish any portion of the material that may cling to it. It is not necessary that the stirring should be all in one direction, as many cooks suppose. The object of the stirring is to thoroughly blend the ingredients, and this may be accomplished as well by stirring—in one direction as in another.

Beating is for the purpose of incorporating as much air in the mixture as possible. It should be done by dipping the spoon in and out, cutting clear through and lifting from the bottom with each stroke. The process must be continuous, and must never be interspersed with any stirring if it is desired to retain the air within the mixture.

Kneading is the mode by which materials already in the form of dough are more thoroughly blended together; it also serves to incorporate air. The process is more fully described in the chapter on "Bread,"

Temperature.—Many a cook fails and knows not why, because she does not understand the influence of temperature upon materials and food. Flour and liquids for unfermented breads cannot be too cold, while for bread prepared with yeast, success is largely dependent upon a warm and equable temperature throughout the entire process.

Cooking Utensils.—The earliest cookery was probably accomplished without the aid of any utensils, the food being roasted by burying it in hot ashes or cooked by the aid of heated stones; but modern cookery necessitates the use of a greater or less variety of cooking utensils to facilitate the preparation of food, most of which are so familiar to the reader as to need no description. (A list of those needed for use will be found onpage 66.) Most of these utensils are manufactured from some kind of metal, as iron, tin, copper, brass, etc. All metals are dissolvable in certain substances, and some of those employed for making household utensils are capable of forming most poisonous compounds when used for cooking certain foods. This fact should lead to great care on the part of the housewife, both in purchasing and in using utensils for cooking purposes.

Iron utensils, although they are, when new, apt to discolor and impart a disagreeable flavor to food cooked in them, are not objectionable from a health standpoint, if kept clean and free from rust. Iron rust is the result of the combination of the iron with oxygen, for which it has so great an affinity that it will decompose water to get oxygen to unite with; hence it is that iron utensils rust so quickly when not carefully dried after using, or if left where they can collect moisture. This is the reason why a coating of tallow, which serves to exclude the air and moisture, will preserve ironware not in daily use from rusting.

"Porcelain ware" is iron lined with a hard, smooth enamel, and makes safe and very desirable cooking utensils. German porcelain ware is unexcelled for culinary purposes.

"Granite ware" is a material quite recently come into use, the composition of which is a secret, although pronounced by eminent chemists to be free from all injurious qualities. Utensils made from it are light in weight, easily kept clean, and for most cooking purposes, are far superior to those made from any other material.

What is termed "galvanized iron" is unsuitable for cooking utensils, it being simply sheet iron coated with zinc, an exceedingly unsafe metal to be used for cooking purposes.

Tin, which is simply thin sheet iron coated with tin by dipping several times into vats of the melted metal, is largely employed in the manufacture of cooking utensils. Tinware is acted upon by acids, and when used for holding or cooking any acid foods, like sour milk, sour fruits, tomatoes, etc., harmful substances are liable to be formed, varying in quantity and harmfulness with the nature of the acid contained in the food.

In these days of fraud and adulteration, nearly all the cheaper grades of tinware contain a greater or less amount of lead in their composition, which owing to its greater abundance and less price, is used as an adulterant of tin. Lead is also used in the solder with which the parts of tinware are united. The action of acids upon lead form very poisonous compounds, and all lead-adulterated utensils should be wholly discarded for cooking purposes.

Test for Lead-Adulterated Tin.—Place upon the metal a small drop of nitric acid, spreading it to the size of a dime, dry with gentle heat, apply a drop of water, then add a small crystal of iodide of potash. If lead is present, a yellowish color will be seen very soon after the addition of the iodide. Lead glazing, which is frequently employed on crockery and ironware in the manufacture of cooking utensils, may also be detected in the same manner.

Cooking utensils made of copper are not to be recommended from the point of healthfulness, although many cooks esteem them because copper is a better conductor of heat than iron or tin. The acids of many fruits combine with copper to form extremely poisonous substances. Fatty substances, as well as salt and sugar, act upon copper to a greater or less degree, also vegetables containing sulfur in their composition and produce harmful compounds.

Utensils made of brass, which is a compound of copper and zinc, are not safe to use for cooking purposes.

TABLE TOPICS.

Bad cooking diminishes happiness and shortens life.—*Wisdom of Ages.*

Says Mrs. Partington: "Many a fair home has been desiccated by poor cooking, and a man's table has been the rock on which his happiness has split."

SIGNIFICANT FACT.—*Lady*—"Have you had much experience as a cook?" *Applicant*—"Oh, indeed I have. I was the cook of Mr. and Mrs. Peterby for three years."

L.—"Why did you leave them?"

A.—"I didn't leave them. They left me. They both died."

L.—"What of?"

A.—"Dyspepsia."

Cooking is generally bad because people falling to routine; habit dulls their appreciation, and they do not think about what they are eating.—*Didsbury.*

Lilly (Secretary of the cooking class)—"Now girls, we've learned nine cakes, two kinds of angel food, and seven pies. What next?"

Susie (engaged)—"Dick's father says I must learn to bake bread."

Indignant chorus—"Bread? How absurd! What are bakers for?"

It is told of Philip Hecgnet, a French, physician who lived in the 17th, century, that when calling upon his wealthy patients, he used often to go to the kitchen and pantry, embrace the cooks and butlers, and exhort them to do their duty well. "I owe you so much gratitude, my dear friends," he would say; "you are so useful to us doctors; for if you did not keep on poisoning the people, we should all have to go to the poorhouse."

There are innumerable books of recipes for cooking, but unless the cook is master of the principles of his art, and unless he knows the why and the wherefore of its processes, he cannot choose a recipe intelligently and execute it successfully.—*Richard Estcourt.*

They who provide the food for the world, decide the health of the world. You have only to go on some errands amid the taverns and hotels of the United States and Great Britain, to appreciate the fact that a vast multitude of the human race are slaughtered by incompetent cookery. Though a young woman may have taken lessons in music, and may have taken lessons in painting, and lessons in astronomy, she is not well educated unless she has taken lessons in dough!—*Talmage*.

HOUSEHOLD WORKSHOP

It is a mistake to suppose that any room, however small and unpleasantly situated, is "good enough" for a kitchen. This is the room where housekeepers pass a great portion of their time, and it should be one of the brightest and most convenient rooms in the house; for upon the results of no other department of woman's domain depend so greatly the health and comfort of the family as upon those involved in this "household workshop." The character of a person's work is more or less dependent upon his surroundings, hence is it to be greatly wondered at that a woman immured in a small, close, dimly-lighted room, whose only outlook may be the back alley or the woodshed, supplies her household with products far below the standard of health and housewifely skill?

Every kitchen should have windows on two sides of the room, and the sun should have free entrance through them; the windows should open from the top to allow a complete change of air, for light and fresh air are among the chief essentials to success in all departments of the household. Good drainage should also be provided, and the ventilation of the kitchen ought to be even more carefully attended to than that of a sleeping room. The ventilation of the kitchen should be so ample as to thoroughly remove all gases and odors, which, together with steam from boiling and other cooking processes, generally invade and render to some degree unhealthful every other portion of the house. It is the steam from the kitchen which gives a fusty odor to the parlor air and provides a wet-sheet pack for the occupant of the "spare bed." The only way of wholly eradicating this evil, is the adoption of the suggestion of the sanitary philosopher who places the kitchen at the top of the house.

To lessen to discomforts from heat, a ventilator may be placed above the range, that shall carry out of the room all superfluous heat, and aid in removing the steam and odors from cooking food. The simplest form of such a ventilator this inverted hopper of sheet iron fitted above the range, the upper and smaller end opening into a large flue adjacent to the smoke flue for the range. Care must be taken, however, to provide an ample ventilating shaft for this purpose, since a strong draft is required to secure the desired results.

There should be ample space for tables, chairs, range, sink, and cupboards, yet the room should not be so large as to necessitate too many steps. A very good size for the ordinary dwelling is 16 x 18 feet.

Undoubtedly much of the distaste for, and neglect of, "housework," so often deplored in these days, arises from unpleasant surroundings. If the kitchen be light, airy, and tidy, and the utensils bright and clean, the work of compounding those articles of food which grace the table and satisfy the appetite will be a pleasant task, and one entirely worthy of the most intelligent and cultivated woman.

It is desirable, from a sanitary standpoint, that the kitchen floor be made impervious to moisture; hence, concrete or tile floors are better than wooden floors. If wooden floors are used, they should be constructed of narrow boards of hard wood, carefully joined and thoroughly saturated with hot linseed oil, well rubbed in to give polish to the surface.

Cleanliness is the great *desideratum*, and this can be best attained by having all woodwork in and about the kitchen coated with varnish; substances which cause stain and grease spots, do not penetrate the wood when varnished, and can be easily removed with a damp cloth. Paint is preferable to whitewash or calcimine for the walls, since it is less affected by steam, and can be more readily cleaned. A carpet on a kitchen floor is as out of place as a kitchen sink would be in a parlor.

The elements of beauty should not be lacking in the kitchen. Pictures and fancy articles are inappropriate; but a few pots of easily cultivated flowers on the window ledge or arranged upon brackets about the window in winter, and a window box arranged as a jardiniere, with vines and blooming plants in summer, will greatly brighten the room, and thus serve to lighten the task of those whose daily labor confines them to the precincts of the kitchen.

The Kitchen Furniture.—The furniture for a kitchen should not be cumbersome, and should be so made and dressed as to be easily cleaned. There should be plenty of cupboards, and each for the sake of order, should be devoted to a special purpose. Cupboards with sliding doors are much superior to closets. They should be placed upon casters so as to be easily moved, as they, are thus not only more convenient, but admit of more thorough cleanliness.

Cupboards used for the storage of food should be well ventilated; otherwise, they furnish choice conditions for the development of mold and germs. Movable cupboards may be ventilated by means of openings in the top, and doors covered with very fine wire gauze which will admit the air but keep out flies and dust. All stationary cupboards and closets should have a ventilating flue connected with the main shaft by which the house is ventilated, or directly communicating with the outer air.

No kitchen can be regarded as well furnished without a good timepiece as an aid to punctuality and economy of time. An eight-day clock with large dial and plain case is the most suitable.

Every kitchen should also be provided with a slate, with sponge and pencil attached, on one side of which the market orders and other memoranda may be jotted down, and on the other the bills of fare for the day or week. In households where servants are kept, the slate will save many a vexatious blunder and unnecessary call to the kitchen, while if one is herself mistress, cook, and housekeeper, it may prove an invaluable aid and time-saver if thus used.

A Convenient Kitchen Table.

Lack of sufficient table room is often a great source of inconvenience to the housekeeper. To avoid this, arrange swinging tables or shelves at convenient points upon the wall, which may be put up or let down as occasion demands. For ordinary kitchen uses, small tables of suitable height on easy-rolling casters, and with zinc tops, are the most convenient and most easily kept clean. It is quite as well that they be made without drawers, which are too apt to become receptacles for a heterogeneous mass of rubbish. If desirable to have some handy place for keeping articles which are frequently required for use, an arrangement similar to that represented in the accompanying cut may be made at very small expense. It may be also an advantage to arrange small shelves about and above the range, on which may be kept various articles necessary for cooking purposes.

One of the most indispensable articles of furnishing for a well-appointed kitchen, is a sink; however, a sink must be properly constructed and well cared for, or it is likely to become a source of great danger to the health of the inmates of the household. Earthen-ware is the best material for kitchen sinks. Iron is very serviceable, but corrodes, and if painted or enameled, this soon wears off. Wood is objectionable from a sanitary standpoint. A sink made of wood lined with copper answers well for a long time if properly cared for.

The sink should if possible stand out from the wall, so as to allow free access to all sides of it for the sake of cleanliness, and under no circumstances should there be any inclosure of woodwork or cupboards underneath to serve as a storage place for pots and kettles and all kinds of rubbish, dust, and germs. It should be supported on legs, and the space below should be open for inspection at all times. The pipes and fixtures should be selected and placed by a competent plumber.

Great pains should be taken to keep the pipes clean and well disinfected. Refuse of all kinds should be kept out. Thoughtless housekeepers and careless domestics often allow greasy water and bits of table waste to find their way into the pipes. Drain pipes usually have a bend, or trap, through which water containing no sediment flows freely; but the melted grease which often passes into the pipes mixed with hot water, becomes cooled and solid as it descends, adhering to the pipes, and gradually accumulating until the drain is blocked, or the water passes through very slowly. A grease-lined pipe is a hotbed for disease germs.

Water containing much grease should be cooled and the grease removed before being turned into the kitchen sink, while bits of refuse should be disposed of elsewhere, since prevention of mischief is in this case, as in most others, far easier than cure. It is customary for housekeepers to pour a hot solution of soda or potash down the sink pipes occasionally, to dissolve any grease which may tend to obstruct the passage; but this is only a partial safeguard, as there is no certainty that all the grease will be dissolved, and any particles adhering to the pipes very soon undergo putrefaction.

A frequent flushing with hot water is important; besides which the pipes should be disinfected two or three times a week by pouring down a gallon of water holding in solution a pound of good chloride of lime.

Stoves and Ranges.—The furnishing of a modern kitchen would be quite incomplete without some form of stove or range. The multiplicity of these articles, manufactured each with some especial merit of its own, renders it a somewhat difficult task to make a choice among them. Much must, however, depend upon the kind of fuel to be used, the size of the household, and various other circumstances which make it necessary for each individual housekeeper to decide for herself what is best adapted to her wants. It may be said, in brief, that economy of fuel, simplicity of construction, and efficiency in use are the chief points to be considered in the selection of stoves and ranges.

A stove or range of plain finish is to be preferred, because it is much easier to keep clean, and will be likely to present a better appearance after a few months' wear than one of more elaborate pattern. But whatever stove or range is selected, its mechanism should be thoroughly understood in every particular, and it should be tested with dampers open, with dampers closed, and in every possible way, until one is perfectly sure she understands its action under all conditions.

Oil and Gas Stoves.—In many households, oil, gas, and gasoline stoves have largely taken the place of the kitchen range, especially during the hot weather of summer. They can be used for nearly every purpose for which a wood or a coal range is used; they require much less labor and litter, and can be instantly started into full force and as quickly turned out when no longer required, while the fact that the heat can be regulated with exactness, makes them superior for certain processes of cooking to any other stove. But while these stoves are convenient and economical, especially in small families, they should be used with much care. Aside from the danger from explosion, which is by no means inconsiderable in the use of gasoline and oil stoves, they are not, unless well cared for altogether healthful. Unless the precaution is taken to use them in well-ventilated rooms or to connect them with a chimney, they vitiate the atmosphere to a considerable extent with the products of combustion. Oil stoves, unless the wicks are kept well trimmed, are apt to smoke, and this smoke is not only disagreeable, but extremely irritating to the mucous membrane of the nose and throat. Oil stoves are constructed on the same principle as ordinary oil lamps, and require the same care and attention.

Quite recently there has been invented by Prof. Edward Atkinson a very unique apparatus for cooking by means of the heat of an ordinary kerosene lamp, called the "Aladdin Cooker." The food to be cooked is placed in a chamber around which hot water, heated by the flame of the lamp, circulates. The uniform heat thus obtained performs the process of cooking, slowly, but most satisfactorily and economically, the result being far superior to that obtained by the ordinary method of cooking by quick heat. The cooker is only used for stewing and steaming; but Mr. Atkinson has also invented an oven in which the heat is conveyed to the place where it is needed by a column of hot air instead of hot water. With this oven, which consists of an outer oven made of non-conducting material, and an inner oven made of sheet iron, with an intervening space between, through which the hot air circulates, no smoke or odor from the lamp can reach the interior.

Kitchen. Utensils.—The list of necessary kitchen utensils must of course be governed somewhat by individual circumstances, but it should not be curtailed for the sake of display in some other department, where less depends upon the results. A good kitchen outfit is one of the foundation-stones of good housekeeping. The following are some of the most essential:—

Two dish pans; two or more *papier-maché* tubs for washing glassware; one kneading board; one bread board; one pair scales, with weights; scrubbing and stove brushes; brooms; dustpans; roller for towel; washbowl; soap dish; vegetable brushes.

For the Tin Closet.-One dipper; one egg-beater; one two-quart pail; one four-quart pail; six brick-loaf bread pans; three shallow tins; three granite-ware pie tins; two perforated sheet iron pans for rolls, etc.; one set of measures, pint, quart, and two quart; two colanders; two fine wire strainers; one flour sifter; one apple corer; one set patty pans; two dripping pans; two sets gem irons; one set muffin rings; one toaster; one broiler; the six saucepans, different sizes; two steamers; six milk-pans; one dozen basins, different sizes; one chopping bowl and knife; six double boilers; two funnels, large and small; one can opener; griddle; kettles, iron and granite ware; two water baths.

For the Dish Closet.—One half dozen iron-stone china cups; three quart bowls; three pint bowls; two large mixing bowls; two quart bowls with lip; six deep plates; three kitchen pitchers; one glass rolling pin; six wooden and six iron spoons, assorted sizes; six kitchen teaspoons; one stone baking pot; glass jars for stores; crocks and jars.

The Pantry.—The pantry and china closet should have direct light and good ventilation. The dark, dingy places sometimes used for this purpose are germ breeders. There should be plenty of shelf room and cupboards for the fine glass and china-ware, with a well-arranged sink for washing the dishes. The sink for this purpose is preferably one lined with tinned or planished copper; for dishes will be less liable to become injured and broken then when washed in an iron or earthen-ware sink. Extension or folding shelves are a great convenience, and can be arranged for the sink if desired. The accompanying cuts illustrate a sink of four compartments for dish-washing, devised by the writer for use in the Sanitarium Domestic Economy kitchen, which can be closed and used as a table. Two zinc trays fit the top, upon which to place the dish drainers. If preferred, the top might be arranged as a drainer, by making it of well-seasoned hard wood, with a number of inclined grooves to allow the water to run into the sink. If the house be heated by steam, a plate-warmer is an important part of the pantry furnishing.

Compartment Sink for Dish-Washing. Open.

The Storeroom.—If possible to do so, locate the room for the keeping of the kitchen supplies on the cool side of the house. Plenty of light, good ventilation, and absolute cleanliness are essential, as the slightest contamination of air is likely to render the food supply unfit for use.

The refrigerator should not be connected with the kitchen drain pipe, and the greatest care should be taken to keep it clean and sweet. It should be thoroughly scrubbed with borax or sal-soda and water, and well aired, at least once a week. Strongly flavored foods and milk should not be kept in the same refrigerator. The ice to be used should always be carefully washed before putting in the refrigerator. Care should also be taken to replenish it before the previous supply is entirely melted, as the temperature rises when the ice becomes low, and double the quantity will be required to cool the refrigerator that would be necessary to keep it of uniform temperature if added before the ice was entirely out.

The Water Supply.—The water used for drinking and cooking purposes should receive equal consideration with the food supply, and from whatever source obtained, it should be frequently tested for impurities, since that which looks the most refreshing may be contaminated with organic poison of the most treacherous character.

A good and simple test solution, which any housewife can use, may be prepared by dissolving twelve grains of caustic potash and three of permanganate of potash in an ounce of distilled water, or filtered soft water. Add a drop of this solution to a glass of the water to be tested. If the pink color imparted by the solution disappears at once, add another drop of the solution, and continue adding drop by drop until the pink color will remain for half an hour or more. The amount of the solution necessary to security permanent color is very fair index to the quality of the water. If the color imparted by the first one or two drops disappears within a half hour, the water should be rejected as probably dangerous. Water which is suspected of being impure may be rendered safe by boiling. Filters are only of service in removing suspended particles and the unpleasant taste of rain water; a really dangerous water is not rendered safe by filtering in the ordinary manner.

Cellars.—Sanitarians tell us that cellars should never be built under dwelling houses. Because of improper construction and neglect, they are undoubtedly the cause of much disease and many deaths. A basement beneath the house is advantageous, but the greatest of care should be given to construct it in accord with sanitary laws. It should be thoroughly drained that there may be no source of dampness, but should not be connected with a sewer or a cesspool. It should have walls so made as to be impervious to air and water. An ordinary brick or stone wall is inefficient unless well covered with good Portland cement polished smooth. The floors should likewise be covered with cement, otherwise the cellar is likely to be filled with impure air derived from the soil, commonly spoken of as "ground air," and which offers a constant menace to the health of those who live over cellars with uncemented walls and floors.

Light and ventilation are quite as essential to the healthfulness of a cellar as to other rooms of the dwelling. Constantly during warm weather, and at least once a day during the winter season, windows should be opened wide, thus effecting a free interchange of air. All mold and mustiness should be kept out by thorough ventilation and frequent coats of whitewash to the walls. Vegetables and other decomposable articles, if stored in the basement, should be frequently sorted, and all decaying substances promptly removed. This is of the utmost importance, since the germs and foul gases arising from decomposing food stuffs form a deadly source of contamination through every crack and crevice.

KITCHEN CONVENIENCES.

In these days of invention and progress, much thought and ingenuity have been expended in making and perfecting labor-saving articles and utensils, which serve to make housework less of a burden and more of a delight.

The Steam-Cooker.—One of the most unique of these conveniences is the steam-cooker, one kind of which is illustrated by the accompanying cut. Steaming is, for many foods, a most economical and satisfactory method of cooking. Especially is this true respecting fruits, grains, and vegetables, the latter of which often have the larger proportion of their best nutritive elements dissolved and thrown away in the water in which they are boiled. In the majority of households it is, however, the method least depended upon, because the ordinary steamer over a pot of boiling water requires too much attention, takes up too much stove room, and creates too much steam in the kitchen, to prove a general favorite. The steam-cooker has an escape-steam tube through which all excess of steam and odors passes into the fire, and thus its different compartments may contain and cook an entire dinner, if need be, and over one stove hole or one burner of an oil or gasoline stove.

The Vegetable Press.—The accompanying cut represents this handy utensil, which is equally useful as a potato and vegetable masher; as a sauce, gruel, and gravy strainer; as a fruit press, and for many other purposes for which a colander or strainer is needed, while it economizes both time and labor.

Lemon Drill.—This little article for extracting the juice of the lemon, and which can be purchased of most hardware dealers, is quite superior to the more commonly used lemon squeezer. Being made of glass, its use is not open to the danger that the use of metal squeezer is are from poisonous combinations of the acid and metal, while the juice extracted is free from pulp, seeds, and the oil of the skin.

A Handy Waiter.—In many households where no help is employed, a labor-saving device like the one represented in the accompanying illustration, will be found of great service. It is a light double table on easy-rolling casters, and can be readily constructed by anyone handy in the use of tools. If preferred, the top may be covered with zinc. In setting or clearing the table, the dishes may be placed on the lower shelf, with the food on the top, and the table rolled from pantry to dining room, and from dining room to kitchen; thus accomplishing, with one trip, what is ordinarily done with hundreds of steps by the weary housewife. If desirable to reset the table at once after a meal, the waiter will be found most serviceable as a place whereon the glassware and silverware may be washed. It is equally serviceable for holding the utensils and material needed when cooking; being so easily moved, they can be rolled to the stove and is always convenient.

Wall Cabinet.

Wall cabinet.—where cupboard space is limited, or where for convenience it is desirable to have some provision for supplies and utensils near the range and baking table, a wall cabinet offers a most convenient arrangement. It may be made of a size to fit in any convenient niche, and constructed plainly or made as ornamental as one pleases, with doors to exclude the dust, shelves on which to keep tin cans filled with rice, oatmeal, cracked wheat, and other grains; glass jars of raisins, sugar, citron, cornstarch, etc.; hooks on which may hang the measures, egg-beater, potato masher, and such frequently needed utensils; and with drawers for paring knives, spoons, and similar articles, the wall cabinet becomes a *multum in parvo* of convenience which would greatly facilitate work in many households.

Percolate Holder.—The accompanying cut illustrates an easily-constructed device for holding a jelly bag or percolate. It may be so made as to be easily screwed to any ordinary table, and will save the housekeeper far more than its cost in time and patience.

Percolate Holder.

Kneading Table.—Much of the tiresome labor of bread-making can be avoided if one is supplied with some convenient table similar to the one represented in the cut, wherein the needed material and utensils may be kept in readiness at all times. The table illustrated has two large tin drawers, each divided into two compartments, in which may be kept corn meal, entire wheat, and Graham and white flours. Two drawers above provide a place for rolling-pin, bread mallet, gem irons, spoons, etc., while a narrow compartment just beneath the hardwood top affords a place for the kneading board. The table being on casters is easily moved to any part of the kitchen for use.

Kneading Table.

Dish-Towel Rack.—Nothing adds more to the ease and facility with which the frequent dish-washings of the household may be accomplished than clean, well-dried towels. For quick drying,—an item of great importance if one would keep the towels fresh and sweet,—the towel rack represented in the cut, and which can be made by any carpenter, is a most handy device. When not in use, it can be turned up against the wall as illustrated. It is light, affords sufficient drying space so that no towel need be hung on top of another, and projecting out from the wall as it does, the free circulation of air between the towels soon dries them.

Dish-Towel Rack.

Kitchen Brushes.—These useful little articles can be put to such a variety of uses that they are among the chiefest of household conveniences. They are also so inexpensive, costing but five cents apiece without handles and seven cents with handles, that no housewife can afford to be without a supply of them. For the washing of dishes with handles, the outside of iron kettles, and other cooking utensils made of iron, they are especially serviceable. The smaller sizes are likewise excellent for cleaning cut glass ware, Majolica ware,—in fact, any kind of ware with raised figures or corrugated surfaces. For cleaning a grater, nothing is superior to one of these little brushes. Such a brush is also most serviceable for washing celery, as the corrugated surface of the stalk makes a thorough cleaning with the hands a difficult operation. Then if one uses a brush with handle, ice water, which adds to the crispness of the celery, may be used for the cleaning, as there will be no necessity for putting the hands in the water. A small whisk broom is also valuable for the same purpose. Such vegetables as potatoes, turnips, etc., are best cleaned with a brush. It makes the work less disagreeable, as the hands need not be soiled by the process, and in no other way can the cleaning be so well and thoroughly done.

All brushes after being used should be carefully scalded and placed brush downward in a wire sponge basket, or hung up on hooks. If left around carelessly, they soon acquire the musty smell of a neglected dishcloth.

TABLE TOPICS.

The kitchen is a chemical laboratory, in which are conducted a number of chemical processes by which our food is converted from its crudest state to condition more suitable for digestion and nutrition, and made more agreeable to the palate.—*Prof. Matthew Williams.*

Half the trouble between mistresses and maids arises from the disagreeable surroundings to which servants are confined. There is no place more dismal than the ordinary kitchen in city dwellings. It is half underground, ill-lighted, and unwholesome. What wonder, then, in the absence of sunlight, there is a lack of sunny temper and cheerful service? An ill-lighted kitchen is almost sure to be a dirty one, where germs will thrive and multiply. Let sanitary kitchens be provided, and we shall have more patient mistresses and more willing servants.—*Sel.*

A sluggish housemaid exclaimed, when scolded for the uncleanliness of her kitchen, "I'm sure the room would be clean enough if it were not for the nasty sun, which is always showing the dirty corners."—*Sel.*

If we would look for ready hands and willing hearts in our kitchens, we should make them pleasant and inviting for those who literally bear the "burden and heat of the day" in this department of our homes, where, emphatically, "woman's work is never done." We should no longer be satisfied to locate our kitchens in the most undesirable corner of the house. We should demand ample light,—sunshine if possible,—and justly too; for the very light itself is inspiring to the worker. It will stir up cheer and breed content in the minds of those whose lot is cast in this work-a-day room.—*Sel.*

Any invention on the part of the housekeeper intended to be a substitute for watchfulness, will prove a delusion and a snare.—*Sel.*

"The first wealth is health," says Emerson.

A knowledge of sanitary principles should be regarded as an essential part of every woman's education, and obedience to sanitary laws should be ranked, as it was in the Mosaic code, as a religious duty.—*Sel.*

Much of the air of the house comes from the cellar. A heated house acts like a chimney. A German experimenter states that one half of the cellar air makes its way into the first story, one third into the second, and one fifth into the third.

CEREALS AND THEIR PREPARATION FOR THE TABLE

Cereal is the name given to those seeds used as food (wheat, rye, oats, barley, corn, rice, etc.), which are produced by plants belonging to the vast order known as the grass family. They are used for food both in the unground state and in various forms of mill products.

The grains are pre-eminently nutritious, and when well prepared, easily digested foods. In composition they are all similar, but variations in their constituent elements and the relative amounts of these various elements, give them different degrees of alimentary value. They each contain one or more of the nitrogenous elements,—gluten, albumen, caseine, and fibrin,—together with starch, dextrine, sugar, and fatty matter, and also mineral elements and woody matter, or cellulose. The combined nutritive value of the grain foods is nearly three times that of beef, mutton, or poultry. As regards the proportion of the food elements necessary to meet the various requirements of the system, grains approach more nearly the proper standard than most other foods; indeed, wheat contains exactly the correct proportion of the food elements.

Being thus in themselves so nearly perfect foods, and when properly prepared, exceedingly palatable and easy of digestion, it is a matter of surprise that they are not more generally used; yet scarcely one family in fifty makes any use of the grains, save in the form of flour, or an occasional dish of rice or oatmeal. This use of grains is far too meager to adequately represent their value as an article of diet. Variety in the use of grains is as necessary as in the use of other food material, and the numerous grain preparations now to be found in market render it quite possible to make this class of foods a staple article of diet, if so desired, without their becoming at all monotonous.

In olden times the grains were largely depended upon as a staple food, and it is a fact well authenticated by history that the highest condition of man has always been associated with wheat-consuming nations. The ancient Spartans, whose powers of endurance are proverbial, were fed on a grain diet, and the Roman soldiers who under Caesar conquered the world, carried each a bag of parched grain in his pocket as his daily ration.

Other nationalities at the present time make extensive use of the various grains. Rice used in connection with some of the leguminous seeds, forms the staple article of diet for a large proportion of the human race. Rice, unlike the other grain foods, is deficient in the nitrogenous elements, and for this reason its use needs to be supplemented by other articles containing an excess of the nitrogenous material. It is for this reason, doubtless, that the Hindoos use lentils, and the Chinese eat peas and beans in connection with rice.

We frequently meet people who say they cannot use the grains,—that they do not agree with them. With all deference to the opinion of such people, it may be stated that the difficulty often lies in the fact that the grain was either not properly cooked, not properly eaten, or not properly accompanied. A grain, simply because it is a grain, is by no means warranted to faithfully fulfil its mission unless properly treated. Like many another good thing excellent in itself, if found in bad company, it is prone to create mischief, and in many cases the root of the whole difficulty may be found in the excessive amount of sugar used with the grain.

Sugar is not needed with grains to increase their alimentary value. The starch which constitutes a large proportion of their food elements must itself be converted into sugar by the digestive processes before assimilation, hence the addition of cane sugar only increases the burden of the digestive organs, for the pleasure of the palate. The Asiatics, who subsist largely upon rice, use no sugar upon it, and why should it be considered requisite for the enjoyment of wheat, rye, oatmeal, barley, and other grains, any more than it is for our enjoyment of bread or other articles made from these same grains? Undoubtedly the use of grains would become more universal if they were served with less or no sugar. The continued use of sugar upon grains has a tendency to cloy the appetite, just as the constant use of cake or sweetened bread in the place of ordinary bread would do. Plenty of nice, sweet cream or fruit juice, is a sufficient dressing, and there are few persons who after a short trial would not come to enjoy the grains without sugar, and would then as soon think of dispensing with a meal altogether as to dispense with the grains.

Even when served without sugar, the grains may not prove altogether healthful unless they are properly eaten. Because they are made soft by the process of cooking and on this account do not require masticating to break them up, the first process of digestion or insalivation is usually overlooked. But it must be remembered that grains are largely composed of starch, and that starch must be mixed with the saliva, or it will remain undigested in the stomach, since the gastric juice only digests the nitrogenous elements. For this reason it is desirable to eat the grains in connection with some hard food. Whole-wheat wafers, nicely toasted to make them crisp and tender, toasted rolls, and unfermented zwieback, are excellent for this purpose. Break two or three wafers into rather small pieces over each individual dish before pouring on the cream. In this way, a morsel of the hard food may be taken with each spoonful of the grains. The combination of foods thus secured, is most pleasing. This is a specially advantageous method of serving grains for children, who are so liable to swallow their food without proper mastication.

Cooking of Grains.—All grains, with the exception of rice, and the various grain meals, require prolonged cooking with gentle and continuous heat, in order to so disintegrate their tissues and change their starch into dextrine as to render them easy of digestion. Even the so-called "steam-cooked" grains, advertised to be ready for use in five or ten minutes, require a much longer cooking to properly fit them for digestion. These so-called quickly prepared grains are simply steamed before grinding, which has the effect to destroy any low organisms contained in the grain. They are then crushed and shredded. Bicarbonate of soda and lime is added to help dissolve the albuminoids, and sometimes diastase to aid the conversion of the starch into sugar; but there is nothing in this preparatory process that so alters the chemical nature of the grain as to make it possible to cook it ready for easy digestion in five or ten minutes. An insufficiently cooked grain, although it may be palatable, is not in a condition to be readily acted upon by the digestive fluids, and is in consequence left undigested to act as a mechanical irritant.

For the proper cooking of grains the double boiler is the best and most convenient utensil for ordinary purposes. If one does not possess a double boiler, a very fair substitute may be improvised by using a covered earthen crock placed within a kettle of boiling water, or by using two pails, a smaller within a larger one containing boiling water.

A closed steamer or steam-cooker is also valuable for the cooking of grains. Grains may be cooked in an ordinary kettle, but the difficulties to be encountered, in order to prolong the cooking sufficiently and prevent burning, make it the least desirable utensil for this purpose.

A Double Boiler.

Water is the liquid usually employed for cooking grains, but many of them are richer and finer flavored when milk is mixed with the water,—one part to two of water. Especially is this true of rice, hominy, and farina. When water is used, soft water is preferable to hard. No salt is necessary, but if used at all, it is generally added to the water before stirring in the grain or meal.

The quantity of liquid required varies with the different grains, the manner in which they are milled, the method by which they are cooked, and the consistency desired for the cooked grain, more liquid being required for a porridge than for a mush. The following table gives the time necessary for cooking and the quantity of liquid required for the various grains, with the exception of rice, when cooked in a double boiler or closed steamer, to produce a mush of ordinary consistency. If an ordinary kettle is used for cooking the grains, a larger quantity of water will be needed:—

TABLE SHOWING PROPORTION OF GRAIN AND LIQUID REQUIRED, WITH APPROXIMATE TIME, WHEN A DOUBLE BOILER IS USED.

	Quantity of Grain.	Water Required.	Hours to Cook.
Graham Grits	1 part	4 parts	3 to 5
Rolled Wheat	1 "	3 "	3 to 4
Cracked Wheat	1 "	4-1/2 "	3 to 4
Pearl Wheat	1 "	4 "	4 to 5
Whole Wheat	1 "	5 "	6 to 8
Rolled Oats	1 "	3 "	3 to 4
Coarse Oatmeal	1 "	4 "	4 to 6
Rolled Rye	1 "	3 "	3 to 4
Pearl Barley	1 "	5 "	4 to 5
Coarse Hominy	1 "	5 "	6 to 10
Fine Hominy	1 "	4 "	4 to 6
Cerealine	1 "	1 part	1/2

All grains should be carefully looked over before being put to cook.

In the cooking of grains, the following points should be observed:—

1. Measure both liquid and grain accurately with the same utensil, or with two of equal size.

2. Have the water boiling when the grain is introduced, but do not allow it to boil for a long time previous, until it is considerably evaporated, as that will change the proportion of water and grain sufficiently to alter the consistency of the mush when cooked. Introduce the grain slowly, so as not to stop the sinking to the bottom, and the whole becomes thickened. If the grain is cooked in a double boiler, this first boiling should be done with the inner dish directly over the fire, and when the grain has thickened or become "set," as it is termed, the dish should at once be placed in the outer boiler, the water in which should be boiling. It will then require no further care during the entire cooking, safe to keep the outer boiler filled and the water boiling. If the grain is to be cooked in a steam-cooker, as soon as set it may be turned into a china or an earthen dish, suitable for use on the table, and placed at once in the steamer to complete the cooking. If an ordinary kettle is used, it is well to place it upon an iron ring or brick on some part of the range were it will just simmer, for the remainder of the cooking.

3. Stir the grain continuously until it has set, but not at all afterward. Grains are much more appetizing if, while properly softened, they can still be made to retain their original form. Stirring renders the preparation pasty, and destroys its appearance. Grains cooked in a double boiler will require no stirring, and there will be little danger of their being lumpy, underdone on top, and scorched at the bottom, as is so often the case when cooked in a single boiler.

4. Cook continuously. If it be necessary to replenish the water in the outer boiler at anytime, let it be done with water of boiling temperature. If it is desired to have the mush quite thick and dry, the boiler should be left uncovered during the latter part of the cooking. If preferred moist, keep the cover on.

In the preparation of all mushes with meal or flour, it is a good plan to make the material into a batter with a portion of the liquid retained from the quantity given, before introducing it into the boiling water. This prevents the tendency to cook in lumps, so frequent when dry meal is scattered into boiling liquid. Care must be taken, however, to add the moistened portion very slowly, stirring vigorously meantime, so that the boiling will not be checked. Use warm water for moistening. The other directions given for the whole or broken grains are applicable to the ground products.

Grains for Breakfast.—Since hasty preparation will not suffice for the grains, they cannot be conveniently cooked in the morning in time for breakfast. This difficulty may be obviated by cooking the day previous, and reheating in the following way:—

Place the grain, when sufficiently cooked, in the refrigerator or in some place where it will cool quickly (as slow cooling might cause fermentation), to remain overnight. If cooked in a porcelain-lined or granite-ware double boiler, it may be left undisturbed, if uncovered. If cooked in tin or iron, turn the grain into a large earthen or china dish. To heat in the morning, fill the outer boiler with boiling water, place the inner dish containing the grain therein, and steam until thoroughly heated. No stirring and no additional liquid will be necessary, and if placed upon the stove when beginning the preparations for breakfast, it will be ready for serving in good season. If the grain has been kept in an earthen dish, it may best be reheated by placing that inside the steam cooker or an ordinary steamer over a kettle of boiling water.

Cracked wheat, pearl wheat, oatmeal, and other course grain preparations to be reheated, require for cooking a half cup of water in addition to the quantity given in the table. For rolled wheat, rolled oats, rolled rye, and other crushed grains, no more is needed. Grains may be used for breakfast without reheating, if served with hot milk or cream. If one has an Aladdin oven, the problem of grains for breakfast may be easily solved by cooking them all night, and if started late in the evening, they may be thus cooked over a single burner oil stove with the flame turned low.

Grains an economical food.—While grains are pre-eminently among the most nutritious of foods, they are also among the most economical, the average price being from five to seven cents a pound, and even less when purchased in bulk. If it be objected that they require much fuel to secure the prolonged cooking necessary, we would say that a few cents' worth of oil a week and a small lamp stove will accomplish the cooking in a most efficient manner. For a hot-weather food there are few articles which give greater satisfaction and require less time and labor on the part of the housewife than grains, cooked by the aid of a small lamp stove.

WHEAT.

Description.—Wheat is the most important of the grain foods. It is probably a native of Southwestern Asia, though like most grains cultivated from the earliest periods, its history is extremely obscure.

Wheat is of two principal kinds, characterized as soft and hard wheat, though there are hundreds of named varieties of the grain. The distinction between many of these is due to variation in the relative proportions of starch and nitrogenous matter. Some contain not more than eight per cent of nitrogenous elements, while others contain eighteen or twenty per cent, with a corresponding decrease in carbonaceous elements. This difference depends upon the soil, cultivation, season, climate, and other conditions under which the grain is produced.

The structure of the wheat grain consists of an external tegument of a hard, woody nature, so coherent that it appears in the form of scales or bran when the wheat is ground, and an inner portion, more soft and friable, consisting of several cellular layers. The layer nearest the outer husk contains vegetable fibrin and fatty matter. The second layer is largely composed of gluten cells; while the center comprising the bulk of the grain, is chiefly made up of starch granules with a small proportion of gluten.

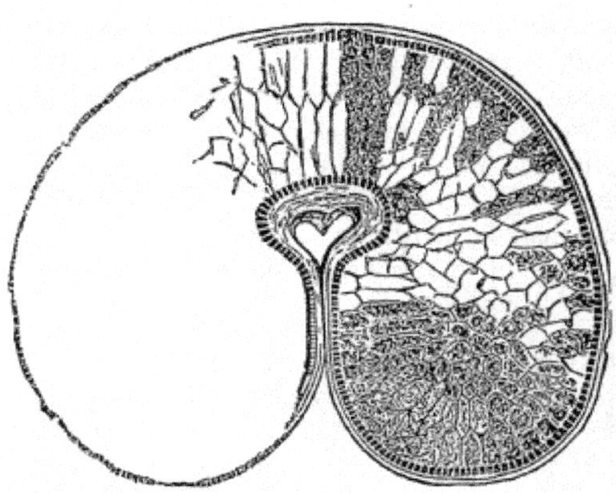

Sectional View of Wheat Kernel.

The structure of a wheat kernel is well illustrated in the are situated in different parts of the grain, and not uniformly distributed throughout its structure. The outer husk of the berry is composed wholly of innutritious and indigestible matter, but the thin layers which lie next this outer covering contain the larger proportion of the nitrogenous elements to be found in the entire kernel. The central portion consists almost wholly of farinaceous matter.

Phosphates and other mineral matter are present to some extent throughout the entire grain, but preponderates in the external part. Here is also found a peculiar, soluble, active principle called diastase, which possesses the power of converting starch into sugar. The dark color and marked flavor of Graham bread is undoubtedly due to the influence of this element.

Until within a few years the unground grain was rarely used as an article of food, but people are beginning to appreciate its wholesomeness, and cracked, rolled, and pearled wheats are coming rapidly into favor. Cracked wheat is the grain cleaned and then cut into two or more pieces; in rolled wheat the grains are mashed between rollers, by which process they are thoroughly softened in every part, and are then easily cooked. Pearl wheat is the whole grain cleaned and dressed. The whole grain is also cooked sometimes in its natural state.

Preparation and cooking.—Few articles of food show greater difference between good and poor cooking than the various grains. Dry, harsh, or underdone, they are as unwholesome as unpalatable. Like most of the grains, wheat, with the exception of new wheat boiled whole, should be put into boiling water and allowed to cook continuously but slowly until done. Any of the unground preparations require prolonged cooking. The average length of time and the approximate amount of water needed in cooking *one cupful* of the various wheat preparations in a double boiler is stated on page 82.

RECIPES.

Pearl Wheat.—Heat a quart of water to boiling in the inner dish of a double boiler, and stir into it one cup or one-half pint of pearl wheat. Let it boil rapidly until thickened and the wheat has ceased settling, then place in the outer boiler, in which the water should be boiling, and cook continuously from three to four hours.

Cracked Wheat.—Cracked wheat may be cooked in the same manner as pearl wheat, by using four and one-half parts of water to one of grain. The length of time required to cook it thoroughly is about the same as for pearl wheat.

Rolled Wheat.—This preparation of wheat requires only three parts water to one of wheat. It should be cooked in the same way as pearled wheat, but requires only three hours' cooking.

Boiled Wheat (sometimes called frumenty).—Select newly-cut wheat, well rubbed or threshed out. Look it over carefully, wash, and put to cook in five times its measure of cold water. Let it come to a boil, and cook gently until the grains burst open, and it can be readily mashed between the thumb and finger. This will require from four to ten hours, depending upon the age and variety of the wheat used. When done, it should be even full of a rich, thick liquor. If necessary, add more boiling water, but stir as little as possible. It may be served with cream, the same as other wheat preparations. It is also excellent served with lemon and other fruit sauces.

Wheat with Raisins.—Raisins or Zante currants may be added to any of the foregoing recipes, if desired. The raisins or currants should be well steamed previously, however, and stirred in lightly and evenly just before dishing. If cooked with the grain, they become soft, broken, and insipid. Figs, well steamed and chopped, may be added in the same way.

Wheat with Fresh Fruit.—Fresh whortleberries, blueberries, and blackberries stirred into any of the well-cooked wheat preparations just before serving, make a very desirable addition. A most delicious dish may be prepared by stirring into well-cooked cracked wheat a few spoonfuls of rather thick cream and some fresh wild blackberries. Serve hot.

Molded wheat.—Cracked wheat, rolled wheat, or pearl wheat, cooked according to the foregoing recipes, and turned into molds until cold, makes a very palatable dessert, and may be served with sugar and cream or with fruit juice. Bits of jelly placed on top of the molds in the form of stars or crosses, add to the appearance. Molded grains are also very nice served with fresh berries, either mashed or whole, arranged around the mold.

FINER MILL PRODUCTS OF WHEAT.

The grain of wheat is inclosed in a woody envelope. The cellular layers just beneath contain the largest proportion of nitrogenous matter, in the form of gluten, and are hard of pulverization, while the starchy heart of the grain is easily crumbled into fine dust. Thus it will be readily understood that when the grain is subjected to an equal pulverizing force, the several portions will be likely to be crushed into particles of different sizes. The outer husk being toughest, will be the least affected, the nitrogenous or glutenous portion will be much finer, while the brittle starch will be reduced to powder. This first simple product of grinding is termed wheat meal, unbolted, or Graham flour, and of course contains all the elements of the grain. In ordinary milling, however, this is subjected to various siftings, boltings, or dressings, to separate the finer from the coarser particles, and then subdivided into various grades of flour, which vary much in composition and properties. The coarser product contains the largest proportion of nutrients, while in the finer portions there is an exclusion of a large part of the nitrogenous element of the grain. The outer portions of the wheat kernel, which contain the greater part of the nitrogenous element, are darker in color than the central, starchy portion. It will be apparent, then, that the finer and whiter the flour, the less nutriment it is likely to contain, and that in the use of superfine white flour the eye is gratified at the expense of the body.

A preparation called farina, is made from the central portion of wheat, freed from bran, and crushed into granules. Another preparation, called Graham grits, is prepared by granulating the outer layers of the kernel together with the germ of the wheat. This preparation, comparatively a new one, includes the most nutritious properties of the grain, and its granular form renders it excellent for mushes as well as for other purposes. Farina is scarcely more nutritious than white flour, and should not be used as a staple food. Graham grits contains the best elements of the wheat grain in good proportion, and is one of the best preparations of wheat. Other preparations of wheat somewhat similar in character are farinose, germlet, etc.

RECIPES.

Farina.—Heat a pint of milk and one of water, or if preferred, a quart of milk, in the inner cup of a double boiler; and when boiling, stir in five tablespoonfuls of farina, moistened evenly with a little milk. Let it boil rapidly until well set, which will be in about five or eight minutes; then place in the outer boiler, and cook one hour. Serve cold or hot with a dressing of cream or fruit juices. Farina may be cooked in water alone, but on account of its lack of nutritive elements, it is more valuable if prepared with milk.

Farina with Fig Sauce.—Cook the farina as in the foregoing recipe, and serve hot with a fig sauce prepared as follows:—

Carefully look over, washed, and chop or cut quite finally, enough good figs to make a cupful. Stew in a pint of water, to which has been added a tablespoonful of sugar, until they are one homogeneous mass. If the figs are not of the best quality and do not readily soften, it is well, after stewing for a time, to rub them through a colander or vegetable press to break up the tough portions and make a smooth sauce. Put a spoonful of the hot fig sauce on each individual dish of farina, and serve with cream or without dressing.

Farina with Fresh Fruit.—Cook the farina as previously directed. Have some sliced yellow peaches, mellow sweet apples, or bananas in a dish, turn the farina over them, stir up lightly with a fork, and serve hot with cream.

Molded Farina.—Farina to be used cold may be cooked in the same manner as before described, with two or three tablespoonfuls of sugar added at the same time with the farina, and when done, molded in cups previously wet with a little cold water. Serve with a dressing of fruit juice, whipped cream flavored with lemon, or mock cream flavored with cocoanut.

Graham Grits.—To four parts of water boiling in the inner dish of a double boiler add slowly, so as not to stop the boiling of the water, one part of Graham grits. Stir until thickened, then place in the outer boiler, and steam from three to five hours. Serve hot with cream, or mold in cups previously dipped in cold water, and serve with a dressing of fruit juice. The fig sauce prepared as previously directed, is also excellent with Graham grits.

Graham Mush No. 1.—Good flour is the first requisite for making good Graham mush. Poor Graham flour cannot be made into first-class mush. Flour made from the best white winter wheat is perhaps the best. It may be used either sifted or unsifted, as preferred. The proportion of flour and liquid to be used will necessarily vary somewhat with the quality of the flour, but in general, three parts water to one of flour will be needed. Too much flour not only makes the mush too thick, but gives it an underdone taste. Stir the dried flour rapidly into boiling water, (which should not cease to boil during the process), until a thick porridge is obtained. It is well to have it a little thinner at first than is desirable for serving, as it will thicken by cooking. Cook slowly at least one hour. A longer time makes it more digestible.

Left-over Graham mush is nice spread on rather shallow tins, and simply heated quickly in a hot oven.

Graham Mush No. 2.—Moisten one pint of good Graham flour with a pint of warm water, or enough to make a batter thin enough to pour. (The quantity of water needed will vary a little with the fineness and quality of the flour.) Pour this batter into a quart of water boiling in the inner cup of a double boiler. Remember to add the batter sufficiently slow, so as not to stop the boiling of the water. When thickened, put into the outer boiler, and cook for one hour.

Graham Mush No. 3.—Prepare in the same way as above, using milk or part milk in the place of water. Left-over Graham mush at breakfast, which has been prepared with water, is very nice if, while it is still warm, a small quantity of hot milk is well stirred into it, and it is then set by to be reheated in a double boiler for dinner.

Graham mush with Dates.—Prepare a mush as for Graham mush No. 2. When done, place in the dish in which the mush is to be served, some nice, fresh dates from which the stones have been removed. Pour the mush over them, and stir up lightly, taking care not to break the fruit, and serve. Raisins previously steamed, or figs steamed and cut into pieces, may be used instead of dates. Serve hot with cream, or mold, and serve cold.

Plum Porridge.—Prepare a Graham mush as previously directed, and when done, add to it a cup of well-steamed raisins and sufficient rich milk to thin it to the consistency of porridge.

Graham Apple Mush.—Prepare a smooth apple sauce of rather tart apples. Sweeten it slightly, and thin with boiling water. Have this mixture boiling, and add to it Graham flour, either sprinkled in dry or moistened with water, sufficient to make a well-thickened mush. Cook, and serve hot with cream.

Granola Mush.—Granola, a cooked preparation of wheat and oats, manufactured by the Sanatarium Food Co., makes a most appetizing and quickly prepared breakfast dish. Into a quart of boiling water sprinkle a pint of granola. Cook for two or three minutes, and serve hot with cream.

Granola Fruit Mush.—Prepare the mush as directed, and stir into it, when done, a large cupful of nicely-steamed, seedless raisins. Serve hot with cream. Milk may be used instead of water, if preferred.

Granola Peach Mush.—Instead of the raisins as directed in the foregoing recipe, add to the mush, when done, a pint of sliced yellow peaches. Finely-cut, mellow sweet apples, sliced bananas, and blueberries may be used in a similar way.

Bran Jelly.—Select some clean wheat bran, sprinkle it slowly into boiling water as for Graham mush, stirring briskly meanwhile with a wooden spoon, until the whole is about the consistency of thick gruel. Cook slowly in a double boiler for two hours. Strain through a fine wire sieve placed over the top of a basin. When strained, reheat to boiling. Then stir into it a spoonful or so of sifted Graham flour, rubbed smooth in a little cold water. Boil up once; turn into molds previously wet in cold water, and when cool, serve with cream or fruit juice.

Description.—The native country of the plant from which our common varieties of the oat are derived, is unknown. Oat grains have been found among the remains of the lake-dwellers in Switzerland, and it is probable that this plant was cultivated by the prehistoric inhabitants of Central Europe.

The ancient Greeks and Romans used oats, ranking them next in value to barley, which they esteemed above all other cereals. Although principally grown as food for horses, the oat, when divested of its husk and broken by a process of milling, is an exceedingly nutritious and valuable article of diet for human beings; and there is no article of food that has increased in general favor more rapidly in the last few years than this grain.

The Scotch have long been famed for their large consumption of oatmeal. It forms the staple article of diet for the peasantry, to which fact is generally attributed the fine physique and uniform health for which they, as a race, are particularly noted. It is related that Dr. Johnson, of dictionary fame, who never lost an opportunity to disparage the Scotch, on one occasion defined oats as, "In Scotland, food for men; in England, food for horses." He was well answered by an indignant Scotchman who replied, "Yes; and where can you find such fine men as in Scotland, or such horses as in England?"

Oatmeal justly ranks high as an alimentary substance. It contains about the same proportion of nitrogenous elements as wheat, and with the exception of maize, is richer in fatty matter than any other of the cultivated cereals. In general structure the oat resembles wheat.

To prepare oats for food, the husk, which is wholly indigestible in character, must be thoroughly removed. To accomplish this, the grain is first kiln-dried to loosen the husk, and afterward submitted to a process of milling. Denuded of its integument, the nutritive part of the grain is termed groats; broken into finer particles, it constitutes what is known as oatmeal; rolled oats, or avena, is prepared by a process which crushes the kernels. Oatmeal varies also in degrees of trituration, some kinds being ground much finer than others. The more finely-ground products are sometimes adulterated with barley meal, which is cheaper than oatmeal and less nutritious. The black specks which are sometimes found in oatmeal are particles of black oats which have been ground in connection with the other.

Oatmeal lacks the tenacity of wheaten flour, and cannot, without the addition of some other flour, be made into light bread. It is, however, largely consumed by the inhabitants of Scotland and the north of England, in the form of oatcakes. The oatmeal is mixed with water, kneaded thoroughly, then rolled into very thin cakes, and baked on an iron plate or griddle suspended over a fire. So much, however, depends upon the kneading, that it is said that the common inquiry before the engagement of a domestic servant in Scotland, is whether or not she is a good kneader of oatcakes.

The most common use of oatmeal in this country is in the form of mush or porridge. For this the coarser grades of meal are preferable. For people in health, there is no more wholesome article of diet than oatmeal cooked in this way and eaten with milk. For growing children, it is one of the best of foods, containing, as it does, a large proportion of bone and muscle-forming material, while to almost all persons who have become accustomed to its use, it is extremely palatable. The time required for its digestion is somewhat longer than that of wheaten meal prepared in the same manner. It is apt to disagree with certain classes of dyspeptics, having a tendency to produce acidity, though it is serviceable as an article of diet in some forms of indigestion. The manner of its preparation for the table has very much to do with its wholesomeness. Indeed, many objectionable dishes are prepared from it. One of these, called *brose*, much used in Scotland, is made by simply stirring oatmeal into some hot liquid, as beef broth, or the water in which a vegetable has been boiled. The result is a coarse, pasty mass of almost raw oatmeal, an extremely indigestible compound, the use of which causes water brash. A preparation called *sowens*, or flummery, made by macerating the husks of the oats in water from twenty-four to thirty-six hours, until the mixture ferments, then boiling down to the consistency of gruel, is a popular article of food among the Scotch and Welsh peasantry. When boiled down still more, so it will form a firm jelly when cold, the preparation is called *budrum*.

Preparation and Cooking.—Oatmeal requires much cooking in order to break its starch cells; and the coarser the meal, the longer it should be allowed to cook. A common fault in the use of oatmeal is that it is served in an underdone state, which makes a coarse, indigestible dish of what, with more lengthy preparation, would be an agreeable and nutritious food. Like most of the grains, it is best put into boiling soft water, and allowed to cook continuously and slowly. It is greatly injured by stirring, and it is therefore preferably cooked in a double boiler or closed steamer. If it is necessary to use an ordinary kettle, place it on some part of the range where the contents will only simmer; or a hot brick may be placed under it to keep it from cooking too fast. It may be cooked the day previous, and warmed for use the same as other grains.

RECIPES.

Oatmeal Mush.—Heat a quart of water to boiling in the inner dish of a double boiler, sift into it one cup of coarse oatmeal, and boil rapidly, stirring continuously until it sets; then place in the outer boiler, the water in which should be boiling, and cook three hours or longer. Serve with cream.

Oatmeal fruit mush.—Prepare the oatmeal as directed above, and stir in lightly, when dishing for the table, some sliced mellow and juicy raw sweet apples. Strawberry apples and other slightly tart apples are likewise excellent for the purpose. Well-ripened peaches and bananas may also be used, if care is taken to preserve the slices whole, so as to present an appetizing appearance. Both this and the plain oatmeal mush are best eaten with toasted whole-wheat wafers or some other hard food.

Oatmeal Blancmange No. 1.—Soak a cupful of coarse oatmeal over night in a pint and a half of water. In the morning, beat the oatmeal well with a spoon, and afterwards pass all the soluble portion through a fine strainer. Place the liquid in the inner dish of a double boiler, and cook for half an hour. Turn into cups, cool fifteen or twenty minutes, and serve warm with cream and sugar, or a dressing of fruit juice. A lemon sauce prepared as directed on page 354 likewise makes an excellent dressing.

Oatmeal Blancmange No. 2.—Take a pint of well-cooked oatmeal, add to it a pint of milk, part cream if obtainable. Beat well together, and strain through a fine wire sieve. Turn the liquid into a saucepan, and boil for a few moments, until it is thick enough to drop from the point of a spoon; then turn into cups previously wet in cold water, and mold. Serve with a dressing of fruit juice or whipped cream slightly sweetened and flavored with lemon.

Jellied Oatmeal.—Cook oatmeal or rolled oats with an additional cup or cup and a half of water, and when done, turned into cups and mold. Serve cold with hot cream.

Mixed Mush.—A cup and a half of rolled wheat, mixed with one-half cup of coarse oatmeal, and cooked the same as oatmeal, forms a mush preferred by some to oatmeal alone.

Rolled Oats.—This preparation of oats should be cooked the same as oatmeal, but requires only three parts water to one of rolled oats, when cooked in a double boiler.

Oatmeal with Apple.—Cold oatmeal which has been left over may be made into an appetising dish by molding in alternate layers with nicely-steamed tart apple, sprinkled lightly with sugar. Serve with cream. Other cooked fruit, such as cherries, evaporated peaches, and apricots may be used in the same way. A very pleasing dish is made by using between the layers ripe yellow peaches and plums sliced together, and lightly sprinkled with sugar.

Oatmeal Porridge.—Into a quart and a half of water, which should be boiling in the inner dish of a double boiler, sprinkle one cup of rather coarse oatmeal. Boil rapidly, stirring meanwhile until the grain is set; then place in the outer boiler, and cook continuously for three hours or longer. A half cup of cream added just before serving, is a desirable addition.

BARLEY.

Description.—Barley is stated by historians to be the oldest of all cultivated grains. It seems to have been the principal bread plant among the ancient Hebrews, Greeks, and Romans. The Jews especially held the grain in high esteem, and sacred history usually uses it interchangeably with wheat, when speaking of the fruits of the Earth.

Among the early Greeks and Romans, barley was almost the only food of the common people and the soldiers. The flour was made into gruel, after the following recipe: "Dry, near the fire or in the oven, twenty pounds of barley flour, then parch it. Add three pounds of linseed meal, half a pound of coriander seeds, two ounces of salt, and the water necessary." If an especially delectable dish was desired, a little millet was also added to give the paste more "cohesion and delicacy." Barley was also used whole as a food, in which case it was first parched, which is still the manner of preparing it in some parts of Palestine and many districts of India, also in the Canary Islands, where it is known as *gofio*. Of this custom a lady from Palestine writes: "The reapers, during barley harvest, take bunches of the half-ripe grain, and singe, or parch, it over a fire of thorns. The milk being still in the grain, it is very sweet, and is considered a delicacy."

In the time of Charles I, barley meal took the place of wheat almost entirely as the food of the common people in England. In some parts of Europe, India, and other Eastern countries, it is still largely consumed as the ordinary farinaceous food of the peasantry and soldiers. The early settlers of New England also largely used it for bread making. At the present day only a very insignificant quantity of barley is used for food purposes in this country, and most of this in the unground state.

Barley is less nutritious than wheat, and to many people is less agreeable in flavor. It is likewise somewhat inferior in point of digestibility. Its starch cells being less soluble, they offer more resistance to the gastric juice.

There are several distinct species of barley, but that most commonly cultivated is designated as two-rowed, or two-eared barley. In general structure, the barley grain resembles wheat and oats.

Simply deprived of its outer husk, the grain is termed *Scotch milled* or *pot barley*. Subjected still further to the process by which the fibrous outer coat of the grain is removed, it constitutes what is known as *pearl barley*. Pearl barley ground into flour is known as *patent barley*. Barley flour, owing to the fact that it contains so small a proportion of gluten, needs to be mixed with wheaten flour for bread-making purposes. When added in small quantity to whole-wheat bread, it has a tendency to keep the loaf moist, and is thought by some to improve the flavor.

The most general use made of this cereal as a food, is in the form of pearl, or Scotch, barley. When well boiled, barley requires about two hours for digestion.

General Suggestions for Cooking Barley.—The conditions requisite for cooking barley are essentially the same as for oatmeal. It is best cooked slowly. Four parts of water to one of grain will be needed for steaming or cooking in a double boiler, and from four to five hours' time will be required, unless the grain has been previously soaked for several hours, in which case three hours will do. If the strong flavor of the grain is objected to, it may be soaked over night and cooked in fresh water. This method will, however, be a sacrifice of some of the nutriment contained in the grain. Barley thus soaked will require only three parts water to one of barley for cooking.

RECIPES.

Baked Barley.—Soak six tablespoonfuls of barley in cold water over night. In the morning, turn off the water, and put the barley in an earthen pudding dish, and pour three and one half pints of boiling water over it; add salt if desired, and bake in a moderately quick oven about two and one half hours, or till perfectly soft, and all the water is absorbed. When about half done, add four or five tablespoonfuls of sugar mixed with grated lemon peel. It may be eaten warm, but is very nice molded in cups and served cold with cream.

Pearl Barley with Raisins.—Carefully look over and wash a cupful of pearl barley. Cook in a double boiler in five cups of boiling water for four hours. Just before serving, add a cupful of raisins which have been prepared by pouring boiling water over them and allowing them to stand until swollen. Serve hot, with cream.

Pearl Barley with Lemon Sauce.—Pearl barley cooked in the same manner, but without the addition of the raisins, is excellent served with cream or with a lemon sauce prepared as directed on page 354.

RICE.

Description.—Rice is one of the most abundantly used and most digestible of all the cereals. It grows wild in India, and it is probable that this is its native home. It is, however, now cultivated in most tropical and sub-tropical climates, and is said to supply the principal food for nearly one third of the human race. It is mentioned in history several hundred years before Christ. According to Soyer, an old writer on foods, the Greeks and Romans held rice in high esteem, believing it to be a panacea for chest and lung diseases.

The grain is so largely grown and used by the Chinese that "fan," their word for rice, has come to enter into many compound words. A beggar is called a "tou-fan-tee," that is, "the rice-seeking one." The ordinary salutation, "Che-fan," which answers to our "How do you do?" means, "Have you eaten your rice?"

Rice requires a wet soil, and the fields in which the grain is raised, sometimes called "paddy" fields, are periodically irrigated. Before ripening, the water is drained off, and the crop is then cut with a sickle, made into shocks, stacked, threshed, and cleaned, much like wheat. The rice kernel is inclosed within two coverings, a course outer husk, which is easily removed, and an inner, reddish, siliceous coating.

"Paddy" is the name given in India to the rice grain when inclosed in its husk. The same is termed "rough rice" in this country. The outer husk of the rice is usually removed in the process of threshing, but the inner red skin, or hull, adheres very closely, and is removed by rubbing and pounding. The rough rice is first ground between large stones, and then conveyed into mortars, and pounded with iron-shod pestles. Thence, by fanning and screening, the husk is fully removed, and the grain divided into three different grades, whole, middlings, and small whole grains, and polished ready for market. The middlings consist of the larger broken pieces of the grain; the small rice, of the small fragments mixed with the chit of the grain. The broken rice, well dried, is sometimes ground into flour of different degrees of fineness. The small rice is much sweeter and somewhat superior in point of nutritive value to the large or head rice usually met with in commerce.

Rice is characterized by a large percentage of starch, and is so deficient in other food elements that if used alone, unless consumed in very large quantities, it will not furnish the requisite amount of nitrogenous material necessary for a perfect health food. For this reason, it is necessary to supplement its use with some other food containing an excess of nitrogenous elements, as peas, beans, milk, etc. Associated with other articles rich in albuminous elements, rice is exceedingly valuable, and one of the most easily digested foods. Boiled or steamed rice requires but a little over one hour for digestion.

Preparation and Cooking.—Rice needs to be thoroughly washed to remove the earthy taste it is so apt to have. A good way to do this is to put it into a colander, in a deep pan of water. Rub the rice well with the hands, lifting the colander in and out the water, and changing the water until it is clear; then drain. In this way the grit is deposited in the water, and the rice left thoroughly clean.

The best method of cooking rice is by steaming it. If boiled in much water, it loses a portion of its already small percentage of nitrogenous elements. It requires much less time for cooking than any of the other grains. Like all the dried grains and seeds, rice swells in cooking to several times its original bulk. When cooked, each grain of rice should be separate and distinct, yet perfectly tender.

RECIPES.

Steamed Rice.—Soak a cup of rice in one and a fourth cups of water for an hour, then add a cup of milk, turn into an earthen dish suitable for serving it from at table, and place in a steam-cooker or a covered steamer over a kettle of boiling water, and steam for an hour. It should be stirred with a fork occasionally, for the first ten or fifteen minutes.

Boiled Rice (Japanese method).—Thoroughly cleanse the rice by washing in several waters, and soak it overnight. In the morning, drain it, and put to cook in an equal quantity of boiling water, that is, a pint of water for a pint of rice. For cooking, a stewpan with tightly fitting cover should be used. Heat the water to boiling, then add the rice, and after stirring, put on the cover, which is not again to be removed during the boiling. At first, as the water boils, steam will puff out freely from under the cover, but when the water has nearly evaporated, which will be in eight to ten minutes, according to the age and quality of the rice, only a faint suggestion of steam will be observed, and the stewpan must then be removed from over the fire to some place on the range, where it will not burn, to swell and dry for fifteen or twenty minutes.

Rice to be boiled in the ordinary manner requires two quarts of boiling water to one cupful of rice. It should be boiled rapidly until tender, then drained at once, and set in a moderate oven to become dry. Picking and lifting lightly occasionally with a fork will make it more flaky and dry. Care must be taken, however, not to mash the rice grains.

Rice With Fig Sauce.—Steam a cupful of best rice as directed above, and when done, serve with a fig sauce prepared as directed on page 89. Dish a spoonful of the fig sauce with each saucer of rice, and serve with plenty of cream. Rice served in this way requires no sugar for dressing, and is a most wholesome breakfast dish.

Orange Rice.—Wash and steam the rice according to directions already given. Prepare some oranges by separating into sections and cutting each section in halves, removing the seeds and all the white portion. Sprinkle the oranges lightly with sugar, and let them stand while the rice is cooking. Serve a portion of the orange on each saucerful of rice.

Rice with raisins.—Carefully wash a cupful of rice, soak it, and cook as directed for Steamed Rice. After the rice has began to swell, but before it has softened, stir into it lightly, using a fork for the purpose, a cupful of raisins, or Zante currents. Serve with cream.

Rice with Peaches.—Steam the rice as previously directed, and when done, serve with cream and a nicely ripened peach pared and sliced on each individual dish.

Browned Rice.—Spread a cupful of rice on a shallow baking tin, and put into a moderately hot oven to brown. It will need to be stirred frequently to prevent burning and to secure a uniformity of color. Each rice kernel, when sufficiently browned, should be of a yellowish brown, about the color of ripened wheat. Steam the same as directed for ordinary rice, using only two cups of water for each cup of browned rice, and omitting the preliminary soaking. When properly cooked, each kernel will be separated, dry, and mealy. Rice prepared in this manner is undoubtedly more digestible than when cooked without browning.

RYE.

Description.—Rye is much more largely grown and used in European countries that in America. In appearance it closely resembles wheat, although somewhat darker in color and smaller in size. Bread made from rye constitutes the staple food of the people in many parts of Europe. In nutritive value such bread nearly equals that made from wheat, but it has an acid taste not relished by persons unaccustomed to its use.

Rye is found in market deprived of its husk and crushed or rolled, and also in the form of meal and flour.

RECIPES.

Rolled Rye.—Into three parts water boiling in the inner dish of a double boiler, stir one part rolled rye. Boil rapidly until set, stirring meanwhile, then place in the outer boiler, and cook for three or more hours.

Rye Mush.—Stir a cupful of rye meal to a smooth batter with a cupful of water, then turn it slowly into three cupfuls of water, which should be boiling on the range, in the inner dish of a double boiler. Stir until thickened, then place in the outer boiler, and cook for an hour or longer.

MAIZE, OR INDIAN CORN.

Description.—There can be little doubt that maize is of American origin. The discoverers of the new world found it cultivated by the aborigines, and from the fact that corn was the generic term then largely used to designate grain (in old English, "corn" means grain), they named it "Indian corn." Since that time it has been carried to nearly every part of the globe, and probably it is more extensively used than any other one of the cereals, with the exception of rice. This is undoubtedly due to the fact that it is the most prolific of the grains, and is adapted to the widest range of climate.

Maize was the chief food of the slaves of Brazil, as it used to be of those in our own Southern States, and is very largely consumed in Mexico and Peru. It was used very little in Europe until the Irish famine in 1847; since then, it has become a staple food with the poorer classes.

The varieties of corn are almost too numerous to be counted. For general purposes, however, they may be classified as field corn, sweet corn, and pop corn.

Corn is characterized by an excess of fatty matter, containing upwards of three times the amount of that element to be found in wheat. Corn requires stronger powers of digestion than wheat, and is unsuited to some stomachs.

The skin of the corn kernel is thin, and when subjected to milling processes, is included in the grinding. When well ground, it can be digested, with the exception of the siliceous coating.

Sweet corn and some of the field varieties, form a nutritious and favorite food while green. The mature grain is used in many forms. The whole grain, hulled, is an agreeable food. Hulled, broken, or split to various degrees of fineness, it is known according to the size to which the grain has been reduced as hominy, fine hominy, or grits; or, if finer still, as samp. Subjected to a process of still finer trituration, it forms meal. Cornstarch consists of the farinaceous portions of the grain.

On account of the large proportion of fatty matter contained in maize, it acquires, if kept for some time and unpleasant, rancid taste, occasioned by the usual change which takes place in fat when exposed to the atmosphere.

The new process granular meal, which is prepared from corn dried for a long period before grinding, becomes rank less quickly than that ground in the old way.

Maize meal is very largely consumed in the form of mush or porridge. This, in Ireland, is termed "stirabout;" in Italy it is called "polenta;" and in British Honduras it is known as "corn lob."

General Suggestions for Cooking—Most of the various preparations from maize require prolonged cooking to render them wholesome; this is equally true respecting mushes prepared from samp or meal, a dish which unfortunately some cook in bygone days saw fit to term "hasty pudding." Unthinking people since, supposing it to have been so named because of the little time required to cook it, have commonly prepared it in fifteen or twenty minutes, whereas from one to two hours, or even longer, are necessary to cook it properly. Hulled corn, hominy, and grits, all require prolonged cooking. The time for cooking these preparations may be somewhat lessened if they are previously soaked over night. They should, however, be cooked in the same water in which they are soaked.

RECIPES.

Corn meal mush.—stir together one pint of cornmeal, one tablespoonful of flour, and one pint of cold milk. Turn this slowly, stirring well meanwhile, into one quart of boiling water, which should not cease to boil during the introduction of the batter. Cook three or four hours. If milk is not obtainable, water alone may be used, in which case two tablespoonfuls of flour will be needed. Cook in a double boiler.

Corn Meal Mush with Fruit.—Mush prepared in the above manner may have some well-steamed raisins or chopped figs added to it just before serving.

Corn meal cubes.—Left-over corn meal mush may be made into an appetizing dish by first slicing into rather thick slices, then cutting into cubes about one inch squares. Put the cubes into a tureen and turn over them a quantity of hot milk or cream. Cover the dish, let them stand until thoroughly heated through, then serve.

Browned Mush.—Slice cold corn meal mush rather thin, brush each slice with thick, sweet cream, and brown in a moderate oven until well heated through.

Samp.—Use one part of samp to four and one half parts of boiling water. It is the best plan to reserve enough of the water to moisten the samp before adding it to the boiling water, as it is much less likely to cook in lumps. Boil rapidly, stirring continuously, until the mush has well set, then slowly for from two to three hours.

Cerealine Flakes.—Into one measure of boiling liquid stir an equal measure of cerealine flakes, and cook in a double boiler from one half to three fourths of an hour.

Hulled Corn.—*To Hull the Corn.*—Put enough wood ashes into a large kettle to half fill it; then nearly fill with hot water, and boil ten minutes. Drain off the water from the ashes, turn it into a kettle, and pour in four quarts of clean, shelled field corn, white varieties preferred. Boil till the hulls rub off. Skim the corn out of the lye water, and put it into a tub of fresh cold water. To remove the hulls, scrub the corn well with a new stiff brush broom kept for the purpose, changing the water often. Put through half a dozen or more waters, and then take the corn out by handfuls, rubbing each well between the hands to loosen the remaining hulls, and drop again into clear water. Pick out all hulls. Cleanse the corn through several more waters if it is to be dried and kept before using. Well hulled corn is found in the markets.

To Cook.—If it is to be cooked at once, it should be parboiled in clear water twice, and then put into new water and cooked till tender. It should be nearly or quite dry when done. It may be served with milk or cream.

Coarse Hominy.—For coarse hominy use four parts of water or milk and water to one of grain. It is best steamed or cooked in a double boiler, though it may be boiled in a kettle over a slow fire. The only objection to this method is the need of frequent stirring to prevent sticking, which breaks and mashes the hominy. From four to five hours' slow cooking will be necessary, unless the grain has been previously soaked; then about one hour less will be required.

Fine Hominy or Grits.—This preparation is cooked in the same manner as the foregoing, using three and one half or four parts of water to one of the grain. Four or five hours will be necessary for cooking the unsoaked grits.

Popped Corn.—The small, translucent varieties of maize known as "pop corn," possessed the property, when gently roasted, of bursting open, or turning inside out, a process which is owing to the following facts: Corn contains an excess of fatty matter. By proper means this fat can be separated from the grain, and it is then a thick, pale oil. When oils are heated sufficiently in a vessel closed from the air, they are turned into gas, which occupies many times the bulk of the oil. When pop corn is gradually heated, and made so hot that the oil inside of the kernel turns to gas, being unable to escape through the hull of the kernel, the pressure finally becomes strong enough to burst the grain, and the explosion is so violent as to shatter it in a most curious manner.

Popped corn forms an excellent food, the starch of the grain being will cooked. It should, however, be eaten in connection with other food at mealtime, and not as a delicacy between meals. Ground pop corn is considered a delectable dish eaten with milk or cream; it also forms the base of several excellent puddings.

To pop the corn, shell and place in a wire "popper" over a bed of bright coals, or on the top of a hot stove; stir or shake continuously, so that each kernel may be subjected to the same degree of heat on all sides, until it begins to burst open. If a popper is not attainable, a common iron skillet covered tightly, and very lightly oiled on the bottom, may be used for the purpose. The corn must be very dry to begin with, and if good, nearly every kernel will pop open nicely. It should be used within twenty-four hours after popping.

MACARONI.

Description.—Macaroni is a product of wheat prepared from a hard, clean, glutenous grain. The grain is ground into a meal called *semolina*, from which the bran is excluded. This is made into a tasty dough by mixing with hot water in the proportion of two thirds *semolina* to one third water. The dough after being thoroughly mixed is put into a shallow vat and kneaded and rolled by machinery. When well rolled, it is made to assume varying shapes by being forced by a powerful plunger through the perforated head of strong steel or iron cylinders arranged above a fire, so that the dough is partially baked as it issues from the holes. It is afterwards hung over rods or laid upon frames covered with cloth, and dried. It is called by different names according to its shape. If in the shape of large, hollow cylinders, it is *macaroni;* if smaller in diameter, it is *spaghetti;* if fine, *vermicelli;* if the paste is cut into fancy patterns, it is termed *pasta d'Italia*.

Macaroni was formerly made only in Italy, but at present is manufactured to a considerable extent in the United States. The product, however, is in general greatly inferior to that imported from Italy, owing to the difference in the character of the wheat from which it is made, the Italian macaroni being produced from a hard, semi-translucent wheat, rich in nitrogenous elements, and which is only grown successfully in a hot climate. Like all cereal foods, macaroni should be kept in a perfectly dry storeroom.

To Select Macaroni.—Good macaroni will keep in good condition for years. It is rough, elastic, and hard; while the inferior article is smooth, soft, breaks easily, becomes moldy with keeping. Inferior macaroni contains a large percentage of starch, and but a small amount of gluten. When put into hot water, it assumes a white, pasty appearance, and splits in cooking. Good macaroni when put into hot water absorbs a portion of the water, swells to nearly double its size, but perfectly retains its shape. Inferior macaroni is usually sold a few cents cheaper per pound than the genuine article. It contains a much smaller amount of gluten. The best quality of any shape one pleases can be bought in most markets for ten or fifteen cents a pound.

To Prepare and Cook Macaroni.—Do not wash macaroni. If dusty, wipe with a clean, dry cloth. Break into pieces of convenient size. Always put to cook in boiling liquid, taking care to have plenty of water in the saucepan (as it absorbs a large quantity), and cook until tender. The length of time required may vary from twenty minutes, if fresh, to one hour if stale. When tender, turn into a colander and drain, and pour cold water through it to prevent the tubes from sticking together. The fluid used for cooking may be water, milk, or a mixture of both; also soup stock, tomato juice, or any preferred liquid.

Macaroni serves as an important adjunct to the making of various soups, and also forms the basis of other palatable dishes.

RECIPES.

Home-Made Macaroni.—To four cupfuls of flour, add one egg well beaten, and enough water to make a dough that can be rolled. Roll thin on a breadboard and cut into strips. Dry in the sun. The best arrangement for this purpose is a wooden frame to which a square of cheese-cloth has been tightly tacked, upon which the macaroni may be laid in such a way as not to touch, and afterwards covered with a cheese-cloth to keep off the dust during the drying.

Boiled Macaroni.—Break sticks of macaroni into pieces about an inch in length, sufficient to fill a large cup; put it into boiling water and cook until tender. When done, drained thoroughly, then add a pint of milk, part cream if it can be afforded, a little salt and one well-beaten egg; stir over the fire until it thickens, and serve hot.

Macaroni with Cream Sauce.—Cook the macaroni as directed in the proceeding, and serve with a cream sauce prepared by heating a scant pint of rich milk to boiling, in a double boiler. When boiling, add a heaping tablespoonful of flour, rubbed smoothed in a little milk and one fourth teaspoonful of salt. If desired, the sauce may be flavored by steeping in the milk before thickening for ten or fifteen minutes, a slice of onion or a few bits of celery, and then removing with a fork.

Macaroni with Tomato Sauce.—Break a dozen sticks of macaroni into two-inch lengths, and drop into boiling milk and water, equal parts. Let it boil for an hour, or until perfectly tender. In the meantime prepare the sauce by rubbing a pint of stewed or canned tomatoes through a colander to remove all seeds and fragments. Heat to boiling, thicken with a little flour; a tablespoonful to the pint will be about the requisite proportion. Add salt and if desired, a half cup of very thin sweet cream. Dish the macaroni into individual dishes, and serve with a small quantity of the sauce poured over each dish.

Macaroni Baked with Granola.—Break macaroni into pieces about an inch in length sufficient to fill a large cup, and cook until tender in boiling milk and water. When done, drain and put a layer of the macaroni in the bottom of an earthen pudding dish, and sprinkle over it a scant teaspoonful of granola. Add a second and third layer and sprinkle each with granola; then turn over the whole a custard sauce prepared by mixing together a pint of milk, the well beaten yolks of two eggs or one whole egg, and one-fourth of a teaspoonful of salt. Care should be taken to arrange the macaroni in layers loosely, so that the sauce will readily permeate the whole. Bake for a few minutes only, until the custard has well set, and serve.

Eggs and macaroni.—Break fifteen whole sticks of macaroni into two-inch lengths, and put to cook in boiling water. While the macaroni is cooking, boil the yolks of four eggs until mealy. The whole egg may be used if caught so the yolks are mealy in the whites simply jellied, not hardened. When the macaroni is done, drain and put a layer of it arranged loosely in the bottom of an earthen pudding dish. Slice the cooked egg yolks and spread a layer of them over the macaroni. Fill the dish with alternate layers of macaroni and egg, taking care to have the top layer of macaroni. Pour over the whole a cream sauce prepared as follows: Heat one and three fourths cup of rich milk to boiling, add one fourth teaspoonful of salt and one heaping spoonful of flour rubbed smooth in a little cold milk. Cook until thickened, then turn over the macaroni. Sprinkle the top with grated bread crumbs, and brown in a hot oven for eight or ten minutes. Serve hot.

TABLE TOPICS.

Sir Isaac Newton, when writing his grail work, "Principia," lived wholly upon a vegetable, diet.

ROBERT COLLYER once remarked; "One great reason why I never had a really sick day in my life was that as boy I lived on oatmeal and milk and brown bread, potatoes and a bit of meat when I could get it, and then oatmeal again."

HOT-WEATHER DIET.—The sultry period of our summer, although comparatively slight and of short duration, is nevertheless felt by some people to be extremely oppressive, but this is mainly due to the practice of eating much animal food or fatty matters, conjoined as it often is with the habit of drinking freely of fluids containing more or less alcoholics. Living on cereals, vegetables, and fruits, and abstaining from alcoholic drinks, the same persons would probably enjoy the temperature, and be free from the thirst which is the natural result of consuming needlessly heating food.—*Sir Henry Thompson.*

Mistress (arranging for dinner)—"Didn't the macaroni come from the grocer's, Bridget?"

Bridget—"Yis, mum, but oi sint it back. Every won av thim leetle stims wuz impty."

Some years since, a great railroad corporation in the West, having occasion to change the gauge of its road throughout a distance of some five hundred miles, employed a force of 3,000 workmen upon the job, who worked from very early in the morning until late at night. Alcoholic drinks were strictly prohibited, but a thin gruel made of oatmeal and water was kept on hand and freely partaken of by the men to quench their thirst. The results were admirable; not a single workmen gave out under the severe strain, and not one lost a day from sickness. Thus this large body of men were kept well and in perfect strength and spirits, and the work was done in considerably less time than that counted on for its completion.

In Scotch households oatmeal porridge is as inevitable as breakfast itself, except perhaps on Sundays, as this anecdote will illustrate. A mother and child were passing along a street in Glasgow, when this conversation was overheard:—

"What day is the morn, mither?"

"Sabbath, laddie."

"An' will wi hae tea to breakfast, mither?"

"Aye, laddie, gin we're spared."

"An' gin we're no spared, will we hae parrich?"

BREADSTUFFS AND BREADMAKING

Although the grains form most nutritious and palatable dishes when cooked in their unground state, this is not always the most convenient way of making; use of them. Mankind from earliest antiquity has sought to give these wonderful products of nature a more portable and convenient form by converting them into what is termed bread, a word derived from the verb *bray*, to pound, beat, or grind small, indicative of the ancient manner of preparing the grain for making bread. Probably the earliest form of bread was simply the whole grain moistened and then exposed to heat. Afterward, the grains were roasted and ground, or pounded between stones, and unleavened bread was made by mixing this crude flour with water, and baking in the form of cakes. Among the many ingenious arrangements used by the ancients for baking this bread, was a sort of portable oven in shape something like a pitcher, in the inside of which a fire was made. When the oven was well heated, a paste made of meal and water was applied to the outside. Such bread was baked very quickly and taken off in small, thin sheets like wafers. A flat cake was the common form in which most of the bread of olden times was baked; being too brittle to be cut with a knife, the common mode of dividing it was by breaking and hence the expression "breaking bread" so common in Scripture.

Various substances have been and are employed for making this needful article. Until the last few decades, barley was the grain most universally used. Chestnuts, ground to a flour, are made into bread in regions where these nuts abound. Quite recently, an immense peanut crop in the Southern States was utilized for bread-making purposes. In ancient times, the Thracians made to bread from a flour made from the *water coltran*, a prickly root of triangular form. In Syria, mulberries were dried and grounded to flour. Rice, moss, palm tree piths, and starch producing roots are used by different nationalities in the preparation of bread. In many parts of Sweden, bread is made from dried fish, using one half fish flour and one half barley flour; and in winter, flour made from the bark of trees is added. Desiccated tomatoes, potatoes, and other vegetables are also mixed with the cereals for bread-making. In India, the lower classes make their bread chiefly from millet. Moss bread is made in Iceland from the reindeer moss, which toward autumn becomes soft, tender, and moist, with a taste like wheat bran. It contains a large quantity of starch, and the Icelanders gather, dry, pulverize it, and thus prepare it for bread-making. The ancient Egyptians often made their bread from equal parts of the whole grain and meal.

The breadstuff's most universally used among civilized nations at the present time are barley, rye, oats, maize, buckwheat, rice, and wheat, of which the last has acquired a decided preference.

If made in the proper manner and from suitable material, bread is, with the exception of milk, the article best fitted for the nourishment of the body, and if need be, can supply the place of all other foods. Good bread does not cloy the appetite as do many other articles of food, and the simplest bill of fare which includes light, wholesome bread, is far more satisfying than an elaborate meal without it. Were the tables of our land supplied with good, nutritious, well-baked bread, there would be less desire for cake, pastry, and other indigestible particles, which, under the present system of cookery, are allowed to compensate for the inferior quality and poor preparation of more wholesome foods.

Bread has been proverbially styled the "staff of life." In nearly all ancient languages the entomology of the word "bread" signifies all, indicating; that the bread of earlier periods was in truth what it should be at the present time,—a staff upon which all the functions of life might with safety depend.

Notwithstanding the important part bread was designed to play in the economy of life, it would be hardly possible to mention another aliment which so universally falls below the standard either through the manner of its preparation or in the material used.

Bread, to answer the requirements of a good, wholesome article of food, beside being palatable, must be light, porous, and friable, so that it can be easily insalivated and digested. It should not contain ingredients which will in any way be injurious if taken into the system, but should contain as many as possible of the elements of nutrition. Wheat, the substance from which bread is most generally made, contains all the necessary food elements in proper proportions to meet the requirements of nutrition, and bread should also contain them. The flour, however, must be made from the whole grain of the wheat, with the exception of the outer husk.

What is ordinarily termed fine flour has a large part of the most nutritive properties of the grain left out, and unless this deficiency is made up by other foods, the use of bread made from such material will leave the most vital tissues of the body poorly nourished, and tend to produce innumerable bad results. People who eat bread made from fine white flour naturally crave the food elements which have been eliminated from the wheat, and are thus led to an excessive consumption of meat, and the nerve-starvation and consequent irritability thus induced may also lead to the use of alcoholic drinks. We believe that one of the strongest barriers women could erect against the inroads of intemperance would be to supply the tables of the land with good bread made from flour of the entire wheat.

The superiority of bread made from the entire wheat or unbolted meal has been attested by many notable examples in history. In England, under the administration of William Pitt, there was for several years such a scarcity of wheat that to make it hold out longer, a law was passed by Parliament that the army should be supplied with bread made of unbolted flour. This occasioned much murmuring on the part of the soldiers, but nevertheless the health of the army improved so greatly as to be a subject of surprise. The officers and the physicians at last publicly declared that the soldiers had never before been so robust and healthy.

According to the eminent Prof. Liebig, whole-wheat bread contains 60 per cent more of the phosphate or bone forming material than does meat, and 200 per cent more gluten than white bread. To the lack of these elements in a food so generally used as white flour bread, is undoubtedly due the great prevalence of early decaying teeth, rickets, and other bone diseases. Indeed, so many are the evils attendant upon a continued use of fine flour bread that we can in a great measure agree with a writer of the last century who says, in a quaint essay still to be seen at the British Museum, that "fine flour, spirituous liquors, and strong ale-house beer are the foundations of almost all the poverty and all the evils that affect the labouring part of mankind."

Bread made from the entire wheat is looked upon with far more favor than formerly, and it is no longer necessary to use the crude products of the grain for its manufacture, since modern invention has worked such a revolution in milling processes that it is now possible to obtain a fine flour containing all the nutritious elements of the grain. The old-time millstone has been largely superceded by machinery with which the entire grain may be reduced to fine flour without the loss of any of its valuable properties. To be sure, the manufacture of fine white flour of the old sort, is still continued, and doubtless will be continued so long as color takes precedence over food value. The improved processes of milling have, however, enabled the millers to utilize a much larger proportion of the nutritious elements of the grain than formerly, and still preserve that whiteness is so pleasing to many consumers. Although it is true that there are brands of white flour which possess a large percentage of the nutrient properties of the wheat, it is likewise true that flour which contains *all* the nutritive elements is *not* white.

Of flours made from the entire grain there are essentially two different varieties, that which is termed *unbolted wheat meal* or *Graham* flour, and that called *wheat-berry, whole-wheat*, or *entire-wheat* flour. The principal difference between the two consists in the preliminary treatment of the wheat kernel before reduction, Graham flour containing more or less of the flinty bran, which is wholly innutritious and to a sensitive stomach somewhat irritating. In the manufacture of *whole* or *entire*-wheat flour, the outer, flinty bran is first removed by special machinery, and then the entire grain pulverized, by some of approved method, to different grades of fineness. The absence of the indigestible bran renders the entire-wheat flour superior in this respect to Graham, though for many persons the latter is to preferred.

How to Select Flour.—The first requisite in the making of good bread is good flour. The quality of a brand of flour will of course depend much upon the kind of grain from which it is prepared—whether new or old, perfect, or deteriorated by rust, mold, or exposure, and also upon the thoroughness with which it has been cleansed from dust, chaff, and all foreign substances, as well as upon the method by which it is ground. It is not possible to judge with regard to all these particulars by the appearance of the flour, but in general, good flour will be sweet, dry, and free from any sour or musty smell or taste. Take up a handful, and if it falls from the hand light and elastic, it is pretty sure to be good. If it will retain the imprint of the fingers and falls and a compact mass or a damp, clammy, or sticky to the touch, it is by no means the best. When and knead a little of it between the fingers; if it works soft and sticky, it is poor. Good flour, when made into dough, is elastic, and will retain its shape. This elastic property of good flour is due to the gluten which it contains. The more gluten and the stronger it is, the better the flour. The gluten of good flour will swell to several times its original bulk, while that of poor flour will not.

In buying white flour, do not select that which is pure white with a bluish tinge, but that which is of a creamy, yellowish-white tint. While the kinds of flour that contain the entire nutritive properties of the wheat will necessarily be darker in color, we would caution the reader not to suppose that because flour is dark in color it is for that reason good, and rich in nutritive elements. There are many other causes from which flour may be dark, such as the use of uncleansed or dark varieties of wheat, and the large admixture of bran and other grains; many unscrupulous millers and flour dealers make use of this fact to palm off upon their unsuspecting customers an inferior article. Much of the so-called Graham flour is nothing more than poor flour mixed with bran, and is in every way inferior to good white flour. Fine flour or made from the entire wheat may generally be distinguished from a spurious article by takinga small portion into the mouth and chewing it. Raw flour made from the entire grain has a sweet taste, and a rich, nutty flavor the same as that experienced in chewing a whole grain of wheat, and produces a goodly quantity of gum or gluten, while a spurious article tastes flat and insipid like starch, or has a bitter, pungent taste consequent upon the presence of impurities. This bitter taste is noticeable in bread made from such flour. A given quantity of poor flour will not make as much bread as the same quantity of good flour, so that adulteration may also be detected in this way. Doubtless much of the prejudice against the use of whole-wheat flour has arisen from the use of a spurious article.

As it is not always possible to determine accurately without the aid of chemistry and a microscope whether flour is genuine, the only safe way is to purchase the product of reliable mills.

It is always best to obtain a small quantity of flour first, and put it to the test of bread-making; then, if satisfactory, purchase that brand so long as it proves good. It is true economy to buy a flour known to be good even though it may cost more than some others. It is not wise to purchase too large a quantity at once unless one has exceptionally good facilities for storage, as flour is subject to many deteriorating influences. It is estimated that a barrel of good flour contains sufficient bread material to last one person one year; and from this standard it can be easily estimated in what proportion it is best to purchase.

To Keep Flour.—Flour should always be kept in a tight receptacle, and in a cool, dry, well-ventilated place. It should not be allowed to remain in close proximity to any substances of strong odor, as it very readily absorbs odors and gaseous impurities. A damp atmosphere will cause it to absorb moisture, and as a result the gluten will lose some of its tenacity and become sticky, and bread made from the flour will be coarser and inferior in quality. Flour which has absorbed dampness from any cause should be sifted into a large tray, spread out thin and exposed to the hot sun, or placed in a warming oven for a few hours.

Deleterious Adulterations of Flour.—Besides the fraud frequently practiced of compounding whole-wheat flour from inferior mill products, white flour is sometimes adulterated—more commonly, however, in European countries that in this—with such substances as alum, ground rice, plaster of Paris, and whiting. Alum is doubtless the most commonly used of all these substances, for the reason that it gives the bread a whiter color and causes the flour to absorb and retain a larger amount of water than it would otherwise hold. This enables the user to make, from an inferior brand of flour, bread which resembles that made from a better quality. Such adulteration is exceedingly injurious, as are other mineral substances used for a similar purpose.

The presence of alum in flour or bread may be detected in the following way: Macerate a half slice of bread in three or four tablespoonfuls of water; strain off the water, and add to it twenty drops of a strong solution of logwood, made either from the fresh chips or the extract. Then add a large teaspoonful of a strong solution of carbonate of ammonium. If alum is present, the mixture will change from pink to lavender blue.

The *Journal of Trade* gives the following simple mode of testing for this adulterant: "Persons can test the bread they buy for themselves, by taking a piece of it and soaking it in water. Take this water and mix it with an equal part of fresh milk, and if the bread contains alum, the mixture will coagulate. If a better test is required, boil the mixture, and it will form perfect clot."

Whiting can be detected by dipping the ends of the thumb and forefinger in sweet oil and rubbing the flour between them. If whiting is present, the flour will become sticky like putty, and remain white; whereas pure flour, when so rubbed, becomes darker in color, but not sticky. Plaster of Paris, chalk, and other alkaline adulterants may be detected by a few drops of lemon juice: if either be present, effervescence will take place.

Chemistry of Bread-Making.—Good flour alone will not insure good bread. As much depends upon its preparation as upon the selection of material; for the very best of flour may be transformed into the poorest of bread through improper or careless preparation. Good bread cannot be produced at random. It is not the fruit of any luck or chance, but the practical result of certain fixed laws and principles to which all may conform.

The first step in the conversion of flour into bread is to incorporate with it a given amount of fluid, by which each atom of flour is surrounded with a thin film of moisture, in order to hydrate the starch, to dissolve the sugar and albumen, and to develop the adhesiveness of the gluten, thus binding the whole into one coherent mass termed *dough*, a word from a verb meaning to wet or moisten. If nothing more be done, and this simple form of dough be baked, the starch granules will be ruptured by the heat and thus properly prepared for food; but the moistening will have developed the glue-like property of the gluten to the extent of firmly cementing the particles of flour together, so that the mass will be hard and tough, and almost incapable of mastication. If, however, the dough be thoroughly kneaded, rolled very thin, made into small cakes, and then quickly baked with sufficient heat, the result will be a brittle kind of bread termed unleavened bread, which, although it requires a lengthy process of mastication, is more wholesome and digestible than soft bread, which is likely to be swallowed insufficiently insalivated.

The gluten of wheat flour, beside being adhesive, is likewise remarkably elastic. This is the reason why wheat flour is much more easily made into light bread than the product of other cereals which contain less or a different quality of gluten. Now if while the atoms of flour are supplied with moisture, they are likewise supplied with some form of gaseous substance, the elastic walls of the gluten cells will become distended, causing the dough to "rise," or grow in bulk, and at the same time become light, or porous, in texture.

This making of bread light is usually accomplished by the introduction of air into the dough, or by carbonic acid gas generated within the mass, either before or during the baking, by a fermentative or chemical process.

When air is the agency used, the gluten, by its glue-like properties, catches and retains the air for a short period; and if heat is applied before the air, which is lighter than the dough, rises and escapes, it will expand, and in expanding distend the elastic glutinous mass, causing it to puff up or rise. If the heat is sufficient to harden the gluten quickly, so that the air cells throughout the whole mass become firmly fixed before the air escapes, the result will be a light, porous bread. If the heat is not sufficient, the air does not properly expand; or if before a sufficient crust is formed to retain the air and form a framework of support for the dough, the heat is lessened or withdrawn, the air will escape, or contract to its former volume, allowing the distended glutinous cell walls to collapse; in either case the bread will be heavy.

If carbonic acid gas, generated within the dough by means of fermentation or by the use of chemical substances, be the means used to lighten the mass, the gluten by virtue of its tenacity holds the bubbles of gas as they are generated, and prevents the large and small ones from uniting, or from rising to the surface, as they seek to do, being lighter than the dough. Being thus caught where they are generated, and the proper conditions supplied to expand them, they swell or raise the dough, which is then termed a loaf. (This word "loaf" is from the Anglo-Saxon *hlifian*, to raise or lift up.) The structure is rendered permanent by the application of heat in baking.

BREAD MADE LIGHT BY FERMENTATION.

For general use, the most convenient form of bread is usually considered to be that made from wheat flour, raised or made light by some method of fermentation, although in point of nutritive value and healthfulness, it does not equal light, unfermented, or aërated bread made without the aid of chemicals.

The Process of Fermentation.—Fermentation is a process of decomposition, and hence more or less destructive to the substances subjected to its influence. When animal and vegetable substances containing large amounts of nitrogenous elements are in a moist state and exposed to air, they very soon undergo a change, the result of which is decomposition or decay. This is occasioned by the action of germs, which feed upon nitrogenous substances, as do the various species of fungi. Meat, eggs, milk, and other foods rich in nitrogenous elements can be preserved but a short time if exposed to the atmosphere. The carbonaceous elements are different in this respect. When pure starch, sugar, or fat is exposed to the air in a moistened state, they exhibit the very little tendency to change or decay. Yet if placed in contact with decomposing substances containing nitrogen, they soon begin to change, and are themselves decomposed and destroyed. This communication of the condition of change from one class of substances to another, is termed fermentation. If a fermenting substance be added to a watery solution containing sugar, the sugar will be changed or decomposed, and two new substances, alcohol and carbonic acid gas, are produced.

The different stages of fermentation are noted scientifically as alcoholic, acetous, and putrefactive. The first is the name given to the change which takes place in the saccharine matter of the dough, which results in the formation of alcohol and carbonic acid gas. This same change takes place in the saccharine matter of fruits under the proper with conditions of warmth, air, and moisture, and is utilized in the production of wines and fermented liquors.

In bread-making, the alcohol and carbonic acid gas produced during the fermentation, are formed from sugar,—that originally contained in the flour and the additional quantity formed from starch during the fermenting process. It is evident, therefore, that bread cannot be fermented without some loss in natural sweetness and nutritive value, and bread made after this method should be managed so as to deteriorate the material as little as possible.

If this fermentation continues long enough, the acetous fermentation is set up, and *acetic* acid, the essential element of vinegar, is formed and the dough becomes sour. If the process of fermentation is very much prolonged, the putrefactive change is set up, and the gluten is more or less decomposed.

If the dough be baked during the alcoholic and carbonic-acid stage of fermentation, the gas will render the loaf light and porous. The alcohol will be dissipated by the heat during the baking, or evaporated shortly afterward, provided the baking be thorough. If the fermentation is allowed to proceed until the acetous fermentation has begun, the loaf, when baked, will be "sad" and heavy, since there is no longer any gas to puff it up. If, however, during the first or alcoholic stage of fermentation, new material be added, the same kind of fermentation will continue for a certain period longer.

These facts serve to show that great care and attention are necessary to produce good bread by a fermentative process. If the fermentation has not been allowed to proceed far enough to generate a sufficient amount of gas to permeate the whole mass, the result will be a heavy loaf; and if allowed to proceed too far, acid fermentation begins, the gas escapes, and we have sour as well as heavy bread. It is not enough, however, to prevent bread from reaching the acetous or sour stage of fermentation. Bread may be over-fermented when there is no appreciable sourness developed. Fermentation may be carried so far as to destroy much of the richness and sweetness of the loaf, and yet be arrested by the baking process just before the acetous stage begins, so that it will be light and porous, but decidedly lacking in flavor and substance. Over-fermentation also develops in the bread various bitter substances which obscure the natural sweetness of the bread and give to it an unpleasant flavor. Many of these substances are more or less harmful in character, and include many poisons known as ptomaines, a class of chemical compounds produced by germs whenever fermentation or decomposition of organic matter takes place. Much skill is required to determine at what point to arrest the fermentation, in order to save the sweetness and richness of the bread.

Fermentative Agents.—Fermentation in vegetable matter is always accompanied by the growth of living organisms. The development of these minute organisms is the exciting cause of fermentation and putrefaction. The germs or spores of some of these fermenting agents are always present in the air. It is well known to housekeepers that if a batter of flour and water and a little salt be kept in a jar of water at a temperature of from 100° to 110°, it will ferment in the course of five or six hours. Scientists assure us that this fermentation is occasioned by the introduction of the spores of certain species of fungi which are continually floating in the atmosphere, and the proper conditions of warmth and moisture being supplied, they at once begin to grow and multiply. This method of securing fermentation is utilized by housewives in making what is termed salt-rising bread. The raising of dough by this process is lengthy and uncertain, and a far more convenient method is to accelerate the fermentation by the addition of some active ferment. The ancient method of accomplishing this was by adding to the dough a leaven, a portion of old dough which had been kept until it had begun to ferment; but since the investigations of modern chemistry have made clear the properties of yeast, that has come to be considered the best agent for setting up the process of alcoholic fermentation in bread. The use of leaven is still practiced to somewhat in some European countries. The bread produced with leaven, although light and spongy in texture, has an unpleasant, sour taste, and is much less wholesome than that produced with fresh yeast.

Yeast is a collection of living organisms or plants belonging to the family of fungi, which, like all other plants, require warmth, moisture, and food, in order to promote growth, and when properly supplied with these, they begin to grow and multiply rapidly. Fermentation will not take place at a temperature below 30°, it proceeds slowly at 45°, but from 70° to 90° it goes on rapidly. Fermentation may be arrested by the exhaustion of either the fermenting agent or the food supply, or by exposure to heat at the temperature of boiling water. This latter fact enables the housewife to arrest the process of fermentation, when the loaf has become sufficiently light, by baking it in a hot oven. Heat destroys most of the yeast cells; a few, however, remain in the loaf unchanged, and it is for this reason that yeast bread is considered less wholesome for dyspeptics than light unleavened bread. It is apparent, then, that the more thoroughly fermented bread is baked, the more wholesome it will be, from the more complete destruction of the yeast germs which it contains.

Yeast.—Next to good flour, the most important requisite in the manufacture of fermented bread is good yeast. The best of flour used in conjunction with poor yeast will not produce good bread. The most convenient and reliable kind of marketable yeast, when fresh, is the compressed yeast. The dry though they are always ready for use, the quality of the bread they produce is generally inferior to that made with either compressed yeast or good liquid yeast. If this sort of yeast must be depended upon, the cakes known as "Yeast Foam" are the best of any with which we are acquainted.

Of homemade yeasts there are almost as many varieties as there are cooks. Their comparative value depends mainly upon the length of time they will keep good, or the facility with which they can be prepared. Essentially the same principles are involved in the making of them all; viz., the introduction of a small quantity of fresh, lively yeast into a mixture of some form of starch (obtained from flour, potato, or a combination of both) and water, with or without the addition of such other substances as will promote fermentation, or aid in preventing the yeast from souring. Under proper conditions of warmth, the small amount of original yeast begins to supply itself with food at once by converting the starch into dextrine, and then into grape sugar, and multiplies itself with great rapidity, and will continue to do so as long as there is material to supply it with the means of growth. While its growth is rapid, its decay is equally so; and unless some means of preservation be employed, the yeast will die, and the mixture become sour and foul. Ordinarily it can be kept good for several days, and under the best conditions, even three or four weeks. After it has been kept from four to six hours, it should be placed in some receptacle as nearly air-tight as possible and set in the cellar or refrigerator, where it can be kept at a temperature not conducive to fermentation. Thus the little yeast organisms will remain in a quiescent state, but yet alive and capable of multiplying themselves when again surrounded with favorable conditions.

The yeast should be kept in glass or glazed earthen ware. The vessel containing it should be washed and scalded with scrupulous care before new yeast is put in, since the smallest particle of sour or spoiled yeast will ruin the fresh supply in a very short time. It is generally conceded that yeast will keep longer if the material of which it is made be mixed with liquid of a boiling temperature, or cooked for a few minutes at boiling heat before adding the yeast. The reason for this undoubtedly lies in the fact that the boiling kills foreign germs, and thus prevents early souring or putrefaction. The yeast must not be added, however, until the liquid has cooled to a little more than blood heat, as too great heat will kill the yeast cells.

The starch of the potato is thought to furnish better material for the promotion of yeast growth than that of wheat flour; but whether the potato be first cooked, mashed, and then combined with the other ingredients, or grated raw and then cooked in boiling water, makes little difference so far as results are concerned, though the latter method may have the advantage of taking less time. If potatoes are used for this purpose, they should be perfectly mature. New ones will not answer.

Sugar assists in promoting the growth of the yeast plant, and a small amount is usually employed in making yeast. Hops serve to prevent the yeast from souring, and an infusion of them is frequently used for this purpose.

While it is essential that the water used should be boiling, it is also necessary that the mixture should cooled to a lukewarm temperature before the introduction of the original yeast, as intense heat will kill the yeast plant. Freezing cold will likewise produced the same result. While a cool temperature is one of the requisites for keeping yeast fresh, care must be taken, especially in winter, that it does not get chilled.

When yeast is needed for bread, it is always the best plan to take a cup to the cellar or refrigerator for the desired quantity, and re-cover the jar as quickly as possible. A half hour in a hot kitchen would be quite likely to spoiled it. Always shake or stir the whole well before measuring out the yeast. In making yeast, used earthen bowls for mixing, porcelain-lined or granite-ware utensils for boiling, and silver or wooden spoons for stirring.

Bitter Yeast.—It sometimes happens that an excessive use of hops in the making of yeast gives to it so bitter a flavor as to communicate a disagreeable taste to the bread. To correct this bitterness, mix with the yeast a considerable quantity of water, and let it stand for some hours, when the thickest portion will have settled at the bottom. The water, which will have extracted much of the bitterness, can then be turned off and thrown away. Yeast also sometimes becomes a bitter from long keeping. Freshly burnt charcoal thrown into the yeast is said to absorb the odors and offensive matter and render the yeast more sweet; however, we do not recommend the use of any yeast so stale as to need sweetening or purifying. Yeast that is new and fresh is always best; old and stale yeast, even though it may still possess the property of raising the dough, will give an unpleasant taste to the bread, and is much less wholesome.

Tests for Yeast.—Liquid yeast, when good, is light in color and looks foamy and effervescent; it has a pungent odor somewhat similar to weak ammonia, and if tasted will have a sharp, biting flavor. Yeast is poor when it looks dull and watery, and has a sour odor. Compressed yeast, if good, breaks off dry and looks white; if poor, it appears moist and stringy.

If there is any question as to the quality of yeast, it is always best to test it before use by adding a little flour to a small quantity and setting it in a warm place. If it begins to ferment in the course of fifteen or twenty minutes, it is good.

Starting the Bread.—Having secured good yeast, it is necessary in some way to diffuse it through the bread material so that it will set up an active fermentation, which, by the evolution of gas, will render the whole mass light and porous. As fermentation is more sure, more rapid, and requires less yeast to start it when set in action in a thin mixture than when introduced into stiff dough, the more common method of starting fermented bread is by "setting a sponge;" viz., preparing a batter of flour and liquid, to which potato is sometimes added, and into which the yeast is introduced. Some cooks, in making the batter, use the whole amount of liquid needed for the bread, and as the sponge rises, add flour in small quantities, beating it back, and allowing it to rise a second, third, or even fourth time, until sufficient flour has been added to knead; others use only half the liquid in preparing the sponge, and when it has well risen, prepare a second one by adding the remainder of the liquid and fresh flour, in which case the fermented batter acts as a double portion of yeast and raises the second sponge very quickly. The requisite amount of flour is then added, the dough kneaded, and the whole allowed to rise a third time in the loaf. Other cooks dispense altogether with the sponge, adding to the liquid at first the requisite amount of flour, kneading it thoroughly and allowing it to rise once in mass and again after molding into loaves. As to the superiority of one method over another, much depends upon their adaptability to the time and convenience of the user; light bread can be produced by either method. Less yeast but more time will be required when the bread is started with a sponge. The end to be attained by all is a complete and equal diffusion of gas bubbles generated during fermentation throughout the whole mass of dough.

The preferable method of combining the materials needed for the batter is by first mingling the yeast with the water or milk. If condensed or dry yeast is used, previously dissolve it well in a half cupful or less of lukewarm water. Stir the flour slowly into the liquid mixture and beat it *very thoroughly* so that the yeast shall be evenly distributed throughout the whole.

Proportion of Materials Needed.—The material needed for making: the bread should all be carefully measured out beforehand and the flour well sifted. Many housekeepers fail in producing good bread, because they guess at the quantity of material to be used, particularly the flour, and with the same quantity of liquid will one time use much more flour that at another, thus making the results exceedingly variable. With this same brand of flour, this same quantity should always be used to produce a given amount of bread. This amount will depend upon the quality of the material used. Good flour will absorb a larger quantity of liquids than that of an inferior quality, and the amount of liquid a given quantity of flour will take up determines the quantity of bread that can be produced from it. This amount is chiefly dependent upon the proportion of gluten contained in the flour. One hundred pounds of good flour will absorb sufficient water to produce one hundred and fifty pounds of bread. One reason why bread retains so much water is that during the baking a portion of starch is converted into gum, which holds water more strongly than starch. Again: the gluten, when wet, is not easily dried, while the dry crust which forms around the bread in baking is merely impervious to water, and, like the skin of a baking potato, prevents the moisture from escaping.

Kinds of flour vary so considerably in respect to their absorbent properties that it is not possible to state the exact proportions of flour and liquid required; approximately, three heaping measures of flour for one scant measure of liquid, including the yeast, will in general be found a good proportion. Bread made from the entire wheat will require from one half to one cupful less flour than that made of white flour. A quart of liquid, including the yeast, is sufficient for three ordinary-sized loaves. One half or two thirds of a cup of homemade yeast, according to its strength, or one half a cake of compressed yeast dissolved in a half cup of lukewarm water, will be sufficient for one quart of liquid. It is a common mistake to use too much yeast. It lessens the time required, but the result is less satisfactory. Bread to be set over night requires less yeast.

Whether water or milk should be used for bread-making, depends upon taste and convenience. Bread retains more nearly the natural flavor of the grain if made with water, and is less apt to sour; at the same time, bread made with milk is more tender than that made with water. Bread made with milk requires from one half to one cupful less of flour.

Potatoes are sometimes used in conjunction with flour for bread-making. They are by no means necessary when good flour is used, but bread made from inferior flour is improved by their use. Only potatoes that are fully matured should be used for this purpose, and they should be well cooked and smoothly mashed. Neither sugar nor salt is essential for the production of good bread, though most cook books recommend the use of one or both. The proportion of the former should not exceed one even tablespoonful to three pints of flour, and the very smallest amount of salt, never more than a half teaspoonful, and better less. No butter or other free fat is required; the tenderness of texture produced by its use can be secured as well by the use of unskimmed milk and thorough kneading.

Utensils.—For bread-making purposes, earthen or china ware is preferable to either tin or wooden utensils: being a poor conductor, it protects the sponge from the cold air much more effectually than tin, and is much more easily kept clean and sweet than wood. The utensil should be kept exclusively for the purpose of bread-making, and should never be allowed to contain any sour substance. The bowl should be thoroughly scalded before and after each using. Use silver or granite-ware spoons for stirring the bread. Iron and tin discolor the sponge. For measuring the material, particularly the liquid and the yeast, half-pint cups, divided by marks into thirds and fourths, as shown in the cut, are especially serviceable.

Measuring Cup.

Measuring Cup.

When to Set the Sponge.—The time to set the sponge for bread-making is a point each housekeeper must determine for herself. The fact before stated, that temperature controls the activity of fermentation, and that it is retarded or accelerated according to the conditions of warmth, enables the housewife, by keeping the bread-mixture at a temperature of about 50° F., to set her bread in the evening, if desired, and find it light and ready for further attention in the morning. In winter, the sponge will need to be prepared early in the evening and kept during the night at as even a temperature as possible. A good way to accomplish this is to cover the bowl with a clean napkin and afterwards wrap it about very closely with several folds of a woolen blanket. In extremely cold weather bottles of hot water may be placed around the bowl outside the wrappings. In case this plan is employed, care must be taken to have sufficient wrappings between the bread and the bottles to prevent undue heat, and the bottles should be covered with an additional blanket to aid in retaining the heat as long as possible.

If the sponge is set in the evening, if in very warm weather, it should be started as late as practicable, and left in a rather cool place. Cover closely to exclude the air, but do not wrap in flannel as in winter. It will be likely to need attention early in the morning.

Temperature for Bread-Making.—Except in very warm weather, the ferment or sponge should be started with liquid at a lukewarm temperature.

The liquid should never be so cold as to chill the yeast. Milk, if used, should be first sterilized by scalding, and then cooled before using.

After the sponge is prepared, the greatest care must be taken to keep it at an equable temperature. From 70° to 90° is the best range of temperature, 75° being considered the golden mean throughout the entire fermentative process of bread-making.

After fermentation has well begun, it will continue, but much more slowly if the temperature be gradually lowered to 45° or 50°. If it is necessary to hasten the rising, the temperature can be raised to 80° or 85°, but it will necessitate careful watching, as it will be liable to over-ferment, and become sour. Cold arrests the process of fermentation, while too great heat carries forward the work too rapidly. Too much stress cannot be laid upon the importance of an equable temperature. The housewife who permits the fermentation to proceed very slowly one hour, forces it rapidly by increased heat the next, and perhaps allows it to subside to a chilling temperature the third, will never be sure of good bread.

Putting the bowl containing the sponge into a dish of warm (not hot) water, or keeping it in the warming oven, or on the back of the range, are all methods which may bring about good results, provided the same degree of heat can be maintained continuously; but if the fire is one which must be increased or diminished to suit the exigencies of household details, nothing but the closest and most careful attention will keep the sponge at uniform temperature. The better way is to cover the bowl with a napkin, and in cold weather wrap closely in several thicknesses of flannel, and place on a stand behind the stove, or in some place not exposed to draughts. A bread-raiser purposely arranged for keeping the bread at proper temperature is a great convenience. Two small and rather thick earthen ware crocks of the same size, serve very well for this purpose. Scald both with hot water, and while still warm, put the sponge in one, invert the other for a cover, and leave in a warm room. All flour used in the bread should be warm when added.

Lightness of the Bread.—The time required for bread in its different stages to grow light will vary according to the quantity and strength of the yeast used and the amount of warmth supplied. A thin batter is light enough when in appearance it resembles throughout a mass of sea foam. It will not greatly increase in bulk, but will be in the state of constant activity, sending up little bubbles of gas and emitting a sharp, pungent odor like fresh yeast.

When the thicker batter or second sponge is sufficiently light, it will have risen to nearly double its original bulk and become cracked over the top like "crazed" china. It should never be allowed to rise to the point of sinking or caving in, and should be kneaded as soon as ready. If for any reason it is not possible to knead the bread at once when it has arrived at this stage, do not allow it to stand, but take a knife or spoon and gently beat it back a little. This dissipates some of the gas and reduces the volume somewhat. Let it rise again, which it will do in a short time, if it has not been allowed to become too light. If dough that has been kneaded and allowed to rise in mass, becomes sufficiently light at some inopportune moment for shaping into loaves, it may be kept from becoming too light and souring, by taking a knife and cutting it away from the sides of the bowl and gradually working it over toward the center. Re-cover and put in a warm place. It will soon assume its former bulk. This "cutting down" may be repeated several times if necessary, provided the bread has not been allowed to become too light at any time, and some cook's recommend it as a uniform practice. We do not, however, except in case of necessity; since, though it may possibly make the bread more light, the long-continued fermentation destroys more than is necessary of the food elements of the flour, and develops an unnecessary amount of the products of fermentation. Lightness is not the only requisite for bread, and should be secured with as little deterioration of the flour as possible.

An important point in the preparation of bread is to decide when it is sufficiently light after having been molded and placed in pans. The length of time cannot be given, because it will vary with the temperature, the quality of the flour, and the quantity added during the kneading. At a temperature of 75°, an hour or an hour and a half is about the average length of time needed. A loaf should nearly double its size after being placed in a pan, before baking; when perfectly risen, the bread feels light when lifted and weighed upon the hand. It is better to begin the baking before it has perfectly risen them to wait until it has become so light as to commence to fall, since if the fermentation proceeds too far, the sweetness of the grain will be destroyed, and the bread will be tasteless and innutritious, even if it does not reach the acetous stage.

The exercise of a little judgment and careful attention to detail will soon enable a person successfully to determine the proper degree of lightness of bread in its various stages. Bread which passes the extreme point of fermentation, or in common phrase gets "too light," will have a strong acid odor, and will pull away from the bowl in a stringy mass, having a watery appearance very different from the fine, spongy texture of properly risen dough. The acidity of such dough may be neutralized by the addition of an alkali, and housewives who through carelessness and inattention have allowed their bread to become "sour," often resort to saleratus or soda to neutralize the acid. The result of such treatment is unwholesome bread, wholly unfit for food. It is better economy to throw away bread material which needs to be sweetened with soda than to run the risk of injury to health by using it.

Kneading the Dough.—As fresh flour is added during the bread-making, it is necessary to mix it in thoroughly. As long as the batter is thin, this can be done by thoroughly beating the mixture with the addition of material; but when it is a thick dough, some other method must be adopted to bring about the desired result. The usual way is by mixing the dough to a proper consistency, and working it with the hands. This is termed *kneading*. Much of the excellence of bread depends upon the thoroughness of this kneading, since if the yeast is not intimately and equally mixed with every particle of flour, the bread will not be uniform; some portions will be heavy and compact, while others will be full of large, open cavities, from the excessive liberation of gas.

The length of time required for kneading depends upon the perfection with which the yeast cells have been previously diffused throughout the sponge, and upon the quality of the flour used in preparing the bread, much less time being required for kneading dough made from good flour. Some consider an hour none too long to knead bread. Such a lengthy process may be advantageous, since one of the objects of kneading is to render the glutinous parts of the flour so elastic that the dough may be capable of expanding to several times its bulk without cracking or breaking, but excellent results can be obtained from good flour with less labor. Bread has been kneaded all that is necessary when it will work clean of the board, and when, after a smart blow with the fist in the center of the mass, it will spring back to its original shape like an India rubber ball. Its elasticity is the surest test of its goodness; and when dough has been thus perfectly kneaded, it can be molded into any shape, rolled, twisted, or braided with ease. Chopping, cutting, stretching, and pulling—the dough are other methods for accomplishing the same end.

If a large mass is to be kneaded, it is better to divide it into several portions and knead each separately. It is less laborious and more likely to result in an equal diffusion of the yeast. Bread is often spoiled by the addition of too much flour during kneading. Dough should always be kneaded as soft as it can be handled, and only sufficient flour added to prevent its sticking to the board. Stiff bread is close in texture, and after a day or two becomes dry and hard.

How to Manipulate the Dough in Kneading.—Sprinkle the board well with flour, and scrape the dough from the bowl with a knife. Dust the hands with flour, and then draw the dough with a rolling motion from the farthest side toward you, using the finger tips for the purpose, but pressing firmly down upon the mass with the palm of the hands. Reach forward again with the finger tips, and again press the ball of the hands upon the dough. Continue this process of manipulation until the mass is very much elongated; then turn at right angles and repeat the process, taking care that the finger tips do not break through the light film which will form upon the outside of soft dough when well managed. *Keep the dough constantly in motion* until it is smooth, elastic, and fine-grained. The hands and the board may need a light dusting of flour at frequent intervals. If the dough sticks, lift it quickly, and clean the board, that it may be kept smooth.

The dough will not stick if kept in constant motion. Do not rub off little wads of dough either from the hands or the board and keep kneading them into the loaf; they will seriously injure the uniform texture of the bread.

How Many Times Shall Bread be Kneaded?—As the objects to be attained in kneading dough are to render the gluten more elastic and thoroughly to diffuse the yeast, it will be seen that there has been sufficient kneading when all the flour necessary for the bread has been added. Furthermore, it must be apparent that continued manipulation of the dough at this stage will dissipate and press out the little vesicles of gas held in place by the elastic gluten, and thus lose in part what so much pains has been taken to secure. At whatever stage the requisite amount of flour be added, the dough should then be thoroughly kneaded once for all. If allowed to rise in bulk, when light it should be shaped into loaves with the greatest care, handled lightly, and worked as little as possible, and if at all diminished, allowed to rise again before baking.

Dryness of the Surface.—Bread in all stages should be covered over the top, since it rises much more evenly, and does not have a stiff, dried surface, as when placed in a warm place exposed to air. It sometimes happens that this precaution is forgotten or not sufficiently attended to, and a dry crust forms and over the dough, which, if kneaded into the loaves, leaves hard, dry spots in the bread. In case of such a mishap, take the dry crust off, dissolve it in a little warm water, add flour enough to mold, make it into a small loaf, and raise it separately.

Size of Loaves.—The lightness of the bread after baking depends upon the perfection with which the little air-cells, formed during the fermenting process, have become fixed by the heat during the baking. The heat expands the carbonic acid gas contained within the open spaces in the dough, and at the same time checks further development of gas by destroying the yeast plant. The sooner, then, that the cells can be made permanent after the arrest of fermentation, the more light and porous the bread will be. Although this fixing of the cells is largely dependent upon the degree of heat maintained, it likewise in a measure depends upon the size of the loaf, as the heat will penetrate and fix the cells of a small loaf throughout much sooner than, those of a large one. Therefore, bake in small loaves, and have a separate pan for each, as that admits of an equal degree of heat to all sides. This aids in a more rapid fixing of the air-cells and likewise gives more crust, which is the sweetest and most digestible part of the bread.

Sheet-iron pans, about eight inches in length, four in width, and five in depth, are the most satisfactory. After the dough is molded, divide it into loaves which will fill such pans to the depth of two inches. Let them rise until double their first volume, and then put them in the oven. In baking, the loaves will rise still higher, and if about five inches high when done, will have expanded to about the right proportions.

Proper Temperature of the Oven.—The objects to be attained in the baking of bread are to break up the starch and gluten cells of the Sour so as to make them easily digestible, to destroy the yeast plant, and render permanent the cells formed by the action of the carbonic acid gas. To accomplish well these ends, the loaf must be surrounded by a temperature ranging from 400° to 600°. The oven should be one in which the heat is equal in all parts, and which can be kept at a steady, uniform heat. Old-fashioned brick ovens were superior in this respect to most modern ranges. The fire for baking bread should be of sufficient strength to keep the oven heated for at least an hour. If the oven has tendency to become too hot upon the bottom, a thin, open grate, broiler, or toasting rack, should be placed underneath the tins to allow a circulation of air and avoid danger of burning. If the heat be insufficient, fermentation will not cease until the bread has become sour; the cells will be imperfectly fixed or entirely collapsed; too little of the moisture will have evaporated, and the result will be a soft, wet, and pasty or sour loaf. If the heat be too great, the bread will be baked before it has perfectly risen, or a thick, burned crust will be produced, forming a non-conducting covering to the loaf, which will prevent the heat from permeating the interior, and thus the loaf will have an overdone exterior, but will be raw and doughy within. If, however, the temperature of the oven be just right, the loaf will continue for a little time to enlarge, owing to the expansion of the carbonic acid gas, the conversion of the water into steam, and the vaporizing of the alcohol, which rises in a gaseous form and is driven off by the heat; a nicely browned crust will be formed over the surface, the result of the rapid evaporation of water from the surface and consequent consolidation of the dough of this portion of the loaf, and a chemical change caused by the action of the heat upon the starch by which is converted into dextrine, finally assuming a brown color due to the production of a substance known to the chemist as *assama*.

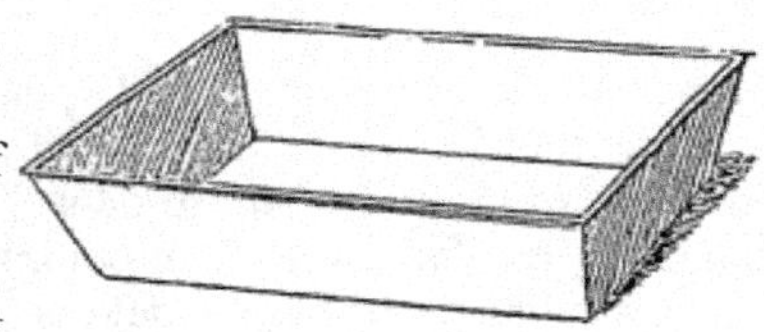

Bread Pan.

Bread is often spoiled in the baking. The dough may be made of the best of flour and yeast, mixed and kneaded in the most perfect manner, and may have risen to the proper degree of lightness' before going to the oven, yet if the oven is either too hot or not hot enough, the bread will be of an inferior quality.

Without an oven thermometer, there is no accurate means of determining the temperature of the oven; but housekeepers resort to various means to form a judgment about it. The baker's old-fashioned method is to throw a handful of flour on the oven bottom. If it blackens without igniting, the heat is deemed sufficient. Since the object for which the heat is desired is to cook the flour, not to burn it, it might be supposed that this would indicate too high a temperature; but the flour within the loaf to be baked is combined with a certain amount of moisture, the evaporation of which lowers the temperature of the bread considerably below that of the surrounding heated atmosphere. The temperature of the inner portion of the loaf cannot exceed 212° so long as it continues moist. Bread might be perfectly cooked at this temperature by steam, but it would lack that most digestible portion of the loaf, the crust.

A common way of ascertaining if the heat of the oven is sufficient, is to hold the bare arm inside it for a few seconds.

If the arm cannot be held within while thirty is counted, it is too hot to begin with. The following test is more accurate: For rolls, the oven should be hot enough to brown a teaspoonful of flour in *one* minute, and for loaves in *five* minutes.

The temperature should be high enough to arrest the fermentation, which it will do at a point considerably below the boiling point of water, and at the same time to form a shell or crust, which will so support the dough as to prevent it from sinking or collapsing when the evolution of carbonic acid gas shall cease; but it should not be hot enough to brown the crust within ten or fifteen minutes. The heat should increase for the first fifteen minutes, remain steady for the next fifteen minutes, and may then gradually decrease during the remainder of the baking. If by any mischance the oven be so hot as to brown the crust too soon, cover the loaf with a clean paper for a few minutes. Be careful that no draught reaches the bread while baking; open the oven door very seldom, and not at all for the first ten minutes. If it is necessary to turn the loaf, try to do so without bringing it to the air. From three fourths of an hour to an hour is usually a sufficient length of time to bake an ordinary sized loaf. Be careful not to remove the bread from the oven until perfectly done. It is better to allow it to bake ten minutes too long than not long enough. The crust of bread, when done, should be equally browned all over.

The common test for well-baked bread is to tap it on the bottom with the finger; if it is light and well done, it will sound hollow; heavy bread will have a dull sound. A thoroughly baked loaf will not burn the hand when lifted upon it from the pan.

Care of Bread after Baking.—When done, remove the loaves from the tins, and tilt them upon edge so that the air may circulate freely on all sides of them to prevent "sweating." Do not, however, lay them on a pine shelf or table to absorb the odor of the wood. A large tin dripping pan turned over upon the table does very well to tilt them on. If they are turned often, so that they will not soften on one side, but a fine wire bread cooler is the best thing. If this is not obtainable, a fair substitute can be easily improvised by tacking window-screen wire to a light frame of sufficient size to hold the requisite number of loaves. If the bread is left exposed to the air until cold, the crust will be crisp; if a soft crust is desired, it can be secured by brushing the top of the loaf while hot, with tepid water, and covering with several thicknesses of a clean bread cloth.

If by accident any portion of the crust is burnt, grate it away as soon as cold; this is preferable to cutting or clipping it off.

Best Method of Keeping Bread.—When the bread is quite cold, put it away in a bread box, which should be of tin, or of wood lined with tin, convenient in form and supplied with a well-fitting cover. Never use an unlined wooden box of any kind, as it cannot easily be kept fresh and free from musty odors, which bread so readily absorbs.

Stone and earthen ware are not open to this objection, but they are likely to collect moisture, and hence are not equal to a tin receptacle. Do not keep bread in the cellar or any other damp place, nor in a close closet, where there are other foods from which it can absorb odors. The bread box should be kept well covered, and free from crumbs and stale bits. It should be carefully washed in boiling soapsuds, scalded, and dried, every two or three days. If cloths are used to wrap or cover the bread, they too should be washed and scalded every week, and oftener if at any time the loaf about which they are wrapped becomes moldy or musty.

Test of Good Fermented Bread.—A loaf of good bread, well risen and perfectly baked, may be taken in the hands, and, with the thumb on the top crust and fingers upon the bottom of the loaf, pressed to less than half its thickness, and when the pressure is removed, it will immediately expand like a sponge, to its former proportions.

Good yeast bread, while it should be firm and preserve a certain amount of moisture, will, when cold, crumble easily when rubbed between the fingers. If, instead, it forms a close, soggy mass, it may be regarded as indigestible. This is one reason why hot, new yeast bread and biscuit are so indigestible. In demonstration of this, take a small lump of new bread, gently roll it into a ball, and put into a glass of water, adding a similar quantity of stale bread of the same kind also. The latter will crumble away very soon, while the former will retain its form for hours, reminding one of its condition in the stomach, "as hard as a bullet," for a long time resisting the action of the gastric juice, although, meanwhile, the yeast germs which have not been killed in the oven are converting the mass into a lump of yeast, by which the whole contents of the stomach are soured. A soluble article like salt or sugar in fine powdered form is much more easily and quickly dissolved than the same article in solid lumps, and so it is with food. The apparent dryness of stale bread is not caused by its loss of moisture; for if carefully weighed, stale bread will be found to contain almost exactly the same proportion of water as new bread that has become cold. The moisture has only passed into a state of concealment, as may be demonstrated by subjecting a stale loaf inclosed in a tightly-sealed receptacle to a temperature equal to boiling heat in an oven for half an hour, when it will again have the appearance of new bread.

Hot bread eaten with butter is still more unwholesome, for the reason that the melted grease fills up the pores of the bread, and further interferes with the action of the digestive fluids.

Whole-Wheat and Graham Breads.—The same general principles are involved in the making of bread with whole-wheat and Graham flours as in the production of bread from white flour. Good material and good care are absolutely essential.

Whole-wheat flour ferments more readily and rises more quickly than does white flour, hence bread made with it needs more careful management, as it is more liable to sour. The novice in bread-making should not undertake the preparation of bread with whole-wheat flour, until she has thoroughly mastered all the details of the art by practical experience, and can produce a perfect loaf from white flour.

Breads from whole-wheat and Graham flours require less yeast and less flour than bread prepared from white flour. A slower process of fermentation is also advantageous.

Such breads will be lighter if at least one third white flour be employed in their manufacture. When the bread is made with a sponge, this white flour may be utilised for the purpose. Thus the length of time the whole-wheat flour will be undergoing fermentation will be somewhat lessened, and its liability to become sour diminished. This plan is a preferable one for beginners in bread-making.

Graham and whole-wheat flour breads must be kneaded longer than white-flour bread, and require a hotter oven at first and a longer time for baking. Much Graham and whole-wheat bread is served insufficiently baked, probably owing to the fact that, being dark in color, the crust appears brown very soon, thus deluding the cook into supposing that the loaf is well baked. For thorough baking, from one to one and a half hours are needed, according to the size of the loaf and the heat of the oven.

Toast.—Toasting, if properly done, renders bread more digestible, the starch being converted into dextrine by the toasting process; but by the ordinary method of preparing toast, that of simply browning each side, only the surfaces of the slices are really toasted, while the action of the heat upon the interior of the slice, it is rendered exactly in the condition of new bread, and consequently quite as indigestible. If butter is added while the toast is hot, we have all the dyspepsia-producing elements of new bread and butter combined. Although considered to be the dish *par excellence* for invalids, nothing could be more unwholesome than such toast. To properly toast the bread, the drying and browning should extend throughout the entire thickness of the slice. Bread may be thus toasted before an open fire, but the process would be such a lengthy and troublesome one, it is far better to secure the same results by browning the bread in a moderate oven.

Such toast is sometimes called *zwieback* (twice baked), and when prepared from good whole-wheat bread, is one of the most nourishing and digestible of foods. Directions for its preparation and use will be found in the chapter on "Breakfast Dishes."

Steamed Bread.—Steaming stale bread is as open to objection as the surface toasting of bread, if steamed so as to be yielding and adhesive. It is not, perhaps, as unwholesome as new bread, but bread is best eaten in a condition dry and hard enough to require chewing, that its starch may be so changed by the action of the saliva as to be easily digested.

LIQUID YEAST.

RECIPES.

Raw Potato Yeast.—Mix one fourth of a cup of flour, the same of white sugar, and a teaspoonful of salt to a paste with a little water. Pare three medium-size, fresh, and sound potatoes, and grate them as rapidly as possible into the paste; mix all quickly together with a silver spoon, then pour three pints of boiling water slowly over the mixture, stirring well at the same time. If this does not rupture the starch cells of the flour and potatoes so that the mixture becomes thickened to the consistency of starch, turn it into a granite-ware kettle and boil up for a minute, stirring well to keep it from sticking and burning. If it becomes too much thickened, add a little more boiling water. It is impossible to give the exact amount of water, since the quality of the flour will vary, and likewise the size of the potatoes; but three pints is an approximate proportion. Strain the mixture through a fine colander into an earthen bread bowl, and let it cool. When lukewarm, add one cup of good, lively yeast. Cover with a napkin, and keep in a moderately warm place for several hours, or until it ceases to ferment. As it begins to ferment, stir it well occasionally, and when well fermented, turn into a clean glass or earthen jar. The next morning cover closely, and put in the cellar or refrigerator, not, however, in contact with the ice. It is best to reserve enough for the first baking in some smaller jar, so that the larger portion need not be opened so soon. Always shake the yeast before using.

Raw Potato Yeast No. 2.—This is made in the same manner as the preceding, with this exception, that one fourth of a cup of loose hops tied in a clean muslin bag, is boiled in the water for five minutes before pouring it into the potato and flour mixture. Many think the addition of the hops aids in keeping the yeast sweet for a longer period. But potato yeast may be kept sweet for two weeks without hops, if cared for, and is preferred by those who dislike the peculiar flavor of the bread made from hop yeast.

Hop Yeast.—Put half a cup of loose hops, or an eighth of an ounce of the pressed hops (put up by the Shakers and sold by druggists), into a granite-ware kettle; pour over it a quart of boiling water, and simmer about five minutes. Meanwhile stir to a smooth paste in a tin basin or another saucepan, a cup of flour, and a little cold water. Line a colander with a thin cloth, and strain the boiling infusion of hops through it onto the flour paste, stirring continually. Boil this thin starch a few minutes, until it thickens, stirring constantly that no lumps be formed. Turn it into a large earthen bowl, add a tablespoonful of salt and two of white sugar, and when it has cooled to blood heat, add one half cup of lively yeast, stirring all well together. Cover the bowl with a napkin, and let it stand in some moderately warm place twenty-four hours, or until it ceases to ferment or send up bubbles, beating back occasionally as it rises; then put into a wide-mouthed glass or earthen jar, which has been previously scalded and dried, cover closely, and set in a cool place.

Yeast made in this manner will keep sweet for two weeks in summer and longer in winter.

Boiled Potato Yeast.—Peel four large potatoes, and put them to boil in two quarts of cold water. Tie two loose handfuls of hops securely in a piece of muslin, and place in the water to boil with the potatoes. When the potatoes are tender, remove them with a perforated skimmer, leaving the water still boiling. Mash them, and work in four tablespoons of flour and two of sugar. Over this mixture pour gradually the boiling hop infusion, stirring constantly, that it may form a smooth paste, and set it aside to cool. When lukewarm, add a gill of lively yeast, and proceed as in the preceding recipe.

Boiled Potato Yeast No. 2.—To one teacupful of very smoothly mashed, mealy potato, add three teaspoonfuls of white sugar, one teaspoonful of salt, and one cup of lively yeast, or one cake of Yeast Foam, dissolved in a very little water. The potatoes should be warm, but not hot enough to destroy the yeast. Allow this to stand until light, when it is ready for use.

FERMENTED BREADS.

In the preparation of breads after the following recipes, the measure of flour should be heaping.

RECIPES.

Milk Bread With White Flour.—Scald and cool on pint of unskimmed milk. Add to the milk when lukewarm, one fourth of a cup, or three tablespoonfuls, of liquid yeast, and three cups of flour. Give the batter a vigorous beating, turn it into a clean bread bowl or a small earthen crock, cover, and let it rise over night. In the morning, when well risen, add two or three cupfuls of warm flour, or sufficient to knead. Knead well until the dough is sufficiently elastic to rebound when struck forcibly with the fist. Allow it to rise again in mass; then shape into loaves; place in pans; let it stand until light, and bake. If undesirable to set the bread over night, and additional tablespoonfuls or two of cheese may be used, to facilitate the rising.

Vienna Bread.—Into a pint of milk sterilized by scalding, turn a cup and a half of boiling water. When lukewarm, add one half cup of warm water, in which has been dissolved a cake of compressed yeast, and a quart of white flour. Beat the batter thus made very thoroughly, and allow it to rise for one hour; then add white flour until the dough is of a consistency to knead. Knead well, and allow it to rise again for about three hours, or until very light. Shape into four loaves, handling lightly. Let it rise again in the pans, and bake. During the baking, wash the tops of the loaves with a sponge dipped in milk, to glaze them.

Water Bread.—Dissolve a tablespoonful of sugar in a pint of boiling water. When lukewarm, add one fourth of a cup full of liquid yeast, and sufficient flour to make a batter thick enough to drop from the spoon. Beat vigorously for ten minutes, turn into a clean, well-scalded bread bowl, cover (wrapping in a blanket if in cold weather), and let it rise over night. In the morning, when well risen, add flour to knead. Knead well for half an hour, cover, and let it become light in mass. When light, shape into loaves, allow it to rise again, and bake.

Fruit Roll.—Take some bread dough prepared as for Milk Bread, which has been sufficiently kneaded and is ready to mold, and roll to about one inch in thickness. Spread over it some dates which have been washed, dried, and stoned, raisins, currants, or chopped figs. Roll it up tightly into a loaf. Let and it rise until very light, and bake.

Fruit Loaf.—Set a sponge with one pint of rich milk, one fourth cup of yeast, and a pint of flour, over night. In the morning, add two cups of Zante currents, one cup of sugar, and three cups of flour, or enough to make a rather stiff dough. Knead well, and set to rise; when light, mold into loaves; let it rise again, and bake.

Potato Bread.—Cook and mash perfectly smooth, potatoes to make a cupful. Add a teaspoonful of best white sugar, one cup and a half of warm water, and when the mixture is lukewarm, one half cup of yeast, prepared as directed for Boiled Potato Yeast No. 2, and flour to make a very thick batter. Allow it to rise over night. In the morning, add a pint of warm water and flour enough to knead. The dough will need to be considerably stiffer than when no potato is used, or the result will be a bread too moist for easy digestion. Knead well. Let it rise, mold into four loaves, and when again light, bake.

Pulled Bread.—Remove a loaf from the oven when about half baked, and lightly pull the partially set dough into pieces of irregular shape, about half the size of one's fist. Do not smooth or mold the pieces; bake in a slow oven until browned and crisp throughout.

Whole Wheat Bread.—The materials needed for the bread are: one pint of milk, scalded and cooled, one quart of wheat berry flour, one pint Minnesota spring wheat flour, one third cup of a soft yeast, or one fourth cake of compressed yeast, dissolved in one third cup of cold water. Stir enough flour into the milk to make a stiff batter, put in the yeast, and let it rise until foamy. Have the milk so warm that, when the flour is put in, the batter will be of a lukewarm temperature. Wrap in a thick blanket, and keep at an equable temperature. When light, stir in, slowly, warm flour to make a soft dough. Knead for fifteen minutes, and return to the bowl (which has been washed and oiled) to rise again. When risen to double its size, form into two loaves, place in separate pans, let rise again, and bake from three fourths to one and one half hours, according to the heat of the oven.

Whole-Wheat Bread No. 2.—Scald one pint of unskimmed milk; when lukewarm, add one half cup of liquid yeast, or one fourth cake of compressed yeast, dissolved in one half cup of warm water, and a pint of Pillsbury's best white flour. Beat this batter thoroughly, and allow it to rise. When well risen, add three and two thirds cups of wheat berry flour. Knead thoroughly, and allow it to become light in mass; then shape into two loaves, allow it to rise again, and bake.

Miss. B's One-Rising Bread.—Sift and measure three and three fourths cups of wheat berry flour. Scald and cool a pint of unskimmed milk. When lukewarm, add one tablespoonful of lively liquid yeast. By slow degrees add the flour, beating vigorously until too stiff to use a spoon, then knead thoroughly for half an hour, shape into a loaf, place in a bread pan, cover with a napkin in warm weather, wrap well with blankets in cold weather, and let rise over night. In the morning, when perfectly light, pat in a well heated oven, and bake.

Potato Bread with Whole Wheat Flour.—Take a half gill of liquid yeast made as for Boiled Potato Yeast No. 2, and add milk, sterilised and cooled to lukewarm, to make a pint. And one cup of well-mashed, mealy potato and one cup of white flour, or enough to make a rather thick batter Beat thoroughly, cover, and set to rise. When well risen, add sufficient whole-wheat flour to knead. The quantity will vary somewhat with the brand of flour used, but about four and one fourth cupfuls will in general be needed. Knead well, let it rise in mass and again in the loaf, and bake.

Rye Bread.—Prepare a sponge over night with white flour as for Water Bread. In the morning, when light, add another tablespoonful of sugar, and rye flour to knead. Proceed as directed for the Water Bread, taking care to use only enough rye flour to make the dough Just stiff enough to mold. Use white flour for dusting than kneading board, as the rye flour is sticky.

Graham Bread.—Take two tablespoonfuls of lively liquid yeast, or a little less than one fourth cake of compressed yeast, dissolved in a little milk, and add new milk, scalded and cooled to lukewarm, to make one pint. Add one pint of white flour, beat very thoroughly, and set to rise. When very light, add three find one half cupfuls of sifted Graham flour, or enough to make a dough that can be molded. Knead well for half an hour. Place in a clean, slightly oiled bread bowl, cover, and allow it to rise. When light, shape into a loaf: allow it to rise again, and bake.

Graham Bread No. 2.—Mix well one pint of white and two pints of best Graham flour. Prepare a batter with a scant pint of milk, scalded and cooled, two table spoonfuls of liquid yeast, or a little less than one fourth of a cake of compressed yeast, dissolved in two table spoonfuls of milk, and a portion of the mixed flour. Give it a vigorous beating, and put it in a warm place to rise. When well risen, add more flour to make a dough sufficiently stiff to knead. There will be some variation in the amount required, dependent upon the brands of flour used, but in general, two and one half pints of the flour will be enough for preparing the sponge and kneading the dough. Knead thoroughly for twenty-five or thirty minutes. Put into a clean and slightly oiled bread bowl, cover, and set to rise again. When double its first bulk, mold into a loaf; allow it to rise again, and bake.

Graham Bread No. 3.—Mix three pounds each of Graham and Minnesota spring wheat flour. Make a sponge of one and a half pints of warm water, one half cake compressed yeast, well dissolved in the water, and flour to form a batter. Let this rise. When well risen, add one and a half pints more of warm water, one half cup full of New Orleans molasses, and sufficient flour to knead. Work the bread thoroughly, allow it to rise in mass; then mold, place in pans, and let it rise again. The amount of material given is sufficient for four loaves of bread.

Raised Biscuit.—These may be made from dough prepared by any of the preceding recipes for bread. They will be more tender if made with milk, and if the dough is prepared expressly for biscuits, one third cream may be used. When the dough has been thoroughly kneaded the last time, divide into small, equal-sized pieces. A quantity of dough sufficient for one loaf of bread should be divided into twelve or sixteen such portions. Shape into smooth, round biscuits, fit closely into a shallow pan, and let them rise until very light. Biscuit should be allowed to become lighter than bread before putting in the oven, since, being so much smaller, fermentation is arrested much sooner, and they do not rise as much in the oven as does bread.

Rolls.—Well kneaded and risen bread dough is made into a variety of small forms termed rolls, by rolling with the hands or with a rolling-pin, and afterward cutting or folding into any shape desired, the particular manner by which they are folded and shaped giving to the rolls their characteristic names. Dough prepared with rich milk or part cream makes the best rolls. It may be divided into small, irregular portions, about one inch in thickness, and shaped by taking each piece separately in the left hand, then with the thumb and first finger of the right hand, slightly stretch one of the points of the piece and draw it over the left thumb toward the center of the roll, holding it there with the left thumb. Turn the dough and repeat the operation until you have been all around the dough, and each point has been drawn in; then place on the pan to rise. Allow the rolls to become very light, and bake. Rolls prepared in this manner are termed *Imperial Rolls*, and if the folding has been properly done, when well baked they will be composed of a succession of light layers, which can be readily separated.

French Rolls may be made by shaping each portion of dough into small oval rolls quite tapering at each end, allowing them to become light, and baking far enough apart so that one will not touch another.

If, when the dough is light and ready to shape, it be rolled on the board until about one eighth of an inch in thickness, and cut into five-inch squares, then divided through the center into triangles, rolled up, beginning with the wide side, and placed in the pan to rise in semicircular shape, the rolls are called *Crescents*.

What are termed *Parker House Rolls* may be made from well-risen dough prepared with milk, rolled upon the board to a uniform thickness of about one forth inch; cut into round or oval shapes with the cutter; folded, one third over the other two thirds; allowed to rise until very light, and baked.

The light, rolled dough, may be formed into a *Braid* by cutting into strips six inches in length and one in width, joining the ends of each three, and braiding.

The heat of the oven should be somewhat greater for roils and biscuit than for bread. The time required will depend upon the heat and the size of the roll, but it will seldom exceed one half hour. Neither rolls nor biscuits should be eaten hot, as they are then open to the same objections as other new yeast bread.

Brown Bread.—To one and one fourth cups of new milk which has been scalded and cooled, add one fourth of a cup of lively yeast, three tablespoonfuls of sugar, and one cup each of white flour, rye flour or sifted rye meal, and yellow corn meal. With different brands of flour there may need to be some variation in the quantity of liquid to be used. The mixture should be thick enough to shape. Allow it to rise until light and cracked over the top; put into a bread pan, and when again well risen, bake for an hour and a half or two hours in an oven sufficiently hot at first to arrest fermentation and fix the bread cells, afterwards allowing the heat to diminish somewhat, to permit a slower and longer baking. Graham flour may be used in place of rye, if preferred.

Date Bread.—Take a pint of light white bread sponge prepared with milk, add two tablespoons of sugar, and Graham flour to make a very stiff batter. And last a cupful of stoned dates. Turn into a bread pan. Let it rise, and bake.

Fruit Loaf With Graham and Whole-Wheat Flour.—Dissolve one fourth cake of compressed yeast in a pint of sterilized milk; and a pint of white flour; heat thoroughly, and set to rise. When well risen, add three and one fourth cups of flour (Graham and whole-wheat, equal proportions, thoroughly mixed), or sufficient to knead. Knead well for half an hour, and just at the last add a cup of raisins, well washed, dried, and dusted with flour. Let the loaf rise in mass; then shape, put in the pan, allow it to become light again, and bake.

Raised Corn Bread.—Into two cupfuls of hot mush made from white granular corn meal, stir two cupfuls of cold water. Beat well, and add one half cup of liquid yeast, or one half cake of compressed yeast, dissolved in one half cup of warm water, and two teaspoonfuls of granulated sugar. Stir in white or sifted Graham flour to make it stiff enough to knead. Knead very thoroughly, and put in a warm place to rise. When light, molded into three loaves, put into pans, and allow it to rise again. When well risen, bake at least for three fourths of an hour.

Corn Cake.—Sterilise a cupful of rich milk or thin cream. Cool to lukewarm, and dissolve in it half a cake of compressed yeast Add two small cupfuls of white flour; beat very thoroughly, and put in a warm place to rise. When light, add a cup of lukewarm water or milk, and two cups of best yellow cornmeal. Turn into a shallow square pan, and leave until again well risen. Bake in a quick oven. A tablespoonful of sugar may be added with the corn meal, if desired.

Oatmeal bread.—Mix a quart of well-cooked oatmeal mush with a pint of water, beating it perfectly smooth; add a cupful of liquid yeast and flour to make a stiff batter. Cover, and let it rise. When light, add sufficient flour to mold; knead as soft as possible, for twenty or thirty minutes; shape into four or more loaves, let it rise again, and bake.

Milk Yeast Bread.—Prepare the yeast the day before by scalding three heaping teaspoonfuls of fresh cornmeal with boiling milk. Set in a warm place until light (from seven to ten hours); then put in a cool place until needed for use. Start the bread by making a rather thick batter with one cupful of warm water, one teaspoonful of the prepared yeast, and white flour. Put in a warm place to rise. When light, add to it a cupful of flour scalded with a cupful of boiling milk, and enough more flour to make the whole into a rather stiff batter. Cover, and allow it to rise. When again well risen, add flour enough to knead. Knead well; shape into a loaf; let it rise, and bake. Three or four cupfuls of white flour will be needed for all purposes with the amount of liquid given; more liquid and flour may be added in forming the second sponge if a larger quantity of bread is desired. In preparing both yeast and bread, all utensils used should first be sterilized by scalding in hot sal-soda water.

Graham Salt-Rising Bread.—Put two tablespoonfuls of milk into a half-pint cup, add boiling water to fill the cup half full, one half teaspoonful of sugar, one fourth teaspoonful of salt, and white flour to make a rather stiff batter. Let it rise over night. In the morning, when well risen, add a cup and a half of warm water, or milk scalded and cooled, and sufficient white flour to form a rather stiff batter. Cover, and allow it again to rise. When light, add enough sifted Graham flour to knead. When well kneaded, shape into a loaf; allow it to become light again in the pan, and bake. All utensils used should be first well sterilized by scalding in hot sal-soda water.

UNFERMENTED BREADS.

The earliest forms of bread were made without fermentation. Grain was broken as fine as possible by pounding on smooth stones, made into dough with pure water, thoroughly kneaded, and baked in some convenient way. Such was the "unleavened breads" or "Passover cakes" of the Israelites. In many countries this bread is the only kind used. Unleavened bread made from barley and oats is largely used by the Irish and Scotch peasantry. In Sweden an unleavened bread is made of rye meal and water, flavored with anise seed, and baked in large, thin cakes, a foot or more in diameter.

Some savage tribes subsists chiefly upon excellent corn bread, made simply of meal and water. Unleavened bread made of corn, called *tortillas*, forms the staple diet of the Mexican Indians. The corn, previously softened by soaking in lime water, is ground to a fine paste between a stone slab and roller called a *metate*, then patted and tossed from hand to hand until flattened into thin, wafer-like cakes, and baked over a quick fire, on a thin iron plate or a flat stone.

Unquestionably, unleavened bread, well kneaded and properly baked, is the most wholesome of all breads, but harder to masticate than that made light by fermentation, but this is an advantage; for it insures more thorough mixing with that important digestive agent, the saliva, than is usually given to more easily softened food.

What is usually termed unfermented bread, however, is prepared with flour and liquid, to which shortening—of some kind is added, and the whole made light by the liberation of gas generated within the dough during the process of baking. This is brought about either by mixing with the flour certain chemical substances, which, when wet and brought into contact, act upon each other so as to set free carbonic acid gas, which expands and puffs up the loaf; or by introducing into the dough some volatile substance as carbonate of ammonia, which the heat during baking will, cause to vaporize, and which in rising produces the same result.

Carbonic acid gas maybe for this purpose developed by the chemical decomposition of bicarbonate of potassa (saleratus), or bicarbonate of soda, by some acid such as sour milk, hydrochloric acid, tartaric acid, nitrate of potassa, or the acid phosphate of lime.

The chemical process of bread-raising originally consisted in adding to the dough definite proportions of muriatic acid and carbonate of soda, by the union of which carbonic acid gas and common salt were produced. This process was soon abandoned, however, on account of the propensity exhibited by the acid for eating holes in the fingers of the baker as well as in his bread pans; and a more convenient one for hands and pans, that of using soda or salaratus with cream of tartar or sour milk, was substituted. When there is an excess of soda, a portion of it remains in the loaf uncombined, giving to the bread a yellow color and an alkaline taste, and doing mischief to the delicate coating of the stomach. Alkalies, the class of chemicals to which soda and salaratus belong, when pure and strong, are powerful corrosive poisons. The acid used with the alkali to liberate the carbonic-acid gas in the process of bread-making, if rightly proportioned, destroys this poisonous property, and unites with it to form a new compound, which, although not a poison, is yet unwholesome.

We can hardly speak too strongly in condemnation of the use of chemicals in bread-making, when we reflect that the majority of housewives who combine sour milk and salaratus, or cream of tartar and soda, more frequently than otherwise *guess* at the proportions, or measure them by some "rule of thumb," without stopping to consider that although two cups of sour milk may at one time be sufficiently acid to neutralize a teaspoonful of saleratus, milk may vary in degree of acidity to such an extent that the same quantity will be quite insufficient for the purpose at another time; or that though a teaspoonful of some brand of cream of tartar will neutralize a half teaspoonful of one kind of soda, similar measures will not always bring about the same result. Very seldom, indeed, will the proportions be sufficiently exact to perfectly neutralise the alkali, since chemicals are subject to variations in degree of strength, both on account of the method by which they are manufactured and the length of time they have been kept, to say nothing of adulterations to which they may have been subjected, and which are so common that it is almost impossible to find unadulterated cream of tartar in the market.

Baking powders are essentially composed of bicarbonate of soda and cream of tartar, mixed in the proper proportions to exactly neutralize each other, and if they were always pure, would certainly be as good as soda and cream of tartar in any form, and possess the added advantage of perfect propotions; but as was demonstrated not long ago by the government chemist, nearly every variety of baking powder in the market is largely adulterated with cheaper and harmful substances. Alum, a most frequent constituent of such baking powders, is exceedingly injurious to the stomach. Out of several hundred brands of baking powder examined, only one was found pure.

Even when in their purest state, these chemicals are not harmless, as is so generally believed. It is a very prevalent idea that when soda is neutralized by an acid, both chemical compounds are in some way destroyed or vaporized in the process, and in some occult manner escape from the bread during the process of baking. This is altogether an error. The alkali and acid neutralize each other chemically, but they do not destroy each other. Their union forms a salt, exactly the same as the Rochelle salts of medicine, a mild purgative, and if we could collected from the bread and weigh or measure it, we would find nearly as much of it as there was of the baking powder in the first place. If two teaspoonfuls of baking powder to the quart of flour be used, we have remaining in the bread made with that amount of flour 165 grains of crystallized Rochelle salts, or 45 grains more than this to be found in a Seidlitz powder. It may be sometimes useful to take a dose of salts, but the daily consumption of such chemical substances in bread can hardly be considered compatible with the conditions necessary for the maintenance of health. These chemical substances are unusable by the system, and must all be removed by the liver and excretory organs, thus imposing upon them an extra and unnecessary burden. It has also been determined by scientific experimentation that the chemicals found in baking powders in bread retard digestion.

Gem Irons.

These substances are, fortunately, not needed for the production of good light bread. The purpose of their use is the production of a gas; but air is a gas much more economical and abundant than carbonic-acid gas, and which, when introduced into bread and subjected to heat, has the property of expanding, and in doing, puffing up the bread and making it light. Bread made light with air is vastly superior to that compounded with soda or baking powder, in point of healthfulness, and when well prepared, will equal it in lightness and palatableness. The only difficulty lies in catching and holding the air until it has accomplished the desired results. But a thorough understanding of the necessary conditions and a little practice will soon enable one to attain sufficient skill in this direction to secure most satisfactory results.

General Directions.—All materials used for making aërated bread should be of the very best quality. Poor flour will not produce good bread by this or by any other process. Aërated breads are of two kinds: those baked while in the form of a batter, and such as are made into a dough before baking.

All breads, whether fermented or unfermented, are lighter if baked in some small form, and this is particularly true of unfermented breads made light with air. For this reason, breads made into a dough are best baked in the form of rolls, biscuits, or crackers, and batter breads in small iron cups similar to those in the accompanying illustration. These cups or "gem irons" as they are sometimes called, are to be obtained in various shapes and sizes, but for this purpose the more shallow cups are preferable. For baking the dough breads a perforated sheet of Russia iron or heavy tin, which any tinner can make to fit the oven, is the most serviceable, as it permits the hot air free access to all sides of the bread at once. If such is not obtainable, the upper oven grate, carefully washed and scoured, may be used Perforated pie tins also answer very well for this purpose.

The heat of the oven for baking should be sufficient to form a slight crust over all sides ofthe bread before the air escapes, but not sufficient to brown it within the first fifteen minutes. To aid in forming the crust on thesides and bottom of batter breads, the iron cups should be heated previous to introducing the batter. The degree of heat required for baking will be about the same as for fermented rolls and biscuit, and the fire should be so arranged as to keep a steady but not greatly increasing heat.

Air is incorporated into batter breads by brisk and continuous agitating and beating; into dough breads by thorough kneading, chopping, or pounding.

Whatever the process by which the air is incorporated, it must be *continuous*. For this reason it is especially essential in making aërated bread that every thing be in readiness before commencing to put the bread together. All the materials should be measured out, the utensils to be used in readiness, and the oven properly heated. Success is also dependent upon the dexterity with which the materials when ready are put together. Batter bread often proves a failure although the beating is kept up without cessation, because it is done slowly and carelessly, or interspersed with stirring, thus permitting the air to escape between the strokes.

If the bread is to be baked at once, the greater the dispatch with which it can be gotten into a properly-heated oven the lighter it will be. Crackers, rolls and other forms of dough breads often lack in lightness because they were allowed to stand some time before baking. The same is true of batter breads. If, for any reason, it is necessary to keep such breads for any length of time after being prepared, before baking, set the dish containing them directly on ice.

The lightness of aërated bread depends not only upon the amount of air incorporated in its preparation, but also upon the expansion of the air during the baking. The colder the air, the greater will be its expansion upon the application of heat. The colder the materials employed, then, for the bread-making, the colder will be the air confined within it, and the lighter will be the bread. For this reason, in making batter bread, it will be found a good plan, when there is time, to put the materials together, and place the dish containing the mixture on ice for an hour or two, or even over night. When ready to use, beat thoroughly for ten or fifteen minutes to incorporate air, and bake in heated irons. Rolls and other breads made into a dough, may be kneaded and shaped and put upon ice to become cold. Thus treated, less kneading is necessary than when prepared to be baked at once.

Many of the recipes given for the batter breads include eggs. The yolk is not particularly essential, and if it can be put to other uses, may be left out. The white of an egg, because of its viscous nature, when beaten, serves as a sort of trap to catch and hold air, and added to the bread, aids in making it light. Very nice light bread may be made without eggs, but the novice in making aërated breads will, perhaps, find it an advantage first to become perfectly familiar with the processes and conditions involved, by using the recipes with eggs before attempting those without, which are somewhat more dependent for success upon skill and practice.

When egg is used in the bread, less heating of the irons will be necessary, and not so hot an oven as when made without.

If the bread, when baked, appears light, but with large holes in the center, it is probable that either the irons or the oven was too hot at first. If the bread after baking, seems sticky or dough-like in the interior, it is an indication that either it was insufficiently baked, or that not enough flour in proportion to the liquid has been used. It should be stated, that although the recipes given have been prepared with the greatest care, and with the same brands of flour, careful measurement, and proper conditions, prove successful every time, yet with different brands of flour some variation in quantity may needed,—a trifle more or less,—dependent upon the absorbent properties of the flour, and if eggs are used, upon the size of the eggs.

A heavy bread may be the result of the use of poor flour, too much flour, careless or insufficient beating, so that not enough air was incorporated, or an oven not sufficiently hot to form a crust over the bread before the air escaped. Breads made into a dough, if moist and clammy, require more flour or longer baking. Too much flour will make them stiff and hard.

The length of time requisite for baking aërated breads made with whole-wheat, wheat berry, or Graham flours, will vary from forty minutes to one hour, according to the kind and form in which the bread is baked, and the heat of the oven.

The irons in which batter breads are to be baked should not be smeared with grease; if necessary to oil them at all, they should only be wiped out lightly with a clean, oiled cloth. Irons well cared for, carefully washed, and occasionally scoured with Sapolio to keep them perfectly smooth, will require no greasing whatever.

In filling the irons, care should be taken to fill each cup at first as full as it is intended to have; it, as the heat of the irons begins the cooking of the batter as soon as it is put in, and an additional quantity added has a tendency to make the bread less light.

RECIPES.

Whole-Wheat Puffs.—Put the yolk of an egg into a basin, and beat the white in a separate dish to a stiff froth. Add to the yolk, one half a cupful of rather thin sweet cream and one cupful of skim milk. Beat the egg, cream, and milk together until perfectly mingled and foamy with air bubbles; then add, gradually, beating well at the same time, one pint of what berry flour. Continue the beating vigorously and without interruption for eight or ten minutes; then stir in, lightly, the white of the egg. Do not beat again after the white of the egg is added, but turn at once into heated, shallow irons, and bake for an hour in a moderately quick oven. If properly made and carefully baked, these puffs will be of a fine, even texture throughout, and as light as bread raised by fermentation.

Whole-Wheat Puffs No. 2.—Make a batter by beating together until perfectly smooth the yolk of one egg, one and one half cups of new or unskimmed milk, and one pint of whole-wheat flour. Place the dish containing it directly upon ice, and leave for an hour or longer. The bread may be prepared and left on the ice over night, if desired for breakfast. When ready to bake the puffs, whip the white of the egg to a stiff froth, and after vigorously beating the batter for ten minutes, stir in lightly the white of the egg; turn at once into heated irons, and bake. If preferred, one third white flour and two thirds sifted Graham flour may be used in the place of the wheat berry flour.

Whole-Wheat Puffs No. 3.—Take one cupful of sweet cream (twelve-hour cream), one half cupful of soft ice water, and two slightly rounded cupfuls of wheat berry flour. Beat the material well together, and set the dish containing it on ice for an hour or more before using. When ready to bake, beat the mixture vigorously for ten minutes, then turn into heated iron cups (shallow ones are best), and bake for about an hour in a quick oven.

Graham Puffs.—Beat together vigorously until full of air bubbles, one pint of unskimmed milk, the yolk of one egg, and one pint and three or four tablespoonfuls of Graham flour, added a little at a time. When the mixture is light and foamy throughout, stir in lightly and evenly the white of the egg, beaten to a stiff froth; turn into heated irons, and bake in a rather quick oven. Instead of all Graham, one third white flour may be used if preferred.

Graham Puffs No. 2.—Beat the yolks of two eggs in two cupfuls of ice water; then add gradually, beating well meantime, three and one fourth cupfuls of Graham flour. Continue the beating, after all the flour is added, until the mixture is light and full of air bubbles. Add last the whites of the eggs, beaten to a stiff froth, and bake at once in heated irons.

Currant Puffs.—Prepare the puffs as directed in any of the foregoing recipes with the addition of one cup of Zante currants which have been well washed, dried, and floured.

Graham Gems.—Into two cupfuls of unskimmed milk which has been made very cold by standing on ice, stir gradually, sprinkling it from the hand, three and one fourth cupfuls of Graham flour. Beat vigorously for ten minutes or longer, until the batter is perfectly smooth and full of air bubbles. Turn at once into hissing hot gem irons, and bake in a hot oven. If preferred, the batter may be prepared, and the dish containing it placed on ice for an hour or longer; then well beaten and baked. Graham gems may be made in this manner with soft water instead of milk, but such, in general, will need a little more flour than when made with milk. With some ovens, it will be found an advantage in baking these gems to place them on the upper grate for the first ten minutes or until the top has been slightly crusted, and then change to the bottom of the oven for the baking.

Crusts.—Beat together very thoroughly one cupful of ice-cold milk, and one cupful of Graham flour. When very light and full of air bubbles, turn into hot iron cups, and bake twenty-five or thirty minutes. The best irons forthis purpose are the shallow oblong, or round cups of the same size at the bottom as at the top. Only a very little batter should be put in each cup. The quantity given is sufficient for one dozen crusts.

Rye Puffs.—Beat together the same as for whole-wheat puffs one cupful of milk, one tablespoonful of sugar, and the yolk of an egg. Add one cupful of good rye flour, mixed with one half cupful of Graham flour, and stir in lastly the well beaten white of the egg. Bake at once, in heated gem-irons.

Rye Puffs No. 2.—Beat together until well mingled one pint of thin cream and the yolk of one egg. Add gradually, beating meanwhile, four cups of rye flour. Continue to beat vigorously for ten minutes, then add the stiffly-beaten white of the egg, and bake in heated irons.

Rye Gems.—Mix together one cupful of corn meal and one cupful of rye meal. Stir the mixed meal into one and a half cupfuls of ice water. Beat the batter vigorously for ten or fifteen minutes, then turn into hot irons, and bake.

Blueberry Gems.—To one cupful of rich milk add one tablespoonful of sugar, and the yolk of an egg. Beat well till full of air bubbles; then add gradually one cupful of Graham flour, and one cupful of white flour, or white corn meal. Beat vigorously until light; stir in the beaten white of the egg, and one cupful of fresh, sound blueberries. Bake in heated irons, in a moderately quick oven. Chopped or sour apples may be used in place of the berries.

Hominy Gems.—Beat one egg until very light, add to it one tablespoonful of thick sweet cream, a little salt if desired, and two cupfuls of cooked hominy (fine). Thin the mixture with one cupful or less of boiling water until it will form easily, beat well, and bake in heated irons.

Sally Lunn Gems.—Beat together the yolk of one egg, two tablespoonfuls of sugar, and one cupful of thin, ice-cold, sweet cream. Add slowly, beating at the same time, one cup and two tablespoonfuls of sifted Graham flour. Beat vigorously, until full of air bubbles, add the white of the egg beaten stiffly, and bake in heated irons.

Corn Puffs.—Mingle the yolk of one egg with one cupful of rich milk. Add to the liquid one cupful of flour, one-half cupful of fine, yellow corn meal, and one-fourth cupful of sugar, all of which have previously been well mixed together. Place the batter on ice for an hour, or until very cold. Then beat it vigorously five or ten minutes, till full of air bubbles; stir in lightly the stiffly beaten white of the egg, and put at once into heated irons. Bake in a moderately quick oven, thirty or forty minutes.

Corn Puffs No. 2.—Scald two cupfuls of fine white corn meal with boiling water. When cold, add three tablespoonfuls of thin sweet cream, and the yolk of one egg. Beat well, and stir in lastly the white of the egg, beaten to a stiff froth. The batter should be sufficiently thin to drop easily from a spoon, but not thin enough to pour. Bake in heated irons, in a moderately quick oven.

Corn Puffs No. 3.—Take one cupful of cold mashed potato, and one cupful of milk, rubbed together through a colander to remove all lumps. Add the yolk of one well beaten, egg, and then stir in slowly, beating vigorously meantime, one cupful of good corn meal. Lastly, stir in the white of the egg beaten to a stiff froth, and bake in heated irons, in a rather quick oven.

Corn Puffs No. 4.—Beat together one and one-half cupfuls of unskimmed milk and the yolks of two eggs, until thoroughly blended. Add two cupfuls of flour, and one cupful best granular corn meal. Beat the batter thoroughly; stir in lightly the whites of the eggs, beaten to a stiff froth, turn into heated irons, and bake.

Corn Dodgers.—Scald one cupful of best granular corn meal, with which a tablespoonful of sugar has been sifted, with one cup of boiling milk. Beat until smooth, and drop on a griddle, in cakes about one inch in thickness, and bake slowly for an hour. Turn when brown.

Corn Dodgers No. 2.—Mix one tablespoonful of sugar with two cups best corn meal. Scald with one cup of boiling water. Add rich milk to make a batter thin enough to drop from a spoon. Lastly, add one egg, yolk and white beaten separately, and bake on a griddle in the oven from three fourth of an hour to one hour.

Cream Corn Cakes.—Into one cup of thin cream stir one and one half cups of granular corn meal, or enough to make a stiff batter; beat well, drop into heated irons, and bake.

Hoe Cakes.—Scald one pint of white corn meal, with which, if desired, a tablespoonful of sugar, and one half teaspoonful of salt have been mixed, with boiling milk, or water enough to make a batter sufficiently thick not to spread. Drop on a hot griddle, in large or small cakes, as preferred, about one half inch in thickness. Cook slowly, and when well browned on the under side, turn over. The cake may be cooked slowly, until well done throughout, or, as the portion underneath becomes well browned the first browned crust may be peeled off with a knife, and the cake again turned. As rapidly as a crust becomes formed and browned, one may be removed, and the cake turned, until the whole is all browned. The thin wafer-like crusts are excellent served with hot milk or cream.

Oatmeal Gems.—To one cupful of well-cooked oatmeal add one half cupful of rich milk or thin cream, and the yolk of one egg. Beat all together thoroughly; then add, continuing to beat, one and one third cupfuls of Graham flour, and lastly the stiffly beaten white of the egg. Bake in heated irons. If preferred, one cupful of white flour may be used in place of the Graham.

Snow Gems.—Beat together lightly but thoroughly two parts clean, freshly fallen, dry snow, and one part best granular corn meal. Turn into hot gem irons and bake quickly. The snow should not be packed in measuring, and the bread should be prepared before the snow melts.

Pop Overs.—For the preparation of these, one egg, one cupful of milk, and one scant cupful of white flour are required. Beat the egg, yolk and white separately. Add to the yolk, when well beaten, one half of the milk, and sift in the flour a little at a time, stirring until the whole is a perfectly smooth paste. Add the remainder of the milk gradually, beating well until the whole is an absolutely smooth, light batter about the thickness of cream. Stir in the stiffly beaten white of the egg, and bake in hot earthen cups or muffin rings, and to prevent them from sticking, sift flour into the rings after slightly oiling, afterward turning them upside down to shake off all of the loose flour.

Granola Gems.—Into three fourths of a cup of rich milk stir one cup of Granola (prepared by the Sanitarium Food Co.). Drop into heated irons, and bake for twenty or thirty minutes.

Bean Gems.—Prepare the gems in the same manner as for Whole-Wheat Puffs, using one half cup of milk, one egg, one cup of cooked beans which have been rubbed through a colander and salted, and one cup and one tablespoonful of white flour. A little variation in the quantity of the flour may be necessary, dependent upon the moisture contained in the beans, although care should be taken to have them quite dry.

Breakfast Rolls.—Sift a pint and a half of Graham flour into a bowl, and into it stir a cupful of very cold thin cream or unskimmed milk. Pour the liquid into the flour slowly, a few spoonfuls at a time, mixing each spoonful to a dough with the flour as fast as poured in. When all the liquid has been added, gather the fragments of dough together, knead thoroughly for ten minutes or longer, until perfectly smooth and elastic. The quantity of flour will vary somewhat with the quality, but in general, the quantity given will be quite sufficient for mixing the dough and dusting the board. When well kneaded, divide into two portions; roll each over and over with the hands, until a long roll about once inch in diameter is formed; cut this into two-inch lengths, prick with a fork and place on perforated tins, far enough apart so that one will not touch another when baking. Each roll should be as smooth and perfect as possible, and with no dry flour adhering. Bake at once, or let stand on ice for twenty minutes. The rolls should not be allowed to stand after forming, unless on ice. From thirty to forty minutes will be required for baking. When done, spread on the table to cool, but do not pile one on top of another.

Very nice rolls may be made in the same manner, using for the wetting ice-cold soft water. They requite a longer kneading, are more crisp, but less tender than those made with cream.

With some brands of Graham flour the rolls will be much lighter if one third white flour be used. Whole-wheat flour may be used in place of Graham, if preferred.

Sticks.—Prepare, and knead the dough the same as for rolls. When ready to form, roll the dough much smaller; scarcely larger than one's little finger, and cut into three or four-inch lengths. Bake the same as rolls, for about twenty minutes.

Cream Graham Rolls.—To one half cup cold cream add one half cup of soft ice water. Make into a dough with three cups of Graham flour, sprinkling in slowly with the hands, beating at the same time, so as to incorporate as much air as possible, until the dough is too stiff to be stirred; then knead thoroughly, form into rolls, and bake.

Corn Mush Rolls.—Make a dough of one cup of corn meal mush, one half cup of cream, and two and one half cups of white flour; knead thoroughly, shape into rolls, and bake.

Fruit Rolls.—Prepare the rolls as directed in the recipe for Breakfast Rolls, and when well kneaded, work into the dough a half cupful of Zante currants which have been well washed, dried, and floured. Form the rolls in the usual manner, and bake.

Cream Mush Rolls.—Into a cupful of cold Graham mush beat thoroughly three tablespoonfuls of thick, sweet cream. Add sufficient Graham flour to make a rather stiff dough, knead thoroughly, shape into roils, and bake. Corn meal, farina, and other mushes may be used in the place of the Graham mush, if preferred.

Beaten Biscuit.—Into a quart of whole-wheat flour mix a large cup of must be very stiff, and rendered soft and pliable by thorough kneading and afterward pounding with a mallet for at least half an hour in the following manner: Pound the dough oat flat, and until of the same thickness throughout; dredge lightly with flour; double the dough over evenly and pound quickly around the outside, to fasten the edges together and thus retain the air within the dough. When well worked, the dough will appear flaky and brittle, and pulling a piece off it quickly will cause a sharp, snapping sound. Mold into small biscuits, making an indenture in the center of each with the thumb, prick well with a fork, and place on perforated sheets, with a space between, and put at once into the oven. The oven should be of the same temperature as for rolls. If they are "sad" inside when cold, they were not well baked, as they should be light and tender. If preferred, use one third white flour, instead of all whole-wheat. Excellent results are also obtained by chopping instead of pounding the dough.

Cream Crisps.—Make a dough of one cupful of thin cream, and a little more than three cups of Graham flour. Knead until smooth, then divide the dough into several pieces, and place in a dish on ice for an hour, or until ice cold. Roll each piece separately and quickly as thin as brown paper. Cut with a knife into squares, prick with a fork, and bake on perforated tins, until lightly browned on both sides.

Cream Crisps No. 2.—Into two and one half cups of cold cream or rich milk, sprinkle slowly with the hands, beating meanwhile to incorporate air, four cups of best Graham flour, sifted with one half cup of granulated sugar. Add flour to knead; about two and one fourth cups will be required. When well kneaded, divide into several portions, roll each as thin as a knife blade, cut into squares, prick well with a fork, and bake.

Graham Crisps.—Into one half cupful of ice-cold soft water, stir slowly, so as to incorporate as much air as possible, enough Graham flour to make a dough stiff enough to knead. A tablespoonful of sugar may be added to the water before stirring in the flour, if desired. After kneading fifteen minutes, divide the dough into six portions; roll each as thin as brown paper, prick with a fork, and bake on perforated tins, turning often until both sides are a light, even brown. Break into irregular pieces and serve.

Oatmeal Crisps.—Make a dough with one cupful of oatmeal porridge and Graham flour. Knead thoroughly, roll very thin, and bake as directed for Graham Crisps. A tablespoonful of sugar may be added if desired.

Graham Crackers.—Make a dough of one cup of cream and Graham flour sufficient to make a soft dough. Knead thoroughly, and place on ice for half an hour; then roll thin, cut into small cakes with a cookie-cutter, prick with a fork, and bake on floured pans, in a brisk oven. A tablespoonful of sugar may be added if desired.

Fruit Crackers.—Prepare a dough with one cup of cold sweet cream and three cups of Graham flour, knead well, and divide into two portions. Roll each quite thin. Spread one thickly with dates or figs seeded and chopped; place the other one on top and press together with the rolling pin. Cut into squares and bake. An additional one fourth of a cup of flour will doubtless be needed for dusting the board and kneading.

TABLE TOPICS.

Behind the nutty loaf is the mill wheel; behind the mill is the wheat field; on the wheat field rests the sunlight; above the sun is God.—*James Russell Lowell.*

Bread forms one of the most important parts of the ration of the German soldier. In time of peace, the private soldier is supplied day by day with one pound and nine ounces of bread; when fighting for the Fatherland, every man is entitled to a free ration of over two pounds of bread, and field bakery trains and steam ovens for providing the large amount of bread required, form a recognized part of the equipment of the German army.

The wandering Arab lives almost entirely upon bread, with a few dates as a relish.

According to Count Rumford, the Bavarian wood-chopper, one of the most hardy and hard-working men in the world, receives for his weekly rations one large loaf of rye bread and a small quantity of roasted meal. Of the meal he makes an infusion, to which he adds a little salt, and with the mixture, which he calls burned soup, he eats his rye bread. No beer, no beef, no other food than that mentioned, and no drink but water; and yet he can do more work and enjoys a better digestion and possesses stronger muscles than the average American or Englishman, with their varied dietary.

The following truthful bit of Scandinavian history well illustrates the influence of habits of frugality upon national character: "The Danes were approaching, and one of the Swedish bishops asked how many men the province of Dalarna could furnish.

"'At least twenty thousand,' was the reply; 'for the old men are just as strong and brave as the young ones.'

"'But what do they live upon?'

"'Upon bread and water. They take little account of hunger and thirst, and when corn is lacking, they make their bread out of tree bark.'

"'Nay,' said the bishop, 'a people who eat tree bark and drink water, the devil himself could not vanquish!' and neither were they vanquished. Their progress was one series of triumphs, till they placed Gustavus Vasa on the throne of Sweden."

The word *biscuit* embodies the process by which this form of bread was made from time immemorial down to within the last century. *Bis* (twice), and *coctus* (cooked), show that they were twice baked.

Fragments of unfermented bread were discovered in the Swiss lake-dwellings, which belong to the Neolithic age.

Fermented bread is seldom seen in Northern Europe and Asia except among the rich or the nobility. At one time, the captain of an English vessel requested a baker of Gottenburg to bake a large quantity of loaves of raised bread. The baker refused to undertake an order of such magnitude, saying it would be quite impossible to dispose of so much, until the captain agreed to take and pay for it all.

I made a study of the ancient and indispensable art of bread-making, consulting such authorities as offered, going back to the primitive days and first invention of the unleavened kind, and traveling gradually down in my studies through that accidental souring of the dough which it is supposed taught the leavening process, and through the various fermentations thereafter till I came to "good, sweet, wholesome bread,"—the staff of life. Leaven, which some deemed the soul of bread, the *spiritus* which fills its cellular tissues, which is religiously preserved like the vestal fire,—some precious bottleful, I suppose, brought over in the Mayflower, did the business for America, and its influence is still rising, swelling, spreading in cerulean billows over the land,—this seed I regularly and faithfully procured from the village, until one morning I forgot the rules and scalded my yeast; by which accident I discovered that even this was not indispensable, and I have gladly omitted it ever since. Neither did I put any soda or other acid or alkali into my bread. It would seem that I made it according to the recipe which Marcus Porcius Cato gave about two centuries before Christ: "Make kneaded bread thus: Wash your hands and trough well. Put the meal into the trough, add water gradually, and knead it thoroughly. When you have needed it well, mold it, and bake it under a cover," that is in a baking kettle.—*Thoreau in Walden.*

FRUITS

Of all the articles which enter the list of foods, none are more wholesome and pleasing than the fruits which nature so abundantly provides. Their delicate hues and perfect outlines appeal to our sense of beauty, while their delicious flavors gratify our appetite. Our markets are supplied with an almost unlimited variety of both native and tropical fruits, and it might be supposed that they would always appear upon the daily bill of fare; yet in the majority of homes this is rarely the case. People are inclined to consider fruit, unless the product of their own gardens, a luxury too expensive for common use. Many who use a plentiful supply, never think of placing it upon their tables, unless cooked. Ripe fruit is a most healthful article of diet when partaken of at seasonable times; but to eat it, or any other food, between meals, is a gross breach of the requirements of good digestion.

Fruits contain from seventy-five to ninety-five per cent of water, and a meager proportion of nitrogenous matter; hence their value as nutrients, except in a few instances, is rather small; but they supply a variety of agreeable acids which refresh and give tone to the system, and their abundant and proper use does much to keep the vital machinery in good working order.

Aside from the skin and seeds, all fruits consist essentially of two parts,—the cellulose structure containing the juice, and the juice itself. The latter is water, with a small proportion of fruit sugar (from one to twenty per cent in different varieties), and vegetable acids. These acids are either free, or combined with potash and lime in the form of acid salts. They are mallic, citric, tartaric, and pectic acids. The last-named is the jelly-producing principle.

While the juice, as we commonly find it, is readily transformable for use in the system, the cellular structure of the fruit is not so easily digested. In some fruits, as the strawberry, grape, and banana, the cell walls are so delicate as to be easily broken up; but in watermelons, apples, and oranges, the cells are coarser, and form a larger bulk of the fruit, hence are less easily digested. As a rule, other points being equal, the fruits which yield the richest and largest quantity of juices, and also possess a cellular framework the least perceptible on mastication, are the most readily digested. A certain amount of waste matter is an advantage, to give bulk to our food; but persons with weak stomachs, who cannot eat certain kinds of fruit, are often able to digest the juice when taken alone.

Unripe fruits differ from ripe fruits in that they contain, starch, which during ripening is changed into sugar, and generally some proportion of tannic acid, which gives them their astringency. The characteristic constituent of unripe fruit, however, is pectose, an element insoluble in water, but which, as maturation proceeds, is transformed into pectic and pectosic acids. These are soluble in boiling water, and upon cooling, yield gelatinous solutions. Their presence makes it possible to convert the juice of ripe fruits into jelly. Raw starch in any form is indigestible, hence unripe fruit should never be eaten uncooked. As fruit matures, the changes it undergoes are such as best fit for consumption and digestion. The following table shows the composition of the fruits in common use:—

ANALYSIS.

	Water.	Albumen.	Sugar.	Free Acid.	Pectose.	Cellulose.	Mineral Matter.
Apples	83.0	0.4	6.8	1.0	5.2	3.2	0.4
Pears	84.0	0.3	7.0	0.1	4.6	3.7	0.3
Peaches	85.0	0.5	1.8	0.7	8.0	3.4	0.6
Grapes	80.0	0.7	(Glucose.) 13.0	(Tartaric.) 0.8	3.1	2.0	0.4
Plums	82.0	0.2	3.6	0.5	5.7	X	0.6
Gooseberries	86.0	0.4	7.0	1.5	1.9	2.7	0.5
Strawberries	87.6	0.5	4.5	1.3	0.1	X	0.6
Raspberries	86.+	0.5	4.7	1.3	1.7	X	0.4
Currants	85.2	0.4	6.4	1.8	0.2	X	0.5
Blackberries	86.4	0.5	4.4	1.1	1.4	X	0.4
Cherries	75.0	0.9	13.1	0.3	2.2	X	0.6
Apricots	85.0	.08	1.0	X	5.9	X	0.8
Oranges	86.0	[A]	8 to 10	X	X	X	X
Dates	20.8	6.6	54.0	(Fat.) 0.2	12.3	5.5	1.6
Bananas	73.9	4.8	19.7[B]	(Fat.) 0.6	X	0.2	0.8
Turkey Figs	17.5	6.1	57.5	(Fat.) 0.9	8.4[C]	7.3	2.3

[Table Note A: Small quantities of albumen, citric acid, citrate of potash, cellulose, etc.]

[Table Note B: Sugar and pectose.]

[Table Note C: Starch, pectose, etc.]

There is a prevailing notion that the free use of fruits, especially in summer, excites derangement of the digestive organs. When such derangement occurs, it is far more likely to have been occasioned by the way in which the fruit was eaten than by the fruit itself. Perhaps it was taken as a surfeit dish at the end of a meal. It may have been eaten in combination with rich, oily foods, pastry, strong coffee, and other indigestible viands, which, in themselves, often excite an attack of indigestion. Possibly it was partaken of between meals, or late at night, with ice cream and other confections, or it was swallowed without sufficient mastication. Certainly, it is not marvelous that stomach and bowel disorders do result under such circumstances. The innocent fruit, like many other good things, being found in "bad company," is blamed accordingly. An excess of any food at meals or between meals, is likely to prove injurious, and fruits present no exception to this rule. Fruit taken at seasonable times and in suitable quantities, alone or in combination with proper foods, gives us one of the most agreeable and healthful articles of diet. Fruit, fats, and meats do not affiliate, and they are liable to create a disturbance whenever taken together.

Partially decayed, stale, and over-ripe, as well as unripe fruit, should never be eaten. According to M. Pasteur, the French scientist, all fruits and vegetables, when undergoing even incipient decay, contain numerous germs, which, introduced into the system, are liable to produce disturbances or disease. Perfectly fresh, ripe fruit, with proper limitations as to quantity and occasion, may be taken into a normal stomach with impunity at any season.

It is especially important that all fruits to be eaten should not only be sound in quality, but should be made perfectly clean by washing if necessary, since fruit grown near the ground is liable to be covered with dangerous bacteria (such as cause typhoid fever or diphtheria), which exist in the soil or in the material used in fertilizing it.

Most fruits, properly used, aid digestion either directly or indirectly. The juicy ones act as dilutents, and their free use lessens the desire for alcohol and other stimulants. According to German analysts, the apple contains a larger percentage of phosphorus than any other fruit, or than any vegetable. In warm weather and in warm climates, when foods are not needed for a heat-producing purpose, the diet may well consist largely of fruits and succulent vegetables, eaten in combination with bread and grains. In case of liver and kidney affections, rheumatism, and gout, the use of fruit is considered very beneficial by many scientific authorities.

To serve its best purpose, raw fruit should be eaten without sugar or other condiments, or with the addition of as small a quantity as possible.

It is a disputed question whether fruits should begin or end the meal; but it is generally conceded by those who have given the matter attention, that fruit eaten at the beginning of a meal is itself the more readily digested, and aids in the digestion of other foods, since fruits, like soups, have the property of stimulating the flow of the digestive juices. Something, however, must depend upon the character of the fruit; oranges, melons, and like juicy fruits, are especially useful as appetizers to begin the meal, while bananas and similar fruits agree better if taken with other food, so as to secure thorough mixture with saliva. This is true of all fruits, except such pulpy fruits as strawberries, peaches, melons, grapes, and oranges. It is often erroneously asserted that fruit as dessert is injurious to digestion. For those people, however, who regulate their bill of fare in accordance with the principles of hygiene, a simple course of fruit is not only wholesome, but is all that is needed after a dinner; and much time, labor, and health will be saved when housekeepers are content to serve desserts which nature supplies all ready for use, instead of those harmful combinations in the preparing of which they spend hours of tiresome toil.

Description.—For convenience, fruits may be grouped together; as, *pomaceous* fruits, including the apple, quince, pear, etc.; the *drupaceous* fruits, those provided with a hard stone surrounded by a fleshy pulp, as the peach, apricot, plum, cherry, olive, and date; the orange or citron group, including the orange, lemon, lime, citron, grape fruit, shaddock, and pomegranate; the *baccate* or berry kind, comprising the grape, gooseberry, currant, cranberry, whortleberry, blueberry, and others; the *arterio* group, to which belong raspberries, strawberries, dewberries, and blackberries; the fig group; the gourd group, including—melons and cantaloupes; and foreign fruits.

It is impossible, in the brief scope of this work, to enumerate the infinite varieties of fruit; but we will briefly speak of some of the most common found in the gardens and markets of this latitude.

Apples.—The origin and first home of the apple, is unknown. If tradition is to be believed, it was the inauspicious fruit to which may be traced all the miseries of mankind. In pictures of the temptation in the garden of Eden, our mother Eve is generally represented as holding an apple in her hand.

We find the apple mentioned in the mythologies of the Greeks, Druids, and Scandinavians. The Thebans offered apples instead of sheep as a sacrifice to Hercules, a custom derived from the following circumstance:—

"At one time, when a sacrifice was necessary, the river Asopus had so inundated the country that it was impossible to take a sheep across it for the purpose, when some youths, recollecting that the Greek word *melon* signified both sheep and an apple, stuck wooden pegs into the fruit to represent legs, and brought this vegetable quadruped as a substitute for the usual offering. After this date, the apple was considered as especially devoted to Hercules."

In ancient times, Greece produced most excellent apples. They were the favorite dessert of Phillip of Macedon and Alexander the Great, the latter causing them to be served at all meals. Doubtless they came to be used to excess; for it is recorded of the Athenian lawgiver, Solon, that he made a decree prohibiting a bridegroom from partaking of more than one at his marriage banquet, a law which was zealously kept by the Greeks, and finally adopted by the Persians. In Homer's time the apple was regarded as one of the precious fruits. It was extensively cultivated by the Romans, who gave to new varieties the names of many eminent citizens, and after the conquest of Gaul, introduced its culture into Southwestern Europe, whence it has come to be widely diffused throughout all parts of the temperate zone.

Apples were introduced into the United States by the early settlers, and the first trees were planted on an island in Boston Harbor, which still retains the name of Apple Island. The wild crab tree is the parent of most of the cultivated varieties.

The Pear.—The origin of the pear, like that of the apple, is shrouded in obscurity, though Egypt, Greece, and Palestine dispute for the honor of having given birth to the tree which bears this prince of fruits. Theophrastus, a Greek philosopher of the fourth century, speaks of the pear in terms of highest praise; and Galen, the father of medical science, mentions the pear in his writings as possessing "qualities which benefit the stomach." The pear tree is one of the most hardy of all fruit trees, and has been known to live several hundred years.

The Quince.—This fruit appears to have been a native of Crete, from whence it was introduced into ancient Greece; and was largely cultivated by both Greeks and Romans. In Persia, the fruit is edible in its raw state; but in this country it never ripens sufficiently to be palatable without being cooked. The fruit is highly fragrant and exceedingly acid, and for these reasons it is largely employed to flavor other fruits.

The Peach.—This fruit, as its botanical name, *prinus Persica*, indicates, is a native of Persia, and was brought from that country to Greece, from whence it passed into Italy. It is frequently mentioned by ancient writers, and was regarded with much esteem by the people of Asia. The Romans, however, had the singular notion that peaches gathered in Persia contained a deadly poison, but if once transplanted to another soil, this injurious effect was lost. In composition, the peach is notable for the small quantity of saccharine matter it contains in comparison with other fruits.

The Plum.—The plum is one of the earliest of known fruits. Thebes, Memphis, and Damascus were noted for the great number of their plum trees in the early centuries. Plum trees grow wild in Asia, America, and the South of Europe, and from these a large variety of domestic plum fruits have been cultivated.

Plums are more liable than most other fruits to produce disorders of digestion, and when eaten raw should be carefully selected, that they be neither unripe nor unripe. Cooking renders them less objectionable.

The Prune.—The plum when dried is often called by its French cognomen, *prune*. The larger and sweeter varieties are generally selected for drying, and when good and properly cooked, are the most wholesome of prepared fruits.

The Apricot.—This fruit seems to be intermediate between the peach and the plum, resembling the former externally, while the stone is like that of the plum. The apricot originated in Armenia, and the tree which bears the fruit was termed by the Romans "the tree of Armenia." It was introduced into England in the time of Henry VIII. The apricot is cultivated to some extent in the United States, but it requires too much care to permit of its being largely grown, except in certain sections.

The Cherry.—The common garden cherry is supposed to have been derived from the two species of wild fruit, and historians tell us that we are indebted to the agricultural experiments of Mithridates, the great king of ancient Pontus, for this much esteemed fruit. It is a native of Asia Minor, and its birthplace.

The Olive.—From time immemorial the olive has been associated with history. The Scriptures make frequent reference to it, and its cultivation was considered of first importance among the Jews, who used its oil for culinary and a great variety of other purposes. Ancient mythology venerated the olive tree above all others, and invested it with many charming bits of fiction. Grecian poets sang its praises, and early Roman writers speak of it with high esteem. In appearance and size the fruit is much like the plum; when ripe, it is very dark green, almost black, and possesses a strong, and, to many people, disagreeable flavor. The pulp abounds in a bland oil, for the production of which it is extensively cultivated in Syria, Egypt, Italy, Spain, and Southern France. The fruit itself is also pickled and preserved in various ways, but, like all other similar commodities when thus prepared, it is by no means a wholesome article of food.

The Date.—The date is the fruit of the palm tree so often mentioned in the Sacred Writings, and is indigenous to Africa and portions of Asia. The fruit grows in bunches which often weigh from twenty to twenty-five pounds, and a single tree will bear from one to three thousand pounds in a season. The date is very sweet and nutritious. It forms a stable article of diet for the inhabitants of some parts of Egypt, Arabia, and Persia, and frequently forms the chief food of their horses, dogs, and camels. The Arabs reduce dried dates to a meal, and make therefrom a bread, which often constitutes their sole food on long journeys through the Great Desert. The inhabitants of the countries where the date tree flourishes, put its various productions to innumerable uses. From its leaves they make baskets, bags, mats, combs, and brushes; from its stalks, fences for their gardens; from its fibers, thread, rope, and rigging; from its sap, a spirituous liquor; from its fruit, food for man and beast; while the body of the tree furnishes them with fuel. The prepared fruit is largely imported to this country. That which is large, smooth, and of a soft reddish yellow tinge, with a whitish membrane between the flesh and stone, is considered the best.

The Orange.—According to some authors, the far-famed "golden fruit of the Hesperides," which Hercules stole, was the orange; but it seems highly improbable that it was known to writers of antiquity. It is supposed to be indigenous to Central and Eastern Asia. Whatever its nativity, it has now spread over all the warmer regions of the earth. The orange tree is very hardy in its own habitat, and is one of the most prolific of all fruit-bearing trees, a single tree having been known to produce twenty thousand good oranges in a season. Orange trees attain great age. There are those in Italy and Spain which are known to have flourished for six hundred years. Numerous varieties of the orange are grown, and are imported to our markets from every part of the globe. Florida oranges are among the best, and when obtained in their perfection, are the most luscious of all fruits.

The Lemon.—This fruit is supposed to be a native of the North of India, although it is grown in nearly all sub-tropical climates. In general, the fruit is very acid, but in a variety known as the sweet lemon, or bergamot (said to be a hybrid of the orange and lemon), the juice is sweet. The sour lemon is highly valued for its antiscorbutic properties, and is largely employed as a flavoring ingredient in culinary preparations, and in making a popular refreshing beverage.

The Citron.—The citron is a fruit very similar to the lemon, though larger in size and less succulent. It is supposed to be identical with the Hebrew *tappuach*, and to be the fruit which is mentioned in the English version of the Old Testament as "apple." The citron is not suitable for eating in its raw state, though its juice is used in connection with water and sugar to form an excellent acid drink. Its rind, which is very thick, with a warty and furrowed exterior, is prepared in sugar and largely used for flavoring purposes.

The Lime.—The fruit of the lime is similar to the lemon, though much smaller in size. It is a native of Eastern Asia, but has long been cultivated in the South of Europe and other sub-tropical countries. The fruit is seldom used except for making acidulous drinks, for which it is often given the preference over the lemon.

The Grape Fruit.—This fruit, a variety of shaddock, belongs to the great *citrus* family, of which there are one hundred and sixty-nine known varieties. The shaddock proper, however, is a much larger fruit, frequently weighing from ten to fourteen pounds. Although a certain quantity of grape fruit is brought from the West Indies, our principal supply is derived from Florida. It is from two to four times the size of an ordinary orange, and grows in clusters. It is rapidly gaining in favor with fruit lovers. Its juice has a moderately acid taste and makes a pleasing beverage. The pulp, carefully separated, is also much esteemed.

The Pomegranate.—This fruit has been cultivated in Asia from earliest antiquity, and is still quite generally grown in most tropical climes. In the Scriptures it is mentioned with the vine, fig, and olive, among the pleasant fruits of the promised land. It is about the size of a large peach, of a fine golden color, with a rosy tinge on one side. The rind is thick and leathery. The central portion is composed of little globules of pulp and seeds inclosed in a thin membrane, each seed being about the size of a red currant. It is sub-acid, and slightly bitter in taste. The rind is strongly astringent, and often used as a medicine.

The Grape.—Undoubtedly the grape was one of the first fruits eaten by mankind, and one highly valued from antiquity down to the present time. Although this fruit is often sadly perverted in the manufacture of wine, when rightly used it is one of the most excellent of all fruits. The skins and seeds are indigestible and should be rejected, but the fresh, juicy pulp is particularly wholesome and refreshing. Several hundred varieties of the grape are cultivated. Some particularly sweet varieties are made into raisins, by exposure to the sun or to artificial heat. Sun-dried grapes make the best raisins. The so-called English or Zante currant belongs to the grape family, and is the dried fruit of a vine which grows in the Ionian Islands and yields a very small berry. The name *currant*, as applied to these fruits, is a corruption of the word *Corinth*, where the fruit was formerly grown.

The Gooseberry.—The gooseberry probably derives its name from gorse or goss, a prickly shrub that grows wild in thickets and on hillsides in Europe, Asia, and America. It was known to the ancients, and is mentioned in the writings of Theocritus and Pliny. Gooseberries were a favorite dish with some of the emperors, and were extensively cultivated in gardens during the Middle Ages. The gooseberry is a wholesome and agreeable fruit, and by cultivation may be brought to a high state of perfection in size and flavor.

The Currant.—This fruit derives its name from its resemblance to the small grapes of Corinth, sometimes called Corinthus, and is indigenous to America, Asia, and Europe. The fruit is sharply acid, though very pleasant to the taste. Cultivation has produced white currants from the red, and in a distinct species of the fruit grown in Northern Europe and Russia, the currants are black or yellow.

The Whortleberry and Blueberry.—These are both species of the same fruit, which grows in woods and waste places in the North of Europe and America. Of the latter species there are two varieties, the high-bush and the low-bush, which are equally palatable. The fruit is very sweet and pleasant to the taste, and is one of the most wholesome of all berries.

The Cranberry.—A German writer of note insists that the original name of this fruit was cram-berry, because after dinner, when one was filled with other food, such was its pleasant and seductive flavor that he could still "cram" quite a quantity thereof, in defiance of all dietetic laws. Other writers consider the name a corruption of craneberry, so called because it is eagerly sought after by the cranes and other birds which frequent the swamps and marshes where it chiefly grows. The fruit is extremely acid, and is highly valued for sauces and jellies. Cranberries are among the most convenient fruits for keeping. Freezing does not seem to hurt them, and they may be kept frozen all winter, or in water without freezing, in the cellar, or other cool places, for a long period.

The Strawberry.—The flavor of antiquity rests upon the wild strawberry. Its fruit was peddled by itinerant dealers about the streets of ancient Grecian and Roman cities. Virgil sings of it in pastoral poems, and Ovid mentions it in words of praise. The name by which the fruit was known to the Greeks indicates its size; with the Latins its name was symbolic of its perfume. The name *strawberry* probably came from the old Saxon *streawberige*, either from some resemblance of the stems to straw, of from the fact that the berries have the appearance when growing of being strewn upon the ground. In olden times, children strung the berries upon straws, and sold so many "straws of berries" for a penny, from which fact it is possible the name may have been derived. The strawberry is indigenous to the temperate regions of both the Eastern and Western Hemispheres, but it seems to have been matured in gardens, only within the last two centuries.

The Raspberry.—This fruit grows in both a wild and a cultivated state. It derives its name from the rough rasps or spines with which the bushes are covered. Among the ancients it was called "the bramble of Mt. Ida," because it was abundant upon that mountain. It is a hardy fruit, found in most parts of the world, and is of two special varieties, the black and the red.

The Blackberry.—This fruit is a native of America and the greater part of Europe. There are one hundred and fifty-one named species, although the high-blackberry and the low-blackberry, or dewberry, are said to have furnished the best cultivated varieties.

The Mulberry.—Different varieties of the mulberry tree produce white, red, and black mulberries of fine aromatic flavor, and acidulous or sweet taste. Persia is supposed to be the native home of this fruit, from whence it was carried, at an early date, to Asia Minor and to Greece. The Hebrews were evidently well acquainted with it. It was also cultivated by the farmers of Attica and Peloponnesus. The ancient mulberry was considered the wisest and most prudent of trees, because it took care not to put forth the smallest bud until the cold of winter had disappeared, not to return. Then, however, it lost no time, but budded and blossomed in a day. Several varieties are found in the United States.

The Melon.—This is the generic name for all the members of the gourd tribe known as cantaloupes, muskmelons, and watermelons. The fruit varies greatly in size and color, and in the character of the rind. When fresh and perfectly ripe, melons are among the most delicious of edible fruits.

The Fig.—In the most ancient histories, the fig tree is referred to as among the most desirable productions of the earth. It was the only tree in the garden of Eden of which the Sacred Writings make particular mention. Among the inhabitants of ancient Syria and Greece, it formed one of the principal articles of food. Its cultivation was, and is still, extensively carried on in nearly all Eastern countries; also in Spain, Southern France, and some portions of the United States. The fruit is pear-shaped, and consists of a pulpy mass full of little seeds. Dried and compressed figs are largely imported, and are to be found in all markets. Those brought from Smyrna are reputed to be the best.

The Banana.—This is essentially a tropical fruit growing very generally in the East, the West Indies, South American countries, and some of the Southern States. The plant is an annual, sending up stems to the height of ten or fifteen feet, while drooping from the top are enormous leaves three or four feet in length, and looking, as one writer has aptly said, like "great, green quill pens." It is planted in fields like corn, which in its young growth it much resembles. Each plant produces a single cluster of from eighty to one hundred or more bananas, often weighing in the aggregate as high as seventy pounds. The banana is exceedingly productive. According to Humboldt, a space of 1,000 feet, which will yield only 38 pounds of wheat, or 462 pounds of potatoes, will produce 4,000 pounds of bananas, and in a much shorter period of time. It is more nutritious than the majority of fruits, and in tropical countries is highly valued as a food, affording in some localities the chief alimentary support of the people. Its great importance as a food product is shown by the fact that three or four good sized bananas are equal in nutritive value to a pound of bread. The amount of albumen contained in a pound of bananas is about the same as that found in a pound of rice, and the total nutritive value of one pound of bananas is only a trifle less than that of an equal quantity of the best beefsteak.

The unripe fruit, which contains a considerable percentage of starch, is often dried in the oven and eaten as bread, which, in this state, it considerably resembles in taste and appearance. Thus prepared, it may be kept for a long time, and is very serviceable for use on long journeys. The variety of the banana thus used is, however, a much larger kind than any of those ordinarily found in our Northern markets, and is known as the plantain. The dried plantain, powdered, furnishes a meal of fragrant odor and bland taste, not unlike common wheat flour. It is said to be easy of digestion, and two pounds of the dry meal or six pounds of the fruit is the daily allowance for a laborer in tropical America.

The Pineapple.—This delicious fruit is a native of South America, where it grows wild in the forests. It is cultivated largely in tropical America, the West Indies, and some portions of Europe. The fruit grows singly from the center of a small plant having fifteen or more long, narrow, serrated, ridged, sharp-pointed leaves, seemingly growing from the root. In general appearance it resembles the century plant, though so much smaller that twelve thousand pineapple plants may be grown on one acre. From the fibers of the leaves is made a costly and valuable fabric called *pina* muslin.

Nothing can surpass the rich, delicate flavor of the wild pineapple as found in its native habitat. It is in every way quite equal to the best cultivated variety. The most excellent pineapples are imported from the West Indies, but are seldom found in perfection in out Northern markets.

FRESH FRUIT FOR THE TABLE.

All fruit for serving should be perfectly ripe and sound. Immature fruit is never wholesome, and owing to the large percentage of water in its composition, fruit is very prone to change; hence over-ripe fruit should not be eaten, as it is liable to ferment and decompose in the digestive tract.

Fruit which has begun, however slightly, to decay, should be rejected. Juice circulates through its tissues in much the same manner as the blood circulates through animal tissues, though not so rapidly and freely. The circulation is sufficient, however, to convey to all parts the products of decomposition, when only a small portion has undergone decay, and although serious results do not always follow the use of such fruit, it certainly is not first-class food.

If intended to be eaten raw, fruit should be well ripened before gathering, and should be perfectly fresh. Fruit that has stood day after day in a dish upon the table, in a warm room, is far less wholesome and tempting than that brought fresh from the storeroom or cellar. All fruits should be thoroughly cleansed before serving. Such fruit as cherries, grapes, and currants may be best washed by placing in a colander, and dipping in and out of a pan of water until perfectly clean, draining and drying before serving.

DIRECTIONS FOR SERVING FRUITS.

Apples.—In serving these, the "queen of all fruits," much opportunity is afforded for a display of taste in their arrangement. After wiping clean with a damp towel, they may be piled in a fruit basket, with a few sprigs of green leaves here and there between their rosy cheeks. The feathery tops of carrots and celery are pretty for this purpose. Oranges and apples so arranged, make a highly ornamental dish.

Raw mellow sweet apples make a delicious dish when pared, sliced, and served with cream.

Bananas.—Cut the ends from the fruit and serve whole, piled in a basket with oranges, grapes, or plums. Another way is to peel, slice, and serve with thin cream. Bananas are also very nice sliced, sprinkled lightly with sugar, and before it had quite dissolved, covered with orange juice. Sliced bananas, lightly sprinkled with sugar, alternating in layers with sections of oranges, make a most delicious dessert.

Cherries.—Serve on stems, piled in a basket or high dish, with bits of green leaves and vines between. Rows of different colored cherries, arranged in pyramidal form, make also a handsome dish.

Currants.—Large whole clusters may be served on the stem, and when it is possible to obtain both red and white varieties, they make a most attractive dish. Put them into cold water for a little time, cool thoroughly, and drain well before using. Currants, if picked from the stems after being carefully washed and drained, may be served lightly sprinkled with sugar. Currants and raspberries served together, half and half, or one third currants two thirds raspberries, are excellent. Only the ripest of currants should be used.

Gooseberries.—When fresh and ripe, the gooseberry is one of the most delicious of small fruits. Serve with stems on. Drop into cold water for a few moments, drain, and pile in a glass dish for the table.

Grapes.—Grapes need always to be washed before serving. Drop the bunches into ice water, let them remain ten of fifteen minutes, then drain and serve. An attractive dish may be made by arranging bunches of different colored grapes together on a plate edged with grape leaves.

Melons.—Watermelons should be served very cold. After being well washed on the outside, put on ice until needed. Cut off a slice at the ends, that each half may stand upright on a plate, and then cut around in even slices. Instead of cutting through the center into even halves, the melon may be cut in points back and forth around the entire circumference, so that when separated, each half will appear like a crown. Another way is to take out the central portion with a spoon, in cone-shaped pieces, and arrange on a plate with a few bits of ice. Other melons may be served in halves, with the seeds removed. The rough skin of the cantaloupe should be thoroughly scrubbed with a vegetable brush, then rinsed and wiped, after which bury the melon in broken ice till serving time; divide into eighths or sixteenths, remove the seeds, reconstruct the melon, and serve surrounded with ice, on a folded napkin, or arranged on a bed of grape leaves. Do not cool the melon by placing ice upon the flesh, as the moisture injures the delicate flavor.

Oranges.—Serve whole or cut the skin into eighths, halfway down, separating it from the fruit, and curling it inward, thus showing half the orange white and the other half yellow; or cut the skin into eighths, two-thirds down, and after loosening from the fruit, leave them spread open like the petals of a lily. Oranges sliced and mixed with well ripened strawberries, in the proportion of three oranges to a quart of berries, make—a palatable dessert.

Peaches and Pears.—Pick out the finest, and wipe the wool from the peaches. Edge a plate with uniform sized leaves of foliage plant of the same tints as the fruit, and pile the fruit artistically upon it, tucking sprays or tips of the plant between. Bits of ice may also be intermingled. Yellow Bartlett pears and rosy-cheeked peaches arranged in this way are most ornamental.

Peaches and Cream.—Pare the peaches just as late as practicable, since they become discolored by standing. Always use a silver knife, as steel soon blackens and discolors the fruit. If sugar is to be used, do not add it until the time for serving, as it will start the juice, and likewise turn the fruit brown, destroying much of its rich flavor. Keep on ice until needed for the table. Add cream with each person's dish.

Pineapples.—The pineapple when fresh and ripened to perfection, is as mellow and juicy as a ripe peach, and needs no cooking to fit it for the table. Of course it must be pared, and have the eyes and fibrous center removed. Then it may be sliced in generous pieces and piled upon a plate, or cut into smaller portions and served in saucers. No condiments are necessary; even the use of sugar detracts from its delicate flavor. Pineapples found in our Northern markets are, however, generally so hard and tough as to require cooking, or are valuable only for their juice, which may be extracted and used for flavoring other fruits. When sufficiently mellow to be eaten raw, they are usually so tart as to seem to require a light sprinkling of sugar to suit most tastes. Pineapples pared, cut into dice or small pieces, lightly sprinkled with sugar, to which just before serving, a cup of orange juice is added, form a delicious dish.

Plums.—Plums make a most artistic fruit piece, served whole and arranged with bunches of choice green grapes, in a basket or glass dish. A fine edge may be made from the velvety leaves of dark purple foliage plants.

Pressed Figs.—Look over carefully, and select only such as are perfectly good. They may be served dry, mixed with bunches of raisins, or steamed over a kettle of boiling water. Steamed figs make an excellent breakfast dish, and are considered much more wholesome then when used dry. Steamed raisins are likewise superior to dried raisins.

Raspberries, Blackberries, Dewberries, Blueberries and Whortleberries, require careful looking over to remove all insects, stems, and over-ripe fruit. Blueberries and whortleberries frequently need to be washed. They are then drained by spreading on a sieve or colander. Perfectly ripe, they are more healthful without condiments; but sugar and cream are usually considered indispensable.

If necessary to wash strawberries, they should be put into cold water, a few at a time, pushed down lightly beneath the water several times until entirely clean, then taken out one by one, hulled, and used at once. Like all other small fruits and berries they are more wholesome served without cream, but if cream is used, each person should be allowed to add it to his own dish, as it quickly curdles and renders the whole dish unsightly; if allowed to stand, it also impairs the flavor of the fruit.

Frosted Fruit.—Prepare a mixture of the beaten white of egg, sugar, and a very little cold water. Dip nice bunches of clean currants, cherries, or grapes into the mixture; drain nearly dry, and roll lightly in powdered sugar. Lay them on white paper to dry. Plums, apricots, and peaches may be dipped in the mixture, gently sprinkled with sugar, then allowed to dry. This method of preparing fruit is not to be commended for its wholesomeness, but it is sometimes desirable for ornament.

KEEPING FRESH FRUIT.

Of the numerous varieties of fruits grown in this country, apples and pears are about the only ones that can be kept for any length of time without artificial means. As soon as fruit has attained its maturity, a gradual change or breaking down of tissues begins. In some fruits this process follows rapidly; in other it is gradual. There is a certain point at which the fruits are best suited for use. We call it mellowness, and say that the fruit is in "good eating condition." When this stage has been reached, deterioration and rotting soon follow. In some fruits, as the peach, plum, and early varieties of apples and pears, these changes occur within a few days after maturity, and it is quite useless to attempt to keep them; in others, like the later varieties of apples and pears, the changes are slow but none the less certain. To keep such fruits we must endeavor to retard or prolong the process of change, by avoiding all conditions likely to hasten decay. Even with ordinary care, sound fruit will keep for quite a length of time; but it can be preserved in better condition and for a longer period by careful attention to the following practical points:—

1. If the fruit is of a late variety, allow it to remain on the tree as long as practicable without freezing.

2. Always pick and handle the fruit with the greatest care.

3. Gather the fruit on a dry, cool day, and place in heaps or bins for two or three weeks.

4. Carefully sort and pack in barrels, placing those most mellow and those of different varieties in different barrels; head the barrels, label, and place in a cool, dry place where the temperature will remain equable. Some consider it better to keep fruit in thin layers upon broad shelves in a cool place. This plan allows frequent inspection and removal of all affected fruit without disturbance of the remainder.

5. Warmth and moisture are the conditions most favorable to decomposition, and should be especially guarded against.

6. The best temperature for keeping fruit is about 34° F., or 2° above freezing.

Another method which is highly recommended is to sprinkle a layer of sawdust on the bottom of a box, and then put in a layer of apples, not allowing them to tough each other. Upon this pack more sawdust; then another layer of apples, and so on until the box is filled. After packing, place up from the ground, in a cellar or storeroom, and they will keep perfectly, retaining their freshness and flavor until brought out. The *Practical Farmer* gives the following rough but good way to store and keep apples: "Spread plenty of buckwheat chaff on the barn floor, and on this place the apples, filling the interstices with the chaff. Cover with the chaff and then with straw two or three feet deep. The advantage of this is that covering and bedding in chaff excludes cold, prevents air currents, maintains a uniform temperature, absorbs the moisture of decay, and prevents the decay produced by moisture."

The ordinary cellar underneath the dwelling house is too warm and damp for the proper preservation of fruit, and some other place should be provided if possible. A writer in the*American Agriculturist* thus calls attention to an additional reason why fruit should not be stored beneath living-rooms: "After late apples are stored for the winter, a gradual change begins within the fruit. It absorbs oxygen from the air of the room, and gives off carbonic acid gas. Another change results in the formation of water, which is given off as moisture. The taking up of oxygen by the fruit and the giving off of carbonic acid, in a short time so vitiates the atmosphere of the room in which the fruit is kept, that it will at once extinguish a candle, and destroy animal life. An atmosphere of this kind tends to preserve the fruit. There being little or no oxygen left in the air of the room, the process of decay is arrested. Hence it is desirable that the room be air tight, in order to maintain such an atmosphere."

The production of carbonic acid shows that a cellar in or under a dwelling, is an improper place for storing fresh fruit. When the gas is present in the air in sufficient proportion, it causes death, and a very small quantity will cause headache, listlessness, and other unpleasant effects. No doubt many troubles attributed to malaria, are due to gases from vegetables and fruits stored in the cellar. A fruit cellar should be underneath some other building rather than the dwelling, or a fruit house may be built entirely above the ground. A house to keep fruit properly must be built upon theprinciple of a refrigerator. Its walls, floor, and ceiling should be double, and the space between filled with sawdust. The doors and windows should be double; and as light is undesirable, the windows should be provided with shutters. There should be a small stove for use if needed to keep a proper temperature in severe weather.

To Keep Grapes.—Select such bunches as are perfect, rejecting all upon which there are any bruised grapes, or from which a grape has fallen. Spread them upon shelves in a cool place for a week or two. Then pack in boxes in sawdust which has been recently well dried in an oven. Bran which has been dried may also be used. Dry cotton is employed by some. Keep in a cool place.

Some consider the following a more efficient method: select perfect bunches, and dip the broken end of the stems in melted paraffine or sealing wax. Wrap separately in tissue paper, hang in a cool place, or pack in sawdust.

To Keep Lemons and Oranges.—Lemons may be kept fresh for weeks by placing them in a vessel of cold water in a very cool cellar or ice house. Change the water every day. Oranges may be kept in the same way. The usual method employed by growers for keeping these fruits is to wrap each one separately in tissue paper, and put in a cool, dry place.

To Keep Cranberries.—Put them in water and keep in a cool place where they will not freeze. Change the water often, and sort out berries which may have become spoiled.

COOKED FRUIT.

Perfectly ripe fruit is, as a rule, more desirable used fresh than in any other way. Fruits which are immature, require cooking. Stewing and baking are the simplest methods of preparation.

General Suggestions for Cooking Fruit.—The utensils for stewing should be porcelain-lined, or granite ware. Fruit cooked in tin loses much of its delicate flavor; while if it be acid, and the tin of poor quality, there is always danger that the acid of the fruit acting upon the metal will form a poisonous compound. Cover with a china plate or granite-ware cover, never with a tin one, as the steam will condense and run down into the kettle, discoloring the contents. Use only silver knives for preparing the fruit, and silver or wooden spoons for stirring. Prepare just before cooking, if you would preserve the fruit perfect in flavor, and unimpaired by discoloration. In preparing apples, pears, and quinces for stewing, it is better to divide the fruit into halves or quarters before paring. The fruit is more easily handled, can be pared thinner and cored more quickly. Peaches, apricots, and plums, if divided and stoned before paring, can be much more easily kept whole.

Cook in a small quantity of boiling water, and if economy is a point to be considered, do not add sugar until the fruit is done. Sugar boiled with an acid will be converted into glucose, two and one half pounds of which only equal one pound of cane sugar in sweetening properties. It will require a much larger amount of sugar to sweeten fruit if added before the cooking process is completed. Fruit should be cooked by stewing, or by gentle simmering; hard boiling will destroy the fine flavor of all fruits, and especially of berries and other small fruits. Cinnamon, cloves, or other spices, should not be added, as their stronger flavors deaden or obliterate the natural flavor, which should always be preserved as perfectly as possible. If desirable to add some foreign flavor, let it be the flavor of another fruit, or the perfume of flowers. For Instance, flavor apple with lemon, pineapple, quince, or rose water.

Unripe fruit is improved by making the cooking quite lengthy, which acts in the place of the ripening process, changing the starchy matter to saccharine elements. In cooking fruit, try to preserve its natural form. The more nearly whole it is, the better it looks, and the more natural will be its flavor.

Apples are best cooked by baking. Pears and quinces are also excellent baked. The oven should be only moderately hot; if the heat is too great, they brown on the outside before they are done throughout. In cooking fruit by any method, pains should be taken to cook together such as are of the same variety, size, and degree of hardness; if it is to be cut in pieces, care should be taken to have the pieces of uniform size.

RECIPES.

Baked Apples.—Moderately tart apples or very juicy sweet ones are best for baking. Select ripe apples, free from imperfections, and of nearly equal size. Wipe carefully and remove the blossom ends. Water sufficient to cover bottom of the baking dish, should be added if the fruit is not very juicy. If the apples are sour and quite firm, a good way is to pare them before baking, and then place them in an earthen pie dish with a little hot water. If they incline to brown too quickly, cover the tops with a granite-ware pie dish. If the syrup dries out, add a little more hot water. When done, set them away till nearly cold, then transfer to a glass dish, pour the syrup, which should be thick and amber colored, over them. Sour apples are excellent pared, cored, and baked with the centers filled with sugar, jelly, or a mixture or chopped raisins and dates. They should be put into a shallow earthen dish with water sufficient to cover the bottom, and baked in a quick oven, basting often with the syrup. Sweet apples are best baked without paring. Baked apples are usually served as a relish, but with a dressing of cream they make a most delicious dessert.

Citron Apples.—Select a few tart apples of the same degree of hardness, and remove the cores. Unless the skins are very tender, it is better to pare them. Fill the cavities with sugar, first placing in each apple a few bits of chopped citron. If the skins have been removed, place the stuffed apples on a flat earthen dish with a tablespoonful of water on the bottom; cover closely, and bake till perfectly tender, but not till they have fallen to pieces. If the skins are left on, they may be baked without covering. When cold, serve in separate dishes, with or without a spoonful or two of whipped cream on each apple.

Lemon Apples.—Prepare tart apples the same as for citron apples. Fill the cavities made by removing the cores with a mixture of grated lemon and sugar, squeeze a few drops of lemon juice over each apple, and bake. Serve with or without whipped cream.

Baked Pears.—Hard pears make an excellent dessert when baked. Pare, halve, remove seeds, and place in a shallow earthen dish, with a cup of water to each two quarts of fruit. If the pears are sour, a little sugar may be added. Bake, closely covered, in a moderate oven until tender. Serve with sugar and cream. Tart pears are the best for baking, as the sweet varieties are often tasteless.

Baked Quinces.—Pare and remove the cores. Fill the cavities with sugar, put in a shallow earthen dish, and add water to cover the bottom; bake till soft, basting often with the syrup. If the syrup dries out before the fruit is perfectly tender, add a little more hot water.

Pippins and Quince.—Pare and quarter nice golden pippins, and cook in boiling water until reduced to a jelly. Add two or three quinces sliced, and simmer slowly in the jelly until the quince is tender. Add sugar to taste. Serve cold.

Baked Apple Sauce.—Pare, core, and quarter apples to fill an earthen crock or deep pudding dish, taking care to use apples of the same degree of hardness, and pieces of the same size. For two quarts of fruit thus prepared, add a cup of water, and if the apples are sour, a cup of sugar. Cover closely, and bake in a moderate oven several hours, or until of a dark red color.

Sweet apples and quinces in the proportion of two parts of apple to one of quince, baked in this way, are also good. Cut the apples into quarters, but slice the quinces much thinner, as they are more difficult to cook. Put a layer of quince on the bottom of the dish, alternating with a layer of apple, until the dish is full. Add cold water to half cover the fruit, and stew in the oven well covered, without stirring, until tender.

Pears may be cooked in a similar way, and both apples and pears thus cooked may be canned while hot and kept for a long period.

Baked Apple Sauce No. 2.—Prepare nice tart apples as for No. 1. Bake, with a small quantity of water, in a covered pudding dish, in a moderate oven, until soft. Mash with a spoon, add sugar, and when cold, a little grated orange rind.

Apples Stewed Whole.—Take six large red apples, wash carefully, and put in a fruit kettle with just enough boiling water to cover. Cover the kettle, and cook slowly until the apples are soft, with the skins broken and the juice a rich red color. After removing the apples, boil the juice to a syrup, sweeten, and pour over the apples.

Steamed Apples.—Select pound sweets of uniform size, wipe, cut out the blossom-ends, and pack in a large pudding dish. Pour in a cupful of water, cover the dish closely, set in a moderate oven, and steam till the apples are tender. Remove from the dish, and pour the liquor over them frequently as they cool.

Compote of Apples.—Pare and extract the cores from moderately tart, juicy apples. Place them in a deep pudding dish with just enough water to cover them. Cover, place in a moderate oven, and stew until they are tender. Remove the apples and place in a deep dish to keep hot. Measure the juice and pour it into a saucepan, add a few bits of lemon rind, and boil up until thickened almost like a jelly. While the juice is boiling, heat some sugar, one tablespoonful to each cup of juice, in the oven, and add to the juice when thickened. Pour scalding hot over the apples, and cover until cold.

Apple Compote No. 2.—Pare eight or ten rather tart, finely flavored and easy-cooking apples, carefully removing the cores, and put them into a broad, shallow, granite-ware saucepan with just enough hot water to cover the bottom. Cover tightly and place over the fire. The steam will cook the apples tender in a short time. Do not allow them to fall to pieces. Make a syrup by dissolving one cup of sugar in a pint of hot water. Add three teaspoonfuls of the juice of canned pineapple, and pour over the apples while both are hot.

Stewed Pears.—Select some fine Bartlett pears which are ripe, but have hardly begun to soften; remove the skins, cut in halves or quarters, and take out the seeds. Put loosely in a granite-ware kettle, and add a pint of water for three and a half quarts of fruit. Cover closely, and when it begins to boil, set it where it will just simmer until the top pieces are tender. Serve cold. Sugar will not be necessary if the fruit is of good quality.

Smooth Apple Sauce.—If fruit is not sufficiently perfect to be cut into uniform quarters, a good way to prepare it is to pare, core, and slice into thin slices. Cook in as small a quantity of water as possible, the fruit covered closely, so that the top portion will steam tender as soon as the bottom, and when done rub through a colander, or beat smooth with a wooden spoon or an egg beater. Let it cool before adding sugar. A little lemon peel may be added to the fruit just long enough before it is done to flavor it, if desired.

Boiled Apples with Syrup.—Halve and remove the cores of a half dozen nice apples, leaving the skins on. Boil till tender in sufficient water to cover them. Take out with a fork into a glass dish. Add to the juice three or four slices of a large lemon; boil for ten or fifteen minutes; sweeten to taste; then pour over the apples, and cool.

Stewed Apples.—Select fine fruit of a sub-acid flavor and not over-ripe. Pare, remove the cores and all blemishes, and divide into sixths if large, into quarters if small. Put into a porcelain or granite-ware kettle with enough boiling water to cook and leave a good liquor. Cover, and simmer gently, without stirring, from one to two hours. Do not add sugar till cold. Be careful not to break the fruit in serving.

Stewed Crab Apples.—Select perfect fruit. Wash and stew in but little water until they are very soft. Rub through a coarse sieve or colander to remove the seeds and skins. Sweeten to taste.

Sweet Apple Sauce with Condensed Apple Juice.—For the juice, wash, divide, and core rather tart apples and cook until softened with one cup of water for every six pounds of fruit. When soft, put into a percolater and drain off the juice or extract it with a fruit press. Boil until it is reduced one half. Skim if needed while boiling, and if not perfectly clear allow it to settle before using. A considerable quantity of the juice may be thus prepared and put into stone jars, to be used as needed. For the sauce, pare, core, and quarter sweet apples. Put into a porcelain kettle with enough of the condensed juice to cover. Cook slowly until tender.

Apples with Raisins.—Pare, core, and quarter a dozen or more medium sized sour apples. Clean thoroughly one fourth as many raisins as apples, and turn over them a quart of boiling water. Let them steep until well swollen, then add the apples, and cook until tender. Sugar to sweeten may be added if desired, although little will be needed unless the apples are very tart. Dried apples soaked over night may be made much more palatable by stewing with raisins or English currants, in the same way.

Apples with Apricots.—Pare, core, and quarter some nice, sour apples. Put them to cook with two halves of dried apricot for each apple. When tender, make smooth by beating or rubbing through a colander, and sweeten. Dried apples may be used in place of fresh ones.

Peaches, Plums, Cherries, Berries, and all small fruits may be cooked for sauce by stewing in a small amount of water, adding sugar to sweeten when done.

Baked Apples.—Take any good tart apples; peel, cut in halves, and remove the cores. Scatter a few spoonfuls of sugar in the bottom of a dish, and lay the apples in, flat side down; add a teacupful of cold water, and bake till tender. Let stand in the dish till cold, then take up the pieces in a vegetable dish, and poor over them what juice remains. Sweet apples are good baked in this way without sugar.

Baked Pears.—Peel ripe pears; cut in halves, and pack in layers in a stone ware jar. Strew a little sugar over each layer, and add a small cupful of water, to prevent burning. Cover tightly, and bake three or four hours in a well-heated oven. Let them get very cold, and serve with sweet cream.

Baked Peaches.—Peaches which are ripe but too hard for eating, are nice baked. Pare, remove the stones, and place in loose layers in a shallow, earthen pudding dish with a little water. Sprinkle each layer lightly with sugar, cover and bake.

Cranberries.—Cranberries make an excellent sauce, but the skins are rather hard of digestion, and it is best to exclude them. Stew in the proportion of a quart of berries to a pint of water, simmering gently until the skins have all burst, and the quantity is reduced to a pint. Put through a colander to remove the skins, and when nearly cool, add for the quart of berries two thirds of a cup of sugar.

Cranberries with Raisins.—Cook the cranberries as in the preceding recipe, and when rubbed through the colander, add for every pound of cranberries before cooking, one fourth pound of raisins which have been steeped for half an hour in just sufficient boiling water to cover. A little less sugar will be needed to sweeten than when served without the raisins.

Cranberries and Sweet Apples.—Stew equal parts of cranberries and sweet apples together. Mash, rub through a fine sieve or colander to remove the skins and make the whole homogeneous. This makes a very palatable sauce without the addition of sugar. California prunes and cranberries stewed together in equal proportion, in a small quantity of water, also make a nice sauce without sugar.

Oranges and Apples.—The mild, easy cooking, tart varieties of apples make an excellent sauce stewed with one third sliced oranges from which the seeds have been removed. Pare, core, and slice the apples, and cook gently so as to preserve the form of both fruits until the apples are tender. Add sugar to sweeten, and if desired a very little of the grated yellow of the orange rind.

Stewed Raisins.—Soak a pint of good raisins, cleaned and freed from stems, in cold water for several hours. When ready to cook, put them, with the water in which they were soaked, in a fruit kettle and simmer until the skins are tender. Three or four good-sized figs, chopped quite fine, cooked with the raisins, gives an additional richness and thickness of juice. No sugar will be needed.

Dried Apples.—Good apples properly dried make a very palatable sauce; but unfortunately the fruit generally selected for drying is of so inferior a quality that if cooked in its fresh state it would not be good. The dried fruit in most of our markets needs to be looked over carefully, and thoroughly washed before using. Put into a granite-ware kettle, cover with boiling water, and cook gently until tender. Fresh steam-dried or evaporated apples will cook in from one half to three fourths of an hour; if older, they may require from one to two more hours. Add boiling water, as needed, during the cooking. If when tender they are lacking in juice, add a little boiling water long enough before lifting from the fire to allow it to boil up once. If the fruit is very poor, a few very thin slices of the yellow portion of lemon or orange rind added a half hour before it is done, will sometimes be an improvement.

Dried Apples with Other Dried Fruit.—An excellent sauce may be made by cooking a few dried plums with dried or evaporated apples. Only enough of the plums to give a flavor to the apples will be needed; a handful of the former to a pound of apples will be sufficient. Dried cherries, raisins, English currants, dried apricots, prunelles, and peaches are also excellent used in combination with dried apples.

Dried Apricots and Peaches.—These fruits, if dried with the skins on, need, in addition to the preparation for cooking recommended for dried apples, a thorough rubbing with the fingers, while being washed, to remove the down. Put into boiling water in about the proportion of two parts of fruit to three of water. If the fruit was pared before drying, a little more water will be required. Cook quickly, but gently, until just tender, and take from the fire as soon as done. If too soft, they will be mushy and insipid.

Evaporated Peach Sauce.—Soak the peaches over night in just enough water to cover. In the morning put to cook in boiling water. When tender, sweeten and beat perfectly smooth with an egg beater.

Dried Pears.—These may be treated in the same way as dried apples.

Small Fruits.—These when dried must be carefully examined, thoroughly washed, and then cooked rather quickly in boiling water. They swell but little, do not require much water, and usually cook in a few minutes. They should be taken from the fire as soon as soft, as long standing makes them insipid.

Prunes.—Use only the best selected prunes. Clean by putting them into warm water; let them stand a few minutes, rubbing them gently between the hands to make sure that all dust and dirt is removed; rinse, and if rather dry and hard, put them into three parts of water to one of prunes; cover closely, and let them simmer for several hours. If the prunes are quite easily cooked, less water may be used. They will be tender, with a thick juice. The sweet varieties need no sugar whatever. Many persons who cannot eat fruit cooked with sugar, can safely partake of sweet prunes cooked in this way. A slice of lemon added just before the prunes are done, is thought an improvement.

Prune Marmalade.—Cook sweet California prunes as directed above. When well done, rub through a colander to remove the skins and stones. No sugar is necessary. If the pulp is too thin when cold, it may be covered in an earthen pudding dish and stewed down by placing in a pan of hot water in a moderate oven.

THE PRESERVATION OF FRUIT.

Fresh fruit is so desirable, while at the same time the season during which most varieties can be obtained is so transient, that various methods are resorted to for preserving it in as nearly a natural state as possible. The old-fashioned plans of pickling in salt, alcohol, or vinegar, or preserving in equal quantities of sugar, are eminently unhygienic. Quite as much to be condemned is the more modern process of keeping fruit by adding to it some preserving agent, like salicylic acid or other chemicals. Salicylic acid is an antiseptic, and like many other substances, such as carbolic acid, creosote, etc., has the power of preventing the decay of organic substances. Salicylic acid holds the preference over other drugs of this class, because it imparts no unpleasant flavor to the fruit. It is nevertheless a powerful and irritating drug, and when taken, even in small doses, produces intense burning in the stomach, and occasions serious disturbances of the heart and other organs. Its habitual use produces grave diseases.

What is sold as antifermentive is simply the well-known antiseptic, salicylate of soda. It should be self-evident to one at all acquainted with the philosophy of animal existence, that an agent which will prevent fermentation and decay must be sufficiently powerful in its influence to prevent digestion also.

The fermentation and decay of fruits as well as that of all other organic substances, is occasioned by the action of those minute living organisms which scientists call germs, and which are everywhere present. These germs are very much less active in a dry, cold atmosphere, and fruit may be preserved for quite a long period by refrigeration, an arrangement whereby the external air is excluded, and the surrounding atmosphere kept at an equal temperature of about 40° F. The most efficient and wholesome method of preserving fruit, however, is destruction of the germs and entire exclusion from the air. The germs are destroyed at a boiling temperature; hence, if fruit be heated to boiling, and when in this condition sealed in air-tight receptacles, it will keep for an unlimited period.

CANNING FRUIT.

Canning consists in sealing in air-tight cans or jars, fruit which has been previously boiled. It is a very simple process, but requires a thorough understanding of the scientific principles involved, and careful management, to make it successful. The result of painstaking effort is so satisfactory, however, it is well worth all the trouble, and fruit canning need not be a difficult matter if attention is given to the following details:—

Select self-sealing glass cans of some good variety. Tin cans give more trouble filling and sealing, are liable to affect the flavor of the fruit, and unless manufactured from the best of material, to impair its wholesomeness. Glass cans may be used more than once, and are thus much more economical. Those with glass covers, or porcelain-lined covers, are best. Test the cans to see if they are perfect, with good rubbers and covers that fit closely, by partly filling them with cold water, screwing on the tops, and placing bottom upward upon the table for some time before using. If none of the water leaks out, they may be considered in good condition. If the cans have been previously used, examine them with special care to see that both cans and covers have been carefully cleaned, then thoroughly sterilize them, and fit with new rubbers when necessary.

Cans and covers should be sterilized by boiling in water for half an hour, or by baking in an oven, at a temperature sufficient to scorch paper, for two hours. The cans should be placed in the water or oven when cold, and the temperature allowed to rise gradually, to avoid breaking. They should be allowed to cool gradually, for the same purpose.

Select only the best of fruit, such as is perfect in flavor and neither green nor over-ripe. Fruit which has been shipped from a distance, and which is consequently not perfectly fresh, contains germs in active growth, and if the least bit musty, it will be almost sure to spoil, even though the greatest care may be taken in canning.

Poor fruit will not be improved by canning; over-ripe fruit will be insipid and mushy; and though cooking will soften hard fruit, it cannot impart to it the delicate flavors which belong to that which is in its prime. The larger varieties of fruit should not be quite soft enough for eating. Choose a dry day for gathering, and put up at once, handling as little as possible. Try to keep it clean enough to avoid washing. If the fruit is to be pared, use a silver knife for the purpose, as steel is apt to discolor the fruit. If the fruit is one needing to be divided or stoned, it will be less likely to become broken if divided before paring.

Cook the fruit slowly in a porcelain-lined or granite-ware kettle, using as little water as possible. It is better to cook only small quantities at a time in one kettle. Steaming in the cans is preferable to stewing, where the fruit is at all soft. To do this, carefully fill the cans with fresh fruit, packing it quite closely, if the fruit is large, and set the cans in a boiler partly filled with cold water, with something underneath them to prevent breaking,—muffin rings, straw, or thick cloth, or anything to keep them from resting on the bottom of the boiler (a rack made by nailing together strips of lath is very convenient); screw the covers on the cans so the water cannot boil into them, but not so tightly as to prevent the escape of steam; heat the water to boiling, and steam the fruit until tender. Peaches, pears, crab apples, etc., to be canned with a syrup, may be advantageously cooked by placing on a napkin dropped into the boiling syrup.

Fruit for canning should be so thoroughly cooked that every portion of it will have been subjected to a sufficient degree of heat to destroy all germs within the fruit, but overcooking should be avoided. The length of time required for cooking fruits for canning, varies with the kind and quality of fruit and the manner of cooking. Fruit is more frequently spoiled by being cooked an insufficient length of time, than by overcooking. Prolonged cooking at a boiling temperature is necessary for the destruction of certain kinds of germs capableof inducing fermentation. Fifteen minutes may be considered as the shortest time for which even the most delicate fruits should be subjected to the temperature of boiling water, and thirty minutes will be required by most fruits. Fruits which are not perfectly fresh, or which have been shipped some distance, should be cooked not less than thirty minutes. The boiling should be very slow, however, as hard, rapid boiling will break up the fruit, and much of its fine flavor will be lost in the steam.

Cooking the sugar with the fruit at the time of canning, is not to be recommended from an economical standpoint; but fruit thus prepared is more likely to keep well than when cooked without sugar; not, however, because of the preservative influence of the sugar, which is too small in amount to prevent the action of germs, as in the case of preserves, but because the addition of sugar to the water or fruit juice increases its specific gravity, and thus raises the boiling point. From experiments made, I have found that the temperature of the fruit is ordinarily raised about 5° by the addition of the amount of sugar needed for sweetening sub-acid fruit. By the aid of this additional degree of heat, the germs are more certainly destroyed, and the sterilization of the fruit will be accomplished in a shorter time.

Another advantage gained in cooking sugar with the fruit at the time of canning, is that the fruit may be cooked for a longer time without destroying its form, as the sugar abstracts the juice of the fruit, and thus slightly hardens it and prevents its falling in pieces.

The temperature to which the fruit is subjected may also be increased by the same method as that elsewhere described for sterilizing milk, the covers of the cans being screwed down tightly before they are placed in the sterilizer, or as soon as the boiling point is approached, so that the steam issues freely from the can. Seepage 396. If this method is employed, it must be remembered that the cans should not be removed from the sterilizer until after they have become cold, or nearly so, by being allowed to stand over night.

Use the best sugar, two tablespoonfuls to a quart of fruit is sufficient for most sub-acid fruits, as berries and peaches; plums, cherries, strawberries, and currants require from five to eight tablespoonfuls of sugar to a quart. Have the sugar hot, by spreading it on tins and heating in the oven, stirring occasionally. See that; it does not scorch. Add it when the fruit is boiling. Pears, peaches, apples, etc., which contain a much smaller quantity of juice than do berries, may be canned in a syrup prepared by dissolving a cup of sugar in two or three cups of water. Perfect fruit, properly canned, will keep without sugar, and the natural 'flavor of the fruit is more perfectly retained when the sugar is left out, adding the necessary amount when opened for use.

If the fruit is to be cooked previous to being put in the cans, the cans should be heated before the introduction of the fruit, which should be put in at a boiling temperature. Various methods are employed for this purpose. Some wrap the can in a towel wrung out of hot water, keeping a silver spoon inside while it is being filled; others employ dry heat by keeping the cans in a moderately hot oven while the fruit is cooking.

Another and surer way is to fill a large dishpan nearly full of scalding (not boiling) water, then gradually introduce each can, previously baked, into the water, dip it full of water, and set it right side up in the pan. Repeat the process with other cans until four or five are ready. Put the covers likewise into boiling water. Have in readiness for use a granite-ware funnel and dipper, also in boiling water; a cloth for wiping the outside of the cans, a silver fork or spoon, a dish for emptyings, and a broad shallow pan on one side of the range, half filled with boiling water, in which to set the cans while being filled. When everything is in readiness, the fruit properly cooked, and *at a boiling temperature,* turn one of the cans down in the water, roll it over once or twice, empty it, and set in the shallow pan of hot water; adjust the funnel, and then place first in the can a quantity of juice, so that when the fruit is put in, no vacant places will be left for air, which is sometimes quite troublesome if this precaution is not taken; then add the fruit. If any bubbles of air chance to be left, work them out with a fork or spoon handle, which first dip in boiling water, and then quickly introduce down the sides of the jar and through the fruit in such a way that not a bubble will remain. Fill the can to overflowing, remembering that any vacuum invites the air to enter; use boiling water or syrup when there is not enough juice. Skim all froth from the fruit, adding more juice if necessary; wipe the juice from the top of the can, adjust the rubber, put on the top, and screw it down as quickly as possible. If the fruit is cooked in the cans, as soon as it is sufficiently heated, fill the can completely full with boiling juice, syrup, or water; run the handle of a silver spoon around the inside of the can, to make sure the juice entirely surrounds every portion of fruit, and that no spaces for air remain, put on the rubbers, wipe off all juice, and seal quickly.

As the fruit cools, the cover can be tightened, and this should be promptly done again and again as the glass contracts, so that no air may be allowed to enter.

If convenient to fill the cans directly from the stove, the fruit may be kept at boiling heat by placing the kettle on a lamp stove on the table, on which the other utensils are in readiness. Many failures in fruit canning are due to neglect to have the fruit boiling hot when put into the cans.

When the cans are filled, set them away from currents of air, and not on a very cold surface, to avoid danger of cracking. A good way is to set the cans on a wet towel, and cover with a woolen cloth as a protection from draughts.

After the cans have cooled, and the tops have been screwed down tightly, place them in a cool place, bottom upward, and watch closely for a few days. If the juice begins to leak out, or any appearance of fermentation is seen, it is a sign that the work has failed, and the only thing to do is to open the can immediately, boil the fruit, and use as quickly as possible; recanning will not save it unless boiled a long time. If no signs of spoiling are observed within two or three weeks, the fruit may be safely stored away in a dark, cool place. If one has no dark storeroom, it is an advantage to wrap each can in brown paper, to keep out the light.

Sometimes the fruit will settle so that a little space appears at the top. If you are perfectly sure that the can is tight, do not open to refill, as you will be unable to make it quite as tight again, unless you reheatthe fruit, in which case you would be liable to have the same thing occur again. Air is dangerous because it is likely to contain germs, though in itself harmless.

If mold is observed upon the top of a can, it should be opened, and the fruit boiled and used at once, after carefully skimming out all the moldy portions. If there is evidence of fermentation, the fruit should be thrown away, as it contains alcohol.

If care be taken to provide good cans, thoroughly sterilized, and with perfectly fitting covers; to use only fruit in good condition; to have it thoroughly cooked, and at boiling temperature when put into the can; to have the cans well baked and heated, filled completely and to overflowing, and sealed at once while the fruit is still near boiling temperature, there will be little likelihood of failure.

Opening Canned Fruit.—Canned fruit is best opened a short time before needed, that is may be will aërated; and if it has been canned without sugar, it should have the necessary quantity added, so that it may be well dissolved before using.

Fruit purchased in tin cans should be selected with the utmost care, since unscrupulous dealers sometimes use cans which render the fruit wholly—unfit for food.

The following rules which we quote from a popular scientific journal should be 'carefully observed in selecting canned fruit:—

"Reject every can that does not have the name of the manufacturer or firm upon it, as well as the name of the company and the town where manufactured. All 'Standards' have this. When the wholesale dealer is ashamed to have his name on the goods, be shy of him.

"Reject every article of canned goods which does not show the line of resin around the edge of the solder of the cap, the same as is seen on the seam at the side of the can.

"Press up the bottom of the can; if decomposition is beginning, the tin will rattle the same as the bottom of your sewing-machine oil can does. If the goods are sound, it will be solid, and there will be no rattle to the tin.

"Reject every can that show any rust around the cap on the inside of the head of the can. Old and battered cans should be rejected; as, if they have been used several times, the contents are liable to contain small amounts of tin or lead"

RECIPES.

To Can Strawberries.—These are generally considered more difficult to can than most other berries. Use none but sound fruit, and put up the day they are picked, if possible. Heat the fruit slowly to the boiling point, and cook fifteen minutes or longer, adding the sugar hot, if any be used, after the fruit is boiling. Strawberries, while cooking, have a tendency to rise to the top, and unless they are kept poshed down, will not be cooked uniformly, which is doubtless one reason they sometimes fail to keep well. The froth should also be kept skimmed off. Fill the cans as directed on page 197, taking special care to let out every air bubble, and to remove every particle of froth from the top of the can before sealing. If the berries are of good size, the may be cooked in the cans, adding a boiling syrup prepared with one cup of water and one of sugar for each quart can of fruit.

If after the cans are cold, the fruit rises to the top, as it frequently does, take the cans and gently shake until the fruit is well saturated with the juice and falls by its own weight to the bottom, or low enough to be entirely covered with the liquid.

To Can Raspberries, Blackberries, and Other Small Fruits.—Select none but good, sound berries; those freshly picked are best; reject any green, over-ripe, mashed, or worm-eaten fruit. If necessary to wash the berries, do so by putting a quart at a time in a colander, and dipping the dish carefully into a pan of clean water, letting it stand for a moment. If the water is very dirty, repeat the process in a second water. Drain thoroughly, and if to be cooked previous to putting in the cans, put into a porcelain kettle with a very small quantity of water, and heat slowly to boiling. If sugar is to be used, have it hot, but do not add it until the fruit is boiling; and before doing so, if there is much juice, dip out the surplus, and leave the berries with only a small quantity, as the sugar will have a tendency to draw out more juice, thus furnishing plenty for syrup.

Raspberries are so juicy that they need scarcely more than a pint of water to two quarts of fruit.

The fruit may be steamed in the cans if preferred. When thoroughly scalded, if sugar is to be used, fill the can with a boiling syrup made by dissolving the requisite amount of sugar in water; if to be canned without sugar, fill up the can with boiling water or juice.

Seal the fruit according to directions previously given.

To Can Gooseberries.—Select such as are smooth and turning red, but not fully ripe; wash and remove the stems and blossom ends. For three quarts of fruit allow one quart of water. Heat slowly to boiling; cook fifteen minutes, add a cupful of sugar which has been heated dry in the oven: boil two or three minutes longer, and can.

To Can Peaches.—Select fruit which is perfectly ripe and sound, but not much softened. Free-stone peaches are the best. Put a few at a time in a wire basket, and dip into boiling water for a moment, and then into cold water, to cool fruit sufficiently to handle with comfort. The skins may then be rubbed or peeled off easily, if done quickly, and the fruit divided into halves; or wipe with a clean cloth to remove all dirt and the wool, and with a silver knife cut in halves, remove the stone, and then pare each piece, dropping into cold water at once to prevent discoloration. Peaches cut before being pared are less likely to break in pieces while removing the stones. When ready, pour a cupful of water in the bottom of the kettle, and fill with peaches, scattering sugar among the layers in the proportion of a heaping tablespoonful to a quart of fruit. Heat slowly, boil fifteen minutes or longer till a silver fork can be easily passed through the pieces; can in the usual way and seal; or, fill the cans with the halved peaches, and place them in a boiler of warm water with something underneath to avoid breaking; cook until perfectly tender. Have ready a boiling syrup prepared with one half cup of sugar and two cups of water, and pour into each can all that it will hold, remove air bubbles, cover and seal. A few of the pits may be cooked in the syrup, and removed before adding to the fruit, when their special flavor is desired.

ANOTHER METHOD.—After paring and halving the fruit, lay a clean napkin in the bottom of a steamer; fill with fruit. Steam until a fork will easily penetrate the pieces. Have ready a boiling syrup prepared as directed above, put a few spoonfuls in the bottom of the hot cans, and dip each piece of fruit gently in the hot syrup; then as carefully place it in the jars. Fill with the syrup, and finish in the usual way.

Peaches canned without sugar, retain more nearly their natural flavor. To prepare in this way, allow one half pint of water to each pound of fruit. Cook slowly until tender, and can in the usual manner. When wanted for the table, open an hour before needed, and sprinkle lightly with sugar.

To Can Pears.—The pears should be perfectly ripened, but not soft. Pare with a silver knife, halve or quarter, remove the seeds and drop into a pan of cold water to prevent discoloration. Prepare a syrup, allowing a cup of sugar and a quart of water to each two quarts of fruit. When the syrup boils, put the pears into it very carefully, so as not to bruise or break them, and cook until they look clear and can be easily pierced with a fork. Have the cans heated, and put in first a little of the syrup, then pack in the pears very carefully; fill to overflowing with the scalding syrup, and finish as previously directed. The tougher and harder varieties of pears must be cooked till nearly tender in hot water, or steamed over a kettle of boiling water, before adding to the syrup, and may then be finished as above. If it is desirable to keep the pears whole, cook only those of a uniform size together; or if of assorted sizes, put the larger ones into the syrup a few minutes before the smaller ones. Some prefer boiling the kins of the pears in the water of which the syrup is to be made, and skimming them out before putting in the sugar. This is thought to impart a finer flavor. Pears which are very sweet, or nearly tasteless, may be improved by using the juice of a large lemon for each quart of syrup. Pears may be cooked in the cans, if preferred.

To Can Plums.—Green Gages and Damsons are best for canning. Wipe clean with a soft cloth. Allow a half cup of water and the same of sugar to every three quarts of fruit, in preparing a syrup. Pick each plum with a silver fork to prevent it from bursting, and while the syrup is heating, turn in the fruit, and boil until thoroughly done. Dip carefully into hot jars, fill with syrup, and cover immediately.

To Can Cherries.—These may be put up whole in the same way as plums, or pitted and treated as directed for berries, allowing about two quarts of water and a scant pint of sugar to five quarts of solid fruit, for the tart varieties, and not quite half as much sugar for the sweeter ones.

To Can Mixed Fruit.—There are some fruits with so little flavor that when cooked they are apt to taste insipid, and are much improved by canning with some acid or strongly flavored fruits.

Blackberries put up with equal quantities of blue or red plums, or in the proportion of one to three of the sour fruit, are much better than either of these fruits canned separately. Black caps are much better if canned with currants, in the proportion of one part currants to four of black caps.

Red and black raspberries, cherries and raspberries, are also excellent combinations.

Quinces with Apples.—Pare and cut an equal quantity of firm sweet apples and quinces. First stew the quinces till they are tender in sufficient water to cover. Take them out, and cook the apples in the same water. Lay the apples and quinces in alternate layers in a porcelain kettle or crock. Have ready a hot syrup made with one part sugar to two and a half parts water, pour over the fruit, and let it stand all night. The next day reheat to boiling, and can.

Quinces and sweet apples may be canned in the same way as directed below for plums and sweet apples, using equal parts of apples and quinces, and adding sugar when opened.

Plums with Sweet Apples.—Prepare the plums, and stew in water enough to cover. When tender, skim out, add to the juice an equal quantity of quartered sweet apples, and stew until nearly tender. Add the plumbs again, boil together for a few minutes, and can. When wanted for the table, open, sprinkle with sugar if any seems needed, let stand awhile and serve.

To Can Grapes.—Grapes have so many seeds that they do not form a very palatable sauce when canned entire. Pick carefully from the stems, wash in a colander the same as directed for berries, and drain. Remove the skins, dropping them into one earthen crock and the pulp into another. Place both crocks in kettles of hot water over the stove, and heat slowly, stirring the pulp occasionally until the seeds will come out clean.

Then rub the pulp through a colander, add the skins to it, and a cupful of sugar for each quart of pulp. Return to the fire, boil twenty minutes until the skins are tender, and can; or, if preferred, the whole grapes may be heated, and when well scalded so that the seeds are loosened, pressed through a colander, thus rejecting both seeds and skins, boiled, then sweetened if desired, and canned.

To Can Crab Apples.—These may be cooked whole, and canned the same way as plums.

To Can Apples.—Prepare and can the same as pears, when fresh and fine in flavor. If old and rather tasteless, the following is a good way:—several thin slices of the yellow part of the rind, four cups of sugar, and three pints of boiling water. Pare and quarter the apples, or if small, only halve them, and cook gently in a broad-bottomed closely-covered saucepan, with as little water as possible, till tender, but not broken; then pour the syrup over them, heat all to boiling, and can at once. The apples may be cooked by steaming over a kettle of hot water, if preferred. Care must be taken to cook those of the same degree of hardness together. The slices of lemon rind should be removed from the syrup before using.

To Can Pineapples.—The writer has had no experience in canning this fruit, but the following method is given on good authority: Pare very carefully with a silver knife, remove all the "eyes" and black specks; then cut the sections in which the "eyes" were, in solid pieces clear down to the core. By doing this all the valuable part of the fruit is saved, leaving its hard, woody center. As, however, this contains considerable juice, it should be taken in the hands and wrung as one wrings a cloth, till the juice is extracted, then thrown away. Prepare a syrup with one part sugar and two parts water, using what juice has been obtained in place of so much water. Let it boil up, skim clean, then add the fruit. Boil just as little as possible and have the fruit tender, as pineapples loses its flavor by overcooking more readily than any other fruit. Put into hot cans, and seal.

FRUIT JELLIES.

The excess of sugar commonly employed in preparing jellies often renders them the least wholesome of fruit preparations, and we cannot recommend our readers to spend a great amount of time in putting up a large stock of such articles.

The juice of some fruits taken at the right stage of maturity may be evaporated to a jelly without sugar, but the process is a more lengthy one, and requires a much larger quantity of juice than when sugar is used.

Success in the preparation of fruit jellies depends chiefly upon the amount of pectose contained in the fruit. Such fruits as peaches, cherries, and others containing but a small proportion of pectose, cannot be made into a firm jelly. All fruit for jelly should, if possible, be freshly picked, and before it is over-ripe, as it has then a much better flavor. The pectose, the jelly-producing element, deteriorates with age, so that jelly made from over-ripe fruit is less certainto "form." If the fruit is under-ripe, it will be too acid to give a pleasant flavor. Examine carefully, as for canning, rejecting all wormy, knotty, unripe, or partially decayed fruit. If necessary to wash, drain very thoroughly.

Apples, quinces, and similar fruits may require to be first cooked in a small amount of water. The juice of berries, currants, and grapes, may be best extracted by putting the fruit in a granite-ware double boiler, or a covered earthen crock placed inside a kettle of boiling water, mashing as much as possible with a spoon, and steaming without the addition of water until the fruit is well scalded and broken.

For straining the juice, have a funnel-shaped bag made of coarse flannel or strong, coarse linen crash. The bag will be found more handy if a small hoop of wire is sewn around the top and two tapes attached to hang it by while the hot juice is draining, or a wooden frame to support the bag may be easily constructed like the one shown on page 74. A dish to receive the juice should be placed underneath the bag, which should first be wrung out of hot water, and the scalded fruit, a small quantity at a time, turned in; then with two large spoons press the sides of the bag well, moving the fruit around in the bag to get out all the juice, and removing the pressed pulp and skins each time before putting in a fresh supply of the hot fruit. If a very clear jelly is desired, the juice must be allowed to drain out without pressing or squeezing. The juice of berries, grapes, and currants may be extracted without the fruit being first scalded, if preferred, by putting the fruit into an earthen or granite-ware dish, and mashing well with a wooden potato masher, then putting into a jelly bag and allowing the juice to drain off for several hours.

When strained, if the jelly is to be prepared with sugar, measure the juice and pour it into a granite or porcelain fruit kettle with a very broad bottom, so that as much surface can be on the stove possible. It is better to boil the juice in quantities of not more than two or three quarts at a time, unless one has some utensil in which a larger quantity can be cooked with no greater depth of liquid than the above quantity would give in a common fruit kettle. The purpose of the boiling is to evaporate the water from the juice, and this can best be accomplished before the sugar is added. The sugar, if boiled with the juice, also darkens the jelly.

The average length of time required for boiling the juice of most berries, currants, and grapes, extracted as previously directed, before adding the sugar, is twenty minutes from the time it begins to bubble all over its surface. It is well to test the jelly occasionally, however, by dropping a small quantity on a plate to cool, since the quantity of juice and the rapidity with which it is boiled, may necessitate some variation in time. In wet season, fruits of all kinds absorb more moisture and a little longer boiling may be necessary. The same is true of the juice of fruits gathered after a heavy rain. Jellies prepared with sugar are generally made of equal measures of juice, measured before boiling, and sugar; but a very scant measure of sugar is sufficient, and a less amount will suffice for many fruits. White granulated sugar is best for all jellies. While the juice is heating, spread the sugar evenly on shallow tins, and heat in the oven, stirring occasionally to keep it from scorching. If portions melt, no great harm will be done, as the melted portions will form in lumps when turned into the juice, and can be removed with a spoon. When the juice has boiled twenty minutes, turn in the sugar, which should be so hot that the hand cannot be borne in it with comfort, stirring rapidly until it is all dissolved. Let the syrup boil again for three or four minutes, then take immediately from the fire. Heat the jelly glasses (those with glass covers are best), by rolling in hot water, and place them in a shallow pan partially filled with hot water, or stand them on a wet, folded towel while filling. If it is desired to have the jelly exceptionally clear and nice, it may be turned through a bag of cheese cloth, previously wrung out of hot water, into the jelly glasses. If the covers of the glasses are not tight fitting, a piece of firm paper should be fitted over the top before putting on the cover, to make it air tight. Pint self-sealing fruit cans are excellent for storing jelly, and if it is sealed in them in the same manner as canned fruit, will keep perfectly, and obviate any supposed necessity for the use of brandied paper as a preservative measure. Label each variety, and keep in some cool, dry place. If the jelly is not sufficiently firm when first made, set the glasses in the sunshine for several days, until the jelly becomes more firm. This is better than reheating and boiling again, as it destroys less of the flavor of the fruit.

RECIPES.

Apple Jelly.—Cut nice tart apples in quarters, but unless wormy, do not peel or core. Put into a porcelain kettle with a cup of water for each six pounds of fruit, and simmer very slowly until the apples are thoroughly cooked. Turn into a jelly-bag, and drain off the juice. If very tart, allow three fourths of a pound of sugar to each pint of juice. If sub-acid, one half pound will be sufficient. Put the sugar into the oven to heat. Clean the kettle, and boil the juice therein twenty minutes after it begins to boil thoroughly. Add the sugar, stirring until well dissolved, let it boil up once again, and remove from the fire. The juice of one lemon may be used with the apples, and a few bits of lemon rind, the yellow portion only, cooked with them to give them a flavor, if liked. One third cranberry juice makes a pleasing combination.

Apple Jelly without Sugar.—Select juicy, white fleshed, sub-acid fruit, perfectly sound and mature but not mellow. The snow apple is one of the best varieties for this purpose. Wash well, slice, and core without removing the skins, and cook as directed in the preceding recipe. Drain off the juice, and if a very clear jelly is desired, filter it through a piece of cheese cloth previously wrung out of hot water. Boil the juice,—rapidly at first, but more gently as it becomes thickened,—until of the desired consistency. The time required will vary with the quantity of juice, the shallowness of the dish in which it is boiled, and the heat employed. One hour at least, will be required for one or two quarts of juice. When the juice has become considerably evaporated, test it frequently by dipping a few drops on a plate to cool; and when it jellies sufficiently, remove at once from the fire. A much larger quantity of juice will be needed for jelly prepared in this manner than when sugar is used, about two quarts of juice being required for one half pint of jelly. Such jelly, however, has a most delicious flavor, and is excellent served with grains. Diluted with water, it forms a most pleasing beverage.

Berry and Currant Jellies.—Express the juice according to the directions already given. For strawberries, red raspberries, and currants, allow three fourths of a pound of sugar to a pint of juice. Black raspberries, if used alone, need less sugar. Strawberry and black raspberry juice make better jelly if a little lemon juice is used. The juice of one lemon to each pint of fruit juice will be needed for black raspberries. Two parts red or black raspberries with one part currants, make a better jelly than either alone. Boil the juice of strawberries, red raspberries, and currants twenty minutes, add the sugar, and finish, as previously directed. Black raspberry juice is much thicker, and requires less boiling.

Cherry Jelly.—Jelly may be prepared from cherries by using with the juice of cherries an equal amount of apple juice, which gives an additional amount of pectose to the juice and does not perceptibly change the flavor.

Crab Apple Jelly.—Choose the best Siberian crab apples; cut into pieces, but do not pare or remove seeds. Place in a porcelain-lined or granite-ware double boiler, with a cup of water for each six pounds of fruit, and let them remain on the back of the range, with the water slowly boiling, seven or eight hours. Leave in the boiler or turn into a large china bowl, and keep well covered, all night. In the morning drain off the juice and proceed as for apple jelly, using from one half to three fourths of a pound of sugar to one of juice.

Cranberry Jelly.—Scald the berries and express the juice for other jellies. Measure the juice, and allow three fourths of a pound of sugar to one of juice. Boil twenty minutes, add the sugar hot, and finish as directed for other jellies.

Grape Jelly.—Jelly from ripe grapes may be prepared in the same manner as that made from the juice of berries. Jelly from green grapes needs one half measure more of sugar.

Orange Jelly.—Express the juice of rather tart oranges, and use with it an equal quantity of the juice of sub-acid apples, prepared in the manner directed for apple jelly. For each pint of the mixed juice, use one half pound of sugar and proceed as for other jellies.

Peach Jelly.—Stone, pare, and slice the peaches, and steam them in a double boiler. Express the juice, and add for each pint of peach juice the juice of one lemon. Measure the juice and sugar, using three fourths of a pound of sugar for each pint of juice, and proceed as already directed. Jelly prepared from peaches will not be so firm as many fruit jellies, owing to the small amount of pectose contained in their composition.

A mixture of apples and peaches, in the proportion of one third of the former to two thirds of the latter, makes a firmer jelly than peaches alone. The apples should be pared and cored, so that their flavor will not interfere with that of the peaches.

Quince Jelly.—Clean thoroughly good sound fruit, and slice thin. Put into a double boiler with one cup of water for each five pounds of fruit, and cook until softened. Express the juice, and proceed as with other jellies, allowing three fourths of a pound of sugar to each pint of juice. Tart or sweet apples may be used with quinces, in equal proportions, and make a jelly of more pleasant flavor than quinces used alone. The seeds of quinces contain considerable gelatinous substance, and should be cooked with the quince for jelly making.

Plum Jelly.—Use Damsons or Green Gages. Stone, and make in the same way as for berry and other small fruit jellies.

Fruit in Jelly.—Prepare some apple jelly without sugar. When boiled sufficiently to form, add to it, as it begins to cool, some nice, stoned dates or seeded raisins. Orange jelly may be used instead of the apple jelly, if preferred.

FRUIT JUICES.

As sauces for desserts and for summer beverages for sick or well, the pure juices of fruits are most wholesome and delicious. So useful are they and so little trouble to prepare, that no housewife should allow the fruit season to pass by without putting up a full stock. Strawberries, raspberries, blackberries, currants, grapes, and cherries are especially desirable. In preparing them, select only the best fruit, ripe, but not over-ripe. Extract the juice by mashing the fruit and slowly heating in the inner cup of a double boiler, till the fruit is well scalded; too long heating will injure its color. Strain through a jelly bag and let it drain slowly for a long time, but do not squeeze, else some of the pulp will be forced through. Reheat slowly to boiling and can the same as fruit. It may be put up with or without sugar. If sugar is to be used, add it hot as for jelly, after the juice is strained and reheated to boiling. For strawberries and currants, raspberries and cherries, use one cup of sugar to a quart of juice. Black raspberries and grapes require less sugar, while blueberries and blackberries require none at all, or not more than a tablespoonful to the quart. A mixed juice, of one part currants and two parts red or black raspberries, has a very superior flavor.

RECIPES.

Grape Juice, or Unfermented Wine.—Take twenty-five pounds of some well ripened very juicy variety of grapes, like the Concord. Pick them from the stems, wash thoroughly, and scald without the addition of water, in double boilers until the grapes burst open; cool, turn into stout jelly bags, and drain off the juice without squeezing. Let the juice stand and settle; turn off the top, leaving any sediment there may be. Add to the juice about four pounds of best granulated sugar, reheat to boiling, skim carefully, and can the same as fruit. Keep in a cool, dark place. The wine, if to be sealed in bottles, will require a corker, and the corks should first be boiled in hot water and the bottles well sterilized.

Grape Juice No. 2.—Take grapes of the best quality, picked fresh from the vines. Wash well after stripping from the stems, rejecting any imperfect fruit. Put them in a porcelain or granite fruit kettle with one pint of water to every three quarts of grapes, heat to boiling, and cook slowly for fifteen minutes or longer, skimming as needed. Turn off the juice and carefully filter it through a jelly bag, putting the seeds and skins into a separate bag to drain, as the juice from them will be less clear. Heat again to boiling, add one cupful of hot sugar to each quart of juice, and seal in sterilized cans or bottles. The juice from the skins and seeds should be canned separately.

Another Method.—Wash the grapes, and express the juice without scalding the fruit. Strain the juice three or four times through muslin or cheese cloth, allowing it to stand and settle for some time between each filtering. To every three pints of juice add one of water and two cupfuls of sugar. Heat to boiling, and keep at that temperature for fifteen minutes, skim carefully, and bottle while at boiling heat. Set away in a cool, dark place.

Fruit Syrup.—Prepare the juice expressed from strawberries, raspberries, currants, or grapes, as directed above for fruit juices. After it has come to a boil, add one pound of sugar to every quart of juice. Seal in pint cans. It may be diluted with water to form a pleasing beverage, and is especially useful in flavoring puddings and sauces.

Currant Syrup.—Boil together a pint of pure currant juice and one half pound of best white sugar for ten minutes, and can or bottle while at boiling temperature. One or two spoonfuls of the syrup in a glass of water makes a most refreshing drink. Two parts currants and one of red raspberries may be used in place of all currants, if preferred.

Orange Syrup.—Select ripe and thin-skinned fruit. To every pint of the juice add one pound of sugar, the juice of one lemon, and a little of the grated rind. Boil for fifteen minutes, removing all scum as it rises. If the syrup is not clear, strain through a piece of cheese cloth, and reheat. Can and seal while boiling hot.

Lemon Syrup.—Grate the yellow portion of the rind of six lemons, and mix with three pounds of best granulated white sugar. Add one quart of water and boil until it thickens. Strain, add the juice of the six lemons, carefully leaving out the pulp and seeds; boil ten minutes, and bottle. Diluted with two thirds cold water, it forms a delicious and quickly prepared lemonade.

Lemon Syrup No. 2.—To every pint of lemon juice add one pound of sugar; boil, skim, and seal in cans like fruit.

Blackberry Syrup.—Crush fresh, well-ripened blackberries, and add to them one fourth as much boiling water as berries; let them stand for twenty-four hours, stirring frequently. Strain, add a cup of sugar to each quart of juice, boil slowly for fifteen minutes, and can.

Fruit Ices.—Express the juice from a pint of stoned red cherries, add the juice of two lemons, one cup of sugar and a quart of cold water. Stir well for five minutes, an freeze in an ice cream freezer. Equal parts currant and red raspberry juice may be used instead of cherry, if preferred.

DRYING FRUIT.

This method of preserving fruit, except in large establishments where it is dried by steam, is but little used, since canning is quicker and superior in every way. Success in drying fruits is dependent upon the quickness with which, they can be dried, without subjecting them to so violent a heat as to burn them or injure their flavor.

Pulpy fruits, such as berries, cherries, plums, etc., should be spread on some convenient flat surface without contact with each other, and dried in the sun under glass, or in a moderate oven. They should be turned daily. They will dry more quickly if first scalded in a hot oven. Cherries should be first stoned and cooked until well heated through and tender, then spread on plates, and the juice (boiled down to a syrup) poured over them. When dried, they will be moist. Pack in jars. Large fruit, such as apples, pears, and peaches, should be pared, divided, and the seeds or stones removed. If one has but a small quantity, the best plan is to dry by mean of artificial heat; setting it first in a hot oven until heated through, which process starts the juice and forms a film or crust over the cut surfaces, thus holding the remaining: quantity of juice inside until it becomes absorbed in the tissues. The drying process may be finished in a warming oven or some place about the range where the fruit will get only moderate heat. If a larger quantity of fruit is to be dried, after being heated in the oven, it may be placed in the hot sun out of doors, under fine wire screens, to keep off the flies; or may be suspended for the ceiling in some way, or placed upon a frame made to stand directly over the stove. As the drying proceeds, the fruit should be turned occasionally, and when dry enough, it should be thoroughly heated before it is packed away, to prevent it from getting wormy.

NUTS.

The nuts, or shell fruits, as they are sometimes termed, form a class of food differing greatly from the succulent fruits. They are more properly seeds, containing, in general, no starch, but are rich in fat and nitrogenous elements in the form of vegetable albumen and casein. In composition, the nuts rank high in nutritive value, but owing to the oily matter which they contain, are difficult of digestion, unless reduced to a very minutely divided state before or during mastication. The fat of nuts is similar in character to cream, and needs to be reduced to the consistency of cream to be easily digested. Those nuts, such as almonds, filberts, and pecans, which do not contain an excess of fat, are the most wholesome. Nuts should be eaten, in moderation, at the regular mealtime, and not partaken of as a tidbit between meals. It is likewise well to eat them in connection with some hard food, to insure their thorough mastication. Almonds and cream crisps thus used make a pleasing combination.

Most of the edible nuts have long been known and used as food. The *Almond* was highly esteemed by the ancient nations of the East, its native habitat, and is frequently referred to in sacred history. It is grown extensively in the warm, temperate regions of the Old World. There are two varieties, known as the bitter and the sweet almond. The kernel of the almond yields a fixed oil; that produced from the bitter almond is much esteemed for flavoring purposes, but it is by no means a safe article to use, at it possesses marked poisonous qualities. Fresh, sweet almonds are a nutritive, and, when properly eaten, wholesome food. The outer brown skin of the kernel is somewhat bitter, rough, and irritating to the stomach but it can be easily removed by blanching.

Blanched almonds, if baked for a short time, become quite brittle, and may be easily pulverized, and are then more easily digested. Bread made from almonds thus baked and pulverized, is considered an excellent food for persons suffering with diabetes.

Brazil Nuts are the seeds of a gigantic tree which grows wild in the valleys of the Amazon, and throughout tropical America. The case containing these seeds is a hard, woody shell, globular in form, and about the size of a man's head. It is divided into four cells, in each of which are closely packed the seeds which constitute the so-called nuts, of commerce. These seeds are exceedingly rich in oil, one pound of them producing about nine ounces of oil.

The *Cocoanut* is perhaps the most important of all the shell fruits, if we may judge by the variety of uses to which the nut and the tree which bears it can be put. It has been said that nature seldom produces a tree so variously useful to man as the cocoanut palm. In tropical countries, where it grows abundantly, its leaves are employed for thatching, its fibers for manufacturing many useful articles, while its ashes produce potash in abundance. The fruit is eaten raw, and in many ways is prepared for food; it also yields an oil which forms an important article of commerce. The milk of the fruit is a cooling beverage, and the woody shell of the nut answers very well for a cup from which to drink it. The saccharine juice of the tree also affords an excellent drink; and from the fresh young stems is prepared a farinaceous substance similar to sago.

The cocoanuts grow in clusters drooping from the tuft of long, fringed leaves which crown the branchless trunk of the stately palm. The cocoanut as found in commerce is the nut divested of its outer sheath, and is much smaller in size than when seen upon the tree. Picked fresh from the tree, the cocoanut consists first of a green outer covering; next of a fibrous coat, which, if the nut is mature, is hairy-like in appearance; and then of the woody shell, inside of which is the meat and milk. For household purposes the nuts are gathered while green, and before the inner shell has become solidified; the flesh is then soft like custard, and can be easily eaten with a teaspoon, while a large quantity of delicious, milk-like fluid is obtainable from each nut.

As found in our Northern markets, the cocoanut is difficult of digestion, as is likewise the prepared or desiccated cocoanut. The cocoanut contains about seventy per cent of oil.

The *Chestnut* is an exception to most nuts in its composition. It contains starch, and about fifteen per cent of sugar. No oil can be extracted from the chestnut. In Italy, and other parts of Southern Europe, the chestnut forms an important article of food. It is sometimes dried and ground into flour, from which bread is prepared. The chestnut is a nutritious food, but owing to the starch it contains, is more digestible when cooked. The same is true of the *Acorn*, which is similar in character to the chestnut. In the early ages, acorns were largely used for food, and are still used as a substitute for bread in some countries.

The *Hazelnut*, with the *Filbert* and *Cobnut*, varieties of the same nut obtained by cultivation, are among the most desirable nuts for general consumption.

The *Walnut*, probably a native of Persia, where in ancient times it was so highly valued as to be considered suited only for the table of the king, is now found very commonly with other species of the same family, the *Butternut* and *Hickory nut*, in most temperate climates.

The *Pecan*, a nut allied to the hickory nut, and grown extensively in the Mississippi Valley and Texas, is one of the most easily digested nuts.

The *Peanut* or *Groundnut* is the seed of an annual, cultivated extensively in most tropical and sub-tropical countries. After the plant has blossomed, the stalk which produced the flower has the peculiarity of bending down and forcing itself under ground so that the seeds mature some depth beneath the surface. When ripened, the pods containing the seeds are dug up and dried. In tropical countries the fresh nuts are largely consumed, and are thought greatly to resemble almonds in flavor. In this country they are more commonly roasted. They are less easily digested than many other nuts because of the large amount of oily matter which they contain.

RECIPES.

To Blanch Almonds.—Shell fresh, sweet almonds, and pour boiling water over them; let them stand for two or three minutes, skim out, and drop into cold water. Press between the thumb and finger, and the kernels will readily slip out of the brown covering. Dry between clean towels. Blanched almonds served with raisins make an excellent dessert.

Boiled Chestnuts.—The large variety, knows as the Italian chestnut, is best for this purpose. Remove the shells, drop into boiling water, and boil for ten minutes, take out, drop into cold water, and rub off the brown skin. Have some clean water boiling, turn the blanched nuts into it, and cook until they can be pierced with a fork. Drain thoroughly, put into a hot dish, dry in the oven for a few minutes, and serve. A cream sauce or tomato sauce may be served with them if liked.

Mashed Chestnuts.—Prepare and boil the chestnuts as in the preceding recipe. When tender, mash through a colander with a potato masher. Season with cream and salt if desired. Serve hot.

Baked Chestnuts.—PutItalian chestnuts in the shell on a perforated tin in a rather hot oven, and bake for ten minutes, until tender. Remove the shells, and serve hot. If preferred, they can be roasted on a clean shovel or in a corn popper over a bed of coals.

To Keep Nuts Fresh.—Chestnuts and other thin-shelled nuts may be kept from becoming too dry by mixing with an equal bulk of dry sand and storing in a box or barrel in some cool place.

TABLE TOPICS.

Who lives to eat, will die by eating.—*Sel.*

Fruit bears the closest relation to light. The sun pours a continuous flood of light into the fruits, and they furnish the best portion of food a human being requires for the sustenance of mind and body.—*Alcott.*

The famous Dr. John Hunter, one of the most eminent physicians of his time, and himself a sufferer from gout, found in apples a remedy for this very obstinate and distressing malady. He insisted that all of his patients should discard wine and roast beef, and make a free use of apples.

Do not too much for your stomach, or it will abandon you.—*Sel.*

The purest food is fruit, next the cereals, then the vegetables. All pure poets have abstained almost entirely from animal food. Especially should a minister take less meat when he has to write a sermon. The less meat the better sermon.—*A. Bronson Alcott.*

There is much false economy: those who are too poor to have seasonable fruits and vegetables, will yet have pie and pickles all the year. They cannot afford oranges, yet can afford tea and coffee daily.—*Health Calendar.*

What plant we in the apple tree?
Fruits that shall dwell in sunny June,
And redden in the August moon,
And drop, when gentle airs come by,
That fan the blue September sky,
While children come, with cries of glee,
And seek there when the fragrant grass
Betrays their bed to those who pass
At the foot of the apple tree—*Bryant.*

LEGUMES

The legumes, to which belong peas, beans, and lentils, are usually classed among vegetables; but in composition they differ greatly from all other vegetable foods, being characterized by a very large percentage of the nitrogenous elements, by virtue of which they possess the highest nutritive value. Indeed, when mature, they contain a larger proportion of nitrogenous matter than any other food, either animal or vegetable. In their immature state, they more nearly resemble the vegetables. On account of the excess of nitrogenous elements in their composition, the mature legumes are well adapted to serve as a substitute for animal foods, and for use in association with articles in which starch or other non-nitrogenous elements are predominant; as, for example, beans or lentils with rice, which combinations constitute the staple food of large populations in India.

The nitrogenous matter of legumes is termed *legumin*, or vegetable casein, and its resemblance to the animal casein of milk is very marked. The Chinese make use of this fact, and manufacture cheese from peas and beans. The legumes were largely used as food by the ancient nations of the East. They were the "pulse" upon which the Hebrew children grew so fair and strong. According to Josephus, legumes also formed the chief diet of the builders of the pyramids. They are particularly valuable as strength producers, and frequently form a considerable portion of the diet of persons in training as athletes, at the present day. Being foods possessed of such high nutritive value, the legumes are deserving of a more extended use than is generally accorded them in this country. In their mature state they are, with the exception of beans, seldom found upon the ordinary bill of fare, and beans are too generally served in a form quite difficult of digestion, being combined with large quantities of fat, or otherwise improperly prepared. Peas and lentils are in some respects superior to beans, being less liable to disagree with persons of weak digestion, and for this reason better suited to form a staple article of diet.

All the legumes are covered with a tough skin, which is in itself indigestible, and which if not broken by the cooking process or by thorough mastication afterward, renders the entire seed liable to pass through the digestive tract undigested, since the digestive fluids cannot act upon the hard skin. Even when the skins are broken, if served with the pulp, much of the nutritive material of the legume is wasted, because it is impossible for the digestive processes to free it from the cellulose material of which the skins are composed. If, then, it be desirable to obtain from the legumes the largest amount of nutriment and in the most digestible form, they must be prepared in some manner so as to reject the skins. Persons unable to use the legumes when cooked in the ordinary way, usually experience no difficulty whatever in digesting them when divested of their skins. The hindrance which even the partially broken skins are to the complete digestion of the legume, is well illustrated by the personal experiments of Prof. Strümpell, a German scientist, who found that of beans boiled with the skins on he was able to digest only 60 per cent of the nitrogenous material they contained. When, however, he reduced the same quantity of beans to a fine powder previous to cooking, he was enabled to digest 91.8 per cent of it.

The fact that the mature legumes are more digestible when prepared in some manner in which the skins are rejected, was doubtless understood in early times, for we find in a recipe of the fourteenth century, directions given "to dry legumes in an oven and remove the skins away before using them."

The green legumes which are more like a succulent vegetable are easily digested with the skins on, if the hulls are broken before being swallowed. There are also some kinds of beans which, in their mature state, from having thinner skins, are more readily digested, as the Haricot variety.

Suggestions for Cooking.—The legumes are best cooked by stewing or boiling, and when mature, require prolonged cooking to render them tender and digestible. Slow cooking, when practicable, is preferable. Dry beans and peas are more readily softened by cooking if first soaked for a time in cold water. The soaking also has a tendency to loosen the skins, so that when boiled or stewed, a considerable portion of them slip off whole, and being lighter, rise to the top during the cooking, and can be removed with a spoon; it likewise aids in removing the strong flavor characteristic of these foods, which is considered objectionable by some persons. The length of time required for soaking will depend upon the age of the seed, those from the last harvest needing only a few hours, while such as have been kept for two or more years require to be soaked twelve or twenty-four hours. For cooking, soft water is best. The mineral elements in hard water have a tendency to harden the casein, of which the legumes a largely composed, thus rendering it often very difficult to soften them.

The dry, unsoaked legumes are generally best put to cook in cold water, and after the boiling point is reached, allowed to simmer gently until done. Boiling water may be used for legumes which have been previously soaked. The amount of water required will vary somewhat with the heat employed and the age and condition of the legume, as will also the time required for cooking, but as a general rule two quarts of soft water for one pint of seeds will be quite sufficient. Salt should not be added until the seeds are nearly done, as it hinders the cooking process.

PEAS.

Description.—The common garden pea is probably a native of countries bordering on the Black Sea. A variety known as the gray pea (*pois chiche*) has been used since a very remote period. The common people of Greece and Rome, in ancient times made it an ordinary article of diet. It is said that peas were considered such a delicacy by the Romans that those who coveted public favor distributed them gratuitously to the people in order to buy votes.

Peas were introduced into England from Holland in the time of Elizabeth, and were then considered a great delicacy. History tells us that when the queen was released from her confinement in the tower, May 19, 1554, she went to Staining to perform her devotions in the church of Allhallows, after which she dined at a neighboring inn upon a meal of which the principal dish was boiled peas. A dinner of the same kind, commemorative of the event, was for a long time given annually at the same tavern.

Peas, when young, are tender and sweet, containing a considerable quantity of sugar. The nitrogenous matter entering into their composition, although less in quantity when unripe, is much more easily digested than when the seeds are mature.

When quite ripe, like other leguminous seeds, they require long cooking. When very old, no amount of boiling will soften them. When green, peas are usually cooked and served as a vegetable; in their dried state, they are put to almost every variety of use in the different countries where they are cultivated.

In the southeast of Scotland, a favorite food is made of ground peas prepared in thick cakes and called peas-bainocks.

In India and southern Europe, a variety of the pea is eaten parched or lightly roasted, or made into cakes, puddings, and sweetmeats. In Germany, in combination with other ingredients, peas are compounded into sausages, which, during the Franco-Prussian war, served as rations for the soldiers.

Dried peas for culinary use are obtainable in two forms; the split peas, which have had the tough envelope of the seed removed, and the green or Scotch peas.

The time required for cooking will vary from five to eight hours, depending upon the age of the seed and the length of time it has been soaked previous to cooking.

RECIPES.

Stewed Split Peas.—Carefully examine and wash the peas, rejecting any imperfect or worm-eaten ones. Put into cold water and let them come to a boil; then place the stewpan back on the range and simmer gently until tender, but not mushy. Season with salt and a little cream if desired.

Peas Puree.—Soak a quart of Scotch peas in cold water over night. In the morning, drain and put them to cook in boiling water. Cook slowly until perfectly tender, allowing them to simmer very gently toward the last until they become as dry as possible. Put through a colander to render them homogeneous and remove the skins. Many of the skins will be loosened and rise to the top during the cooking, and it is well to remove these with a spoon so as to make the process of rubbing through the colander less laborious. Season with salt if desired, and a cup of thin cream. Serve hot.

Mashed Peas.—Soak and cook a quart of peas as for Peas *Puree* When well done, if the Scotch peas, rub through a colander to remove the skins. If the split peas are used, mash perfectly smooth with a potato masher. Season with a teaspoonful of salt and a half cup of sweet cream, if desired. Beat well together, turn into an earthen or granite-ware pudding dish, smooth the top, and bake in a moderate oven until dry and mealy throughout, and nicely browned on top. Serve hot like mashed potato, or with a tomato sauce prepared as follows: Heat a pint of strained, stewed tomato, season lightly with salt, and when boiling, thicken with a tablespoonful of flour rubbed smooth in a little cold water.

Peas Cakes.—Cut cold mashed peas in slices half an inch in thickness, brush lightly with cream, place on perforated tins, and brown in the oven. If the peas crumble too much to slice, form them into small cakes with a spoon or knife, and brown as directed. Serve hot with or without a tomato sauce. A celery sauce prepared as directed in the chapter on Sauces, is also excellent.

Dried Green Peas.—Gather peas while young and tender and carefully dry them. When needed for use, rinse well, and put to cook in cold water. Let them simmer until tender. Season with cream the same as fresh green peas.

BEANS.

Description.—Some variety of the bean family has been cultivated and used for culinary purposes from time immemorial. It is frequently mentioned in Scripture; King David considered it worthy of a place in his dietary, and the prophet Ezekiel was instructed to mix it with the various grains and seeds of which he made his bread.

Among some ancient nations the bean was regarded as a type of death, and the priests of Jupiter were forbidden to eat it, touch it, or even pronounce its name. The believer in the doctrine of transmigration of souls carefully avoided this article of food, in the fear of submitting beloved friends to the ordeal of mastication.

At the present day there is scarcely a country in hot or temperate climates where the bean is not cultivated and universally appreciated, both as a green vegetable and when mature and dried.

The time required to digest boiled beans is two and one half hours, and upwards.

In their immature state, beans are prepared and cooked like other green vegetables. Dry beans may be either boiled, stewed, or baked, but whatever the method employed, it must be very slow and prolonged. Beans to be baked should first be parboiled until tender. We mention this as a precautionary measure lest some amateur cook, misled by the term "bake," should repeat the experiment of the little English maid whom we employed as cook while living in London, a few years ago. In ordering our dinner, we had quite overlooked the fact that baked beans are almost wholly an American dish, and failed to give any suggestions as to the best manner of preparing it. Left to her own resources, the poor girl did the best she knew how, but her face was full of perplexity as she placed the beans upon the table at dinner, with, "Well, ma'am, here are the beans, but I don't see how you are going to eat them." Nor did we, for she had actually baked the dry beans, and they lay there in the dish, as brown as roasted coffee berries, and as hard as bullets.

Beans to be boiled or stewed do not need parboiling, although many cooks prefer to parboil them, to lessen the strong flavor which to some persons is quite objectionable.

From one to eight hours are required to cook beans, varying with the age and variety of the seed, whether it has been soaked, and the rapidity of the cooking process.

RECIPES.

Baked Beans.—Pick over a quart of best white beans and soak in cold water over night. Put them to cook in fresh water, and simmer gently till they are tender, but not broken. Let them be quite juicy when taken from the kettle. Season with salt and a teaspoonful of molasses. Put them in a deep crock in a slow oven. Let them bake two or three hours, or until they assume a reddish brown tinge, adding boiling water occasionally to prevent their becoming dry. Turn, into a shallow dish, and brown nicely before sending to the table.

Boiled Beans.—Pick over some fresh, dry beans carefully, and wash thoroughly. Put into boiling water and cook gently and slowly until tender, but not broken. They should be moderately juicy when done. Serve with lemon juice, or season with salt and a little cream as preferred.

The colored varieties, which are usually quite strong in flavor, are made less so by parboiling for fifteen or twenty minutes and then pouring the water off, adding more of boiling temperature, and cooking slowly until tender.

Beans Boiled in a Bag.—Soak a pint of white beans over night. When ready to cook, put them into a clean bag, tie up tightly, as the beans have already swelled, and if given space to move about with the boiling of the water will become broken and mushy. Boil three or four hours. Serve hot.

Scalloped Beans.—Soak a pint of white beans over night in cold water. When ready to cook, put into an earthen baking dish, cover well with new milk, and bake in a slow oven for eight or nine hours; refilling the dish with milk as it boils away, and taking care that the beans do not at any time get dry enough to brown over the top till they are tender. When nearly done, add salt to taste, and a half cup of cream. They may be allowed to bake till the milk is quite absorbed, and the beans dry, or may be served when rich with juice, according to taste. The beans may be parboiled in water for a half hour before beginning to bake, and the length of time thereby lessened. They should be well drained before adding the milk, however.

Stewed Beans.—Soak a quart of white beans in water over night. In the morning drain, turn hot water over them an inch deep or more, cover, and place on the range where they will only just simmer, adding boiling water if needed. When nearly tender, add salt to taste, a tablespoonful of sugar if desired, and half a cup of good sweet cream. Cook slowly an hour or more longer, but let them be full of juice when taken up, never cooked down dry and mealy.

Mashed Beans.—Soak over night in cold water, a quart of nice white beans. When ready to cook, drain, put into boiling water, and boil till perfectly tender, and the water nearly evaporated. Take up, rub through a colander to remove the skins, season with salt and a half cup of cream, put in a shallow pudding dish, smooth the top with a spoon, and brown in the oven.

Stewed Lima Beans.—Put the beans into boiling water, and cook till tender, but not till they fall to pieces. Fresh beans should cook an hour or more, and dry ones require from two to three hours unless previously soaked. They are much better to simmer slowly than to boil hard. They should be cooked nearly dry. Season with salt, and a cup of thin cream, to each pint of beans. Simmer for a few minutes after the cream is turned in. Should it happen that the beans become tender before the water is sufficiently evaporated, do not drain off the water, but add a little thicker cream, and thicken the whole with a little flour. A little flour stirred in with the cream, even when the water is nearly evaporated may be preferred by some.

Succotash.—Boil one part Lima beans and two parts sweet corn separately until both are nearly tender. Put them together, and simmer gently till done. Season with salt and sweet cream. Fresh corn and beans may be combined in the same proportions, but as the beans will be likely to require the most time for cooking, they should be put to boil first, and the corn added when the beans are about half done, unless it is exceptionally hard, in which case it must be added sooner.

Pulp Succotash.—Score the kernels of some fresh green corn with a sharp knife blade, then with the back of a knife scrape out all the pulp, leaving the hulls on the cob. Boil the pulp in milk ten or fifteen minutes, or until well done. Cook some fresh shelled beans until tender, and rub them through a colander. Put together an equal quantity of the beans thus prepared and the cooked corn pulp, season with salt and sweet cream, boil together for a few minutes, and serve. Kornlet and dried Lima beans may be made into succotash in a similar manner.

LENTILS.

Description.—Several varieties of the lentil are cultivated for food, but all are nearly alike in composition and nutritive value. They have long been esteemed as an article of diet. That they were in ordinary use among the Hebrews is shown by the frequent mention of them in Scripture. It is thought that the red pottage of Esau was made from the red variety of this legume.

The ancient Egyptians believed that a diet of lentils would tend to make their children good tempered, cheerful, and wise, and for this reason constituted it their principal food. A gravy made of lentils is largely used with their rice by the natives of India, at the present day.

The meal which lentils yield is of great richness, and generally contains more casein than either beans or peas. The skin, however, is tough and indigestible, and being much smaller than peas, when served without rejecting the skins, they appear to be almost wholly of tough, fibrous material; hence they are of little value except for soups, *purees*, toasts, and other such dishes as require the rejection of the skin. Lentils have a stronger flavor than any of the other legumes, and their taste is not so generally liked until one has become accustomed to it.

Lentils are prepared and cooked in the same manner as dried peas, though they require somewhat less time for cooking.

The large dark variety is better soaked for a time previous to cooking, or parboiled for a half hour and then put into new water, to make them less strong in flavor and less dark in color.

RECIPES.

Lentil Puree.—Cook the lentils and rub through a colander as for peas *puree*. Season, and serve in the same manner.

Lentils Mashed with Beans.—Lentils may be cooked and prepared in the same manner as directed for mashed peas, but they are less strong in flavor if about one third to one half cooked white beans are used with them.

Lentil Gravy with Rice.—Rub a cupful of cooked lentils through a colander to remove the skins, add one cup of rich milk, part cream if it can be afforded, and salt if desired. Heat to boiling, and thicken with a teaspoonful of flour rubbed smooth in a little cold milk. Serve hot on nicely steamed or boiled rice, or with well cooked macaroni.

TABLE TOPICS.

The men who kept alive the flame of learning and piety in the Middle Ages were mainly vegetarians.—*Sir William Axon.*

According to Xenophon, Cyrus, king of Persia, was brought up on a diet of water, bread, and cresses, till his fifteenth year, when honey and raisins were added; and the family names of Fabii and Lentuli were derived from their customary diet.

Thomson, in his poem, "The Seasons," written one hundred and sixty years ago, pays the following tribute to a diet composed of seeds and vegetable products:—

"With such a liberal hand has Nature flung
These seeds abroad, blown them about in winds— ...
But who their virtues can declare? who pierce,
With vision pure, into those secret stores
Of health and life and joy—the food of man,
While yet he lived in innocence and told
A length of golden years, unfleshed in blood?
A stranger to the savage arts of life—
Death, rapine, carnage, surfeit, and disease—
The *lord*, and not the *tyrant* of the world."

Most assuredly I do believe that body and mind are much influenced by the kind of food habitually depended upon. I can never stray among the village people of our windy capes without now and then coming upon a human being who looks as if he had been split, salted, and dried, like the salt fish which has built up his arid organism. If the body is modified by the food which nourishes it, the mind and character very certainly will be modified by it also. We know enough of their close connection with each other to be sure of what without any statistical observation to prove it.—*Oliver Wendell Holmes.*

The thoughts and feelings which the food we partake of provokes, are not remarked in common life, but they, nevertheless, have their significance. A man who daily sees cows and calves slaughtered, or who kills them himself, hogs "stuck," hens "plucked," etc., cannot possibly retain any true feeling for the sufferings of his own species....Doubtless, the majority of flesh-eaters do not reflect upon the manner in which this food comes to them, but this thoughtlessness, far from being a virtue, is the parent of many vices....How very different are the thoughts and sentiments produced by the non-flesh diet!—*Gustav Von Struve.*

That the popular idea that beef is necessary for strength is not a correct one, is well illustrated by Xenophon's description of the outfit of a Spartan soldier, whose dietary consisted of the very plainest and simplest vegetable fare. The complete accoutrements of the Spartan soldier, in what we would call heavy marching order, weighed seventy-five pounds, exclusive of the camp, mining, and bridge-building tools and the rations of bread and dried fruit which were issued in weekly installments, and increased the burden of the infantry soldier to ninety, ninety-five, or even to a full hundred pounds. This load was often carried at the rate of four miles an hour for twelve hours *per diem*, day after day, and only when in the burning deserts of southern Syria did the commander of the Grecian auxiliaries think prudent to shorten the usual length of the day's march.

DIET OF TRAINERS.—The following are a few of the restrictions and rules laid down by experienced trainers:—

Little salt. No course vegetables. No pork or veal. Two meals a day; breakfast at eight and dinner at two. No fat meat is allowed, no butter or cheese, pies or pastry.

VEGETABLES

Vegetables used for culinary purposes comprise roots and tubers, as potatoes, turnips, etc.; shoots and stems, as asparagus and sea-kale; leaves and inflorescence, as spinach and cabbage; immature seeds, grains, and seed receptacles, as green peas, corn, and string-beans; and a few of the fruity products, as the tomato and the squash. Of these the tubers rank the highest in nutritive value.

Vegetables are by no means the most nutritious diet, as water enters largely into their composition; but food to supply perfectly the needs of the vital economy, must contain water and indigestible as well as nutritive elements. Thus they are dietetically of great value, since they furnish a large quantity of organic fluids. Vegetables are rich in mineral elements, and are also of service in giving bulk to food. An exclusive diet of vegetables, however, would give too great bulk, and at the same time fail to supply the proper amount of food elements. To furnish the requisite amount of nitrogenous material for one day, if potatoes alone were depended upon as food, a person would need to consume about nine pounds; of turnips, sixteen pounds; of parsnips, eighteen pounds; of cabbage, twenty-two pounds. Hence it is wise to use them in combination with other articles of diet—grains, whole-wheat bread, etc.—that supplement the qualities lacking in the vegetables.

To Select Vegetables.—All roots and tubers should be plump, free from decay, bruises, and disease, and with fresh, unshriveled skins. They are good from the time of maturing until they begin to germinate. Sprouted vegetables are unfit for food. Potato sprouts contain a poison allied to belladonna. All vegetables beginning to decay are unfit for food.

Green vegetables to be wholesome should be freshly gathered, crisp, and juicy; those which have lain long in the market are very questionable food. In Paris, a law forbids a market-man to offer for sale any green vegetable kept more than one day. The use of stale vegetables is known to have been the cause of serious illness.

Keeping Vegetables—If necessary to keep green vegetables for any length of time, do not put them in water, as that will dissolve and destroy some of their juices; but lay them in a cool, dark place,—on a stone floor is best,—and do not remove their outer leaves until needed. They should be cooked the day they are gathered, if possible. The best way to freshen those with the stems when withered is to cut off a bit of the stem or stem-end, and set only the cut part in water. The vegetables will then absorb enough water to replace what has been lost by evaporation.

Peas and beans should not be shelled until wanted. If, however, they are not used as soon as shelled, cover them with pods and put in a cool place.

Winter vegetables can be best kept wholesome by storing in a cool, dry place of even temperature, and where neither warmth, moisture, nor light is present to induce decay or germination. They should be well sorted, the bruised or decayed, rejected, and the rest put into clean bins or boxes; and should be dry and clean when stored. Vegetables soon absorb bad flavors if left near anything odorous or decomposing, and are thus rendered unwholesome. They should be looked over often, and decayed ones removed. Vegetables, to be kept fit for food, should on no account be stored in a cellar with barrels of fermenting pickle brine, soft soap, heaps of decomposing rubbish, and other similar things frequently found in the dark, damp vegetable cellars of modern houses.

Preparation and Cooking.—Most vegetables need thorough washing before cooking. Roots and tubers should be well cleaned before paring. A vegetable brush or a small whisk broom is especially serviceable for this purpose. If necessary to wash shelled beans and peas, it can best be accomplished by putting them in a colander and dipping in and out of large pans of water until clean. Spinach, lettuce, and other leaves may be cleaned the same way.

Vegetables admit of much variety in preparation for the table, and are commonly held to require the least culinary skill of any article of diet. This is a mistake. Though the usual processes employed to make vegetables palatable are simple, yet many cooks, from carelessness or lack of knowledge of their nature and composition, convert some of the most nutritious vegetables into dishes almost worthless as food or almost impossible of digestion. It requires no little care and skill to cook vegetables so that they will neither be underdone nor overdone, and so that they will retain their natural flavors.

A general rule, applicable to all vegetables to be boiled or stewed, is to cook them in as little water as may be without burning. The salts and nutrient juices are largely lost in the water; and if this needs to be drained off, much of the nutriment is apt to be wasted. Many cooks throw away the true richness, while they serve the "husks" only. Condiments and seasonings may cover insipid taste, but they cannot restore lost elements. Vegetables contain so much water in their composition that it is not necessary to add large quantities for cooking, as in the case of the grains and legumes, which have lost nearly all their moisture in the ripening process. Some vegetables are much better cooked without the addition of water.

Vegetables to be cooked by boiling should be put into boiling water; and since water loses its goodness by boiling, vegetables should be put in as soon as the boiling begins. The process of cooking should be continuous, and in general gentle heat is best. Remember that when water is boiling, the temperature is not increased by violent bubbling. Keep the cooking utensil closely covered. If water is added, let it also be boiling hot.

Vegetables not of uniform size should be so assorted that those of the same size may be cooked together, or large ones may be divided. Green vegetables retain their color best if cook rapidly. Soda is sometimes added to the water in which the vegetables are cooked, for the purpose of preserving their colors, but this practice is very harmful.

Vegetables should be cooked until they are perfectly tender but not overdone. Many cooks spoil their vegetables by cooking them too long, while quite as many more serve them in an underdone state to preserve their form. Either plan makes them less palatable, and likely to be indigestible.

Steaming or baking is preferable for most vegetables, because their finer flavors are more easily retained, and their food value suffers less diminution. Particularly is this true of tubers.

The time required for cooking depends much upon the age and freshness of the vegetables, as well as the method of cooking employed. Wilted vegetables require a longer time for cooking than fresh ones.

Time Required for Cooking.—The following is the approximate length of time required for cooking some of the more commonly used vegetables:—

Potatoes, baked, 30 to 45 minutes.

Potatoes, steamed, 20 to 40 minutes.

Potatoes, boiled (in jackets), 20 to 25 minutes after the water is fairly boiling.

Potatoes, pared, about 20 minutes if of medium size; if very large, they will require from 25 to 45 minutes.

Green corn, young, from 15 to 20 minutes.

Peas, 25 to 30 minutes.

Asparagus, 15 to 20 minutes, young; 30 to 50 if old.

Tomatoes, 1 to 2 hours.

String beans and shelled beans, 45 to 60 minutes or longer.

Beets, boiled, 1 hour if young; old, 3 to 5 hours.

Beets, baked, 3 to 6 hours. Carrots, 1 to 2 hours.

Parsnips, 45 minutes, young; old, 1 to 2 hours.

Turnips, young, 45 minutes; old, 1-1/2 to 2 hours.

Winter squash, 1 hour. Cabbage, young, 1 hour; old, 2 to 3 hours.

Vegetable oysters, 1 to 2 hours.

Celery, 20 to 30 minutes.

Spinach, 20 to 60 minutes or more.

Cauliflower, 20 to 40 minutes.

Summer squash, 20 to 60 minutes.

If vegetables after being cooked cannot be served at once, dish them up as soon as done, and place the dishes in a *bain marie* or in pans of hot water, where they will keep of even temperature, but not boil. Vegetables are never so good after standing, but they spoil less kept in this way than any other. The water in the pans should be of equal depth with the food in the dishes. Stewed vegetables and others prepared with a sauce, may, when cold, be reheated in a similar manner.

If salt is to be used to season, one third of a teaspoonful for each pint of cooked vegetables is an ample quantity.

THE IRISH POTATO.

Description.—The potato, a plant of the order *Solanaceae*, is supposed to be indigenous to South America. Probably it was introduced into Europe by the Spaniards early in the sixteenth century, but cultivated only as a curiosity. To Sir Walter Raleigh, however, is usually given the credit of its introduction as a food, he having imported it from Virginia to Ireland in 1586, where its valuable nutritive qualities were first appreciated. The potato has so long constituted the staple article of diet in Ireland, that it has come to be commonly, though incorrectly, known as the Irish potato.

The edible portion of the plant is the tuber, a thick, fleshy mass or enlarged portion of an underground stem, having upon its surface a number of little buds, or "eyes," each capable of independent growth. The tuber is made up of little cells filled with starch granules, surrounded and permeated with a watery fluid containing a small percentage of the albuminous or nitrogenous elements. In cooking, heat coagulates the albumen within and between the cells, while the starch granules absorb the watery portion, swell, and distend the cells. The cohesion between these is also destroyed, and they easily separate. When these changes are complete, the potato becomes a loose, farinaceous mass, or "mealy." When, however, the liquid portion is not wholly absorbed, and the cells are but imperfectly separated, the potato appears waxen, watery, or soggy. In a mealy state the potato is easily digested; but when waxy or water-soaked, it is exceedingly trying to the digestive powers.

It is obvious, then, that the great *desideratum* in cooking the potato, is to promote the expansion and separation of its cells; in other words, to render it mealy. Young potatoes are always waxy, and consequently less wholesome than ripe ones. Potatoes which have been frozen and allowed to thaw quickly are much sweeter and more watery, because in thawing the starch changes into sugar. Frozen potatoes should be thawed in cold water and cooked at once, or kept frozen until ready for use.

Preparation and Cooking.—Always pare potatoes very thin. Much of the most nutritious part of the tuber lies next its outer covering; so care should be taken to waste as little as possible. Potatoes cooked with the skins on are undoubtedly better than those pared. The chief mineral element contained in the potato is potash, an important constituent of the blood. Potash salts are freely soluble in water, and when the skin is removed, there is nothing to prevent these salts from escaping into the water in which the potato is boiled. If the potato is cooked in its "jacket," the skin, which does not in general burst open until the potato is nearly done, serves to keep this valuable element largely inside the potato while cooking. For the same reason it is better not to pare potatoes and put them in water to soak over night, as many cooks are in the habit of doing, to have them in readiness for cooking for breakfast.

Potatoes to be pared should be first washed and dried. It is a good plan to wash quite a quantity at one time, to be used as needed. After paring, drop at once into cold water and rinse them thoroughly. It is a careless habit to allow pared potatoes to fall among the skins, as in this way they become stained, and appear black and discolored after cooking. Scrubbing with a vegetable brush is by far the best means for cleaning potatoes to be cooked with the skins on.

When boiled in their skins, the waste, according to Letheby, is about three per cent, while without them it is not less than fourteen per cent, or more than two ounces in every pound. Potatoes boiled without skins should be cooked very gently.

Steaming, roasting, and baking are much better methods for cooking potatoes than boiling, for reasons already given. Very old potatoes are best stewed or mashed. When withered or wilted, they are freshened by standing in cold water for an hour or so before cooking. If diseased or badly sprouted, potatoes are wholly unfit for food.

RECIPES.

Boiled Potatoes (in Jackets).—Choose potatoes of uniform size, free from specks. Wash and scrub them well with a coarse cloth or brush; dig out all eyes and rinse in cold water; cook in just enough water to prevent burning, till easily pierced with a fork, not till they have burst the skin and fallen in pieces. Drain thoroughly, take out the potatoes, and place them in the oven for five minutes, or place the kettle back on the range; remove the skins, and cover with a cloth to absorb all moisture, and let them steam three or four minutes. By either method they will be dry and mealy. In removing the skins, draw them off without cutting the potatoes.

Boiled Potatoes (without Skins).—Pare very thin, and wash clean. If not of an equal size, cut the larger potatoes in two. Cook in only sufficient water to prevent burning until a fork will easily pierce their center; drain thoroughly, place the kettle back on the range, cover with a cloth to absorb the moisture, and let them dry four or five minutes. Shake the kettle several times while they are drying, to make them floury.

Steamed Potatoes.—Potatoes may be steamed either with or without the skin. Only mature potatoes can be steamed. Prepare as for boiling; place in a steamer, over boiling water, and steam until tender. If water is needed to replenish, let it always be boiling hot, and not allow the potatoes to stop steaming, or they will be watery. When done, uncover, remove the potatoes to the oven, and let them dry a few minutes. If peeled before steaming, shake the steamer occasionally, to make them floury.

Roasted Potatoes.—Potatoes are much more rich and mealy roasted than cooked in any other way. Wash them very carefully, dry with a cloth, and wrap in tissue paper; bury in ashes not too hot, then cover with coals and roast until tender. The coals will need renewing occasionally, unless the roasting is done very close to the main fire.

Baked Potatoes.—Choose large, smooth potatoes as near the same size as possible; wash and scrub with a brush until perfectly clean; dry with a cloth, and bake in a moderately hot oven until a fork will easily pierce them, or until they yield to pressure between the fingers. They are better turned about occasionally. In a slow oven the skins become hardened and thickened, and much of the most nutritious portion is wasted. When done, press each one till it bursts slightly, as that will allow the steam to escape, and prevent the potatoes from becoming soggy. They should be served at once, in a folded napkin placed in a hot dish. Cold baked potatoes may be warmed over by rebaking, if of good quality and not overdone the first time.

Stuffed Potato.—Prepare and bake large potatoes of equal size, as directed in the preceding recipe. When done, cut them evenly three fourths of an inch from the end, and scrape out the inside, taking care not to break the skins. Season the potato with salt and a little thick sweet cream, being careful not to have it too moist, and beat thoroughly with a fork until light; refill the skins with the seasoned potato, fit the broken portions together, and reheat in the oven. When hot throughout, wrap the potatoes in squares of white tissue paper fringed at both ends. Twist the ends of the paper lightly together above the fringe, and stand the potatoes in a vegetable dish with the cut end uppermost. When served, the potatoes are held in the hand, one end of the paper untwisted, the top of the potato removed, and the contents eaten with a fork or spoon.

Stuffed Potatoes No. 2.—Prepare large, smooth potatoes, bake until tender, and cut them in halves; scrape out the inside carefully, so as not to break the skins; mash smoothly, mix thoroughly with one third freshly prepared cottage cheese; season with nice sweet cream, and salt if desired. Fill the shells with the mixture, place cut side uppermost, in a pudding dish, and brown in the oven.

Mashed Potatoes.—Peel and slice potatoes enough to make two quarts; put into boiling water and cook until perfectly tender, but not much broken; drain, add salt to taste; turn into a hot earthen dish, and set in the oven for a few moments to dry. Break up the potatoes with a silver fork; add nearly a cup of cream, and beat hard at least five minutes till light and creamy; serve at once, or they will become heavy. If preferred, the potatoes may be rubbed through a hot sieve into a hot plate, or mashed with a potato beetle, but they are less light and flaky when mashed with a beetle. If cream for seasoning is not obtainable, a well-beaten egg makes a very good substitute. Use in the proportion of one egg to about five potatoes. For mashed potatoes, if all utensils and ingredients are first heated, the result will be much better.

New Potatoes.—When potatoes are young and freshly gathered, the skins are easiest removed by taking each one in a coarse cloth and rubbing it; a little coarse salt used in the cloth will be found serviceable for this purpose. If almost ripe, scrape with a blunt knife, wash very clean, and rinse in cold water. Boiling is the best method of cooking; new potatoes are not good steamed. Use only sufficient water to cover, and boil till tender. Drain thoroughly, cover closely with a clean cloth, and dry before serving.

Cracked Potatoes.—Prepare and boil new potatoes as in the preceding recipe, and when ready to serve, crack each by pressing lightly upon it with the back of a spoon, lay them in a hot dish, salt to taste, and pour over them a cup of hot thin cream or rich milk.

Creamed Potatoes.—Take rather small, new potatoes and wash well; rub off all the skins; cut in halves, or if quite large, quarter them. Put a pint of divided potatoes into a broad-bottomed, shallow saucepan; pour over them a cup of thin sweet cream, add salt if desired; heat just to the boiling point, then allow them to simmer gently till perfectly tender, tossing them occasionally in the stewpan to prevent their burning on the bottom. Serve hot.

Scalloped Potatoes.—Pare the potatoes and slice thin; put them in layers in an earthen pudding dish, dredge each layer lightly with flour, and salt, and pour over all enough good, rich milk to cover well. Cover, and bake rather slowly till tender, removing the cover just long enough before the potatoes are done, to brown nicely. If preferred, a little less milk may be used, and a cup of thin cream added when the potatoes are nearly done.

Stewed Potato.—Pare the potatoes and slice rather thin. Put into boiling water, and cook until nearly tender, but not broken. Have some rich milk boiling in the inner dish of a double boiler, add to it a little salt, then stir in for each pint of milk a heaping teaspoonful of corn starch or rice flour, rubbed smooth in a little cold milk. Stir until it thickens. Drain the potatoes, turn them into the hot sauce, put the dish in the outer boiler, and cook for a half hour or longer. Cold boiled potatoes may be sliced and used in the same way. Cold baked potatoes sliced and stewed thus for an hour or more, make a particularly appetizing dish.

Potatoes Stewed with Celery.—Pare and slice the potatoes, and put them into a stewpan with two or three tablespoonfuls of minced celery. Use only the white part of the celery and mince it finely. Cover the whole with milk sufficient to cook and prevent burning, and stew until tender. Season with cream and salt.

Potato Snowballs.—Cut largo potatoes into quarters; if small, leave them undivided; boil in just enough water to cover. When tender, drain and dry in the usual way. Take up two or three pieces at a time in a strong, clean cloth, and press them compactly together in the shape of balls. Serve in a folded napkin on a hot dish.

Potato Cakes.—Make nicely seasoned, cold mashed potato into small round cakes about one half an inch thick. Put them on a baking tin, brush them over with sweet cream, and bake in a hot oven till golden brown.

Potato Cakes with Egg.—Bake nice potatoes till perfectly tender; peel, mash thoroughly, and to each pint allow the yolks of two eggs which have been boiled until mealy, then rubbed perfectly smooth through a fine wire sieve, and one half cup of rich milk. Add salt to taste, mix all well together, form the potato into small cakes, place them on oiled tins, and brown ten or fifteen minutes in the oven.

Potato Puff.—Mix a pint of mashed potato (cold is just as good if free from lumps) with a half cup of cream and the well-beaten yolk of an egg; salt to taste and beat till smooth; lastly, stir in the white of the egg beaten to a stiff froth. Pile up in a rocky form on a bright tin dish, and bake in a quick oven until heated throughout and lightly browned. Serve at once.

Browned Potatoes.—Slice cold potatoes evenly, place them on an oiled tin, and brown in a very quick oven; or slice lengthwise and lay on a wire broiler or bread-toaster, and brown over hot coals. Sprinkle with a little salt if desired, and serve hot with sweet cream as dressing.

Ornamental Potatoes.—No vegetable can be made palatable in so many ways as the potato, and few can be arranged in such pretty shapes. Mashed potatoes made moist with cream, can easily be made into cones, pyramids, or mounds. Cold mashed potatoes may be cut into many fancy shapes with a cookie-cutter, wet with a little cold water, and browned in the oven.

Mounds of potatoes are very pretty smoothed and strewn with well-cooked vermicelli broken into small bits, and then lightly browned in the oven.

Scoring the top of a dish of mashed potato deeply in triangles, stars, and crosses, with the back of a carving knife, and then browning lightly, gives a very pretty effect.

Broiled Potato.—Mashed potatoes, if packed firmly while warm into a sheet-iron bread tin which has been dipped in cold water, may be cut into slices when cold, brushed with cream, and browned on a broiler over hot coals.

Warmed-over Potatoes.—Cut cold boiled potatoes into very thin slices; heat a little cream to boiling in a saucepan; add the potato, season lightly with salt if desired, and cook until the cream is absorbed, stirring occasionally so as to prevent scorching or breaking the slices.

Vegetable Hash.—With one quart finely sliced potato, chop one carrot, one red beet, one white turnip, all boiled, also one or two stalks of celery. Put all together in a stewpan, cover closely, and set in the oven; when hot, pour over them a cup of boiling cream, stir well together, and serve hot.

THE SWEET POTATO.

Description.—The sweet potato is a native of the Malayan Archipelago, where it formerly grew wild; thence it was taken to Spain, and from Spain to England and other parts of the globe. It was largely used in Europe as a delicacy on the tables of the rich before the introduction of the common potato, which has now taken its place and likewise its name. The sweet potato is the article referred as potato by Shakespeare and other English writers, previous to the middle of the seventeenth century.

Preparation and Cooking.—What has been said in reference to the common potato, is generally applicable to the sweet potato; it may be prepared and cooked in nearly all the ways of the Irish potato.

In selecting sweet potatoes, choose firm, plump roots, free from any sprouts; if sprouted they will have a poor flavor, and are likely to be watery.

The sweet potato is best cooked with the skin on; but all discolored portions and the dry portion at each end, together with all branchlets, should be carefully removed, and the potato well washed, and if to be baked or roasted, well dried with a cloth before placing in the oven.

The average time required for boiling is about fifty minutes; baking, one hour; steaming, about one hour; roasting, one and one half hours.

RECIPES.

Baked Sweet Potatoes.—Select those of uniform size, wash clean, cutting out any imperfect spots, wipe dry, put into moderately hot oven, and bake about one hour, or until the largest will yield to gentle pressure between the fingers. Serve at once without peeling. Small potatoes are best steamed, since if baked, the skins will take up nearly the whole potato.

Baked Sweet Potato No. 2.—Select potatoes of medium size, wash and trim but do not pare, and put on the upper grate of the oven. For a peek of potatoes, put in the lower part of the oven in a large shallow pan a half pint of hot water. The water may be turned directly upon the oven bottom if preferred. Bake slowly, turning once when half done. Serve in their skins, or peel, slice, and return to the oven until nicely browned.

Boiled Sweet Potatoes.—Choose potatoes of equal size; do not pare, but after cleaning them well and removing any imperfect spots, put into cold water and boll until they can be easily pierced with a fork; drain thoroughly, and lay them on the top grate in the oven to dry for five or ten minutes. Peel as soon as dry, and send at once to the table, in a hot dish covered with a folded napkin. Sweet potatoes are much better baked than boiled.

Steamed Sweet Potatoes.—Wash the potatoes well, cut out any discolored portions, and steam over a kettle of boiling water until they can be easily pierced with a fork, not allowing the water in the pot to cease boiling for a moment. Steam only sufficient to cook them, else they will be watery.

Browned Sweet Potatoes.—Slice cold, cooked sweet potatoes evenly, place on slightly oiled tins in a hot oven, and brown.

Mashed Sweet Potatoes.—Either bake or steam nice sweet potatoes, and when tender, peel, mash them well, and season with cream and salt to taste. They may be served at once, or made into patties and browned in the oven.

Potato Hash.—Take equal parts of cold Irish and sweet potatoes; chop fine and mix thoroughly; season with salt if desired, and add sufficient thin cream to moisten well. Turn into a stewpan, and heat gently until boiling, tossing continually, that all parts become heated alike, and serve at once.

Roasted Sweet Potatoes.—Wash clean and wipe dry, potatoes of uniform size, wrap with tissue paper, cover with hot ashes, and then with coals from a hardwood fire; unless near the main fire, the coals will need renewing a few times. This will require a longer time than by any other method, but they are much nicer. The slow, continuous heat promotes their mealiness. When tender, brush the ashes off with a broom, and wipe with a dry cloth. Send to the table in their jackets.

To Dry Sweet Potatoes.—Carefully clean and drop them into boiling water. Let them remain until the skins can be easily slipped off; then cut into slices and spread on racks to dry. To prepare for cooking, soak over night, and boil the next day.

TURNIPS.

Description.—The turnip belongs to the order *Cruciferæ*, signifying "cross flowers," so called because their four petals are arranged in the form of a cross. It is a native of Europe and the temperate portions of Asia, growing wild in borders of fields and waste places. The ancient Roman gastronomists considered the turnip, when prepared in the following manner, a dish fit for epicures: "After boiling, extract the water from them, and season with cummin, rue or benzoin, pounded in a mortar; afterward add honey, vinegar, gravy, and boiled grapes. Allow the whole to simmer, and serve."

Under cultivation, the turnip forms an agreeable culinary esculent; but on account of the large proportion of water entering into its composition, its nutritive value is exceedingly low. The Swedish, or Rutabaga, variety is rather more nutritive than the white, but its stronger flavor renders it less palatable. Unlike the potato, the turnip contains no starch, but instead, a gelatinous substance called pectose, which during the boiling process is changed into a vegetable jelly called pectine. The white lining just inside the skin is usually bitter; hence the tuber should be peeled sufficiently deep to remove it. When well cooked, turnips are quite easily digested.

Preparation and Cooking.—Turnips are good for culinary purposes only from the time of their ripening till they begin to sprout. The process of germination changes their proximate elements, and renders them less fit for food. Select turnips which are plump and free from disease. A turnip that is wilted, or that appears spongy, pithy, or cork-like when cut, is not fit for food.

Prepare turnips for cooking by thoroughly washing and scraping, if young and tender, or by paring if more mature. If small, they may be cooked whole; if large, they should be cut across the grain into slices a half inch in thickness. If cooked whole, care must be taken to select those of uniform size; and if sliced, the slices must be of equal thickness.

RECIPES.

Boiled Turnips.—Turnips, like other vegetables, should be boiled in as small an amount of water as possible. Great care must be taken, however, that the kettle does not get dry, as scorched turnip is spoiled. An excellent precaution, in order to keep them from scorching in case the water becomes low, is to place an inverted saucer or sauce-dish in the bottom of the kettle before putting in the turnips. Put into boiling water, cook rapidly until sufficiently tender to pierce easily with a fork; too much cooking discolors and renders them strong in flavor. Boiled turnips should be drained very thoroughly, and all water pressed out before preparing for the table. The age, size, and variety of the turnip will greatly vary the time necessary for its cooking. The safest rule is to allow plenty of time, and test with a fork. Young turnips will cook in about forty-five minutes; old turnips, sliced, require from one and a quarter to two hours. If whole or cut in halves, they require a proportionate length of time. White turnips require much, less cooking than yellow ones.

Baked Turnips.—Select turnips of uniform size; wash and wipe, but do not pare; place on the top grate of a moderately hot oven; bake two or more hours or until perfectly tender; peel and serve at once, either mashed or with cream sauce. Turnips are much sweeter baked than when cooked in any other way.

Creamed Turnips.—Pare, but do not cut, young sweet white turnips; boil till tender in a small quantity of water; drain and dry well. Cook a tablespoonful of flour in a pint of rich milk or part cream; arrange the turnips in a baking dish, pour the sauce over them, add salt if desired, sprinkle the top with grated bread crumbs, and brown in a quick oven.

Chopped Turnips.—Chop well-boiled white turnips very fine, add salt to taste and sufficient lemon juice to moisten. Turn into a saucepan and heat till hot, gently lifting and stirring constantly. Cold boiled turnip may be used advantageously in this way.

Mashed Turnips.—Wash the turnips, pare, and drop into boiling water. Cook until perfectly tender; turn into a colander and press out the water with a plate or large spoon; mash until free from lumps, season with a little sweet cream, and salt if desired. If the turnips are especially watery, one or two hot, mealy potatoes mashed with them will be an improvement.

Scalloped Turnips.—Prepare and boil whole white turnips until nearly tender; cut into thin slices, lay in an earthen pudding dish, pour over them a white sauce sufficient to cover, made by cooking a tablespoonful of flour in a pint of milk, part cream if preferred, until thickened. Season with salt, sprinkle the top lightly with grated bread crumbs, and bake in a quick oven until a rich brown. Place the baking dish on a clean plate, and serve. Rich milk or cream may be used instead of white sauce, if preferred.

Steamed Turnips.—Select turnips of uniform size, wash, pare, and steam rapidly till they can be easily pierced with a fork; mash, or serve with lemon juice or cream sauce, as desired.

Stewed Turnips.—Prepare and slice some young, fresh white turnips, boil or steam about twenty minutes, drain thoroughly, turn into a saucepan with a cup of new milk for each quart of turnips; simmer gently until tender, season with salt if desired, and serve.

Turnips in Juice.—Wash young white turnips, peel, and boil whole in sufficient water to keep them from burning. Cover closely and cook gently until tender, by which time the water in the kettle should be reduced to the consistency of syrup. Serve at once.

Turnips with Cream Sauce.—Wash and pare the turnips, cut them into half-inch dice, and cook in boiling water until tender. Meanwhile prepare a cream sauce as directed for Scalloped Turnips, using thin cream in place of milk. Drain the turnips, pour the cream sauce over them, let them boil up once, and serve.

PARSNIPS.

Description.—The common garden parsnip is derived by cultivation from the wild parsnip, indigenous to many parts of Europe and the north of Asia, and cultivated since Roman times. It is not only used for culinary purposes, but a wine is made from it. In the north of Ireland a table beer is brewed from its fermented product and hops.

The percentage of nutritive elements contained in the parsnip is very small; so small, indeed, that one pound of parsnips affords hardly one fifth of an ounce of nitrogenous or muscle-forming material. The time required for its digestion, varies from two and one half to three and one half hours.

Preparation and Cooking.—Wash and trim off any rough portions: scrape well with a knife to remove the skins, and drop at once into cold water to prevent discoloration. If the parsnips are smooth-skinned, fresh, and too small to need dividing, they need only be washed thoroughly before cooking, as the skins can be easily removed by rubbing with a clean towel. Reject those that are wilted, pithy, coarse, or stringy. Large parsnips should be divided, for if cooked whole, the outside is likely to become soft before the center is tender. They may be either split lengthwise or sliced. Parsnips may be boiled, baked, or steamed; but like all other vegetables containing a large percentage of water, are preferable steamed or baked.

The time required for cooking young parsnips, is about forty-five minutes; when old, they require from one to two hours.

RECIPES.

Baked Parsnips.—Wash, thoroughly, but do not scrape the roots; bake the same as potatoes. When tender, remove the skins, slice, and serve with cream or an egg sauce prepared as directed for Parsnips with Egg Sauce. They are also very nice mashed and seasoned with cream. Baked and steamed parsnips are far sweeter than boiled ones.

Baked Parsnips No. 2.—Wash, scrape, and divide; drop into boiling water, a little more than sufficient to cook them, and boil gently till thoroughly tender. There should remain about one half pint of the liquor when the parsnips are done. Arrange on an earthen plate or shallow pudding dish, not more than one layer deep; cover with the juice, and bake, basting frequently until the juice is all absorbed, and the parsnips delicately browned. Serve at once.

Boiled Parsnips.—Clean, scrape, drop into a small quantity of boiling water, and cook until they can be easily pierced, with a fork. Drain thoroughly, cut the parsnips in slices, and mash or serve with a white sauce, to which a little lemon juice may be added if desired.

Browned Parsnips.—Slice cold parsnips into rather thick pieces, and brown as directed for browned potatoes.

Creamed Parsnips.—Bake or steam the parsnips until tender; slice, add salt if desired, and a cup of thin sweet cream. Let them stew slowly until nearly dry, or if preferred, just boil up once and serve.

Mashed Parsnips.—Wash and scrape, dropping at once into cold water to prevent discoloration. Slice thinly and steam, or bake whole until perfectly tender. When done, mash until free from lumps, removing all hard or stringy portions; add salt to taste and a few spoonfuls of thick sweet cream, and serve.

Parsnips with Cream Sauce.—Bake as previously directed. When tender, slice, cut into cubes, and pour over them a cream sauce prepared as for Turnips with Cream Sauce. Boil up together once, and serve.

Parsnips with Egg Sauce.—Scrape, wash, and slice thinly, enough parsnips to make three pints; steam, bake, or boil them until very tender. If boiled, turn into a colander and drain well. Have ready an egg sauce, for preparing which heat a pint of rich milk or very thin cream to boiling, stir into it a level tablespoonful of flour rubbed smooth with a little milk. Let this boil a few minutes, stirring constantly until the flour is well cooked and the sauce thickened; then add slowly the well-beaten yolk of one egg, stirring rapidly so that it shall be well mingled with the whole; add salt to taste; let it boil up once, pour over the parsnips, and serve. The sauce should be of the consistency of thick cream.

Parsnips with Potatoes.—Wash, scrape, and slice enough parsnips to make two and a half quarts. Pare and slice enough potatoes to make one pint. Cook together in a small quantity of water. When tender, mash smoothly, add salt, the yolks of two eggs well beaten, and a cup of rich milk. Beat well together, put into an earthen or china dish, and brown lightly in the oven.

Stewed Parsnips.—Prepare and boil for a half hour; drain, cover with rich milk, add salt if desired, and stew gently till tender.

Stewed Parsnips with Celery.—Prepare and steam or boil some nice ones until about half done. If boiled, drain thoroughly; add salt if desired, and a tablespoonful of minced celery. Turn rich boiling milk over them, cover, and stew fifteen or twenty minutes, or till perfectly tender.

CARROTS.

Description.—The garden carrot is a cultivated variety of a plant belonging to the *Umbettiferæ*, and grows wild in many portions of Europe. The root has long been used for food. By the ancient Greeks and Romans it was much esteemed as a salad. The carrot is said to have been introduced into England by Flemish refugees during the reigns of Elizabeth and James I. Its feathery leaves were used by the ladies as an adornment for their headdresses, in place of plumes. Carrots contain sugar enough for making a syrup from them; they also yield by fermentation and distillation a spirituous liquor. In Germany they are sometimes cut into small pieces, and roasted as a substitute for coffee.

Starch does not enter into the composition of carrots, but a small portion of pectose is found instead. Carrots contain more water than parsnips, and both much cellulose and little nutritive material. Carrots when well cooked form a wholesome food, but one not adapted to weak stomachs, as they are rather hard to digest and tend to flatulence.

Preparation and Cooking.—The suggestions given for the preparation of parsnips are also applicable to carrots; and they may be boiled, steamed, or browned in the same manner. From one to two hours time will be required, according to age, size, variety, and method of cooking.

RECIPES.

Boiled Carrots.—Clean, scrape, drop into boiling water, and cook till tender; drain thoroughly, slice, and serve with a cream sauce. Varieties with strong flavor are better parboiled for fifteen or twenty minutes, and put into fresh boiling water to finish.

Carrots with Egg Sauce.—Wash and scrape well; slice and throw into boiling water, or else steam. When tender, drain thoroughly, and pour over them a sauce prepared the same as for parsnips (page 244), with the addition of a tablespoonful of sugar. Let them boil up once, and serve.

Stewed Carrots.—Prepare young and tender carrots, drop into boiling water, and cook for fifteen or twenty minutes. Drain, slice, and put into a stewpan with rich milk or cream nearly to cover; simmer gently until tender; season with salt and a little chopped parsley.

BEETS.

Description.—The beet is a native of the coasts of the Mediterranean, and is said to owe its botanical name, *beta*, to a fancied resemblance to the Greek letter B. Two varieties are in common use as food, the white and the red beet; while a sub-variety, the sugar beet, is largely cultivated in France, in connection with the beet-sugar industry in that country. The same industry has recently been introduced into this country. It is grown extensively in Germany and Russia, for the same pose, and is also used there in the manufacture of alcohol.

The beet root is characterized by its unusual amount of sugar. It is considered more nutritive than any other esculent tuber except the potato, but the time required for its digestion exceeds that of most vegetables, being three and three fourths hours.

Preparation and Cooking.—Beets, like other tubers, should be fresh, unshriveled, and healthy. Wash carefully, scrubbing with a soft brush to remove all particles of dirt; but avoid scraping, cutting, or breaking, lest the sweet juices escape. In handling for storage, be careful not to bruise or break the skins; and in purchasing from the market, select only such as are perfect.

Beets may be boiled, baked, or steamed. In boiling, if the skin is cut or broken, the juice will escape in the water, and the flavor will be injured; for this reason, beets should not be punctured with a fork to find if done. When tender, the thickest part will yield readily to pressure of the fingers. Beets should be boiled in just as little water as possible, and they will be much better if it has all evaporated by the time they are cooked.

Young beets will boil in one hour, while old beets require from three to five hours; if tough, wilted, and stringy, they cannot be boiled tender. Baked beets require from three to six hours.

RECIPES.

Baked Beets.—Beets are far better baked than boiled, though it takes a longer time to cook properly. French cooks bake them slowly six hours in a covered dish, the bottom of which is lined with well-moistened rye straw; however, they may be baked on the oven grate, like potatoes. Wipe dry after washing, and bake slowly. They are very nice served with a sauce made of equal quantities of lemon juice and whipped cream, with a little salt.

Baked Beets No. 2.—Wash young and tender beets, and place in an earthen baking dish with a very little water; as it evaporates, add more, which must be of boiling temperature. Set into a moderate oven, and according to size of the beets, bake slowly from two to three hours. When tender, remove the skins and dress with lemon juice or cream sauce.

Beets and Potatoes.—Boil newly matured potatoes and young beets separately till tender; then peel and slice. Put thorn in alternate layers in a vegetable dish, with salt to taste, and enough sweet cream nearly to cover. Brown in the oven, and serve at once.

Beet Hash.—Chop quite finely an equal quantity of cold boiled or baked beets and boiled or baked potatoes. Put into a shallow saucepan, add salt and sufficient hot cream to moisten. Toss frequently, and cook until well heated throughout. Serve hot.

Beet Greens.—Take young, tender beets, clean thoroughly without separating the tops and roots. Examine the leaves carefully, and pick off inferior ones. Put into boiling water, and cook for nearly an hour. Drain, press out all water, and chop quite fine. Serve with a dressing of lemon juice or cream, as preferred.

Beet Salad, or Chopped Beets.—Cold boiled or baked beets, chopped quite fine, but not minced, make a nice salad when served with a dressing of lemon juice and whipped cream in the proportion of three tablespoonfuls of lemon juice to one half cup of whipped cream, and salt if desired.

Beet Salad No. 2.—Chop equal parts of boiled beets and fresh young cabbage. Mix thoroughly, add salt to taste, a few tablespoonfuls of sugar, and cover with diluted lemon juice. Equal quantities of cold boiled beets and cold boiled potatoes, chopped fine, thoroughly mixed, and served with a dressing of lemon juice and whipped cream, make a palatable salad. Care should be taken in the preparation of these and the preceding salad, not to chop the vegetables so fine as to admit of their being eaten without mastication.

Boiled Beets.—Wash carefully, drop into boiling water, and cook until tender. When done, drop into cold water for a minute, when the skins can be easily rubbed off with the hand. Slice, and serve hot with lemon juice or with a cream sauce.

Stewed Beets.—Bake beets according to recipe No. 2. Peel, cut in slices, turn into a saucepan, nearly cover with thin cream, simmer for ten or fifteen minutes, add salt if desired, and thicken the gravy with a little corn starch or flour.

CABBAGE.

Description.—The common white garden cabbage is one of the oldest of cultivated vegetables. A variety of the plant known as red cabbage was the delight of ancient gourmands more than eighteen centuries ago. The Egyptians adored it, erected altars to it, and made it the first dish at their repasts. In this they were imitated by the Greeks and Romans.

Hippocrates, the Father of Medicine, considered the cabbage one of the most valuable of remedies, and often prescribed a dish of boiled cabbage to be eaten with salt for patients suffering with violent colic. Erasistratus looked upon it as a sovereign remedy against paralysis, while Cato in his writings affirmed it to be a panacea for all diseases, and believed the use the Romans made of it to have been the means whereby they were able, during six hundred years, to do without the assistance of physicians, whom they had expelled from their territory. The learned philosopher, Pythagoras, composed books in which he lauded its wonderful virtues.

The Germans are so fond of cabbage that it enters into the composition of a majority of their culinary products. The cabbage was first raised in England about 1640, by Sir Anthony Ashley. That this epoch, important to the English horticultural and culinary world, may never be forgotten, a cabbage is represented upon Sir Anthony's monument.

The nutritive value of the cabbage is not high, nearly ninety per cent being water; but it forms an agreeable variety in the list of vegetable foods, and is said to possess marked antiscorbutic virtue. It is, however, difficult of digestion, and therefore not suited to weak stomachs. It would be impossible to sustain life for a lengthened period upon cabbage, since to supply the body with sufficient food elements, the quantity would exceed the rate of digestion and the capacity of the stomach.

M. Chevreul, a French scientist, has ascertained that the peculiar odor given off during the boiling of cabbage is due to the disengagement of sulphureted hydrogen. Cabbage is said to be more easily digested raw than cooked.

Preparation and Cooking.—A good cabbage should have a well-developed, firm head, with fresh, crisp leaves, free from worm-holes and decayed portions. To prepare for cooking, stalk, shake well to free from dirt, and if there are any signs of insects, lay in cold salted water for an hour or so to drive them out. Rinse away the salt water, and if to be boiled, drop into a small quantity of boiling water. Cover closely and boil vigorously until tender. If cooked slowly, it will be watery and stringy, while overdone cabbage is especially insipid and flavorless. If too much water has been used, remove the cover, that evaporation may go on more rapidly; if too little, replenish with boiling water. Cabbage should be cooked in a porcelain-lined or granite-ware sauce pan or a very clean iron kettle. Cabbage may also be steamed, but care must be taken to have the process as rapid as possible. Fresh young cabbage will cook in about one hour; old cabbage requires from two to three hours.

RECIPES.

Baked Cabbage.—Prepare and chop a firm head of young white cabbage, boil until tender, drain, and set aside until nearly cold. Then add two well-beaten eggs, salt to taste, and a half cup of thin cream or rich milk. Mix and bake in a pudding dish until lightly browned.

Boiled Cabbage.—Carefully clean a nice head of cabbage, divide into halves, and with a sharp knife slice very thin, cutting from the center of the head outward. Put into boiling water, cover closely, and cook rapidly until tender; then turn into a colander and drain, pressing gently with the back of a plate. Return to the kettle, add salt to taste, and sufficient sweet cream to moisten well, heat through if at all cooled, dish, and serve at once. If preferred, the cream may be omitted, and the cabbage served with tomato sauce or lemon juice as a dressing.

Cabbage and Tomatoes.—Boil finely chopped cabbage in as little water as possible. When tender, add half the quantity of hot stewed tomatoes, boil together for a few minutes, being careful to avoid burning, season with salt if desired, and serve. If preferred, a little sweet cream may be added just before serving.

Cabbage Celery.—A firm, crisp head of cabbage cut in slices half an inch or an inch thick, and then again into pieces four or five inches long and two or three inches wide, makes a quite appetizing substitute for celery.

Cabbage Hash.—Chop fine, equal parts of cold boiled potatoes and boiled cabbage, and season with salt. To each quart of the mixture add one half or three fourths of a cup of thin cream; mix well and boil till well heated.

Chopped Cabbage or Cabbage Salad.—Take one pint of finely chopped cabbage; pour over it a dressing made of three tablespoonfuls of lemon juice, two tablespoonfuls of sugar, and a half cup of whipped cream, thoroughly beaten together in the order named; or serve with sugar and diluted lemon juice.

Mashed Cabbage.—Cut a fine head of cabbage into quarters, and cook until tender. A half hour before it is done, drop in three good-sized potatoes. When done, take all up in a colander together, press out the water, and mash very fine. Season with cream, and salt if desired.

Stewed Cabbage. Chop nice cabbage quite fine, and put it into boiling water, letting it boil twenty minutes. Turn into a colander and drain thoroughly; return to the kettle, cover with milk, and let it boil till perfectly tender; season with salt and cream to taste. The beaten yolk of an egg, stirred in with the cream, is considered an improvement by some.

CAULIFLOWER AND BROCCOLI.

Description.—These vegetables are botanically allied to the cabbage, and are similar in composition. They are entirely the product of cultivation, and constitute the inflorescence of the plant, which horticultural art has made to grow into a compact head of white color in the cauliflower, and of varying shades of buff, green, and purple in the broccoli. There is very little difference between the two aside from the color, and they are treated alike for culinary purposes. They were known to the Greeks and Romans, and highly appreciated by connoisseurs. They are not as nutritious as the cabbage, but have a more delicate and agreeable flavor.

Preparation and Cooking.—The leaves should be green and fresh, and the heads of cauliflower creamy white; when there are dark spots, it is wilted. The color of broccoli will depend upon the variety, but the head should be firm, with no discolorations. To prepare, pick off the outside leaves, cut the stalk squarely across, about two inches below the flower, and if very thick, split and wash thoroughly in several waters; or better still, hold it under the faucet, flower downward, and allow a constant stream of water to fall over it for several minutes; then place top downward in a pan of lukewarm salted water, to drive out any insects which may be hidden in it; examine carefully for worms just the color of the stalk; tie in a net (mosquito netting, say) to prevent breaking, or place the cauliflower on a plate in a steamer, and boil, or steam, as is most convenient. The time required for cooking will vary from twenty to forty minutes.

RECIPES.

(The recipes given are applicable to both broccoli and cauliflower.)

Boiled Cauliflower.—Prepare, divide into neat branches, and tie securely in a net. Put into boiling milk and water, equal quantities, and cook until the main stalks are tender. Boil rapidly the first five minutes, afterward more moderately, to prevent the flower from becoming done before the stalks. Serve on a hot dish with cream sauce or diluted lemon juice.

Browned Cauliflower.—Beat together two eggs, a little salt, four tablespoonfuls of sweet cream, and a small quantity of grated bread crumbs well moistened with a little milk, till of the consistency of batter. Steam the cauliflower until tender, separate it into small bunches, dip each top in the mixture, and place in nice order in a pudding dish; put in the oven and brown.

Cauliflower with Egg Sauce.—Steam the cauliflower until tender, separate into small portions, dish, and serve with an egg sauce prepared as directed for parsnips on page 244.

Cauliflower with Tomato Sauce.—Boil or steam the cauliflower until tender. In another dish prepare a sauce with a pint of strained stewed smooth in a little water, and salted to taste. When the cauliflower is tender, dish, and pour over it the hot tomato sauce. If preferred, a tablespoonful of thick sweet cream may be added to the sauce before using.

Stewed Cauliflower.—Boil in as little water as possible, or steam until tender; separate into small portions, add milk, cream and salt to taste; stew together for a few minutes, and serve.

Scolloped Cauliflower.—Prepare the cauliflower, and steam or boil until tender. If boiled, use equal quantities of milk and water. Separate into bunches of equal size, place in a pudding dish, cover with a white or cream sauce, sprinkle with grated bread crumbs, and brown in the oven.

SPINACH.

Description.—This plant is supposed to be a native of western Arabia. There are several varieties which are prepared and served as "greens." Spinach is largely composed of water. It is considered a wholesome vegetable, with slightly laxative properties.

Preparation and Cooking.—Use only tender plants or the tender leaves of the older stalks, and be sure to have enough, as spinach shrinks greatly. A peck is not too much for a family of four or five. Pick it over very carefully, trim off the roots and decayed leaves, and all tough, stringy stalks, and the coarse fibers of the leaves, as those will not cook tender until the leaves are overdone. Wash in several waters, lifting grit. Shake each bunch well. Spinach is best cooked in its own juices; this may be best accomplished by cooking it in a double boiler, or if placed in a pot and slowly heated, it will however, be stirred frequently at first, to prevent burning; cover closely and cook until tender. The time required will vary from twenty minutes to half an hour or more. If water is used in the cooking, have a half kettleful boiling when the spinach is put in, and continue to boil rapidly until the leaves are perfectly tender; then drain in a colander, press with the back of a plate to extract all water, chop very fine, and either serve with lemon juice as a dressing, or add a half cup of sweet cream with or without a teaspoonful of sugar. Boil up once, stirring constantly, and serve very hot. A garnish of sliced boiled eggs is often employed with this vegetable.

CELERY.

Description.—The common celery is a native of Great Britain. In its wild state it has a strong, disagreeable taste and smell, and is known as *smallage*. By cultivation it becomes more mild and sweet. It is usually eaten uncooked as a salad herb, or introduced into soups as a flavouring. In its raw state, it is difficult of digestion.

Celery from the market may be kept fresh for some time by wrapping the bunches in brown paper, sprinkling them with water, then wrapping in a damp cloth and putting in some cool, dark place.

RECIPES.

Celery Salad.—Break the stems apart, cut off all green portions, and after washing well put in cold water for an hour or so before serving.

Stewed Celery.—Cut the tender inner parts of celery heads into pieces about a finger long. The outer and more fibrous stalks may be saved to season soups. Put in a stewpan, and add sufficient water to cover; then cover the pan closely, and set it where it will just simmer for an hour, or until the celery is perfectly tender. When cooked, add a pint of rich milk, part cream if you have it, salt to taste, and when boiling, stir in a tablespoon of flour rubbed smooth in a little milk. Boil up once and serve.

Stewed Celery No. 2.—Cut the white part of fine heads of celery into small pieces, blanch in boiling water, turn into a colander, and drain. Heat a cup and a half of milk to boiling in a stewpan; add the celery, and stew gently until tender. Remove the celery with a skimmer, and stir into the milk the beaten yolks of two eggs and one half cup of cream. Cook until thickened; pour over the celery, and serve.

Celery with Tomato Sauce.—Prepare the celery as in the preceding recipe, and cook until tender in a small quantity of boiling water. Drain in a colander, and for three cups of stewed celery prepare a sauce with a pint of strained stewed tomato, heated to boiling and thickened with a tablespoonful of flour rubbed smooth in a little cold water. If desired, add a half cup of thin cream. Turn over the celery, and serve hot.

Celery and Potato Hash.—To three cups of cold boiled or baked potato, chopped rather fine, add one cup of cooked celery, minced. Put season. Heat to boiling, tossing and stirring so that the whole will be heated throughout, and serve hot.

ASPARAGUS.

Description.—The asparagus is a native of Europe, and in its wild state is a sea-coast plant. The young shoots form the edible portion. The plant was known to the ancient Greeks and Romans, who not only used it as a table delicacy but considered it very useful in the treatment of internal diseases. Roman cooks provided themselves with a supply of the vegetable for winter use by cutting fine heads and drying them. When wanted, they were put into hot water and gently cooked.

The asparagus is remarkable as containing a crystalline alkaloid called *asparagin*, which is thought to possess diuretic properties.

Preparation and Cooking.—Select fresh and tender asparagus. Those versed in its cultivation, assert that it should be cut at least three times a week, and barely to the ground. If it is necessary to keep the bunches for some time before cooking, stand them, tops uppermost, in water about one half inch deep, in the cellar or other cool place. Clean each stalk separately by swashing back and forth in a pan of cold water till perfectly free from sand, then break off all the tough portions, cut in equal lengths, tie in bunches of half a dozen or more with soft tape, drop into boiling water barely sufficient to cover, and simmer gently until perfectly tender.

If the asparagus is to be stewed, break: (not cut) into small pieces; when it will not snap off quickly, the stalk is too tough for use.

Asparagus must be taken from the water just as soon as tender, while yet firm in appearance. If boiled soft, it loses its flavor and is uninviting. It is a good plan when it is to be divided before cooking, if the stalks are not perfectly tender, to boil the hardest portions first. Asparagus cooked in bunches is well done, if, when held by the thick end in a horizontal position between the fingers, it only bends lightly and does not fall heavily down.

The time required for boiling asparagus depends upon its freshness and age. Fresh, tender asparagus cooks in a very few minutes, so quickly, indeed, that the Roman emperor Augustus, intimating that any affair must be concluded without delay, was accustomed to say, "Let that be done quicker than you can cook asparagus." Fifteen or twenty minutes will suffice if young and fresh; if old, from thirty to fifty minutes will be required.

RECIPES.

Asparagus and Peas.—Asparagus and green peas make a nice dish served together, and if of proportionate age, require the same length of time to cook. Wash the asparagus, shell and look over the peas, put together into boiling water, cook, and serve as directed for stewed asparagus.

Asparagus Points.—Cut of enough heads in two-inch lengths to make three pints. Put into boiling water just sufficient to cover. When tender, drain off the water, add a half cup of cream, and salt if desired. Serve at once.

Asparagus on Toast.—Cook the asparagus in bunches, and when tender, drain and place on slices of nicely browned toast moistened in the asparagus liquor. Pour over all a cream sauce prepared as directed below.

Asparagus with Cream Sauce.—Thoroughly wash, tie in small bunches, and put into boiling water; boil till perfectly tender. Drain thoroughly, untie the bunches, place the stalks all the same way upon a hot plate, with a dressing prepared as follows: Let a pint of sweet cream (about six hours old is best) come to the boiling point, and stir into it salt to taste and a level tablespoonful of flour rubbed smooth with a little cold cream.

Asparagus with Egg Sauce.—Prepare and cook asparagus as directed above. When tender, drain thoroughly, and serve on a hot dish or on slices of nicely browned toast, with an egg sauce prepared in the following manner: Heat a half cup of rich milk to boiling, add salt, and turn into it very slowly the well-beaten yolk of an egg, stirring constantly at the same time. Let the whole just thicken, and remove from the fire at once.

Stewed Asparagus.—Wash, break into inch pieces, simmer till tender in water just to cover, add sufficient rich milk, part cream if convenient, to make a gravy, thicken slightly with flour, a teaspoonful to a pint of milk; add salt if desired, boil up together once, and serve.

SEA-KALE.

Description.—This plant, a native of Britain, and much esteemed as a vegetable in England and on the Continent, is also in its wild state a sea-coast plant. When properly cooked, it is nutritious and easy of digestion. In appearance and flavor it greatly resembles asparagus, and the suggestions for cooking and recipes given for that vegetable are applicable to sea-kale.

LETTUCE AND RADISH.

Description.—These two vegetables, although wholly different, the one being the leaf of a plant, the other the root, are both so commonly served as relishes that we will speak of them together. Both have long been known and used.

Wild lettuce is said to be the bitter herb which the Hebrews ate with the Paschal lamb. The ancient Greek and Roman epicures valued lettuce highly, and bestowed great care upon its cultivation, in some instances watering the plants with sweet wine instead of water, in order to communicate to them a delicate perfume and flavor. The common garden lettuce of the present day is a hardy plant, which supplies an agreeable, digestible, and, when served with a wholesome dressing, unobjectionable salad.

The common radish is supposed to be indigenous to China. Ancient writers on foods mention the radish as used by the early Greeks and Romans, who fancied that at the end of three years its seed would produce cabbages. They had also the singular custom of making the radish the ignominious projectile with which in times of tumult the mob pursued persons whose political opinions had made them obnoxious. When quiet was restored, the disgraced vegetable was boiled and eaten with oil and vinegar. Common garden radishes are of different shapes and of various colors on the outside, there being black, violet, red, and white radishes. The inside portion of all, however, is white. They are sometimes cooked, but more commonly served raw. A dish of crisp, coral radishes adds beauty to the appearance of the table, but they are not possessed of a high nutritive value, being very similar to the turnip in composition, and unless very young, tender, and when eaten thoroughly masticated, are quite difficult of digestion.

RECIPES.

Lettuce.—Wash well, put into cold water, and set on ice or on the cellar bottom for an hour or more before using. Dry the leaves with a soft towel and use whole or tear into convenient pieces with a silver fork; never cut with a knife. Serve with a dressing prepared of equal quantities of lemon juice and sugar, diluted with a little ice water; or, with a dressing of cream and sugar, in the proportion of three or four tablespoonfuls of thin cream to a teaspoonful of sugar. The dressing may be prepared, and after the sugar is dissolved, a very little lemon juice (just enough to thicken the cream slightly, but not sufficient to curdle it) may be added if desired.

Radishes.—Wash thoroughly young and tender radishes, and arrange in a glass dish with the taper ends meeting. Scatter bits of cracked ice among them. An inch of the stem, if left on, serve as a convenience in handling.

CYMLING, SUMMER SQUASH, or VEGETABLE MARROW.

Description.—The vegetable marrow (sometimes called cymling) is thought to be a variety of the common gourd, from which also the pumpkin and winter squash appear to have been derived. It is easily digested, but on account of the abundance of water in its composition, its nutritive value is very low.

Preparation and Cooking.—When very young, most varieties need no preparation for cooking, aside from washing thoroughly. After cooking, the skin can be easily rubbed off and the seeds removed. If more mature, pare thinly, and if large, divide into halves or quarters and scoop out the seeds. Summer squashes are better steamed than boiled. If boiled, they should be cooked in so little water that it will be quite evaporated when they are tender. From twenty to sixty minutes will be required for cooking.

RECIPES.

Mashed Squash.—Wash, peel, remove seeds, and steam until tender. Place the squash in a clean cloth, mash thoroughly, squeeze until the squash is quite dry, or rub through a fine colander and afterward simmer until neatly dry; season with cream, and a little salt if desired, and heat again before serving. A teaspoonful of sugar may be added with the cream, if desired.

Squash with Egg Sauce.—Prepare, steam till tender, cut into pieces, and serve with an egg sauce made the same as directed for asparagus, page 256.

Stewed Squash.—Prepare, cut into pieces, and stew until tender in a small quantity of boiling water; drain, pressing out all the water; serve on toast with cream or white sauce. Or, divide in quarters, remove the seeds, cook in a double boiler, in its own juices, which when done may be thickened with a little flour. Season with salt if desired, and serve hot.

WINTER SQUASHES.

The winter squash and pumpkin are allied in nature to the summer squash.

Preparation and Cooking.—Select squashes of a firm texture, wash, break in pieces with a hatchet if hard-shell, or if the shell is soft, divide with a knife; remove all seeds, and boil, stew, steam, or bake, as preferred.

To boil or steam, from thirty minutes to one hour's time will be needed; to bake, one to two hours.

RECIPES.

Baked Squash..—The hard-shell varieties are best for baking. Wash, divide, and lay, shells downward, on the top grate of the oven, or place in a shallow baking dish with a little boiling water. Boil until tender, serve in the shell, or scrape out the soft part, mash and serve with two largo tablespoonful of cream to a pint of squash. If preferred, the skins may be removed before baking, and the squash served the same as sweet potato, for which it makes a good substitute.

Steamed Squash.—Prepare the squash, and steam until tender. Mash and season as for baked squash.

THE PUMPKIN.

Description.—When our forefathers came to this country, they found the pumpkin growing in the Indian cornfields, and at once made use of it. Although as food it did not supply what its handsome exterior promised, yet in the absence of other fruits and relishes, of which the exigencies of a new country deprived them, they soon found the pumpkin quite palatable; and the taste, cultivated through necessity, has been handed down through generations, until the pumpkin stewed and baked in pies, has become an established favorite.

RECIPES.

Baked Pumpkin.—Wash the pumpkin well on the outside, divide into quarters if small, into sixths or eighths if large; remove the seeds but not the rind. Bake as directed for squash. Serve in the rind, dishing it out by spoonfuls.

Stewed Pumpkin—Select a good, ripe pumpkin, and cut in halves; remove the seeds, slice halfway around, pare, cut into inch pieces, put over the fire in a kettle containing a small quantity of boiling water, and stew gently, stirring frequently until it breaks to pieces. Cool, rub through a colander, and place where it will just simmer, but not burn, until the water is all evaporated and the pumpkin dry. Pumpkin for pies is much richer baked like squash, and rubbed through a colander after the skin has been removed.

Dried Pumpkin.—Pumpkin may be dried and kept for future use. The best way is first to cut and stew the pumpkin, then spread on plates, and dry quickly in the oven. Dried in this manner, it is easily softened, when needed, by soaking in a small quantity of water, and is considered nearly as good as that freshly stewed.

TOMATO.

Description.—The tomato, or "love apple," as it was called in the early part of the century, is a native of South America and Mexico. It was formerly regarded as poisonous, and though often planted and prized as a curiosity in the flower garden, it has only within the last half century come to be considered as a wholesome article of diet. Botanically, it is allied to the potato. It is an acid fruit, largely composed of water, and hence of low nutritive value; but it is justly esteemed as a relish, and is very serviceable to the cook in the preparation of soups and various mixed dishes.

Preparation and Cooking.—Tomatoes to be served in an uncooked state should be perfectly ripe and fresh. The medium-sized, smooth ones are the best. To peel, pour scalding water over them; let them remain for half a minute, plunge into cold water, allow them to cool, when the skins can be easily rubbed off. Tomatoes should always be cooked in porcelain or granite ware; iron makes them look dark, and being slightly acid in character, they are not wholesome cooked in tin vessels.

Tomatoes require cooking a long time; one hour is needed, and two are better.

RECIPES.

Baked Tomatoes.—Fill a pudding dish two thirds full of stewed tomatoes; season with salt, and sprinkle grated crumbs of good whole-wheat or Graham bread over it until the top looks dry. Brown in the oven, and serve with a cream dressing.

Baked Tomatoes No. 2. Wash and wipe a quantity of smooth, even-sized tomatoes; remove the stems with a sharp-pointed knife. Arrange on an earthen pudding or pie dish, and bake whole in a moderate oven. Serve with cream.

Scalloped Tomatoes.—Take a pint of stewed tomatoes, which have been rubbed through a colander, thicken with one and one fourth cups of lightly picked crumbs of Graham or whole-wheat bread, or a sufficient quantity to make it quite thick, add salt if desired, and a half cup of sweet cream, mix well, and bake for twenty minutes. Or, fill a pudding dish with alternate layers of peeled and sliced tomatoes and bread crumbs, letting the topmost layer be of tomatoes. Cover, and bake in a moderate oven for an hour or longer, according to depth. Uncover, and brown for ten or fifteen minutes.

Stewed Corn and Tomatoes.—Boil dried or fresh corn until perfectly tender, add to each cup of corn two cups of stewed, strained tomatoes, either canned or freshly cooked. Salt to taste, boil together for five or ten minutes, and serve plain or with a little cream added.

Tomato Gravy.—Heat to boiling one pint of strained stewed tomatoes, either canned or fresh, and thicken with a tablespoonful of flour rubbed smooth in a little water; add salt and when thickened, if desired, a half cup of hot cream. Boil together for a minute or two and serve at once.

Tomato Salad.—Select perfectly ripe tomatoes, and peel at least an hour before using. Slice, and place on ice or in a cool place. Serve plain or with lemon juice or sugar as preferred.

Tomato Salad No. 2.—Use one half small yellow tomatoes and one half red. Slice evenly and lay in the dish in alternate layers. Powder lightly with sugar, and turn over them a cupful of orange juice to a pint of tomato, or if preferred, the juice of lemons may be used instead. Set on ice and cool before serving.

Broiled Tomatoes.—Choose perfectly ripened but firm tomatoes of equal size. Place them on a wire broiler, and broil over glowing coals, from three to eight minutes, according to size, then turn and cook on the other side. Broil the stem end first. Serve hot with salt to season, and a little cream.

Tomato Pudding.—Fill an earthen pudding dish with alternate layers of stale bread and fresh tomatoes, peeled, sliced, and sprinkled lightly with sugar. Cover the dish and bake.

Stewed Tomatoes.—Peel and slice the tomatoes. Put them into a double boiler, without the addition of water, and stew for an hour or longer. When done, serve plain with a little sugar added, or season with salt and a tablespoonful of rather thick sweet cream to each pint of tomatoes. If the tomatoes are thin and very juicy, they may be thickened with a little flour rubbed smooth in a little cold water. They are much better, however, to stew a longer time until the water they contain is sufficiently evaporated to make them of the desired consistency. The stew may also be thickened, if desired, by the addition of bread crumbs, rice, or macaroni.

Tomato with Okra.—Wash the okra, cut off the stem and nibs, and slice thin. For a quart of sliced okra, peel and slice three large tomatoes. Stew the tomatoes for half an hour, then add the okra, and simmer together for half an hour longer. Season with salt and a little cream.

EGG PLANT.

Description.—The egg plant, a vegetable indigenous to the East Indies, is somewhat allied in character to the tomato. In shape, it resembles an egg, from which fact it doubtless derives its name. It ranks low in nutritive value. When fresh, the plant is firm and has a smooth skin.

RECIPES.

Scalloped Egg Plant.—Pare a fresh egg plant. If large, divide in quarters, if small, in halves, and put to cook in boiling water. Cook until it can be easily pierced with a straw, and drain in a colander. Turn into a hot dish, and beat with a silver fork until finely broken. Measure the egg plant, and add to it an equal quantity of graded bread crumbs, a little salt, and a tablespoonful of thick sweet cream. Lastly, add one well beaten egg. Put in an earthen pudding dish, and brown in the oven until the egg is set, and the whole is heated throughout but not dry.

Baked Egg Plant.—Wash and cook whole in boiling water until tender. Divide in halves, remove the inside with a spoon, taking care not to break the skin. Beat the egg plant smooth with a fork. Season with salt and cream, and if desired, a stalk of celery or a small slice of onion very finely minced, for flavor. Put back in the skin, sprinkle the top with bread crumbs, and brown the outside uppermost in the oven.

CUCUMBER.

Description.—The cucumber is a native of Southern Asia, although it is quite commonly cultivated in most civilized countries. It formed a part of the dietary of the Israelites when in Egypt, where it grew very plentifully. The ancient Greeks held the cucumber in high esteem, and attributed to it wonderful properties.

The cucumber is not a nutritious vegetable, and when served in its raw state, as it so generally is, dressed with salt, vinegar, pepper, and similar condiments, it is an exceedingly indigestible article. If it is to be eaten at all, it should first be cooked. It may be pared, divided in quarters, the seeds removed, and cooked in a small quantity of water until perfectly tender, and served on toast with an egg sauce or a cream sauce; or it may be prepared the same as directed for Escalloped Egg Plant.

SALSIFY, OR VEGETABLE OYSTER.

Description.—The vegetable oyster plant, sometimes called purple goat's-beard, or salsify, is indigenous to some portions of Great Britain. The long, slender root becomes fleshy and tender under cultivation, with a flavor, when cooked, somewhat resembling that of the mollusk for which it is named. On this account, it is much esteemed for soups. A variety of the plant grows near the line of perpetual snow, and forms the principal article of fresh vegetable food in the dietary of Kurdistan.

Preparation and Cooking.—Select fresh and unshriveled roots, wash and scrape well, dropping into cold water as soon as cleaned, to prevent discoloration. If the roots are covered with cold water for a half hour or more before scraping, they can be cleaned much easier. Use a porcelain-lined kettle, for cooking, as an iron one will discolor it and injure its flavor. From twenty minutes to one hour, according to age, is required to cook it tender.

RECIPES.

Scalloped Vegetable Oysters.—Boil two quarts of sliced vegetable oysters in about two quarts of water until very tender. Skim them out, and fill a pudding dish with alternate layers of crumbs and oysters, having a layer of crumbs for the top. To the water in which they were boiled, add a pint and a half of thin cream, salt to taste, boil up, and thicken with a heaping tablespoonful or two of flour rubbed smooth in a little cold cream. Pour this over the oysters and crumbs, and bake a half hour. If this is not enough to cover well, add more cream or milk. Stewed tomatoes are a nice accompaniment for escalloped vegetable oysters.

Stewed Vegetable Oysters.—Wash, scrape, and cut into slices not more than one half inch in thickness. Put into a small quantity of boiling water and cook until tender. If a large quantity of water is used, the savory juices escape, and leave the roots very insipid. When tender, pour in a cup of rich milk and simmer for five or ten minutes; add a little flour rubbed smooth in milk, and salt if desired; boil up once, and serve as a vegetable or on slices of nicely browned toast. If preferred, a well-beaten egg may be used in the place of flour.

GREEN CORN, PEAS, AND BEANS.

Description.—Corn, peas, and beans in their immature state are so nearly allied to vegetables, that we give in this connection recipes for cooking green corn, green beans, and green peas. A general rule applicable to all is that they should, when possible, be cooked and eaten the day they are gathered, as otherwise they lose much of their sweetness and flavor. For corn, select young, tender, well-filled ears, from which the milk will spurt when the grain is broken with the finger nail. Beans and peas are fresh only when the pods are green, plump, snap crisply when broken, and have unshriveled stems. If the pods bend and appear wilted, they are stale. Corn, peas, and beans are wholesome and nutritious foods when thoroughly cooked and sufficiently masticated, but they are almost indigestible unless the hull, or skin, of each pea, bean, or grain of corn, be broken before being swallowed.

RECIPES FOR CORN.

Baked Corn.—Select nice fresh ears of tender corn of as nearly equal size as possible. Open the husks and remove all the silk from the corn; replace and tie the husks around the ears with a thread. Put the corn in a hot oven, and bake thirty minutes or until tender. Remove the husks before serving.

Baked Corn No. 2.—Scrape enough corn from the cob (as directed below for Corn Pulp) to make one and a half quarts. Put into a baking dish, season with salt if desired, add enough milk, part cream if convenient, barely to cover the corn, and bake in a hot oven twenty-five or thirty minutes.

Boiled Green Corn.—Remove the husks and every thread of the silk fiber. Place in a kettle, the larger ears at the bottom, with sufficient boiling water nearly to cover. Cover with the clean inner husks, and cook from twenty to thirty minutes, according to the age of the corn; too much cooking hardens it and detracts from its flavor. Try a kernel, and when the milk has thickened, and a raw taste is no longer apparent, it is sufficiently cooked. Green corn is said to be sweeter, boiled with the inner husks on. For cooking in this way, strip off all outer husks, and remove the silk, tying the inner husk around the ear with a bit of thread, and boil. Remove from the kettle, place in a heated dish, cover with a napkin and serve at once on the cob. Some recommend scoring or splitting the corn by drawing a sharp knife through each row lengthwise. This is a wise precaution against insufficient mastication.

Stewed Corn Pulp.—Take six ears of green corn or enough to make a pint of raw pulp; with a sharp knife cut a thin shaving from each row of kernels or score each kernel, and with the back of the knife scrape out the pulp, taking care to leave the hulls on the cob. Heat a cup and a half of rich milk—part cream if it can be afforded—to boiling, add the corn, cook twenty or thirty minutes; season with salt and a teaspoonful of sugar if desired.

Corn Cakes.—To a pint of corn pulp add two well-beaten eggs and two tablespoonfuls of flour; season with salt if desired, and brown on a griddle. Canned corn finely chopped can be used, but two tablespoonfuls of milk should be added, as the corn is less moist.

Corn Pudding.—One quart of corn pulp prepared as for stewing, one quart of milk, three eggs, and a little salt. Mix the corn with a pint of the milk, and heat it to boiling. Break the eggs into the remainder of the milk, and add it to the corn, turn all into an oiled pudding dish, and bake slowly until the custard is well set.

Roasted Green Corn.—Remove the husks and silk, and place the corn before an open grate or in a wire broiler over hot coals until the kernels burst open, or bury in hot ashes without removing the husks. Score the grains, and serve from the cob.

Stewed Green Corn.—Cut the corn from the cob and with the back of the knife scrape off all the pulp, being careful to leave the hull on the cob. Put into a stewpan with half as much water as corn, cover closely and stew gently until thoroughly cooked, stirring frequently to prevent the corn from sticking to the pan; add cream or milk to make the requisite amount of juice, and season with salt if desired. A teaspoonful of white sugar may be added if desired.

Cold boiled corn cut from the cob and stewed a few minutes in a little milk, makes a very palatable dish.

Summer Succotash.—This maybe made by cooking equal quantities of shelled beans and corn cut from the cob, separately until tender, and then mixing them; or the beans may be cooked until nearly soft, an equal quantity of shaved corn added, and the whole cooked fifteen or twenty minutes or longer. Season with cream, and salt if desired.

Dried Corn.—The sweet varieties of corn taken when young and tender and properly dried, furnish an excellent material for nearly all purposes to which green corn is put. Take green corn, just right for eating, have it free from silk; cut the fleshy portion from the cob with a sharp knife, then with the back of the knife gently press the remaining pulp from the cob. Spread thinly on plates and put into an oven hot enough to scald, not scorch it. Watch closely for a half hour or more, turning and stirring frequently with a fork. When thus thoroughly scalded, the corn may be left without further attention if placed in a moderate oven, save an occasional stirring to prevent its sticking to the plate, until the drying is complete, which ought to be in about forty-eight hours; however, if one can spend the time to watch closely and stir very frequently, the drying may be completed in a single afternoon in a rather hot oven. Be careful that it does not scorch.

When needed for use, soak over night and cook in accordance with recipes for Stewed Corn, Succotash, etc., pages 265, 234, only remembering to allow a longer time.

RECIPES FOR PEAS.

Stewed Peas.—If from the garden, pick and shell the peas with clean hands; if from the market, wash the pods before shelling, so that the peas will not require washing, as they are much better without. When shelled, put into a colander and sift out the fine particles and undeveloped blossoms. If not of equal growth, sort the peas and put the older ones to cook ten minutes before the others. Use a porcelain kettle, with one half pint of boiling water for each quart of peas, if young and tender; older ones, which require longer stewing, need more. Cover closely, and simmer gently till tender. The time required for young peas is from twenty-five to thirty minutes; older ones require forty to fifty minutes. Serve without draining, season with salt and enough sweet cream to make them as juicy as desired. If preferred, the juice may be thickened with a little flour.

The peas may be purposely stewed in a larger quantity of water, and served in their own juices thickened with a little flour and seasoned with salt.

RECIPES FOR BEANS.

Lima Beans.—Lima beans are not good until they are full grown and have turned white. Shell, wash, cover with boiling water, and cook about one hour or until tender. Let the water nearly evaporate, and add milk or cream thickened with a little flour. Season with salt to taste, boil up once, and serve.

Shelled Beans.—Shell, wash, drop into boiling water sufficient to cover, and cook until tender. Let the water boil nearly away, and serve without draining. Season with thin cream, and salt if desired.

String Beans.—Wash well in cold water. Remove the strong fiber, or strings, as they are called, by paring both edges with a sharp knife; few cooks do this thoroughly. Break off stems and points, carefully rejecting any imperfect or diseased pods. Lay a handful evenly on a board and cut them all at once into inch lengths. Put in a porcelain kettle, cover with boiling water, and cook from one to three hours, according to age and variety, testing frequently, as they should be removed from the kettle just as soon as done. When very young and tender, only water sufficient to keep them from burning will be needed. When done, add a half cup of thin cream, and salt to taste. If the quantity of juice is considerable, thicken with a little flour.

THE ONION.

The onion belongs to a class of foods containing an acrid oil of a strongly irritating character, on which account it cannot be considered a wholesome food when eaten raw, as it so generally is. The essential oil is, however, quite volatile, so that when cooked, after being first parboiled in two or three waters, its irritating properties are largely removed. The varieties grown in warm climates are much milder and sweeter than those grown in colder countries. The onion is valuable for flavoring purposes. It may also be boiled and served whole with a cream sauce, or cut in quarters and prepared as directed for Scalloped Turnips, page 242.

CANNING VEGETABLES.

Most housekeepers experience more difficulty in canning and keeping vegetables than fruit. This is frequently owing to lack of care to secure perfect cans, covers, and rubbers, and to cook the vegetables thoroughly. Whatever is to be canned must be cooked sufficiently to be eaten, and must be boiling at the time it is put into the cans. Care as to the cleanliness of the cans and their sterilization is also important, and after the canning process is completed, all vegetables put up in glass should be kept in a cool, dark place. The general directions given for canning fruits should be followed in canning vegetables.

RECIPES.

Canned Corn.—Select corn just ripe enough for table use, and prepare as directed for stewed corn. It will require from twelve to fifteen ears to fill sufficiently each quart can. To insure success, the cans should be so full that when the corn is shrunken by the cooking, the can will still be well filled. Pack the corn in the cans, working it down closely by means of the small end of a potato masher, so the milk will cover the corn and completely fill the can; heap a little more corn loosely on the top, and screw the covers on sufficiently tight to prevent water from getting into the can. Place the cans in a boiler, on the bottom of which has been placed some straw or a rack; also take care not to let the cans come in contact with each other, by wrapping each in a cloth or by placing a chip between them. A double layer of cans may be placed in the boiler, one on top of the other, if desirable, provided there is some intervening substance. Fill the boiler with cold water so as completely to cover the cans; place over the fire, bring gradually to a boil, and keep boiling steadily for four hours. Remove the boiler from the fire, and allow the cans to cool gradually, tightening the covers frequently as they cool.

If the corn in the can shrinks, do not open to refill. If cooked thoroughly, and due care is taken in other particulars, there need be no failure. Wrap closely in brown paper, and put away in a dark, cool, dry place.

Canned Corn and Tomatoes.—Use about one third corn and two thirds tomatoes, or in equal portions if preferred. Cook the tomatoes in a double boiler for an hour and a half or longer; and in another double boiler, when the tomatoes are nearly done, cook the corn in its own juices until thoroughly done. Turn them together, heat to boiling, and can at once.

Canned Peas.—Select peas which are fresh, young, and tender. Shell, pack into perfect cans, shaking and filling as full as possible, add sufficient cold water to fill them to overflowing, screw on the covers, and cook and seal the same as directed for canning corn.

Canned Tomatoes.—Tomatoes for canning should be freshly gathered, ripe, but not at all softened.

As they are best cooked in their own juices, peel, slice, put into a double boiler or a porcelain fruit-kettle set inside a dish filled with boiling water, and cook from one to two hours. Cooked in the ordinary way, great care will be required to keep the fruit from burning. When thoroughly cooked—simple scalding will not do—put into cans, and be sure that all air bubbles are expelled before sealing. Wrap in dark brown paper, and put in a cool, dry, dark place.

Canned Tomatoes No. 2.—Cut the fruit into thick slices, let it stand and drain until a large portion of the juice has drained off; then pack solid in new or perfect cans. Allow them to stand a little time, then again drain off the juice; fill up a second time with sliced tomatoes, and screw on the top of the cans without the rubbers. Pack into a wash boiler as directed for canning corn, and boil for two hours, then put on the rubbers and seal. When cold, tighten the covers and put away.

String Beans.—Select young and tender beans, string them, and cut into pieces about one half inch in length. Pack the cans as full as possible, and fill with water until every crevice between the beans is full. Screw on the covers and can in the same manner as corn.

Shelled beans may be canned in the same way.

Canned Pumpkin and Squash.—These fruits when canned are quite as desirable for pies as the fresh material. The same general rules should be followed as in canning other vegetables and fruits.

TABLE TOPICS.

The word "vegetarian" is not derived from "vegetable," but from the Latin, *homo vegetus*, meaning among the Romans a strong, robust, thoroughly healthy man.

AN INTELLECTUAL FEAST.—Professor Louis Agassiz in his early manhood visited Germany to consult Oken, the transcendentalist in zoölogical classification. "After I had delivered to him my letter of introduction," he once said to a friend, "Oken asked me to dine with him, and you may suppose with what joy I accepted the invitation. The dinner consisted only of potatoes, boiled and roasted; but it was the best dinner I ever ate; for there was Oken. Never before were such potatoes grown on this planet; for the mind of the man seemed to enter into what we ate sociably together, and I devoured his intellect while munching his potatoes."

Dr. Abernethy's recipe for using cucumbers: "Peel the cucumber, slice it, pepper it, put vinegar to it, then throw it out the window."

A green son of the Emerald Isle was eating sweet corn from the cob for the first time. He handed the cob to the waiter, and asked, "Will you plaze put some more beans on my shtick?"

A French physician styles spinach, *le balai de l'estomac* (broom of the stomach).

An ox is satisfied with the pasture of an acre or two; one wood suffices for several elephants. Man alone supports himself by the pillage of the whole earth and sea. What? Has Nature indeed given us so insatiable a stomach, while she has given us so insignificant bodies? No; it is not the hunger of our stomachs, but insatiable covetousness which costs so much.—*Seneca.*

The oftener we go to the vegetable world for our food, the oftener we go to the first and therefore the cheapest source of supply. The tendencies of all advanced scholars in thrift should be to find out plans for feeding all the community, as far as possible, direct from the lap of earth; to impress science into our service so that she may prepare the choicest viands minus the necessity of making a lower animal the living laboratory for the sake of what is just a little higher than cannibal propensities.

—*Dr. B.W. Richardson.*

A VOICE FROM THE CORN.

I was made to be eaten, not to be drank,
To be husked in a barn, not soaked in a tank;
I come as a blessing when put in a mill,
As a blight and a curse when run through a still.
Make me up into loaves, and your children are fed;
But made into drink, I will starve them instead.
In bread I'm a servant the eater shall rule,
In drink I'm a master, the drinker a fool.
Then remember my warning; my strength I'll employ,
If eaten, to strengthen, if drunk, to destroy.—*Sel.*

SOUPS

Soup is an easily made, economical, and when properly prepared from healthful and nutritious material, very wholesome article of diet, deserving of much more general use than is commonly accorded it.

In general, when soup is mentioned, some preparation of meat and bones is supposed to be meant; but we shall treat in this chapter of a quite different class of soups, viz., those prepared from the grains, legumes, and vegetables, without the previous preparation of a "stock." Soups of this character are in every way equal, and in many points superior to those made from meat and bones. If we compare the two, we shall find that soups made from the grains and legumes rank much higher in nutritive value than do meat soups. For the preparation of the latter, one pound of meat and bones, in about equal proportion, is required for each quart of soup. In the bone, there is little or no nourishment, it being valuable simply for the gelatine it contains, which gives consistency to the soup; so in reality there is only one half pound of material containing nutriment, for the quart of soup. Suppose, in comparison we take a pea soup. One half pound of peas will be amply enough for a quart. As we take an equal amount of material as basis for each soup, we can easily determine their relative value by comparing the amount of nutritive material contained in peas with that of beef, the most commonly used material for meat soups. As will be seen by reference to the table of food analyses on page 486, peas contain 87.3 parts nutritive material, while lean beef contains only 28 parts in one hundred. Thus the pea soup contains more than three times as much nourishment as does the beef soup.

Soups prepared from grains and legumes are no more expensive than meat soups, and many kinds cost much less, while they have the added advantage of requiring less time and no more labor to prepare.

The greater bulk of all meat soups is water, holding in solution the essence of meat, the nutritive value of which is of very doubtful character.

When properly prepared, the solid matter which enters into the composition of vegetable soups, is so broken up in the process of cooking, that it is more easily digested than in any other form.

Taken hot at the beginning of a meal, soup stimulates the flow of the digestive juices, and on account of the bulk, brings a sense of satiety before an excessive quantity of food has been taken.

In preparing soups from grains, legumes, and vegetables, the material should be first cooked in the ordinary manner, using as small an amount of water as practicable, so as the more thoroughly to disintegrate or break it up. If the material be legumes or grains, the cooking should be slow and prolonged. The purpose to be attained in the cooking of all foods is the partial digestion of the food elements; and in general, with these foods, the more slowly (if continuous) the cooking is done, the more completely will this be brought about.

When the material is cooked, the next step is to make it homogeneous throughout, and to remove any skins or cellulose material it may contain. To do this, it should be put through a colander. The kind of colander depends upon the material. Peas and beans require a fine colander, since the skins, of which we are seeking to rid them, would easily go through a coarse one. To aid in this sifting process, if the material be at all dry, a small quantity of liquid may be added from time to time. When the colander process is complete, a sufficient amount of milk or other liquid may be added to make the whole of the consistency of rather thick cream.

If the material is now cold, it must be reheated, and the salt, if any is to be used, added. The quantity of salt will depend somewhat upon the taste of the consumer; but in general, one half teaspoonful to the pint of soup will be an ample supply. If any particular flavor, as of onion or celery, is desired, it may be imparted to the soup by adding to it a slice of onion or a few stalks of celery, allowing them to remain during the reheating. By the time the soup is well heated, it will be delicately flavored, and the pieces of onion or celery may be removed with a fork or a skimmer. It is better, in general, to cook the soup all that is needed before flavoring, since if allowed to boil, all delicate flavors are apt to be lost by evaporation. When reheated, add to the soup a quantity of cream as seasoning, in the proportion of one cup of thin cream for every quart or three pints of soup.

To avoid the possibility of any lumps or fragments in the soup, pour it again through a colander or a Chinese soup strainer into the soup tureen, and serve. It is well to take the precaution first to heat the strainer and tureen, that the soup be not cooled during the process.

If it is desired to have the soup especially light and nice, beat or whip the cream before adding, or beat the hot soup with an egg beater for a few minutes after adding the cream. The well-beaten yolk of an egg for every quart or three pints of soup, will answer as a very fair substitute for cream in potato, rice, and similar soups. It should not be added to the body of the soup, but a cupful of the hot soup may be turned slowly onto the egg, stirring all the time, in order to mix it well without curdling, and then the cupful stirred into the whole. Soups made from legumes are excellent without cream.

The consistency of the soup when done should be about that of single cream, and equal throughout, containing no lumps or fragments of material. If it is too thick, it may be easily diluted with hot milk or water; if too thin, it will require the addition of more material, or may be thickened with a little flour or cornstarch rubbed to a cream with a small quantity of milk, used in the proportion of one tablespoonful for a quart of soup,—heaping, if flour; scant, if cornstarch,—and remembering always to boil the soup five or ten minutes after the flour is added, that there may be no raw taste.

The addition of the flour or cornstarch gives a smoothness to their consistency which is especially desirable for some soups. A few spoonfuls of cooked oatmeal or cracked wheat, added and rubbed through the colander with the other material, is valuable for the same purpose. Browned flour prepared by spreading a cupful thinly on shallow tins, and placing in a moderately hot oven, stirring frequently until lightly and evenly browned, is excellent to use both for thickening and flavoring certain soups.

If whole grains, macaroni, vermicelli, or shredded vegetables are to be used in the soup, cook them separately, and add to the soup just before serving.

The nutritive value of soup depends of course upon its ingredients, and these should be so chosen and combined as to produce the best possible food from the material employed. Milk is a valuable factor in the preparation of soups. With such vegetables as potatoes, parsnips, and others of the class composed largely of starch, and containing but a small proportion of the nitrogenous food elements, its use is especially important as an addition to their food value, as also to their palatableness. Very good soups may, however, be made from legumes, if carefully cooked with water only.

Soups offer a most economical way of making use of the "left-over" fragments which might otherwise be consigned to the refuse bucket. A pint of cold mashed potatoes, a cupful of stewed beans, a spoonful or two of boiled rice, stewed tomatoes, or other bits of vegetables and grains, are quite as good for soup purposes as fresh material, provided they have been preserved fresh and sweet. To insure this it is always best to put them away in clean dishes; if retained in the dish from which they were served, the thin smears and small crumbs on the sides which spoil much sooner than the larger portion, will help to spoil the rest. One may find some difficulty in rubbing them through the colander unless they are first moistened. Measure the cold food, and then determine how much liquid will be needed, and add a part of this before attempting to put through the colander.

It is difficult to give specific directions for making soups of fragments, as the remnants to be utilized will vary so much in character as to make such inapplicable, but the recipes given for combination soups will perhaps serve as an aid in this direction. Where a sufficient amount of one kind of food is left over to form the basis of a soup or to serve as a seasoning, it can be used in every way the same as fresh material. When, however, there is but a little of various odds and ends, the general rule to be observed is to combine only such materials as harmonize in taste.

Soups prepared from the grains, legumes, and vegetables, are so largely composed of food material that it is important that they be retained in the mouth long enough for proper insalivation; and in order to insure this, it is well to serve with the soup *croutons*, prepared by cutting stale bread into small squares or cubes, and browning thoroughly in a moderate oven. Put a spoonful or two of the *croutons* in each plate, and turn the hot soup over them. This plan also serves another purpose,—that of providing a means whereby the left-over bits of stale bread may be utilized to advantage.

RECIPES.

Asparagus Soup.—Wash two bunches of fresh asparagus carefully, and cut into small pieces. Put to cook in a quart of boiling water, and simmer gently till perfectly tender, when there should remain about a pint of the liquor. Turn into a colander, and rub all through except the hard portion. To a pint of asparagus mixture add salt and one cup of thin cream and a pint of milk; boil up for a few minutes, and serve.

Baked Bean Soup.—Soak a half pint of white beans over night. In the morning turn off the water, and place them in an earthen dish with two or two and one half quarts of boiling water; cover and let them simmer in a moderate oven four or five hours. Also soak over night a tablespoonful of pearl tapioca in sufficient water to cover. When the beans are soft, rub through a colander, after which add the soaked tapioca, and salt if desired; also as much powdered thyme as can be taken on the point of a penknife and sufficient water to make the soup of proper consistency if the water has mostly evaporated. Return to the oven, and cook one half hour longer. A little cream may be added just before serving.

Bean and Corn Soup.—Cold boiled or stewed corn and cold baked beans form the basis of this soup. Take one pint of each, rub through a colander, add a slice of onion, three cups of boiling water or milk, and boil for ten minutes. Turn through the colander a second time to remove the onion and any lumps or skins which may remain. Season with salt and a half cup of cream. If preferred, the onion may be omitted.

Bean and Hominy Soup.—Soak separately in cold water over night a cupful each of dry beans and hominy. In the morning, boil them together till both are perfectly tender and broken to pieces. Rub through a colander, and add sufficient milk to make three pints. Season with salt, and stir in a cup of whipped cream just before serving. Cold beans and hominy may be utilized for this soup.

Bean and Potato Soup.—Soak a half pint of dry white beans over night; in the morning drain and put to cook in boiling water. When tender, rub through a colander. Prepare sliced potato sufficient to make one quart, cook in as small a quantity of water as possible, rub through a colander, and add to the beans. Add milk or water sufficient to make two quarts, and as much prepared thyme as can be taken on the point of a penknife, with salt to season. Boil for a few minutes, add a teacup of thin cream, and serve.

Bean and Tomato Soup.—Take one pint of boiled or a little less of mashed beans, one pint of stewed tomatoes, and rub together through a colander. Add salt, a cup of thin cream, one half a cup of nicely steamed rice, and sufficient boiling water to make a soup of the proper consistency. Reheat and serve.

Black Bean Soup.—Soak a pint of black beans over night in cold water. When ready to cook, put into two and one half quarts of fresh water, which should be boiling, and simmer until completely dissolved, adding more boiling water from time to time if needed. There should be about two quarts of all when done. Rub through a colander, add salt, a half cup of cream, and reheat. When hot, turn through a soup strainer, add two or more teaspoonfuls of lemon juice, and serve.

Black Bean Soup No. 2.—Soak a pint of black beans in water over night. Cook in boiling water until tender, then rub through a colander. Add sufficient boiling water to make about two quarts in all. Add salt, and one half a small onion cut in slices to flavor. Turn into a double boiler and reheat. When sufficiently flavored, remove the onion with a skimmer, thicken the soup with two teaspoonfuls of browned flour, turn through the soup strainer and serve. If desired, a half cup of cream may be added, and the onion flavor omitted.

Bran Stock.—For every quart of stock desired, boil a cup of good wheat bran in three pints of water for two or three hours or until reduced one third. This stock may be made the base of a variety of palatable and nutritious soups by flavoring with different vegetables and seasoning with salt and cream. An excellent soup may be prepared by flavoring the stock with celery, or by the addition of a quantity of strained stewed tomato sufficient to disguise the taste of the stock. It is also valuable in giving consistence to soups, in the preparation of some of which it may be advantageously used in place of other liquid.

Brown Soup.—Simmer together two pints of sliced potatoes and one third as much of the thin brown shavings (not thicker than a silver dime) from the top of a loaf of whole-wheat bread, in one quart of water. The crust must not be burned or blackened, and must not include any of the soft portion of the loaf. When the potatoes are tender, mash all through a colander. Flavor with a cup of strained, stewed tomatoes, a little salt, and return to the fire; when hot, add a half cup of cream, and boiling water to make the soup of proper consistency, and serve at once. If care has been taken to prepare the crust as directed, this soup will have a brown color and a fine, pungent flavor exceedingly pleasant to the taste.

Canned Green Pea Soup.—Rub a can of green peas through a colander to remove the skins. Add a pint of milk and heat to boiling. If too thin, thicken with a little flour rubbed smooth in a very little cold milk. Season with salt and a half cup of cream. A small teaspoonful of white sugar may be added if desired.

Green peas, instead of canned, may be used when procurable. When they have become a little too hard to serve alone, they can be used for soup, if thoroughly cooked.

Canned Corn Soup.—Open a can of green corn, turn it into a granite-ware dish, and thoroughly mash with a potato-masher until each kernel is broken, then rub through a colander to remove the skins. Add sufficient rich milk to make the soup of the desired consistency, about one half pint for each pint can of corn will be needed. Season with salt, reheat, and serve. If preferred, a larger quantity of milk and some cream may be used, and the soup, when reheated, thickened with a little corn starch or flour. It may be turned through the colander a second time or not, as preferred.

Carrot Soup.—For a quart of soup, slice one large carrot and boil in a small quantity of water for two hours or longer, then rub it through a colander, add a quart of rich milk, and salt to season. Reheat, and when boiling, thicken with two teaspoonfuls of flour rubbed smooth in a little cold milk.

Celery Soup.—Chop quite fine enough fresh, crisp celery to make a pint, and cook it until tender in a very little boiling water. When done, heat three cupfuls of rich milk, part cream if it can be afforded, to boiling, add the celery, salt to season, and thicken the whole with a tablespoonful of flour rubbed smooth in a little cold milk; or add to the milk before heating a cupful of mashed potato, turn through a colander to remove lumps, reheat, add salt and the celery, and serve.

Celery Soup No. 2.—Cook in a double boiler a cupful of cracked wheat in three pints of water for three or four hours. Rub the wheat through a colander, add a cup of rich milk, and if needed, a little boiling water, and a small head of celery cut in finger lengths. Boil all together for fifteen or twenty minutes, until well flavored, remove the celery with a fork, add salt, and serve with or without the hard-boiled yolk of an egg in each soup plate.

Chestnut Soup.—Shell and blanch a pint of Italian chestnuts, as directed on page 215, and cook in boiling milk until tender. Rub the nuts through a colander, add salt and sufficient milk and cream to make a soup of the proper consistency, reheat and serve.

Combination Soup.—This soup is prepared from material already cooked, and requires two cups of cracked wheat, one and one half cups of Lima beans, one half cup of black beans, and one cup of stewed tomato. Rub the material together through a colander, adding, if needed, a little hot water to facilitate the sifting. Add boiling water to thin to the proper consistency, season with salt and if it can be afforded a little sweet cream,—the soup is, however, very palatable without the cream.

Combination Soup No. 2.—Take three and one half cups of mashed (Scotch) peas, one cup each of cooked rice, oatmeal, and hominy, and two cups of stewed tomato. Rub the material through a colander, add boiling water to thin to the proper consistency, season with salt, reheat, and add, just before serving, two cups of cooked macaroni. If preferred, a cup of cream may be used in place of the tomato, or both may be omitted.

Another.—One half cup of cold mashed potato, one cup each of cooked pearl wheat, barley and dried peas. Rub all through a colander, add boiling milk to thin to the proper consistency, season with salt and a half cup of cream.

Another.—Take three cups of cooked oatmeal, two of mashed white beans, and one of stewed tomato. Rub the ingredients through a colander, add boiling milk to thin to the proper consistency, season with salt and a little cream.

Cream Pea Soup.—Soak three fourths of a pint of dried Scotch peas over night in a quart of water. In the morning put to cook in boiling water, cover closely and let them simmer gently four or five hours, or until the peas are very tender and well disintegrated; then rub through a colander to remove the skins. If the peas are very dry, add a little water or milk occasionally, to moisten them and facilitate the sifting. Just before the peas are done, prepare potatoes enough to make a pint and a half, after being cut in thin slices. Cook the potatoes until tender in a small amount of water, and rub them through a colander. Add the potatoes thus prepared to the sifted peas, and milk enough to make three and one half pints in all. Return to the fire, and add a small head of celery cut finger lengths, and let the whole simmer together ten or fifteen minutes, until flavored. Remove the celery with a fork, add salt and a cup of thin cream. This should make about two quarts of soup. If preferred, the peas may be cooked without soaking. It will, however, require a little longer time.

Cream Barley Soup.—Wash a cup of pearl barley, drain and simmer slowly in two quarts of water for four or five hours, adding boiling water from time to time as needed. When the barley is tender, strain off the liquor, of which there should be about three pints; add to it a portion of the cooked barley grains, salt, and a cup of whipped cream, and serve. If preferred, the beaten yolk of an egg may be used instead of cream.

Green Corn Soup.—Take six well-filled ears of tender green corn. Run a sharp knife down the rows and split each grain; then with the back of a knife, scraping from the large to the small end of the ear, press out the pulp, leaving the hulls on the cob. Break the cobs if long, put them in cold water sufficient to cover, and boil half an hour. Strain off the water, of which there should be at least one pint. Put the corn water on again, and when boiling add the corn pulp, and cook fifteen minutes, or until the raw taste is destroyed. Rub through a rather coarse colander, add salt and a pint of hot unskimmed milk; if too thin, thicken with a little cornstarch or flour, boil up, and serve. If preferred, a teaspoonful of sugar may be added to the soup. A small quantity of cooked macaroni, cut in rings, makes a very pretty and palatable addition to the soup. The soup is also excellent flavored with celery.

Green Pea Soup.—Gently simmer two quarts of shelled peas in sufficient water to cook, leaving almost no juice when tender. Rub through a colander, moistening if necessary with a little cold milk. Add to the sifted peas an equal quantity of rich milk and a small onion cut in halves. Boil all together five or ten minutes until the soup is delicately flavored, then remove the onion with a skimmer; add salt if desired, and serve. If preferred, a half cup of thin cream may be added just before serving. Celery may be used in place of the onion, or both may be omitted.

Green Bean Soup.—Prepare a quart of fresh string beans by pulling off ends and strings and breaking into small pieces. Boil in a small quantity of water. If the beans are fresh and young, three pints will be sufficient; if wilted or quite old, more will be needed, as they will require longer cooking. There should be about a teacupful and a half of liquid left when the beans are perfectly tender and boiled in pieces. Rub through a colander, return to the kettle, and for each cup of the bean pulp add salt, a cup and a half of unskimmed milk; boil together for a few minutes, thicken with a little flour, and serve. The quart of beans should be sufficient for three pints of soup.

Kornlet Soup.—Kornlet or canned green corn pulp, may be made into a most appetizing soup in a few minutes by adding to a pint of kornlet an equal quantity of rich milk, heating to boiling, and thickening it with a teaspoonful of flour rubbed smooth in a little cold milk.

Kornlet and Tomato Soup—Put together equal quantities of kornlet and strained stewed tomato, season with salt and heat to boiling; add for each quart one fourth to one half cup of hot thin cream, thicken with a tablespoonful of flour rubbed smooth in a little water, and serve. Cooked corn rubbed through a colander may also be used for this soup.

Lentil Soup.—Simmer a pint of lentils in water until tender. If desired to have the soup less dark in color and less strong in flavor, the lentils may be first parboiled for a half hour, and then drained and put into fresh boiling water. Much valuable nutriment is thus lost, however. When perfectly tender, mash through a colander to remove all skins; add salt and a cup of thin cream, and it too thick, sufficient boiling milk or water to thin to the proper consistency, heat again to boiling, and serve. If preferred, an additional quantity of liquid may be added and the soup slightly thickened with browned flour.

Lentil and Parsnip Soup.—Cook together one pint of lentils and one half a small parsnip, sliced, until tender in a small quantity of boiling water. When done, rub through a colander, and add boiling water to make a soup of the proper consistency. Season with salt and if desired a little cream.

Lima Bean Soup.—Simmer a pint of Lima beans gently in just sufficient water to cook and not burn, until they have fallen to pieces. Add more boiling water as needed. When done, rub the beans through a colander. Add rich milk or water to make of the proper consistency, and salt to season; reheat and serve. White beans may be used in place of Lima beans, but they require more prolonged cooking. A heaping tablespoonful of pearl tapioca or sago previously soaked in cold water, may be added to the soup when it is reheated, if liked, and the whole cooked until the sago is transparent.

Macaroni Soup.—Heat a quart of milk, to which has been added a tablespoonful of finely grated bread crust (the brown part only, from the top of the loaf) and a slice of onion to flavor, in a double boiler. When the milk is well flavored, remove the onion, turn through a colander, add salt, and thicken with two teaspoonfuls of flour rubbed smooth in a little cold milk. Lastly add one cupful of cooked macaroni, and serve.

Oatmeal Soup.—Put two heaping tablespoonfuls of oatmeal into a quart of boiling water, and cook in a double boiler for two hours or longer. Strain as for gruel, add salt if desired, and two or three stalks of celery broken into finger lengths, and cook again until the whole is well flavored with the celery, which may then be removed with a fork; add a half cup of cream, and the soup is ready to serve. Cold oatmeal mush may be thinned with milk, reheated, strained, flavored, and made into soup the same as fresh material. A slice or two of onion may be used with the celery for flavoring the soup if desired, or a cup of strained stewed tomato may be added.

Parsnip Soup.—Take a quart of well scraped, thinly sliced parsnips, one cup of bread crust shavings (prepared as for Brown Soup), one head of celery, one small onion, and one pint of sliced potatoes. The parsnips used should be young and tender, so that they will cook in about the same length of time as the other vegetables. Use only sufficient water to cook them. When done, rub through a colander and add salt and sufficient rich milk, part cream if desired, to make of the proper consistency. Reheat and serve.

Parsnip Soup No. 2.—Wash, pare, and slice equal quantities of parsnips and potatoes. Cook, closely covered, in a small quantity of water until soft. If the parsnips are not young and tender, they must be put to cook first, and the potatoes added when they are half done. Mash through a colander. Add salt, and milk to make of the proper consistency, season with cream, reheat and serve.

Pea and Tomato Soup.—Soak one pint of Scotch peas over night. When ready to cook, put into a quart of boiling water and simmer slowly until quite dry and well disintegrated. Rub through a colander to remove the skins. Add a pint of hot water, one cup of mashed potato, two cups of strained stewed tomato, and one cup of twelve-hour cream. Turn into a double-boiler and cook together for a half hour or longer; turn a second time through a colander or soup strainer and serve. The proportions given are quite sufficient for two quarts of soup. There may need to be some variation in the quantity of tomato to be used, depending upon its thickness. If very thin, a larger quantity and less water will be needed. The soup should be a rich reddish brown in color when done. The peas may be cooked without being first soaked, if preferred.

Plain Rice Soup.—Wash and pick over four tablespoonfuls of rice, put it in an earthen dish with a quart of water, and place in a moderate oven. When the water is all absorbed, add a quart of rich milk, and salt if desired; turn into a granite kettle and boil ten minutes, or till the rice is done. Add a half cup of sweet cream and serve. A slice of onion or stalk of celery can be boiled with the soup after putting in the kettle, and removed before serving, if desired to flavor.

Potato and Rice Soup.—Cook a quart of sliced potatoes in as little water as possible. When done, rub through a colander. Add salt, a quart of rich milk, and reheat. If desired, season with a slice of onion, a stalk of celery, or a little parsley. Just before serving, add a half cup of cream and a cup and a half of well-cooked rice with unbroken grains. Stir gently and serve at once.

Potato Soup.—For each quart of soup required, cook a pint of sliced potatoes in sufficient water to cover them. When tender, rub through a colander. Return to the fire, and add enough rich, sweet milk, part cream if it can be afforded to make a quart in all, and a little salt. Let the soup come to a boil, and add a teaspoonful of flour or corn starch, rubbed to a paste with a little water; boil a few minutes and serve. A cup and a half of cold mashed potato or a pint of sliced baked potato can be used instead of fresh material; in which case add the milk and heat before rubbing through the colander. A slice of onion or a stalk of celery may be simmered in the soup for a few minutes to flavor, and then removed with a skimmer or a spoon. A good mixed potato soup is made by using one third sweet and two thirds Irish potatoes, in the same manner as above.

Potato and Vermicelli Soup.—Breakup a cupful of vermicelli and drop into boiling water. Let it cook for ten or fifteen minutes, and then turn into a colander to drain. Have ready a potato soup prepared the same as in the proceeding; stir the vermicelli lightly into it just before serving.

Sago and Potato Soup.—Prepare the soup as directed for Potato Soup, from fresh or cold mashed potato, using a little larger quantity of milk or cream, as the sago adds thickness to the soap. When seasoned and ready to reheat, turn a second time through the colander, and add for each quart of soup, one heaping tablespoonful of sago which has been soaked for twenty minutes in just enough water to cover. Boil together five or ten minutes, or until the sago is transparent, and serve.

Scotch Broth.—Soak over night two tablespoonfuls of pearl barley and one of coarse oatmeal, in water sufficient to cover them. In the morning, put the grains, together with the water in which they were soaked, into two quarts of water and simmer for several hours, adding boiling water as needed. About an hour before the soup is required, add a turnip cut into small dice, a grated carrot, and one half cup of fine pieces of the brown portion of the crust of a loaf of whole-wheat bread. Rub all through a colander, and add salt, a cup of milk, and a half cup of thin cream. This should make about three pints of soup.

Split Pea Soup.—For each quart of soup desired, simmer a cupful of split peas very slowly in three pints of boiling water for six hours, or until thoroughly dissolved. When done, rub through a colander, add salt and season with one half cup of thin cream. Reheat, and when boiling, stir into it two teaspoonfuls of flour rubbed smooth in a little cold water. Boil up until thickened, and serve. If preferred, the cream may be omitted and the soup flavored with a little celery or onion.

Sweet Potato Soup.—To a pint of cold mashed sweet potato add a pint and a half of strained stewed tomato, rub together through a colander, add salt to season, and half a cup of cream. Reheat and serve.

Swiss Potato Soup.—Pare and cut up into small pieces, enough white turnips to fill a pint cup, and cook in a small quantity of water. When tender, add three pints of sliced potatoes, and let them boil together until of the consistency of mush. Add hot water if it has boiled away so that there is not sufficient to cook the potatoes. When done, drain, rub through a colander, add a pint and a half of milk and a cup of thin cream, salt if desired, and if too thick, a little more milk or a sufficient quantity of hot water to make it of the proper consistency. This should be sufficient for two and a half quarts of soup.

Swiss Lentil Soup.—Cook a pint of brown lentils in a small quantity of boiling water. Add to the lentils when about half done, one medium sized onion cut in halves or quarters. When the lentils are tender, remove the onion with a fork, and rub the lentils through a colander. Add sufficient boiling water to make three pints in all. Season with salt, reheat to boiling, and thicken the whole with four table spoonfuls of browned flour, rubbed to a cream in a little cold water.

Tomato and Macaroni Soup.—Break a half dozen sticks of macaroni into small pieces, and drop into boiling water. Cook for an hour, or until perfectly tender. Rub two quarts of stewed or canned tomatoes through a colander, to remove all seeds and fragments. When the macaroni is done, drain thoroughly, cut each piece into tiny rings, and add it to the strained tomatoes. Season with salt, and boil for a few minutes. If desired, just before serving add a cup of thin cream, boil up once, and serve immediately. If the tomato is quite thin, the soup should be slightly thickened with a little flour before adding the macaroni.

Tomato Cream Soup.—Heat two quarts of strained, stewed tomatoes to boiling; add four tablespoonfuls of flour rubbed smooth in a little cold water. Let the tomatoes boil until thickened, stirring constantly that no lumps form; add salt to season. Have ready two cups of hot rich milk or thin cream. Add the cream or milk hot, and let all boil together for a minute or two, then serve.

Tomato and Okra Soup.—Take one quart of okra thinly sliced, and two quarts of sliced tomatoes. Simmer gently from one to two hours. Rub through a colander, heat again to boiling, season with salt and cream if desired, and serve.

Canned okra and tomatoes need only to be rubbed through a colander, scalded and seasoned, to make a most excellent soup. If preferred, one or two potatoes may be sliced and cooked, rubbed through a colander, and added.

Tomato Soup with Vermicelli—Cook a cupful of broken vermicelli in a pint of boiling water for ten minutes. Turn into a colander to drain. Have boiling two quarts of strained, stewed tomatoes, to which add the vermicelli. If preferred, the tomato may be thickened slightly with a little cornstarch rubbed smooth in cold water before adding the vermicelli. Salt to taste, and just before serving turn in a cup of hot, thin cream. Let all boil up for a moment, then serve at once.

Vegetable Oyster Soup.—Scrape all the outer covering and small rootlets from vegetable oysters, and lay them in a pan of cold water to prevent discoloration. The scraping can be done much easier if the roots are allowed first to stand in cold water for an hour or so. Slice rather thin, enough to make one quart, and put to cook in a quart of water. Let them boil slowly until very tender. Add a pint of milk, a cup of thin cream, salt, and when boiling, a tablespoonful or two of flour, rubbed to a cream with a little milk. Let the soup boil a few minutes until thickened, and serve.

Vegetable Soup.—Simmer together slowly for three or four hours, in five quarts of water, a quart of split peas, a slice of carrot, a slice of white turnip, one cup of canned tomatoes, and two stalks of celery cut into small bits. When done, rub through a colander, add milk to make of proper consistency, reheat, season with salt and cream, and serve.

Vegetable Soup No. 2.—Prepare and slice a pint of vegetable oysters and a pint and a half of potatoes. Put the oysters to cook first, in sufficient water to cook both. When nearly done, add the potatoes and cook all till tender. Rub through a colander, or if preferred, remove the pieces of oysters, and rub the potato only through the colander, together with the water in which the oysters were cooked, as that will contain all the flavor. Return to the fire, and add salt, a pint of strained, stewed tomatoes, and when boiling, the sliced oysters if desired, a cup of thin cream and a cup of milk, both previously heated; serve at once.

Vegetable Soup No. 3.—Soak a cupful of white beans over night in cold water. When ready to cook, put into fresh boiling water and simmer until tender. When nearly done, add three large potatoes sliced, two or three slices of white turnip, and one large parsnip cut in slices. When done, rub through a colander, add milk or water to make of proper consistency, season with salt and cream, reheat and serve. This quantity of material is sufficient for two quarts of soup.

Vegetable Soup No. 4.—Prepare a quart of bran stock as previously directed. Heat to boiling, and add to it one teaspoonful of grated carrot, a slice of onion, and a half cup of tomato. Cook together in a double boiler for half an hour. Remove the slice of onion, and add salt and a half cup of turnip previously cooked and cut in small dice.

Velvet Soup.—Pour three pints of hot potato soup, seasoned to taste, slowly over the well-beaten yolks of two eggs, stirring briskly to mix the egg perfectly with the soup. It must not be reheated after adding the egg. Plain rice or barley soup may be used in place of potato soup, if preferred.

Vermicelli Soup.—Lightly fill a cup with broken vermicelli. Turn it into a pint of boiling water, and cook for ten or fifteen minutes. Drain off all the hot water and put into cold water for a few minutes. Turn into a colander and drain again; add three pints of milk, salt to taste, and heat to boiling. Have the yolks of three eggs well beaten, and when the soup is boiling, turn it gradually onto the eggs, stirring briskly that they may not curdle. Return to the kettle, reheat nearly to boiling, and serve at once.

Vermicelli Soup No. 2.—Cook a cupful of sliced vegetable oysters, a stalk or two of celery, two slices of onion, a parsnip, and half a carrot in water just sufficient to cover well. Meanwhile put a cupful of vermicelli in a quart of milk and cook in a double boiler until tender. When the vegetables are done, strain off the broth and add it to the vermicelli when cooked. Season with salt and a cup of cream. Beat two eggs light and turn the boiling soup on the eggs, stirring briskly that they may not curdle. Reheat if not thickened, and serve.

White Celery Soup.—Cut two heads of celery into finger lengths, and simmer in a quart of milk for half an hour. Remove the pieces of celery with a skimmer. Thicken the soup with a tablespoonful of cornstarch braided with a little milk, add salt if desired, and a teacup of whipped cream.

TABLE TOPICS.

Soup rejoices the stomach, and disposes it to receive and digest other food.—*Brillat Savarin.*

To work the head, temperance must be carried into the diet.—*Beecher.*

To fare well implies the partaking of such food as does not disagree with body or mind. Hence only those fare well who live temperately.—*Socrates.*

The aliments to which the cook's art gives a liquid or semi-liquid form, are in general more digestible.—*Dictionaire de Medicine.*

In the most heroic days of the Grecian army, their food was the plain and simple produce of the soil. When the public games of ancient Greece were first instituted, the *athleta*, in accordance with the common dietetic habits of the people, were trained entirely on vegetable food.

The eating of much flesh fills us with a multitude of evil diseases and multitudes of evil desires.
—*Perphyrises, 233 A.D.*

No flocks that range the valley free
To slaughter I condemn;
Taught by the Power that pities me,
I learn to pity them.
But from the mountain's grassy side
A guiltless feast I bring;
A scrip with herbs and fruits supplied
And water from the spring.

—*Goldsmith.*

BREAKFAST DISHES

A good breakfast is the best capital upon which people who have real work to do in the world can begin the day. If the food is well selected and well cooked, it furnishes both cheer and strength for their daily tasks. Poor food, or good food poorly prepared, taxes the digestive powers more than is due, and consequently robs brain and nerves of vigor. Good food is not rich food, in the common acceptation of the term; it is such food as furnishes the requisite nutriment with the least fatigue to the digestive powers. It is of the best material, prepared in the best manner, and with pleasant variety, though it may be very simple.

"What to get for breakfast" is one of the most puzzling problems which the majority of housewives have to solve. The usually limited time for its preparation requires that it be something easily and quickly prepared; and health demands that the bill of fare be of such articles as require but minimum time for digestion, that the stomach may have chance for rest after the process of digestion is complete, before the dinner hour. The custom of using fried potatoes or mushes, salted fish or meats, and other foods almost impossible of digestion, for breakfast dishes, is most pernicious. These foods set completely at variance all laws of breakfast hygiene. They are very difficult of digestion, and the thirst-provoking quality of salted foods makes them an important auxiliary to the acquirement of a love of intoxicating drinks. We feel very sure that, as a prominent temperance writer says, "It very often happens that women who send out their loved ones with an agony of prayer that they may be kept from drink for the day, also send them with a breakfast that will make them almost frantic with thirst before they get to the first saloon."

The foods composing the breakfast *menu* should be simple in character, well and delicately cooked, and neatly served. Fruits and grains and articles made from them offer the requisites for the ideal breakfast. These afford ample provision for variety, are easily made ready, and easily digested, while at the same time furnishing excellent nutriment in ample quantity and of the very best quality. Meats, most vegetables, and compound dishes, more difficult of digestion, are better reserved for the dinner bill of fare. No vegetable except the potato is especially serviceable as a breakfast food, and it is much more readily digested when baked than when prepared in any other manner. Stewing requires less time for preparation, but about one hour longer for digestion.

As an introduction to the morning meal, fresh fruits are most desirable, particularly the juicy varieties, as oranges, grape fruit, melons, grapes, and peaches, some one of which are obtainable nearly the entire year. Other fruits; such as apples, bananas, pears, etc., though less suitable, may be used for the same purpose. They are, however, best accompanied with wafers or some hard food, to insure their thorough mastication.

For the second course, some of the various cereals, oatmeal, rye, corn, barley, rice, or one of the numerous preparations of wheat, well cooked and served with cream, together with one or more unfermented breads (recipes for which have been given in a previous chapter), cooked fruits, and some simple relishes, are quite sufficient for a healthful and palatable breakfast.

If, however, a more extensive bill of fare is desired, numerous delicious and appetizing toasts may be prepared according to the recipes given in this chapter, and which, because of their simple character and the facility with which they can be prepared, are particularly suitable as breakfast dishes. The foundation of all these toasts is*zwieback*, or twice-baked bread, prepared from good whole-wheat or Graham fermented bread cut in uniform slices not more than a half inch thick, each slice being divided in halves, placed on tins, or what is better, the perforated sheets recommended for baking rolls, and baked or toasted in a slow oven for a half hour or longer, until it is browned evenly throughout the entire slice. The zwieback may be prepared in considerable quantity and kept on hand in readiness for use. It will keep for any length of time if stored in a dry place.

Stale bread is the best for making zwieback, but it should be good, light bread; that which is sour, heavy, and not fit to eat untoasted, should never be used. Care must be taken also not to scorch the slices, as once scorched, it is spoiled. Properly made, it is equally crisp throughout, and possesses a delicious, nutty flavor.

Its preparation affords an excellent opportunity for using the left-over slices of bread, and it may be made when the oven has been heated for other purposes, as after the baking of bread, or even during the ordinary cooking, with little or no additional heat. If one possesses an Aladdin oven, it can be prepared to perfection.

Zwieback may also be purchased in bulk, all ready for use, at ten cents a pound, from the Sanitarium Food Co., Battle Creek, Mich., and it is serviceable in so many ways that it should form a staple article of food in every household.

For the preparation of toasts, the zwieback must be first softened with some hot liquid, preferably thin cream. Heat the cream (two thirds of a pint of cream will be sufficient for six half slices) nearly to boiling in some rather shallow dish. Put the slices, two or three at a time, in it, dipping the cream over them and turning so that both sides will become equally softened. Keep the cream hot, and let the slices remain until softened just enough so that the center can be pierced with a fork, but not until at all mushy or broken. With two forks or a fork and a spoon, remove each slice from the hot cream, draining as thoroughly as possible, and pack in a heated dish, and repeat the process until as much zwieback has been softened as desired. Cover the dish, and keep hot until ready to serve. Special care should be taken to drain the slices as thoroughly as possible, that none of them be wet and mushy. It is better to remove them from the cream when a little hard than to allow them to become too soft, as they will soften somewhat by standing after being packed in the dish. Prepare the sauce for the toast at the same time or before softening the slices, and pour into a pitcher for serving. Serve the slices in individual dishes, turning a small quantity of the hot sauce over each as served.

RECIPES.

Apple Toast.—Fresh, nicely flavored apples stewed in a small quantity of water, rubbed through, a colander, sweetened, then cooked in a granite-ware dish in a slow oven until quite dry, make a nice dressing for toast. Baked sweet or sour apples rubbed through a colander to remove cores and skins, are also excellent. Soften slices of zwieback in hot cream, and serve with a spoonful or two on each slice. If desired, the apple may be flavored with a little pineapple or lemon, or mixed with grape, cranberry, or apricot, thus making a number of different toasts.

Apricot Toast.—Stew some nice dried apricots as directed on page 191. When done, rub through a fine colander to remove all skins and to render them homogeneous. Add sugar to sweeten, and serve as a dressing on slices of zwieback which have been previously softened in hot cream. One half or two thirds fresh or dried apples may be used with the apricots, if preferred.

Asparagus Toast.—Prepare asparagus as directed on page 255. When tender, drain off the liquor and season it with a little cream, and salt if desired. Moisten nicely browned zwieback in the liquor and lay in a hot dish; unbind the asparagus, heap it upon the toast, and serve.

Banana Toast.—Peel and press some nice bananas through a colander. This may be very easily done with a potato masher, or if preferred a vegetable press may be used for the purpose. Moisten slices of zwieback with hot cream and serve with a large spoonful of the banana pulp on each slice. Fresh peaches may be prepared and used on the toast in the same way.

Berry Toast.—Canned strawberries, blueberries, and blackberries may be made into an excellent dressing for toast.

Turn a can of well-kept berries into a colander over an earthen dish, to separate the juice from the berries. Place the juice in a porcelain kettle and heat to boiling. Thicken to the consistency of cream with flour rubbed smooth in a little water; a tablespoonful of flour to the pint of juice will be about the right proportion. Add the berries and boil up just sufficiently to cook the flour and heat the berries; serve hot. If cream for moistening the zwieback is not obtainable, a little juice may be reserved without thickening, and heated in another dish to moisten the toast; of if preferred, the fruit may be heated and poured over the dry zwieback without being thickened, or it may be rubbed through a colander as for Apricot Toast.

Berry Toast No. 2.—Take fresh red or black raspberries, blueberries, or strawberries, and mash well with a spoon. Add sugar to sweeten, and serve as a dressing on slices of zwieback previously moistened with hot cream.

Celery Toast.—Cut the crisp white portion of celery into inch pieces, simmer twenty minutes or half an hour, or until tender, in a very little water; add salt and a cup of rich milk. Heat to boiling, and thicken with a little flour rubbed smooth in a small quantity of milk—a teaspoonful of flour to the pint of liquid. Serve hot, poured over slices of zwieback previously moistened with cream or hot water.

Cream Toast—For this use good Graham or whole-wheat zwieback. Have a pint of thin sweet cream scalding hot, salt it a little if desired, and moisten the zwieback in it as previously directed packing it immediately into a hot dish; cover tightly so that the toast may steam, and serve. The slices should be thoroughly moistened, but not soft and mushy nor swimming in cream; indeed, it is better if a little of the crispness still remains.

Cream Toast with Poached Egg.—Prepare the cream toast as previously directed, and serve hot with a well-poached egg on each slice.

Cherry Toast.—Take a quart of ripe cherries; stem, wash and stew (if preferred the stones may be removed) until tender but not broken; add sugar to sweeten, and pour over slices of well-browned dry toast or zwieback. Serve cold.

Gravy Toast.—Heat a quart and a cupful of rich milk to boiling, add salt, and stir into it three scant tablespoonfuls of flour which has been rubbed to a smooth paste in a little cold milk. This quantity will be sufficient for about a dozen slices of toast. Moisten slices of zwieback with hot water and pack in a heated dish. When serving, pour a quantity of the cream cause over each slice.

Dry Toast with Hot Cream.—Nicely prepared zwieback served in hot saucers with hot cream poured over each slice at the table, makes a most delicious breakfast dish.

Grape Toast.—Stem well-ripened grapes, wash well, and scald without water in a double boiler until broken; rub through a colander to remove sends and skins, and when cool, sweeten to taste. If the toast is desired for breakfast, the grapes should be prepared the day previous. Soften the toast in hot cream, as previously directed, and pack in a tureen. Heat the prepared grapes and serve, pouring a small quantity over each slice of toast. Canned grapes may be used instead of fresh ones, if desired.

Lentil Toast.—Lentils stewed as directed for Lentil Gravy onpage 226 served as a dressing on slices of zwieback moistened with hot cream or water, makes a very palatable toast. Browned flour may be used to thicken the dressing if preferred.

Prune Toast.—Cook prunes as directed on page 191, allowing them to simmer very slowly for a long time. When done, rub through a colander, and if quite thin, they should be stewed again for a time, until they are about the consistency of marmalade. Moisten slices of zwieback with hot cream, and serve with a spoonful or two of the prune dressing on each. One third dried apple may be used with the prune, if preferred.

Peach Toast.—Stew nice fresh peaches in a small quantity of water; when tender, rub through a colander, and if quite juicy, place on the back of the range where they will cook very slowly until nearly all the water has evaporated, and the peach is of the consistency of marmalade. Add sugar to sweeten, and serve the same as prunes, on slices of zwieback previously moistened with hot cream. Canned peaches may be drained from their juice and prepared in the same manner. Dried or evaporated peaches may also be used. Toast with dried-peach dressing will be more delicate in flavor if one third dried apples be used with the peaches.

Snowflake Toast.—Heat to boiling a quart of milk to which a half cup of cream, and a little salt have been added. Thicken with a tablespoonful of flour rubbed smooth in a little cold milk. Have ready the whites of two eggs beaten to a stiff froth; and when the sauce is well cooked, turn a cupful of it on the beaten egg, stirring well meanwhile so that it will form a light, frothy mixture, to which add the remainder of the sauce. If the sauce is not sufficiently hot to coagulate the albumen, it may be heated again almost to the boiling point, but should not be allowed to boil. The sauce should be of a light, frothy consistency throughout. Serve as dressing on nicely moistened slices of zwieback.

Tomato Toast.—Moisten slices of zwieback in hot cream, and serve with a dressing prepared by heating a pint of strained stewed tomato to boiling, and thickening with a tablespoonful of corn starch or flour rubbed smooth in a little cold water. Season with salt and a half cupful of hot cream. The cream may be omitted, if preferred.

Vegetable Oyster Toast.—Cook a quart of cleaned, sliced vegetable oysters in a quart of water until very tender; add a pint and a half of rich milk, salt to taste, and thicken the whole with two tablespoonfuls of flour rubbed to a smooth paste with a little milk. Let it boil for a few minutes, and serve as a dressing on slices of well-browned toast previously moistened with hot water or cream.

MISCELLANEOUS BREAKFAST DISHES.

Brewis.—Heat a pint of rich milk to boiling, remove from fire, and beat into it thoroughly and quickly a cup of very fine stale rye or Graham bread crumbs. Serve at once with cream.

Blackberry Mush.—Rub a pint of canned or fresh stewed and sweetened blackberries, having considerable juice, through a fine colander or sieve to remove the seeds. Add water to make a pint and a half cupful in all, heat to boiling, and sprinkle into it a cupful of sifted Graham flour, or sufficient to make a mush of desired thickness. Cook as directed for Graham Mush, page 90. Serve hot with cream.

Dry Granola.—This prepared food, made from wheat, corn, and oats, and obtainable from the Sanitarium Food Co., Battle Creek, Mich., forms an excellent breakfast dish eaten with cold or hot milk and cream. Wheatena, prepared wholly from wheat; Avenola, made from oats and wheat; and Gofio, made from parched grains, all obtainable from the same firm, are each delicious and suitable foods for the morning meal.

Frumenty.—Wash well a pint of best wheat, and soak for twenty-four hours in water just sufficient to cover. Put the soaked wheat in a covered earthen baking pot or jar, cover well with water, and let it cook in a very slow oven for twelve hours. This may be done the day before it is wanted, or if one has a coal range in which a fire may be kept all night, or an Aladdin oven, the grain may be started in the evening and cooked at night. When desired for use, put in a saucepan with three pints of milk, a cupful of well-washed Zante currants, and one cup of seeded raisins. Boil together for a few minutes, thicken with four tablespoonfuls of flour rubbed smooth in a little cold milk, and serve.

Macaroni with Raisins.—Break macaroni into inch lengths sufficient to fill a half-pint cup. Heat four cups of milk, and when actively boiling, put in the macaroni and cook until tender. Pour boiling water over a half cup of raisins, and let them stand until swelled. Ten or fifteenminutes before the macaroni is done, add the raisins. Serve hot with or without the addition of cream. Macaroni cooked in the various ways as directed in the chapter on Grains, is also suitable for breakfast dishes.

Macaroni with Kornlet.—Break macaroni into inch lengths and cook in boiling milk and water. Prepare the kornlet by adding to it an equal quantity of rich milk or thin cream, and thickening with a little flour, a tablespoonful to the pint. When done, drain the macaroni, and add the kornlet in the proportion of a pint of kornlet mixture to one and one half cups of macaroni. Mix well, turn into an earthen dish, and brown in a moderate oven. Left-over kornlet soup, if kept on ice, may be utilized for this breakfast dish, and the macaroni may be cooked the day before. Green corn pulp may be used in place of the kornlet.

Peach Mush.—Prepare the same as Blackberry Mush using very thin peach sauce made smooth by rubbing through a colander. Freshly stewed or canned peaches or nicely cooked dried peaches are suitable for this purpose. Apples and grapes may be likewise used for a breakfast mush.

Rice with Lemon.—Wash a cup of rice and turn it into three pints of boiling water, let it boil vigorously until tender, and turn into a colander to drain. While still in the colander and before the rice has become at all cold, dip quickly in and out of a pan of cold water several times to separate the grains, draining well afterward. All should be done so quickly that the rice will not become too cold for serving; if necessary to reheat, place for a few moments in a dish in a steamer over a kettle of boiling water. Serve with a dressing of lemon previously prepared by cutting two fresh lemons in thin, wafer-like slices, sprinkling each thickly with sugar, and allowing them to stand for an hour or more until a syrup is formed. When the rice is ready to serve, lay the slices of lemon on top of it, pouring the syrup over it, and serve with a slice or two of the lemon for each dish.

TABLE TOPICS.

The lightest breakfast is the best.—*Oswald.*

A NEW NAME FOR BREAKFAST.—"Tum, mamma, leth's go down to tupper," said a little toddler to her mother, one morning, recently.

"Why, we don't have supper in the morning," replied the mother.

"Den leth's do down to dinner," urged the little one.

"But we don't have dinner in the morning," corrected the mother.

"Well, den, leth's do down any way," pleaded the child.

"But try and think what meal we have in the morning," urged mamma.

"I know," said the toddler, brightening up.

"What meal do we have in the morning?"

"Oatmeal. Tum on; leth's do."—*Sel.*

Seneca, writing to a friend of his frugal fare which he declares does not cost a sixpence a day, says:—

"Do you ask if that can supply due nourishment? Yes; and pleasure too. Not indeed, that fleeting and superficial pleasure which needs to be perpetually recruited, but a solid and substantial one. Bread and polenta certainly is not a luxurious feeding, but it is no little advantage to be able to receive pleasure from a simple diet of which no change of fortune can deprive one."

Breakfast: Come to breakfast!
Little ones and all,—
How their merry footsteps
Patter at the call!
Break the bread; pour freely
Milk that cream-like flows;
A blessing on their appetites
And on their lips of rose.

Dinner may be pleasant
So may the social tea,
But yet, methinks the breakfast
Is best of all the three.
With its greeting smile of welcome,
Its holy voice of prayer,
It forgeth heavenly armor
To foil the hosts of care.—*Mrs. Sigourney.*

Health is not quoted in the markets because it is without price.—*Sel.*

It is a mistake to think that the more a man eats, the fatter and stronger he will become.—*Sel.*

DESSERTS

Custom has so long established the usage of finishing the dinner with a dessert of some kind, that a *menu* is considered quite incomplete without it; and we shall devote the next few pages to articles which may be deemed appropriate and healthful desserts, not because we consider the dessert itself of paramount importance, for indeed we do not think it essential to life or even to good living, but because we hope the hints and suggestions which our space permits, may aid the housewife in preparing more wholesome, inexpensive dishes in lieu of the indigestible articles almost universally used for this purpose.

We see no objection to the use of a dessert, if the articles offered are wholesome, and are presented before an abundance has already been taken. As usually served, the dessert is but a "snare and delusion" to the digestive organs.

Compounded of substances "rich," not in food elements, but in fats, sweets, and spices, and served after enough has already been eaten, it offers a great temptation to overeat; while the elements of which it is largely composed, serve to hamper the digestive organs, to clog the liver, and to work mischief generally. At the same time it may be remarked that the preparation of even wholesome desserts requires an outlay of time and strength better by far expended in some other manner. Desserts are quite unnecessary to a good, healthful, nutritious dietary. The simplest of all desserts are the various nuts and delicious fruits with which nature has so abundantly supplied us, at no greater cost than their harmful substitutes, and which require no expenditure of time or strength in their preparation. If, however, other forms of dessert are desired, a large variety may be prepared in a simple manner, so as to be both pleasing and appetizing.

GENERAL SUGGESTIONS.

In the preparation of desserts, as in that of all other foods it is essential that all material used shall be thoroughly good of its kind. If bread is to be used, the crumbs should be dry and rather stale, but on no account use that which is sour or moldy. Some housekeepers imagine that if their bread happens to spoil and become sour, although it is hardly palatable enough for the table, it may be advantageously used to make puddings. It is indeed quite possible to combine sour bread with other ingredients so as to make a pudding agreeable to the palate; but disguising sour bread makes sweets and flavors by no means changes it into a wholesome food. It is better economy to throw sour bread away at once than to impose it upon the digestive organs at the risk of health and strength.

Bread which has begun to show appearance of mold should never be used; for mold is a poison, and very serious illness has resulted from the eating of puddings made from moldy bread.

Eggs, to be used for desserts, should always be fresh and good. Cooks often imagine that an egg too stale to be eaten in any other way will do very well for use in cakes and puddings, because it can be disguised so as not to be apparent to the taste; but stale eggs are unfit for food, either alone or in combination with other ingredients. Their use is often the occasion of serious disturbances of the digestive organs. Most desserts in which eggs are used will be much lighter if the yolks and whites are beaten separately. If in winter, and eggs are scarce, fewer may be used, and two tablespoonfuls of dry snow for each omitted egg stirred in the last thing before baking.

Milk, likewise, should always be sweet and fresh. If it is to be heated, use a double boiler, so that there will be no danger of scorching. If fresh milk is not available, the condensed milk found at the grocer's is an excellent substitute. Dissolve according to directions, and follow the recipe the same as with fresh milk, omitting one half or two thirds the given amount of sugar.

If dried sweet fruits, raisins, or currants are to be used, look them over carefully, put them in a colander, and placing it in a pan of warm water, allow the currants to remain until plump. This will loosen the dirt which, while they are shriveled, sticks in the creases, and they may then be washed by dipping the colander in and out of clean water until they are free from sediment; rinse in two waters, then spread upon a cloth, and let them get perfectly dry before using.

It is a good plan, after purchasing raisins and currants, to wash and dry a quantity, and store in glass cans ready for use. To facilitate the stoning of raisins, put them into a colander placed in a dish of warm water until plump; then drain, when the seeds can be easily removed.

For desserts which are to be molded, always wet the molds in cold water before pouring in the desserts.

SUGGESTIONS FOR FLAVORING, ETC.

To Prepare Almond Paste.—Blanch the nuts according to directions given on page 215. Allow them to dry thoroughly, and pound in a mortar to a smooth paste. They can be reduced much easier if dried for a day or two after blanching. During the pounding, sprinkle with a few drops of cold water, white of egg, rose water, or lemon juice, to prevent them from oiling.

Cocoanut Flavor.—Cocoanut, freshly grated or desiccated, unless in extremely fine particles, is a very indigestible substance, and when its flavor is desired for custards, puddings, etc., it is always better to steep a few tablespoonfuls in a pint of milk for twenty minutes or a half hour, and strain out the particles. The milk should not be allowed to boil, as it will be likely to curdle. One tablespoonful of freshly grated cocoanut or two of the desiccated will give a very pleasant and delicate flavor; and if a more intense flavor is desired, use a larger quantity.

Orange and Lemon Flavor.—Orange or lemon flavor may be obtained by steeping a few strips of the yellow part of the rind of lemon or orange in milk for twenty minutes. Skim out the rind before using for desserts. Care should be taken to use only the yellow part, as the white will impart a bitter flavor. The grated rind may also be used for flavoring, but in grating the peel, one must be careful to grate very lightly, and thus use only the outer yellow portion, which contains the essential oil of the fruit. Grate evenly, turning and working around the lemon, using as small a surface of the grater as possible, in order to prevent waste. Generally, twice across the grater and back will be sufficient for removing all the yellow skin from one portion of a lemon. A well-grated lemon should be of exactly the same shape as before, with no yellow skin remaining, and no deep scores into the white. Remove the yellow pulp from the grater with a fork.

To Color Sugar.—For ornamenting the meringues of puddings and other desserts, take a little of the fresh juice of cranberries, red raspberries, currants, black raspberries, grapes, or other colored juices of fruits, thicken it stiff with the sugar, spread on a plate to dry, or use at one. It may be colored yellow with orange peel strained through a cloth, or green with the juice of spinach. Sugar prepared in this manner is quite as pretty and much more wholesome than the colored sugars found in market, which are often prepared with poisonous chemicals.

FRUIT DESSERTS.

RECIPES.

Apple Dessert.—Pare some large tart apples, remove the cores, put into the cavities a little quince jelly, lemon flavored sugar, or grated pineapple and sugar, according to the flavor desired. Have as many squares of bread with the crust taken off as there are apples, and place a filled apple on each piece of bread, on earthen pie plates; moisten well with a little quince jelly dissolved in water, lemon juice, or pineapple juice, according to the filling used. Cover closely, and bake in a rather quick oven till the apples are tender. Serve with whipped cream and sugar.

Apple Meringue Dessert.—Pare and core enough tart, easy-cooking apples to make a quart when stewed. Cover closely and cook slowly till perfectly tender, when they should be quite dry. Mash through a colander, add a little sugar and a little grated pineapple or lemon peel. Beat light with a silver fork, turn into a pudding dish, and brown in a moderate oven ten or fifteen minutes. Then cover with a meringue made with two tablespoonfuls of sugar and the beaten whites of two eggs, and return to the oven for a moment to brown. Serve cold.

Apple Rose Cream.—Wash, core, slice, and cook without paring, a dozen fresh snow apples until very dry. When done, rub through a colander to remove the skins, add sugar to sweeten, and the whites of two eggs; beat vigorously with an egg beater until stiff, add a teaspoonful of rose water for flavoring, and serve at once, or keep on ice. It is especially important that the apples be very dry, otherwise the cream will not be light. If after rubbing through the colander, there is still much juice, they should be cooked again until it has evaporated; or they may be turned into a jelly bag and drained. Other varieties of apple may be used, and flavored with pineapple or vanilla. Made as directed of snow apples or others with white flesh and red skins, the cream should be of a delicate pink color, making a very dainty as well as delicious dessert.

Apple Snow.—Pare and quarter some nice tart apples. Those that when cooked will be whitest in color are best. Put them into a china dish, and steam until tender over a kettle of boiling water. When done, rub through a colander or beat with a fork until smooth, add sugar to sweeten and a little grated lemon rind, and beat again. For every cup and a half of the prepared apple allow the white of one egg, which beat to a stiff froth, adding the apple to it a little at a time, beating all together until, when taken up in a spoon, it stands quite stiff. Serve cold, with or without a simple custard prepared with a pint of hot milk, a tablespoonful of sugar, and the yolks of two eggs.

Baked Apples with Cream.—Pare some nice juicy sweet apples, and remove the cores without dividing. Bake until tender in a covered dish with a spoonful or two of water on the bottom. Serve with whipped cream. Or, bake the apples without paring and when done, remove the skins, and serve in the same manner. The cream may be flavored with a little lemon or rose if desired. Lemon apples and Citron apples, prepared as directed on pages 186 and 187, make a most delicious dessert served with whipped cream and sugar, or with mock cream flavored with cocoanut.

Baked Sweet Apple Dessert.—Wash and remove the cores from a dozen medium-sized sweet apples, and one third as many sour ones, and bake until well done. Mash through a colander to make smooth and remove the skins. Put into a granite-ware dish, smooth the top with a knife, return to the oven and bake very slowly until dry enough to keep its shape when cut. Add if desired a meringue made by heating the white of one egg with a tablespoonful of sugar. Cut into squares, and serve in individual dishes. The meringue may be flavored with lemon or dotted with bits of colored sugar.

Bananas in Syrup.—Heat in a porcelain kettle a pint of currant and red raspberry juice, equal parts, sweetened to taste. When boiling, drop into it a dozen peeled bananas, and simmer very gently for twenty minutes. Remove the bananas, boil the juice until thickened to the consistency of syrup, and pour over the fruit. Serve cold.

Baked Bananas—Bake fresh, firm, yelow bananas with the skins on fifteen minutes in a moderate oven. Serve hot.

Fresh Fruit Compote.—Flavor three tablespoonfuls of sugar by mixing with it a little of the grated yellow rind of an orange, or by rubbing it over the orange to extract the oil. If the latter method is used, the square lump sugar will be preferable. Pare, quarter, and slice three medium-sized tart apples. Peel, remove the seeds, and cut in quite fine pieces three oranges. Put the fruit in alternate layers in a glass dish. Sweeten a cupful of fresh or canned raspberry juice with the flavored sugar, and turn it over the fruit. Put the dish on ice to cool for a half hour before serving.

Grape Apples.—Sweeten a pint of fresh grape juice with a pint of sugar, and simmer gently until reduced one third. Pare and core without dividing, six or eight nice tart apples, and stew very slowly in the grape juice until tender, but not broken. Remove the apples and boil the juice (if any remain) until thickened to the consistency of syrup. Serve cold with a dressing of whipped cream. Canned grape pulp or juice may be utilized for this purpose. Sweet apples may be used instead of tart ones, and the sugar omitted.

Peach Cream.—Pare and stone some nice yellow peaches, and mash with a spoon or press through a colander with a potato masher. Allow equal quantities of the peach pulp and cream, add a little sugar to sweeten, and beat all together until the cream is light. Serve in saucers or glasses with currant buns. A banana cream may be prepared in the same manner.

Prune Dessert.—Prepare some prune marmalade as directed on page 191. Put in a square granite-ware dish, which place inside another dish containing hot water, and cook it in a slow oven until the marmalade is dry enough to retain its shape when cut with a knife. If desired add a meringue as for baked sweet apple dessert, dotting the top with pink sugar. Serve in squares in individual dishes.

DESSERTS MADE OF FRUIT WITH GRAINS, BREAD, ETC.

RECIPES.

Apple Sandwich.—Mix half a cup of sugar with the grated yellow rind of half a lemon. Stir half a cup of cream into a quart of soft bread crumbs; prepare three pints of sliced apples, sprinkled with the sugar; fill a pudding dish with alternate layers of moistened crumbs and sliced apples, finishing with a thick layer of crumbs. Unless the apples are very juicy, add half a cup of cold water, and unless quite tart, have mixed with the water the juice of half a lemon. Cover and bake about one hour. Remove the cover toward the last, that the top may brown lightly. Serve with cream. Berries or other acid fruits may be used in place of apples, and rice or cracked wheat mush substituted for bread crumbs.

Apple Sandwich No. 2.—Prepare and stew some apples as for sauce, allowing them to become quite dry; flavor with lemon, pineapples, quince, or any desired flavor. Moisten slices of zwieback in hot cream as for toast. Spread a slice with the apple mixture, cover with a second slice of the moistened zwieback, then cut in squares and serve, with or without a dressing of mock cream. If desired to have the sandwiches particularly dainty, cut the bread from which the zwieback is prepared in rounds, triangles, or stars before toasting.

Baked Apple Pudding.—Pour boiling water over bread crumbs; when soft, squeeze out all the water, and line the bottom and sides of an oiled earthen pudding dish with the crumbs. Fill the interior with sliced apples, and cover with a layer of bread crumbs. Bake in a covered dish set in a pan of hot water, until the apples are tender; then remove the cover and brown. Loosen the pudding with a knife, invert on a plate, and it will turn out whole. Serve with sugar and cream.

Barley Fruit Pudding.—Mix together a pint of cold, well steamed pearl barley, a cup of finely minced tart apples, three fourths of a cup of chopped and seeded raisins, a third of a cup of sugar, and a cup of boiling water and turn into a pudding dish; cover, and place the dish in the oven in a pan of hot water, and bake slowly an hour and a half, or until the water has become quite absorbed and the fruit tender. Serve warm with a water, adding sugar to taste, and thickening with a half teaspoonful of cornstarch. Any tart fruit jelly may be used, or the pudding may be served with cream and sugar flavored with a little grated lemon rind.

Barley Fig Pudding.—One pint of well-steamed pearl barley, two cups of finely chopped best figs, one half cup of sugar, one half cup of thin sweet cream, and one and one half cups of fresh milk. Mix allthoroughly, turn into an earthen pudding dish; place it in the oven in a pan half full of hot water, and bake slowly till the milk is nearly absorbed. The pudding should be stirred once or twice during the baking, so that the figs will be distributed evenly, instead of rising to the top.

Blackberry Cornstarch Pudding.—Take two quarts of well-ripened blackberries which have been carefully looked over, put them into a granite-ware boiler with half a cup of water, and stew for twenty minutes. Add sugar to sweeten, and three heaping tablespoonfuls of cornstarch rubbed to a cream with a little cold water. Cook until thickened, pour into molds, and cool. Serve cold with milk or cream. Other fresh or canned berries may be used in the same way.

Cocoanut and Cornstarch Blancmange.—Simmer two tablespoonfuls of desiccated cocoanut in a pint of milk for twenty minutes, and strain through a fine sieve. If necessary, add more cold milk to make a full pint. Add a tablespoonful of sugar, heat to boiling, and stir in gradually two tablespoonfuls of cornstarch rubbed smooth in a very little cold milk. Cook five minutes, turn into cups, and serve cold with fruit sauce or cream.

Cornstarch Blancmange.—Stir together two tablespoonfuls of cornstarch, half a cup of sugar, the juice and a little of the grated rind of one lemon; braid the whole with cold water enough to dissolve well. Then pour boiling water over the mixture, stirring meanwhile, until it becomes transparent. Allow it to bubble a few minutes longer, pour into molds, and serve cold with cream and sugar.

Cornstarch with Raisins.—Measure out one pint of rich milk. Rub two tablespoonfuls of cornstarch perfectly smooth with a little of the milk, and heat the remainder to boiling, adding to it a tablespoonful of sugar. Add the braided cornstarch, and let it cook until it thickens, stirring constantly. Then add a half cup of raisins which have been previously steamed. This may be served hot with sugar and cream, or turned into cups and molded, and served cold with lemon, orange, or other fruit sauce for dressing.

Cornstarch with Apples.—Prepare the cornstarch as in the preceding recipe, omitting the raisins. Place in a pudding dish some lemon apple sauce, without juice, about two inches deep. Pour the cornstarch over it, and serve hot or cold with cream.

Cornstarch Fruit Mold.—Heat a quart of strawberry, raspberry, or currant juice, sweetened to taste, to boiling. If the pure juice of berries is used, it may be diluted with one cup of water to each pint and a half of juice. Stir in four tablespoonfuls of cornstarch well braided with a little of the juice reserved for this purpose. Boil until the starch is well cooked, stirring constantly. Pour into molds previously wet with cold water, and cool. Serve with cream and sugar. A circle of fresh berries around the mold when served adds to its appearance.

Cornstarch Fruit Mold No. 2.—Wash, stone, and stew some nice French prunes, add sugar to sweeten, and if there is not an abundance of juice, a little boiling water. For every one fourth pound of prunes there should be enough juice to make a pint in all, for which add two tablespoonfuls of cornstarch, rubbed smooth in a little cold water, and boil three or four minutes. Pour into cups previously wet in cold water, and mold. Serve cold with whipped cream. Other dried or canned fruits, as apricots, peaches, cherries, etc., may be used in place of prunes, if preferred.

Cracked-Wheat Pudding.—A very simple pudding may be made with two cups of cold, well-cooked cracked wheat, two and a half cups of milk, and one half cup of sugar. Let the wheat soak in the milk till thoroughly mixed and free from lumps, then add the sugar and a little grated lemon peel, and bake about three fourths of an hour in a moderate oven. It should be of a creamy consistency when cold, but will appear quite thin when taken from the oven. By flavoring the milk with cocoanut, a different pudding may be produced. Rolled or pearl wheat may be used for this pudding. A cupful of raisins may be added if desired.

Cracked-Wheat Pudding No. 2.—Four and one half cups of milk, a very scant half cup of cracked wheat, one half cup of sugar; put together in a pudding dish, and bake slowly with the dish covered and set in a pan of hot water for three or four hours, or until the wheat is perfectly tender, as may be ascertained by dipping a few grains with a spoon out from the side of the dish.

Farina Blancmange.—Heat a quart of milk, reserving one half cup, to boiling. Then add two tablespoonfuls of sugar, and four heaping tablespoonfuls of farina, previously moistened with the reserved half cup of milk. Let all boil rapidly for a few minutes till the farina has well set, then place in a double boiler, or a dish set in a pan of boiling water, to cook an hour longer. Mold in cups previously wet with cold water. Serve with sugar and cream flavored with vanilla or a little grated lemon rind, mock cream, or cocoanut sauce.

Much variety may be given this simple dessert by serving it with a dressing of fruit juices; red raspberry, strawberry, grape, current, cranberry, cherry, and plum are all very good. If desired, the milk with which the blancmange is prepared may be first flavored with cocoanut, thus making a different blancmange. Fresh fruit, as sliced banana, blueberries, or strawberries, lightly stirred in just before molding, make other excellent varieties.

Farina Fruit Mold.—Put a quart of well-sweetened red raspberry juice into the inner cup of a double boiler. Heat to boiling, and stir in four heaping tablespoonfuls of farina first moistened with a little of the juice. Boil up until thickened, then set into the outer boiler, the water in which should be boiling, and cook for one hour. Pour into molds previously wet in cold water, and cool. Serve with whipped cream or mock cream. Currant, strawberry, cherry, or blackberry juice may be used instead of raspberry. If water be added to dilute the juice, a little more farina will be needed.

Fruit Pudding.—Measure out one quart of rich new milk, reserving half a pint to wet five large rounded tablespoonfuls of sifted flour. Add to the milk one even cup of sugar, turn in the flour mixture and heat to boiling in a farina kettle, stirring all the while to prevent lumps, and cook till it thickens, which will be about ten minutes after it begins to boil. Remove from the stove, and beat while it is cooling. When cool, add sliced bananas or whole strawberries, whortleberries, raspberries, blackberries, sliced apricots, or peaches. Serve cold.

Jam Pudding.—Make a jam by mashing well some fresh raspberries or blueberries and sweetening to taste. Spread over slices of fresh, light bread or buns, and pile in layers one above another in a pudding dish. Pour over the layers enough rich milk or thin cream heated to scalding, to moisten the whole. Turn a plate over the pudding, place a weight upon it, and press lightly till cold. Cut in slices, and serve with or without a cream dressing.

Plain Fruit Pudding or Brown Betty.—Chop together one part seeded raisins and two parts good tart apples. Fill a pudding dish with alternate layers of the fruit and bread crumbs, finishing with the bread crumbs on top. Unless the apples are very juicy, moisten the whole with a tablespoonful of lemon juice in a cup of cold water, for a pudding filling a three-pint dish. Cover the dish and place it in a moderate oven in a pan of hot water, and bake nearly an hour; then remove from the pan, uncover, and brown nicely. Serve warm with cream and sugar, or with an orange or lemon sauce. Seeded cherries may be used in place of the apples and raisins. In that case, each layer of fruit should be sprinkled lightly with sugar, and the water omitted.

Prune Pudding.—Moisten rather thin slices of stale bread in hot milk and place in a pudding dish with alternate layers of stewed prunes from which the stones have been removed, finishing with bread on top. Pour over the whole a little more hot milk or pure juice or both, and bake in a moderate over three fourths of an hour. Serve hot or cold with orange or lemon sauce.

Rice Meringue.—Steam a cupful of rice as directed on page 99 until tender and dry. Heap it loosely on a glass dish, and dot with squares of cranberry or currant jelly. Beat with the whites of two eggs to a stiff froth with one third cup of sugar, and pile it roughly over the rice. Serve with cream.

Rice Snowball.—Wash a cupful of good rice and steam until half done. Have pared and cored without dividing, six large, easy cooking tart apples. Put a clean square of cheese cloth over a plate, place the apples on it, and fill them and all the interstices between with rice. Put the remainder of the rice over and around the apples; tie up the cloth, and cook in a kettle of boiling water until the apples are tender. When done, lift from the water and drain well, untie the cloth, invert the pudding upon a plate and remove the cloth. Serve hot with cream and sugar or cocoanut sauce.

Rice Fruit Dessert.—Cold boiled rice, molded so that it can be sliced, may be utilized in making a variety of delicious desserts. A nice pudding may be prepared by filling a dish with alternate layers of half-inch slices of molded rice and grated tart raw apples the same thickness. Grate a little lemon rind over each layer. Cover, and place in the oven in a pan of boiling water, and bake for an hour. Serve with sugar and cream. Stoned cherries or peaches may be used instead of the apple.

Rice Dumpling.—Steam a teacup of rice until tender, and line an oiled earthen pudding dish, pressing it up around the sides and over the bottom. Fill the crust thus made with rather tart apples cut in small slices; cover with rice, and steam until the apples are tender, which may be determined by running a broom-straw through them. Let stand until cold, then turn from the dish, and serve with sugar and cream. Any easy cooking tart fruit, as stoned cherries, gooseberries, etc., may be used in place of the apples when preferred.

Rice Cream Pudding.—Take one cup of good well-washed rice, one scant cup of sugar, and eight cups of new milk, with a little grated lemon rind for flavoring. Put all into an earthen pudding dish, and place on the top of the range. Heat very slowly until the milk is boiling, stirring frequently, so that the rice shall not adhere to the bottom of the dish. Then put into a moderately hot oven, and bake without stirring, till the rice is perfectly tender, which can be ascertained by dipping a spoon in one side and taking out a few grains. It should be, when cold, of a rich, creamy consistency, with each grain of rice whole. Serve cold. It is best if made the day before it is needed. If preferred, the milk may be first flavored with cocoanut, according to the directions given on page 298.

Rice Pudding with Raisins.—Wash thoroughly one half cup of rice, and soak for two hours in warm water. Drain off the water, add two tablespoonfuls of sugar, one half cup of raisins, and four cups of milk. Put in an earthen pudding dish and cook for two hours in a moderate oven, stirring once or twice before the rice begins to swell, then add a cup of hot milk, and cook for an hour longer.

Red Rice Mold.—Take one and one half pints of red currants and one half pint of red raspberries, and follow directions on page 209 for extracting their juice. The juice may be diluted with one part water to two of juice if desired. Sweeten to taste, and for each pint when boiling stir in two tablespoonfuls of ground rice or rice flour rubbed smooth in a little of the juice which may be retained for the purpose. Pour into molds, cool, and serve with whipped cream.

Rice and Fruit Dessert.—Steam a cup of good well-washed rice in milk till tender. Prepare some tart apples by paring, dividing midway between the stem and blow ends, and removing the cores. Fill the cavities with quince or pineapple jelly; put the apples in a shallow stewpan with a half cup of water, cover, and steam till nearly tender. Put the rice, which should be very moist, around the bottom and sides of a pudding dish; place the apples inside, cover, and bake ten minutes. Serve with cream flavored with quince or lemon.

Rice and Tapioca Pudding.—Soak one half cup of tapioca over night in a cup of water; in the morning drain off the water if any remains. Add to the tapioca half a cup of rice, one cup of sugar, one cup of raisins, and eight cups of new milk, with a little grated lemon rind for flavoring. Put all in an earthen pudding dish on the top of the range, where it will heat very gradually to the boiling point, stirring frequently. When the milk boils, put the pudding in the oven, and bake till the rice grains are perfectly tender but not broken and mushy. From twenty minutes to half an hour is usually sufficient. When taken from the oven, it will appear quite thin, but after cooling will be of a delicious, creamy consistency. Serve cold.

Rice-Flour Mold.—Braid two tablespoonfuls of rice flour with a little milk and stir the mixture into a pint of boiling milk to which has been added three tablespoonfuls of sugar, and a little salt if desired. Let this boil until it thickens, then mold, and serve with cream and sugar or with lemon, orange, or other fruit sauce.

Rice and Stewed Apple Dessert.—Steam or bake some rice in milk until tender, sweeten slightly and spread a layer of the rice half an inch thick on the bottom of a pudding dish, then a layer of lemon-flavored apple sauce, which has been rubbed through a colander and afterward simmered on the range until stiff. If preferred, the sauce may be prepared by first baking the apples, and then rubbing the pulp through a colander. Add another layer of rice, then one of sauce, and so on until the dish is full. Bake in a moderate oven and serve hot. If the apples are not very tart, part stewed and sifted cranberries may be used with them.

Rice and Strawberry Dessert.—Soak a cup of rice in one and a half cups of new milk; place all in an earthen dish, and steam an hour, or until dry and tender, stirring occasionally for the first fifteen minutes. When the rice is done, place in the bottom of cups previously moistened with cold water, five nice hulled strawberries in the shape of a star. Carefully fill the interstices between the berries with the cooked rice, and put in a layer of rice. Add next a layer of strawberries, then another of rice. Press firmly into the cups, and set away to cool. When well molded, turn into saucers, and pile whipped cream around each mold; sprinkle with sugar and serve.

A little care in forming the stars and filling the molds makes this a delicious and pretty dessert. If preferred, the dessert may be prepared in one large mold, and a larger number of berries arranged in the form of a cross in the bottom of the dish, covering with rice, and adding as many alternate layers of berries and rice as desired.

Stewed Fruit Pudding.—Take a deep, square or oblong granite-ware or earthen dish; cut strips of stale bread uniformly an inch in width and three fourths of an inch in thickness, and place them in the mold with spaces between them equal to their width. Or, fit the strips around the bottom of a round, earthen pudding dish, like the spokes of a wheel, with stewed or canned fruit, sweetened to taste; whortleberries are best, but apricots, cherries, currants, strawberries, and gooseberries may all be used. Separate the juice from the berries by turning them into a colander. Fill the interstices between the bread with hot fruit, using just as little juice as possible. Cover with another layer, this time placing the strips of bread over the fruit in the first layer, and leaving the spaces for fruit over the bread in the first layer. Fill the dish with these layers of fruit and bread, and when full, pour over all the hot fruit juice. Put a plate with a weight on it on the top to press it firmly. Dip off any juice that may be pressed out, and set the pudding in the refrigerator to cool and press. When cold, it will turn out whole, and can be cut in slices and served with whipped cream or cocoanut sauce.

Strawberry Minute Pudding.—Cook a quart of ripe strawberries in a pint of water till well scalded. Add sugar to taste. Skim out the fruit, and into the boiling juice stir a scant cup of granulated wheat flour previously rubbed to a paste with a little cold water; cook fifteen or twenty minutes, pour over the fruit, and serve cold with cream sauce.

Sweet Apple Pudding.—Pare, core, and slice enough ripe, juicy sweet apples to fill a pint bowl. Heat a quart of new milk to scalding in a double boiler. Pour it hot over one cup of good granulated cornmeal, and beat very thoroughly to remove all lumps. Return to the double boiler, and cook until the meal is set. The batter then should be about the consistency of corn mush. Remove from the fire, add a pint of cold milk, stir in the sliced apples, one third of a cup of sugar or molasses, and a teaspoonful of flour rubbed smooth in a very little milk. Turn all into a deep earthen crock or pudding dish, and bake slowly from three to four hours, stirring frequently the first hour. It should be moderately browned on top when done. Serve warm or cold.

Whortleberry Pudding.—One quart of new milk, one quart of fine bread crumbs, two quarts of fresh whortleberries, one or two tablespoonfuls of sugar. Heat the milk to boiling; fill a pudding dish with alternate layers of bread crumbs and berries, beginning and ending with crumbs. Add the sugar to the milk, let it dissolve, and pour the whole over the pudding. Cover closely, and bake in a slow oven within a pan of hot water nearly an hour. Serve warm with cream or cocoanut sauce.

DESSERTS WITH TAPIOCA, SAGO, MONICA, AND SEA MOSS.

Both pearl and flake tapioca are suitable for these desserts. They should be soaked for some hours before using, and it is always best to soak over night if convenient. The flake tapioca requires longer soaking and cooking than the pearl tapioca. For soaking, use one and a half cups of water for each cup of flake tapioca, and one pint of water for a cup of pearl tapioca. For cooking, three or four additional cups of water will be required for each cup of tapioca, depending upon, the articles used with it. A double boiler should be used for the cooking.

RECIPES.

Apple Tapioca.—Soak a cupful of pearl tapioca over night. In the morning simmer in a quart of boiling water until transparent and thickened. Arrange in the bottom of a pudding dish four or five good-sized tart apples, which have been pared, cored, and the cavities filled with sugar. Squeeze the juice of a lemon and grate a very little of the rind over the apples. Pour the tapioca over the fruit. Set the dish inside a pan filled with hot water, cover, and bake one hour, or until the apples are done. Serve with sugar and cream. It is best nearly cold. Fresh peaches, pared and stewed, may be used in place of apples, if preferred.

Apple Tapioca No. 2.—Soak a half cup of tapioca in a cap of tepid water, for at least three hours. Pare, core, and quarter nice tart apples to fill a two-quart pudding dish nearly half full. Add four cups of water and one of sugar to the soaked tapioca, pour it over the apples, and bake two or three hours in a slow oven. Serve with whipped cream.

Banana Dessert.—Soak a cup of tapioca over night. In the morning cook in a double boiler in a quart of water until transparent. When done, add a cup of sugar and three or four sliced bananas. Serve cold with cream.

Blackberry Tapioca.—Soak a cup of tapioca over night. When ready to cook, add three cups of boiling water and cook in a double boiler until transparent and smooth. Sprinkle a quart of fresh blackberries with sugar, and stir lightly into the tapioca. Pour into molds and serve cold with cream and sugar. Other fresh berries may be used in the same way.

Cherry Pudding.—Soak and cook a half cup of tapioca in a pint of water until transparent. Have a pint of fresh pitted cherries in an earthen pudding dish. Sprinkle them well with sugar, pour over them the cooked tapioca, and bake for an hour in a moderate oven. Serve hot with or without cream.

Fruit Tapioca.—Cook three fourths of a cup of tapioca in four cups of water until smooth and transparent Stir into it lightly a pint of fresh strawberries, raspberries, currants, or any small fruit, adding sugar as required. For variety a cup of canned quinces or apricots may be substituted for fresh fruit. Serve warm or cold with whipped cream or mock cream.

Molded Tapioca with Fruit.—Simmer one half cup of desiccated cocoanut in a pint of milk for twenty minutes. Strain out the cocoanut, and add milk to make a full pint. Add one half cup of sugar and one half cup of tapioca previously soaked over night. Let the whole simmer until the tapioca is transparent. Dip some cups in cold water, drain, and lay fresh strawberries, currants, or cherries in the bottom of each in the form of a star or cross. Pour the tapioca into the molds gently, so as not to displace the fruit. When cold, turn out and serve with whipped cream or fruit sauce. Raisins may be substituted for fresh fruit, or bits of jelly may be placed around the mold after it has cooled, if preferred.

Pineapple Tapioca.—Soak one cup of tapioca over night in one and one half cups of water. Add two and one half cups of water and cook in a double boiler until transparent, then add one cup of sugar and one juicy pineapple minced fine with a sharp knife. Mold, and serve cold with or without cream.

Prune and Tapioca Pudding.—Soak one half cup of tapioca over night. In the morning cook until transparent in two cups of water. Stew two cups of well-washed and stoned prunes in a quart of water till perfectly tender; then add the juice of a good lemon and two tablespoonfuls of sugar, and boil till the syrup becomes thick and rich. Turn the prunes into a pudding dish, cover with the cooked tapioca, and add a little grated lemon rind. Bake lightly. Serve without dressing or with sugar and cream or almond sauce. If preferred, the prunes and tapioca may be placed in the dish in alternate layers, having the top one of tapioca.

Tapioca and Fig Pudding.—Cook three fourths of a cup of tapioca as for Apple Tapioca. Have ready two cups of finely sliced or chopped tart apples, and one cup of chopped figs, which have first been lightly steamed. If preferred, raisins may be used in place of half the figs. Put the fruit in the bottom of the pudding dish, turn the tapioca over it, and bake till the fruit is very soft. If the apples are not very tart, sprinkle the juice of a lemon over them before adding the figs and tapioca.

A nice fruit pudding can also be made by using half canned pears and half apples, or canned quinces may be substituted for figs.

Peach Tapioca.—For this will be needed a quart of nicely canned peaches, a cup of tapioca, and from one half to three fourths of a cup of sugar, according to the sweetness of the peaches. Soak the tapioca over night in just enough water to cover. When ready to cook, put in a double boiler with three cups of water, and cook for an hour. Remove from the fire and add to it the juice from the peaches, of which there should be a cup and a half, which has been secured by draining the peaches in a colander, and stir it well into the tapioca. Place a layer of this mixture in an oiled pudding dish, add the peaches, cover with the remainder of the tapioca, and bake for an hour in a moderate oven.

Tapioca Jelly.—Soak a cup of tapioca in a pint of water over night. Add another pint and cook until transparent and smooth. Add three tablespoonfuls of lemon juice and four tablespoonfuls of sugar; beat well together and tun into molds. Serve cold. No dressing is required. This may be varied by using unsweetened currant, grape, or other acid fruit juice in place of lemon. Fruit jelly may be used if the juice is not easily obtained. Add when the tapioca is well cooked, and stir until dissolved.

Apple Sago Pudding.—Soak one cup of sago in six cups of water; stew ten small apples, mix with the sago, and bake three quarters of an hour. Serve with cream and sugar. It is better warm than cold, but acceptable either way.

Red Sago Mold.—Take a quart of red raspberry juice, pure or diluted with one third water, and sweeten to taste. Have ready one half cup of best sago which has soaked for twenty minutes in just enough water to cover. Drain off any water that may remain. Add the sago to the juice, and cook until the sago is transparent, then turn into molds. Serve cold with cream. Cranberry or strawberry juice may be used in place of the raspberry, if preferred.

Sago Fruit Pudding.—Soak a small cup of sago an hour in just enough water to cover. Drain off any water that may not be absorbed. Mix two thirds of a cup of sugar with this sago, and stir all into a quart of boiling water. Let it boil until the sago is perfectly transparent and pour in a pint of nicely hulled strawberries. Turn into molds to cool, or serve warm with cream, as preferred. Tapioca can be used instead of sago, but needs longer soaking. Raspberries, stoned cherries, or currants can be used in place of strawberries.

Sago Pudding.—Soak a cupful of sago for twenty minutes in a cup of cold water; then pour over it a quart and a cup of boiling water, add a cup of sugar and one half cup of raisins. Cook till the sago is perfectly transparent, flavor with vanilla, and set away to cool. Serve with whipped cream.

Manioca with Fruit.—Pare, core, and quarter six medium-sized tart apples, and put them to cook in a quart of boiling water. Add a cup of sugar, and cook without stirring until softened, then sprinkle into the water in which they are cooking five tablespoonfuls of manioca, and cook until it is transparent, which will be in about ten minutes. Flavor with a little grated lemon rind, and serve hot with sugar and cream, or mold, as preferred. Canned peaches, apricots, or cherries may be used in a similar manner, adding boiling water if there is not sufficient juice to properly cook the manioca. Or the manioca may be first cooked in boiling water, using four scant tablespoonfuls for a pint of water, and when transparent, turning it over sliced bananas, pineapples, or oranges, molding and serving with cream and sugar.

Raspberry Manioca Mold.—Heat a pint of water, and when boiling, sprinkle into it four scant tablespoonfuls of manioca and cook for ten minutes or until transparent, stirring continually. When transparent and thickened, remove from the fire and add a tablespoonful of lemon juice and one cup of sugar. Place a layer of the cooked manioca in the bottom of a pudding dish, add a layer of freshly picked red raspberries, then another of the manioca, filling the dish in alternate layers with one of manioca for the top. Set away in some cool place until well molded. Serve in slices with cream flavored with rose. Other fresh berries may be used instead of raspberries.

Sea Moss Blancmange.—Wash the moss well in several waters, and soak in a very little cold water for an hour before using. It is hardly possible to give exact directions for making this blancmange, owing to the difficulty of accurately measuring the moss, but in general, a small handful will be ample for a quart of milk. Add the moss, when washed, to the milk, and cook in a double boiler until the milk has become thickened and glutinous. Add sugar to sweeten, flavor with vanilla or rose water, and strain through a fine sieve into cups previously wet in cold water, and mold. This may be varied by using boiling water instead of milk for cooking, adding the juice of one or two lemons and a little grated rind to flavor.

DESSERTS MADE WITH GELATINE.

Gelatine is an article largely employed in making delicate and dainty dishes. It is economical and convenient, because the dessert can be prepared several hours before needed; but it must be stated that it has in itself little or no food value, and there is great liability of its being unwholesome. A writer in the *Anti-Adulteration Journal*, a short time since, speaking of the use of gelatine, says:—

"The nutritive value of pure gelatine has been shown to be very low in the scale of foods. The beef gelatine of the markets that is used by bakers, is far from being pure gelatine. It frequently has a very disagreeable, fetid odor, and has evidently begun to decompose during the process of manufacture. After a thorough drying, putrefaction does not take place as long as it remains dry. But suppose that gelatine which has thus begun to decompose during the drying process, containing, perhaps, putrefactive germs in the dried state, be dissolved in water, and in hot weather, kept in this condition for a few hours previous to being used; the result would be rapid putrefaction. The putrefaction would be checked by freezing; but the bacteria causing it are not killed by the low temperature. As soon as the dessert is melted or eaten, they resume their activity in the body, and may cause sickness. It is a well-known fact that gelatine is an excellent medium in which to cultivate various kinds of micro-organisms; and if the conclusions here mentioned be correct, it seems that gelatine should be used with great care in connection with food preparations. When used carelessly, it may do a great deal of harm. I wish to impress those who use it with the importance of guarding against its dangers. Gelatine should not be allowed to remain in solution for many hours before using, especially in hot weather.

"When used at all, the best varieties should be employed, and such as are free from putrefactive odor."

A "box" of gelatine is used to signify a two-ounce package. If half a box is called for, divide it by cutting the box and its contents in halves rather than by emptying the box and then attempting to make a division.

To prepare gelatine for desserts, first soak it till soft in a small quantity of cold water (a cupful to one box of gelatine is sufficient); fifteen minutes will suffice if it is stirred frequently; then dissolve in boiling liquid. Do not cook the gelatine, and after it is dissolved, always strain through a cloth strainer before using.

In winter, a two-ounce package will solidify two quarts of liquid, including the water in which the gelatine is soaked. In summer, a little less liquid should be used. Gelatine desserts must be left on ice or in a cool place until hardened, but they should not be served at the table so cold as to interfere with the digestion of other foods.

RECIPES.

Apples in Jelly.—Pare and core without cutting open, a half dozen medium-sized tart apples of the same degree of hardness. Fill the centers with a little grated lemon rind and sugar. Steam until tender but not broken. Have ready half a package of gelatine which has been soaked for an hour in just enough water to cover. Prepare a syrup with one cup of sugar and a pint of water. When boiling, turn the syrup over the gelatine, stirring well to dissolve it, and add the juice of half a lemon. Strain, place the apples in a deep dish with a little space between each; turn the mixture over them, and set in the ice box to cool. Serve with or without a little whipped cream.

Apple Shape.—Steam some nice tart apples. When tender, rub through a colander. Have two thirds of a box of gelatine soaked in just enough water to cover; pour over it a cup and a half of boiling water; when well dissolved, strain and add a pint of the sifted apples sweetened to taste, and one half cup of grated fresh or canned pineapple, or if preferred, one half cup of the juice of canned pineapple. Turn into cups previously wet in cold water, and mold. Serve with a little cream. Canned peaches, apricots, and other fruit may be used the same as apples, if preferred. Rub the fruit with but little juice through a colander, and proceed as above.

Banana Dessert.—Dissolve half a box of gelatine in a half cup of warm water. Heat three cups of rich milk to boiling, and add to it one cup of sugar and turn over the well-dissolved gelatine and strain. Let it partly cool, and mix in three or four bananas, sliced thin or chopped fine. Turn all into a mold previously wet with cold water, and leave till hardened, which may require several hours unless the mold be placed on ice. When well molded, turn into a glass dish, serve with whipped cream flavored with vanilla or lemon.

Clear Dessert—Soak a box of gelatine in a large bowl with half a cup of cold water. When soft, pour over it three pints of boiling water, add the juice of three large lemons and two cups of sugar. Stir well, strain, and pour into molds previously wet with cold water. Put into the refrigerator until hardened. Serve with whipped cream. Quince, apricot, orange, or pineapple juice may be substituted for lemon, and thus a variety of desserts may be made.

Fruit Foam Dessert.—Soak half a package of gelatine in half a cup of cold water until soft. Heat to boiling two and one half cups of red raspberry, currant, strawberry, or grape juice, sweetened to taste, and pour over the soaked gelatine. Stir until perfectly dissolved, then strain, and set the dish in ice water to cool. When it is cold and beginning to thicken, beat the whites of three eggs to a stiff froth and stir into the thickening gelatine. Beat thoroughly for fifteen minutes with an egg beater, or whip till the whole is of a solid foam stiff enough to retain its shape. Turn into molds previously wet with cold water, or pile roughly in large spoonfuls in a glass dish. Set away in the refrigerator until needed. Serve with a little whipped cream piled lightly around it.

Fruit Shape.—Take a quart of nicely canned red raspberries, sweetened to taste; turn into a colander and drain off the juice, taking care to keep the fruit as perfect as possible. Put two thirds of a box of gelatine to soak in just enough of the juice to cover. When the gelatine is ready, heat the remainder of the juice to boiling and pour over it. When well dissolved, add the fruit, turn into cups, and mold. Serve with cream. Peaches, strawberries, apricots, and other canned fruit may be used in place of the raspberries, if preferred.

Gelatine Custard.—Soak a quarter of a box of gelatine in one fourth of a cup of cold water till soft; then pour over it three fourths of a cup of boiling water, and stir until dissolved. Beat the yolks of two eggs and three tablespoonfuls of sugar to a cream; pour over it slowly, stirring continuously, a pint of boiling milk, and cook in a double boiler until it thickens. Then add the gelatine mixture, which should first be strained, the whites of the two eggs beaten stiff, and a little vanilla for flavoring. Beat all well together, turn into molds previously wet in cold water, and place on iceto harden. Serve with fruit sauce.

Layer Pudding.—Divide a package of gelatine into three portions, and put each to soak in one third of a cup of cold water. Heat one and one fourths cups of water to boiling, add the juice of one lemon and two thirds of a cup of sugar. Turn this slowly, stirring well meanwhile, over the well-beaten yolks of two eggs. Cook in a double boiler five minutes, or until the mixture thickens. Pour the hot custard over one portion of the soaked gelatine, and stir it until dissolved. Strain, add a little grated lemon rind for flavoring, and turn into a broad, shallow dish to mold. A square granite-ware baking tin is admirable for this purpose.

Take one and one half cups of raspberry, strawberry, grape, or currant juice, sweetened to taste; heat to boiling and pour over the second portion of the soaked gelatine. Stir till well dissolved, strain, and turn into a shallow mold like that containing the first portion.

Heat one and one half cups of rich milk to boiling, add one half cup of sugar, and pour over the third portion of soaked gelatine. Strain and cool a little, flavor with vanilla or a few chopped bananas; or, if preferred, flavor the milk with cocoanut before using, as directed on page 298. Pour into a third mold like the others to cool. When all are cold, arrange in layers, the yellow at the bottom and the white at the top. The whites of the eggs may be used for meringue, or for making a whipped cream sauce to serve with the pudding.

Lemon Jelly.—Soak one half box of gelatine in a scant cup of cold water until soft. Then pour over it one pint of boiling water and stir until well dissolved. Add one cup of sugar, the yellow rind of one lemon, and one half cup of lemon juice. Strain, put into molds previously wet in cold water, and place in the ice chest to harden. If preferred, the above may be cooled in a shallow dish and cut into irregular shapes to be served with a custard sauce. Use only the yolks of eggs in making the custard, that it may have a rich color, using two yolks in place of one whole egg.

Jelly with Fruit.—Soak a package of gelatine in a cup of cold water until soft; then pour over it one quart and a cup of boiling water. Strain, add the juice of four lemons and twelve tablespoonfuls of sugar. Cool a little of the gelatine in a mold, and as soon as set, scatter in some nice currants or seedless raisins; add another layer of gelatine, and when set, scatter in more fruit; continue until the mold is full, having gelatine at the top. Fresh fruit, currants, grapes, cherries, plums, peaches, etc., may be used in place of raisins, if preferred.

Orange Dessert.—Soak one third of a cup of gelatine in one third of a cup of cold water until soft; then pour over it one third of a cup of boiling water. Add a scant cup of sugar, the juice of one lemon, and a cupful of orange juice and pulp. Set the dish containing the mixture in a pan of ice water until it begins to harden. Have ready the whites of three eggs well whipped, add to the jelly, and beat all together until light and stiff enough to drop. Pour into molds wet in cold water, and lined with sections of oranges, from which seeds and white fiber have been removed.

Oranges in Jelly.—Pare divide, and take out the seeds from four or five sweet oranges, being careful to remove all the white rind and shreds. Place in a deep dish and pour over them a syrup prepared as for Apples in Jelly, using the juice of a whole lemon. Set in the ice box over night. A very little orange peel may be grated into the syrup if liked; and if the oranges are very sweet, less sugar will be required. If one can afford to use orange juice in place of the water in making the syrup, the dessert will be greatly improved.

Orange Jelly.—Soak one quarter of a box of gelatine until soft in just enough cold water to cover. Then pour over it one half cup of boiling water. Stir until well dissolved, add the juice of one small lemon, one cupful of orange juice, and one half cup of sugar. Strain, turn into molds previously wet in cold water, and set on ice to harden. Strawberry, raspberry, and other fruit juices may be used in a similar manner.

Snow Pudding.—Soak one fourth of a box of gelatine until soft in an equal measure of cold water. Then pour over it one cup of boiling water, and add one fourth of a cup of strained lemon juice and one cup of sugar; stir till the sugar is all dissolved. Strain into a large china dish, and set in ice water to cool. Let it stand until cold and beginning to thicken. Have ready the whites of three eggs beaten to a stiff froth, and add to the gelatine as it begins to thicken; beat all together for fifteen or twenty minutes, until it is of a solid foam and stiff enough to hold its shape. Turn into molds and keep in a cool place till needed. A half dozen finely sliced or chopped bananas stirred in toward the last, makes a nice variation. Serve with custard sauce made with the yolks of the eggs and flavored with rose or vanilla. Orange, quince, or pineapple juice may be substituted for lemon, for a change.

This dessert is best if made several hours before it is needed and set in the refrigerator to keep cold.

DESSERTS WITH CRUSTS.

RECIPES.

Apple Tart.—Pare and slice some quick-cooking, tart apples, and place them in the bottom of a pudding dish, with a tablespoonful of water. Cover with a crust prepared in the following manner: Into a cup of thin cream stir a gill of yeast and two cups of flour; let this become very light, then add sufficient flour to mix soft. Knead for fifteen or twenty minutes very thoroughly, roll evenly, and cover the apples; put all in a warm place until the crust has become very light, then bake. If the apples do not bake easily, they may be partially cooked before putting on the crust. Dish so that the fruit will be uppermost, and serve cold with cream and sugar, cocoanut sauce, or mock cream.

Gooseberry Tart.—Fill a pudding dish with well prepared green gooseberries, adding a tablespoonful or two of water. Cover with a crust as for Apple Tart, and when light, bake in a moderately quick oven. Cut the crust into the required number of pieces, and dish with gooseberries heaped on top. Serve cold with sugar and cream.

Cherry Tart.—Prepare the same as for Apple Tart, with stoned cherries, only omitting the water, as the cherries will be sufficiently juicy of themselves. If the fruit is very juicy, sprinkle a tablespoonful of flour over it before putting on the crust. Plum and peach tart may be made in the same manner, and are both very nice.

Strawberry and other Fruit Shortcakes.—Beat together one cup of thin cream, slightly warmed, a tablespoonful of yeast, and two small cups of flour. Set in a warm place till very light. Add sufficient warm flour to mix soft, and knead thoroughly for fifteen or twenty minutes. Divide into two equal portions, and roll into sheets about one half inch in thickness, making the center a very little thinner than the edges, so that when risen, the center will not be highest. Place in tins, and set in a warm place until perfectly risen, or until they have doubled their first thickness. Bake quickly. When cold, spread one cake with fruit, and cover with the other. If the fruit is large, it may be chopped fine with a knife, or mashed with a spoon. A little lemon juice added to peaches is an addition for shortcake.

Banana Shortcake.—Prepare the crust as previously directed. Fill with sliced bananas, for every three of which add the juice of one orange, a little of the grated rind, and a half cup of sugar.

Lemon Shortcake.—Prepare the crust as for Fruit Shortcake. For the filling, grate the yellow portion only of the lemon, and squeeze the juice into a bowl; add a cupful of sugar. Braid a tablespoonful of flour smooth with two tablespoonfuls of water, add enough boiling water, stirring well meanwhile, to make a teacupful. Add this to the other ingredients, beat well together, and place the bowl in a basin of boiling water or over the teakettle. Cook until about as thick as boiled custard. Fill this between the shortcakes and serve.

Berry Shortcake with Prepared Cream.—Prepare the shortcake as previously directed. Sweeten the berries and spread on the lower crust, then pour over them a "cream" prepared as follows, and add top crust:—

Cream.—Heat one half cup of milk and the same of thin cream to boiling, add two tablespoonfuls of sugar, and thicken with one teaspoonful of cornstarch rubbed smooth in a little cold milk. Turn the hot sauce over the beaten white of two eggs, stirring rapidly meanwhile, until the egg is thoroughly mingled with the whole. Allow it to become cold before using.

Raised Pie.—Prepare the dough as for shortcake. Divide in two portions, spread one on the tin, and cover with a layer of easy-cooking tart apples sliced in eighths. Put two or three spoonfuls of rather thick sweet cream over the apples, and cover with the top crust. Let the crusts rise until very light, and bake. Peaches may be used in the same manner.

Baked Apple Loaf.—Prepare some dough as for buns on page 347, leaving out the sugar, and when ready for the last melding, cut it into three portions. Put some flour on the bread board, mold the dough well, and roll as thin as pie crust in such shape as will fit a shallow baking tin. Spread over the tin, and cover the dough with a layer of easy-cooking, sour apples sliced very thin, or with very stiff apple marmalade. Cover this with a second layer of dough, then add another layer of apples, and cover with the third portion of the dough. Pinch the edges of the dough well together, let the loaf rise till very light, then bake. Eat cold with sugar and cream. If the apples will not cook quickly, they may be first steamed until nearly tender. If the crust appears too hard when taken from the oven, cover with a wet napkin and allow it to steam for a little time until softened.

CUSTARD PUDDINGS.

Very much depends upon the baking in all puddings made with milk and eggs.

A custard pudding made with one egg, and slowly baked, will be much thicker and nicer than one made with more eggs, baked in too hot an oven.

A custard pudding baked too quickly or too long will have the eggs mixed with the farinaceous substance and the milk turned to whey, while one more carefully baked will have eggs and milk formed into a thick custard on the top.

Custard puddings and all other baked puddings which require to be cooked slowly, are best cooked in an earthen dish set in the oven in a pan of hot water, and baked only till the pudding is set. If it is desirable to use with eggs any ingredient which requires a lengthy cooking, it is much better to cook it partially before adding the eggs. Many custard desserts are much more dainty and more easily served when cooked in cups than when baked in a large dish. The blue willow pattern stoneware cups and the blue and white Japanese ware are very suitable for this purpose. When cooking, set the cups, allowing one for each person, in the oven in a dripping pan containing hot water, and bake. Serve without removing from the cups.

If desired to stir beaten eggs into heated milk, add a few spoonfuls of cold milk to the eggs, and pour the mixture, a little at a time, into the hot milk, taking care to stir it constantly.

A nice way to flavour custards and meringues for custard puddings is to beat fruit jelly with the whites of the eggs; red raspberry, quince, and pineapple jellies give especially nice flavours.

RECIPES.

Apple Custard.—Bake good tart apples; when done, remove the pulp, and rub through a sieve; sweeten, and flavour with grated pineapple or grated orange or lemon rind. Put in a glass dish, and cover with a plain custard prepared as directed on page 328. Bits of jelly may be scattered over the top of the custard.

Apple Custard No. 2.—Peel, halve, and core eight or ten medium-sized sour apples. Have prepared a syrup made with a cup of water, the juice of one lemon, a little grated rind, and a half cup of sugar. When the sugar is dissolved, add the fruit, and simmer till tender but not fallen to pieces. Skim out the apples, draining thoroughly, and lay them in a glass dish. Boil up the syrup until thick, and poor it over the apples. Make a soft boiled custard with a pint of milk, yolks of three eggs, and two tablespoonfuls of sugar. When cold, spread over the apples; whip the whites to a stiff froth, flavor with lemon, and pile irregularly upon the top. Brown lightly in the oven.

Apple Custard No. 3.—Pare and remove the cores from a dozen tart apples, and fill the cavities with black raspberry, quince, or grape jelly. Put them in a covered baking dish with a tablespoonful of water, and steam in the oven till tender but not fallen to pieces. Then cover the apples with a raw custard made by cooking two tablespoonfuls of flour rubbed smooth with a little milk, in a quart of milk, till just thickened, and adding, when cold, the yolks of two eggs well beaten with two heaping tablespoonfuls of sugar, and lastly the whites of the eggs whipped to a stiff froth. Bake in a dish set in a pan of hot water, until the custard has set, but not till it separates.

Apple Cornstarch Custard.—Cover the bottom of a small earthen-ware pudding dish an inch or more in depth with apples stewed until very dry, sweetened and flavored with a teaspoonful of rose water. Heat a cup of milk to boiling, and stir into it a tablespoonful of cornstarch rubbed smooth in a little cold milk, and one fourth cup of sugar; cook until thickened, then add the yolk of one egg, and pour the whole over the apple. Meringue the top with the white of the egg beaten stiff with a tablespoonful of sugar, and flavored with a little rose water.

Apple and Bread Custard.—For this is required one cup of finely rolled bread crumbs, two eggs, one half cup of sugar, one cup minced sour apples, and one quart of milk. Beat the sugar and yolks together, add the milk, bread, and fruit, and lastly the well-beaten whites of the eggs. Bake in a dish set in a pan of hot water till firm but not dry.

Almond Cornstarch Pudding.—Blanch one and one half ounces of sweet almonds, and reduce them to a paste as directed on page 298; or if obtainable, almondine may be used instead of the prepared almonds. Heat a quart of milk, and while boiling, stir into it four tablespoonfuls of cornstarch which has been braided smooth with a little cold milk; let it thicken over the fire, stirring all the time. Then add two tablespoonfuls of thick, sweet cream. Lastly, stir in two or three well-beaten eggs and a tablespoonful of rose water. Let it come just to the boiling point, and remove from the stove. Keep in a cold place till needed. Serve with hot mock cream or with grape pulp as dressing.

Almond Cream.—Heat a pint of milk, and when boiling stir into it two tablespoonfuls of cornstarch rubbed smooth in a little cold milk, also one fourth cup of sugar and three tablespoonfuls of almondine. Cook until thickened, and pour it, stirring constantly meanwhile, over the beaten whites of two eggs. Set on ice to cool, and serve with grape pulp as dressing. A cupful of blanched and chopped almonds may be used instead of almondine if that is not obtainable. The pudding will then require an additional one fourth cup of sugar.

Apple Charlotte.—Take three cups of nicely stewed tart apples which have been beaten smooth or rubbed through a colander and sweetened to taste. If the sauce is thin and very juicy, place it upon the range, and simmer slowly till it is of the consistency of thick marmalade or jelly. Add to the apples four tablespoonfuls of grated fresh or canned pineapple for flavoring. Remove the hard crusts from slices of light whole-wheat bread, spread them quite thickly with the prepared apple, and pack in layers in a pudding mold. Cover with a simple custard made of a quart of milk, three tablespoonfuls of sugar, and two eggs. Let it stand half an hour, then bake. Do not press the bread or beat it after the custard is turned on, as that will be likely to make the pudding heavy. Other fruit marmalade may be used in place of the apple preparation if preferred.

Banana Custard.—Prepare a custard as directed for Plain Custard with a quart of milk, two well-beaten eggs, four tablespoonfuls of sugar, and one of cornstarch. When the custard is cool, pour it over four thinly sliced yellow bananas, over which a tablespoonful of sugar and a teaspoonful of water have been sprinkled. Serve cold.

Boiled Custard.—Beat thoroughly together one pint of milk, two eggs, and a tablespoonful or two of sugar, until thoroughly mingled. Turn the mixture into a double boiler, and cook until the custard is set.

Boiled Custard Bread Pudding.—Crumble enough of the soft portion of stale whole-wheat bread to lightly fill a pint bowl. Heat a pint of milk to boiling. Stir into it, as soon as it boils, two eggs, yolks and whites well beaten separately, two heaping tablespoonfuls of sugar, a little grated lemon rind, and the light bread crumbs; stir rapidly till the whole thickens, pour into a deep dish, and when cold, dot the top with bits of currant or cranberry jelly.

Bread and Fruit Custard.—Take for this, two cups of grated bread crumbs, two cups of finely chopped tart apples, one cup of English currants or stoned raisins, mixed with a very little chopped citron for flavor, two tablespoonfuls of sugar, three cups of milk, and two eggs. Beat the yolks of the eggs and the sugar together, then add the milk, bread, fruit, and lastly the well-beaten whites of the eggs. Bake in a dish set within a pan of hot water, until the custard is set.

Bread Custard Pudding.—Take one cup of finely powdered bread crumbs, one half cup of sugar, one quart of milk, and the beaten yolks of three eggs and whites of two. Mix the bread and milk, and when well softened, add the beaten yolks, sugar, and lastly the well-beaten whites; beat all together thoroughly, season with a little grated lemon rind; place the pudding dish in the oven in a pan of hot water, and bake till firm and lightly brown. Take from the oven, cover the top with a layer of apple marmalade made without sugar, or with some tart fruit jelly; add to this a meringue made of the white of the remaining egg and a tablespoonful of sugar, beaten to a stiff froth, and place in the oven a moment to brown lightly.

Fresh fruit, strawberries, raspberries, chopped peaches, currants, cherries, or shredded oranges are equally as good as the marmalade or jelly for the top dressing, and may be used to vary this pudding in a number of different ways. Canned fruits, if well drained from juice, especially apricots and peaches, are excellent for this purpose. A cocoanut custard pudding may be made of the above by flavoring the milk before using, with two tablespoonfuls of desiccated cocoanut Another variety still may be made by adding to the first recipe half a cup of Zante currants and the same of seedless raisins, or a half cup of finely shredded, tender citron.

Bread and Fig Pudding.—Put together two cups of finely grated bread crumbs, two cups of milk, one cup of finely chopped figs previously steamed or cooked, one fourth cup of sugar, and lastly, two well-beaten eggs. Bake in a moderate oven till the custard is set.

Bread and Apricot Pudding.—Fill a pudding dish with alternate layers of bread crumbs and canned apricots well drained from juice. Pour over it a custard made with two eggs, one half cup of sugar, and a pint of milk. Bake one half hour, or only until the custard is set. Canned peaches, to which a teaspoonful of lemon juice has been added after draining, may be used in place of apricots.

Caramel Custard.—Turn one fourth of a cup of sugar into a stewpan, and stir it over the fire until it becomes liquid and brown. Scald a cup and a half of milk, and add the browned sugar. Beat two eggs thoroughly, add to them one half cup cold milk, and turn the mixture slowly, stirring constantly that no lumps form, into the scalding milk; continue to stir until the custard thickens. Set away to cool, and serve in glasses.

Carrot Pudding.—Take two cups of carrots, boiled tender and rubbed through a colander, one pint of milk, two thirds of a cup of sugar, and two well beaten eggs. Flavor with vanilla, and having beaten all well together, turn into an earthen pudding dish, set the dish in a pan of hot water, and place in the oven. Bake only till the custard sets.

Cocoanut Cornstarch Pudding.—Simmer a cupful of grated cocoanut in a quart of milk for twenty minutes. Strain the milk to remove the cocoanut, adding enough more milk to make a full quart. With a small portion of it braid smoothly one and one half tablespoonfuls of cornstarch or rice flour, and put the remainder in a saucepan over the fire. When the milk is boiling, add the cornstarch, stirring constantly until it thickens; then remove from the fire and cool. Next add two tablespoonfuls of sugar and two well-beaten eggs. Bake in a moderate oven, in a dish set in a pan of hot water, until the custard is well set.

Cocoanut Custard.—Flavor a pint of milk with cocoanut, add a tablespoonful of sugar and two well-beaten eggs, and boil till set in a double boiler or a bowl set in a dish of boiling water. Richer custards may be made by using three or four eggs, but the richer the custard the more likely it is to curdle and become watery, as well as being less wholesome.

Coconut Rice Custard.—Flavor one quart of milk quite strongly with coconut, as previously directed. Add to it one and one half cups of boiled rice, one cup of raisins, one half cup of sugar, and lastly three well-beaten eggs. Set the pudding dish in a pan of hot water, and bake till the custard is well set.

Corn Meal Pudding.—Heat a quart of milk lacking two thirds of a cupful, to boiling. Moisten three tablespoonfuls of nice granulated corn meal with the two thirds of a cup of milk, and stir gradually into the boiling milk. Let it boil up until set, turn into a double boiler, and cook for an hour. Then add a tablespoonful of thick sweet cream, one half a cup of molasses or sugar, a quart of cold milk, a little salt if desired, and lastly, two well-beaten eggs. Mix thoroughly. Pour into a pudding dish and bake one hour. A cup of currants or seeded raisins may be used to give variety.

Corn Meal Pudding No. 2.—Crumble cold corn puffs or corn cake to make a cupful; add a pint of sweet milk, three teaspoonfuls of sugar, the yolks of two eggs and the white of one, and bake slowly in a dish set inside a pan of hot water for an hour.

Corn Meal and Fig Pudding.—Beat together a scant cup of best sifted corn meal with a cupful of molasses, and stir the mixture gradually into a quart of boiling milk. Cook ten or twelve minutes, or until well thickened, then set aside to cool. Add a cupful of finely chopped figs, one and two thirds cups of cold milk, part cream if it can be afforded, and when the mixture is cool, add two well-beaten eggs. Pour into a pudding dish and bake in a moderate, steady oven for three or more hours; the longer the better. When the pudding has baked an hour, pour over it a cupful of cold milk. Do not stir the pudding, but allow the milk to soak in gradually, a pint of finely sliced or chopped sweet apples may be used in place of figs for variety, or if preferred, both may be omitted.

Cornstarch Meringue.—Heat one and one half pints of milk to boiling, and then stir in gradually two tablespoonfuls of cornstarch which has been previously rubbed smooth in a little cold milk. When the starch has thickened, allow it partially to cool, and then add, stirring continuously meanwhile, the yolks of two eggs which have been previously well beaten with three table spoonfuls of sugar. Let the whole simmer for a minute or two longer, turn into a dish, meringue with the whites of the eggs, and when cold, dot with lumps of strawberry jelly.

Cracked Wheat Pudding.—Beat two cups of cold steamed cracked wheat in two cups of rich milk until so thoroughly mingled that no lumps remain. Add one cup of canned sweet cherries well drained from juice, one half cup of sugar, and two eggs, whites and yolks beaten separately. Bake in a slow oven till the custard is set.

Cup Custard.—Into four cups of milk stir the yolks of three eggs and one whole one well beaten. Add four tablespoonfuls of sugar, and strain the mixture into cups; place these in a dripping pan full of hot water, grate a little lemon rind over the top of each, and bake in a moderate oven. If preferred, the milk may be first flavoured with cocoanut. It is also better to have the milk nearly hot when stirring in the egg. Half a cupful of the milk should be reserved to add to the egg before turning into the heated portion.

Farina Custard.—Flavor a quart of milk with cocoanut as directed on page 298. Cook two tablespoonfuls of farina in the flavored milk for twenty minutes, in a double boiler; then set aside to cool. When nearly cold, add two tablespoonfuls of sugar and the well-beaten yolks of two eggs. Beat all together very thoroughly, and lastly stir in the whites of the eggs which have been previously beaten to a stiff froth. Bake in one dish set inside another filled with hot water, just long enough to set the custard. Serve cold.

Farina Pudding.—Take a cup of cold cooked farina and soak it in four cups of milk until there are no lumps, or rub through a colander; add two well-beaten eggs, one scant cup of sugar and one cup of raisins; bake in a moderate oven until the custard is well set.

Floating Island.—Make a custard of a pint of milk flavored with cocoanut, and the yolks of three eggs; sweeten to taste, and steam in a double boiler. When done, turn into a glass dish. Have the whites of the eggs whipped to a stiff froth, and drop for a few seconds on the top of a pan of scalding hot water, turning so that both sides may be alike coagulated but not hardened; skim off, and put in islands on the top of the custard. When quite cold, drop bits of different colored jellies on the islands, and keep in a cool place till needed. Or put a spoonful of fruit jelly in the bottom of small glasses, and fill with the custard with a spoonful of the white on top.

Fruit Custard.—Heat a pint of red raspberry, strawberry, or currant juice to boiling, and stir into it two tablespoonfuls or cornstarch rubbed smooth in a little cold water. Stir constantly until thickened, then add half a cup of sugar, or less if the fruit juice has been sweetened; take from the fire and stir in the stiffly beaten whites of three eggs, stirring all the time so that the hot mixture will coagulate the egg. Make a custard of a pint of milk, the yolks of the three eggs, and three tablespoonfuls of sugar. When done, set on the ice to cool. Dish in a glass dish when cold, placing the fruit mixture by spoonfuls on top, and serve.

Graham Grits Pudding.—Heat two cups of milk in a double boiler. When boiling, stir in one cup of Graham grits moistened with one cup of cold milk. Cook for an hour and a half in a double boiler, then remove from the fire and cool. Add three tablespoonfuls of sugar, three fourths of a cup of finely chopped apples, and one fourth of a cup of chopped raisins, and two well-beaten eggs. Bake three fourths of an hour in a moderate oven.

Ground Rice Pudding.—Simmer a few pieces of thinly cut lemon rind or half a cup of cocoanut, very slowly in a quart of milk for twenty minutes, or until the milk is well flavored. Strain the milk through a fine strainer to remove the lemon rind or cocoanut, and put into a saucepan to boil. Mix four large tablespoonfuls of ground rice smooth with a little cold milk, and add to the boiling milk. Cook until the whole has thickened, then set aside to cool. When nearly cold, add two tablespoonfuls of sugar and two well-beaten eggs. Bake in a gentle oven in a dish placed in a pan of hot water, until the whole is lightly browned.

Lemon Pudding.—Grate the rind of one lemon; soften one pint of bread crumbs in one quart of sweet milk, add the yolks of two eggs, and half a cup of sugar mixed with grated lemon rind. Bake twenty minutes. Beat to a froth the whites of the eggs, the juice of the lemon, and half a cup of sugar. Spread over the top, and return to the oven for five minutes. This may be baked in cups if preferred.

Lemon Cornstarch Pudding.—Beat the yolks of two eggs in a pudding dish; add a cupful of sugar; dissolve four tablespoonfuls of cornstarch in a little cold water, stir it into two teacupfuls of actively boiling water; when thickened, add the juice of two lemons with a little grated peel; turn over the eggs and sugar, beating well to mix all together, and bake about fifteen minutes. If desired, the beaten whites of the eggs may be used to meringue the top. Serve either cold or hot.

Lemon Cornstarch Pudding No. 2.—Mix together one half cup of cornstarch, one half cup of sugar, the juice and a portion of the grated rind of one medium-sized lemon. Add to these ingredients just enough cold water to dissolve thoroughly, then pour boiling water over the mixture until it becomes thickened and looks transparent. Stir continuously and boil for a few minutes until the starch is cooked. Take from the fire, and add gradually, with continuous stirring, the well-beaten yolks of three eggs. Whip the whites of the eggs with a teaspoonful of quince jelly to a stiff froth, and pour over the pudding; then brown in the oven. Orange juice with a very little of the grated rind, or pineapple juice may be substituted for the lemon, if preferred.

Macaroni Pudding.—Break sufficient macaroni to make a pint in inch lengths, put into a double boiler, turn over it three pints of milk, and cook until tender. Turn into a pudding dish, add a pint of cold milk, two thirds of a cup of sugar, one egg, and the yolks of two others well beaten. Bake from twenty minutes to one half hour. When done, cool a little, spread the top with some mashed fresh berries or grape marmalade, and meringue with the whites of the eggs and a tablespoonful of sugar.

Molded Rice or Snow Balls.—Steam a pint of well-cleaned rice until tender, as directed on page 99, and tarn Into cups previously wet in cold water, to mold. When perfectly cold, place in a glass dish, and pour over them a cold custard made of a pint of milk, half a cup of sugar, a teaspoonful of cornstarch, and one egg. Or, if preferred, the rice balls may be served in individual dishes with the custard sauce, or with a dressing of fruit juice.

Orange Float.—Heat one quart of water, the juice of two lemons, and one and one half cupfuls of sugar. When boiling, stir into it four tablespoonfuls of cornstarch rubbed smooth in a very little water. Cook until the whole is thickened and clear. When cool, stir into the mixture five nice oranges which have been sliced, and freed from seeds and all the white portions. Meringue, and serve cold.

Orange Custard.—Turn a pint of hot milk over two cups of stale bread crumbs and let them soak until well softened: add the yolks of two eggs, and beat all together until perfectly smooth; add a little of the grated rind and the juice of three sweet oranges, and sugar to taste. Lastly add the whites of the eggs beaten to a stiff froth, turn into cups, which place into a moderate oven in a pan of hot water, and bake twenty minutes, or until the custard is well set but not watery.

Orange Pudding.—Pare and slice six sweet Florida oranges, removing the seeds and all the white skin and fibers. Place in the bottom of a glass dish. Make a custard by stirring two table spoonfuls of cornstarch braided with a little milk into a pint of boiling milk, and when thickened, adding gradually, stirring constantly meanwhile, one egg and the yolk of a second egg well beaten with one fourth cup of sugar. When partially cool, pour over the oranges. Whip the white of the second egg to a stiff froth with one fourth cup of sugar which has been flavored by rubbing over some orange peel, and meringue the top of the pudding. Fresh strawberries, raspberries, or peaches may be substituted for oranges in making this dessert, if preferred.

Peach Meringue.—To every pint of stewed or canned peaches, sweetened to taste, stir in the beaten yolks of two eggs. Bake in a deep pudding dish fifteen minutes, then cover with the whites of the two eggs beaten till very light with two tablespoonfuls of sugar. Brown in the oven, and serve cold with whipped cream. For peaches, substitute any other stewed fruit desired.

Picnic Pudding.—Thicken a pint of strawberry or raspberry juice, sweetened to taste, with two tablespoonfuls of corn starch, as for Fruit Custard. Turn into the bottom of cups previously wet with cold water, or a large mold, as preferred. In a second dish heat to boiling a pint of milk, flavored with cocoanut, to which a tablespoonful of sugar has been, added. Stir into it two tablespoonfuls of cornstarch rubbed smooth in a little cold milk, and cook thoroughly. When done, cool slightly and turn into the molds on the top of the pink portion, which should be sufficiently cool so that it will not mix. A third layer may be added by cooking two tablespoonfuls of cornstarch and one of sugar, rubbed smooth in a little milk, in a pint of boiling milk, and stirring in, just as it is taken from the stove, the well-beaten yolks of two eggs.

Plain Cornstarch Pudding.—Heat to boiling a pint and a half of milk, with a few bits of the yellow rind of a lemon to flavor it. While the milk is heating, rub four large spoonfuls of cornstarch to a cream with half a cup of cold milk; beat well together the yolks of three eggs, three tablespoonfuls of sugar, and half a cup of cold milk, and whip the whites of the eggs to a stiff froth. When the milk is actively boiling, remove the bits of lemon rind with a skimmer, and stir in the starch mixture; stir constantly and boil three or four minutes—until the starch is well cooked; then add gradually, stirring well meanwhile, the yolks and sugar. Remove from the fire, and stir the beaten whites lightly through the whole. Serve with a dressing of fruit juice or fruit syrup; if in the season of fresh berries, the pudding may be dressed with a few spoonfuls of mashed strawberries, raspberries, or currants.

Plain Custard.—Heat a pint of milk to boiling, and stir in a tablespoonful of cornstarch nabbed smooth in a little milk; let the milk and starch boil together till they thicken; then cool and add one well-beaten egg and two tablespoonfuls of sugar. Cook in the oven in a dish set inside another filled with hot water, or in a double boiler. The milk may be previously flavored with orange, lemon, or cocoanut.

Prune Pudding.—Heat two and one half cups of milk to boiling, then stir in gradually a heaping tablespoonful of cornstarch which has been rubbed smooth in a little cold milk; let this boil and thicken for a minute, then remove from the fire. When cool, add three well-beaten eggs, two tablespoonfuls of sugar, and a cupful of prunes which have been stewed, then drained of all juice, the stones removed, and the prunes chopped fine. Pour into a pudding dish and bake twenty minutes. Serve with or without cream.

Prime Whip.—Sift through a colander some stewed sweet California prunes which have been thoroughly drained from juice, and from which the stones have been removed. Beat the whites of three eggs to a stiff froth, and add two cups of the sifted prunes; beat all together thoroughly; turn into a pudding dish, and brown in the oven fifteen minutes. Serve cold, with a little cream or custard for dressing. Almond sauce also makes an excellent dressing.

Rice Apple Custard Pudding.—Pare, and remove the cores without dividing from a sufficient number of apples to cover the bottom of a two-quart pudding dish. Fill the cavities of the apples with a little grated lemon rind and sugar, and put them into the oven with a tablespoon of water on the bottom of the dish. Cover, and steam till the apples are tender, but not fallen to pieces. Then pour over them a custard made with two cups of boiled rice, a quart of milk, half a cup of sugar, and two eggs.

Rice Custard Pudding.—Take one and one half cups of nicely steamed rice, four tablespoonfuls of sugar, and a pint of milk; heat to boiling in a saucepan. Then stir in very carefully the yolk of one egg and one whole egg, previously well beaten together with a few spoonfuls of milk reserved for the purpose. Let the whole boil up till thickened, but not longer, as the custard will whey and separate. When partly cool, flavor with a little vanilla or lemon, turn into a glass dish, and meringue with the white of the second egg beaten to a stiff froth. Cold steamed rice may be used by soaking it in hot milk until every grain is separate.

Rice Snow.—Into a quart of milk heated to boiling, stir five tablespoonfuls of rice flour previously braided with a very little cold milk; add one half cup of sugar. Let the whole boil up together till well cooked and thickened; then remove from the stove, and stir in lightly the beaten whites of four eggs. Mold, and serve cold with foam sauce.

Rice Snow with Jelly.—Steam or bake a teacupful of best rice in milk until the grains are tender. Pile it up on a dish roughly. When cool, lay over it squares of jelly. Beat the whites of two eggs and one third of a cup of sugar to a stiff froth, and pile like snow over the rice. Serve with cream sauce.

Rice with Eggs.—Steam rice as previously directed, and when sufficiently cooked, stir into half of it while hot, the yolks of one or two eggs well beaten with a little sugar. Into the other half, the whites of the eggs, sweetened and beaten to a stiff froth, may be lightly stirred while the rice is still hot enough to set the eggs. Serve with the yellow half in the bottom of the dish, and the white part piled on top covered with whipped cream flavored with lemon or vanilla.

Snow Pudding.—Heat one half pint each of water and milk together, to boiling, stir into this a tablespoonful of cornstarch rubbed smooth in a little cold milk, and cook for five minutes. Cool partially and add the whites of two well-beaten eggs. Turn into molds and set in the ice box to cool. Serve with a cream made by stirring into a half pint of boiling milk the yolks of two eggs, a teaspoonful of cornstarch rubbed smooth in a little cold milk, and half a cup of sugar. Cook until well thickened. Cool and flavor with a little lemon or vanilla. Or, if preferred, serve with a dressing of fruit juice.

Steamed Custard.—Heat a pint of milk, with which has been well beaten two eggs and one third of a cup of sugar, in a double boiler until well thickened. When done, turn into a glass dish, and grate a little of the yellow rind of lemon over the top to flavor. If desired to have the custard in cups, remove from the fire when it begins to thicken, turn into cups, and finish in a steamer over a kettle of boiling water.

Strawberry Charlotte.—Fit slices of nice plain buns (those made according to recipe on page 347 are nice for this) in the bottom of a pudding dish, and cover with a layer of hulled strawberries; add another layer of the buns cut in slices, a second layer of strawberries, and then more slices of buns. Make a custard in the following manner: Heat a scant pint of milk to boiling in the inner cup of a double boiler, and stir into it gradually, beating thoroughly at the same time, an egg which has been previously well beaten with half a cup of sugar, a teaspoonful of cornstarch, and a spoonful or two of milk until perfectly smooth. Cook together in the double boiler until well set. Cool partially, and pour over the buns and strawberries. Place a plate with a weight upon it on the top of the charlotte, and set away to cool.

Pop Corn Pudding.—Take a scant pint of the pop corn which is ground and put up in boxes, or if not available, freshly popped corn, rolled fine, is just as good. Add to it three cups of new milk, one half cup of sugar, two whole eggs and the yolk of another, well beaten. Bake in a pudding dish placed inside another filled with hot water, till the custard is set. Cover with a meringue made of the remaining white of egg, a teaspoonful of sugar, and a sprinkling of the pop corn.

Sago Custard Pudding.—Put one half cup of sago and a quart of rich milk into the inner cup of a double boiler, or a basin set inside a pan of boiling water, and let it simmer until the sago has thickened the milk and become perfectly transparent. Allow it to cool, then add a cup of sugar, two well-beaten eggs, and a little of the grated rind of a lemon. Turn into a pudding dish, and bake only till the custard has set.

Sago and Fruit Custard Pudding.—Soak six table spoonfuls of sago in just enough water to cover it, for twenty minutes. Meanwhile pare and remove the cores from half a dozen or more tart apples, and fill the cavities with a mixture of grated lemon rind and sugar. Place the apples in the bottom of a pudding dish, with a tablespoonful of water; cover, and set in the oven to bake. Put the soaked sago with a quart of milk into a double boiler. Let it cook until the sago is clear and thick; then add three fourths of a cup of sugar and two well-beaten eggs. Pour the sago custard over the apples, which should be baked tender but not mushy. Put the pudding dish in the oven in a pan of hot water, and bake till the custard is well set. Serve cold.

Snowball Custard.—Flavor a pint of milk by sleeping in it three or four slices of the yellow rind of a lemon for twenty minutes or more. Skim out the rind; let the milk come to the boiling point, and drop into it the well-beaten whites of two eggs, in tablespoonfuls, turning each one over carefully, allowing them to remain only long enough to become coagulated but not hardened, and then place the balls upon a wire sieve to drain. Afterward stir into the scalding milk the yolks of the eggs and one whole one well beaten, together with two tablespoonfuls of sugar. Stir until it thickens. Pour this custard into a glass dish, and lay the white balls on top.

Tapioca Custard.—Soak a cup of pearl tapioca over night in sufficient water to cover. When ready to prepare the custard, drain off the water if any remain, and add one quart of milk to the tapioca; place in a double boiler and cook until transparent; then add the well-beaten yolks of three eggs or the yolks of two and one whole one, mixed with three fourths of a cup of sugar. Let it cook a few minutes, just long enough for the custard to thicken and no more, or it will whey and be spoiled; flavor with a little vanilla and turn into a glass dish. Cover the top with the whites beaten stiffly with a tablespoonful of sugar, and dot with bits of jelly, or colored sugar prepared by mixing sugar with cranberry or raspberry juice and allowing it to dry. For variety, the custard may be flavored with grated lemon rind and a tablespoonful of lemon juice whipped up with the whites of the eggs, or other flavor may be dispensed with, and the meringue flavored by beating with a tablespoonful of quince jelly with the whites of the eggs.

Tapioca Pudding.—Soak a cupful of tapioca over night in just enough water to cover. In the morning, add to it one quart of milk, and cook in a double boiler until transparent. Add three eggs well beaten, one half cup of sugar, one half cup of chopped raisins, and a very little chopped citron. Bake till the custard is set. Serve warm or cold as preferred.

Vermicelli Pudding.—Flavor two and one half cups of milk with lemon as directed on page 229. Drop into it, when boiling, four ounces of vermicelli, crushing it lightly with one hand while sprinkling it in, and stir to keep it from gathering in lumps. Let it cook gently in a double boiler, stirring often until it is tender and very thick. Then pour it into a pudding dish, let it cool, and add a tablespoonful of rather thick sweet cream if you have it (it does very well without), half a cup of sugar, and lastly, two well-beaten eggs. Bake in a moderately hot oven till browned over the top.

White Custard.—Beat together thoroughly one cup of milk, the whites of two eggs, one tablespoonful of sugar, and one and one half tablespoonfuls of almondine. Turn into cups and steam or bake until the custard is set.

White Custard No. 2.—Cook a half cup of farina in a quart of milk in a double boiler, for an hour. Remove from the stove, and allow it to become partially cool, then add one half cup of sugar, the whites of two eggs, and one half the yolk of one egg. Turn into a pudding dish, and bake twenty minutes or until the custard is well set.

STEAMED PUDDING.

The following precautions are necessary to be observed in steaming puddings or desserts of any sort:—

1. Have the water boiling rapidly when the pudding is placed in the steamer, and keep it constantly boiling.

2. Replenish, if needed, with boiling water, never with cold.

3. Do not open the steamer and let in the air upon the pudding, until it is done.

RECIPES.

Batter Pudding.—Beat four eggs thoroughly; add to them a pint of milk, and if desired, a little salt. Sift a teacupful of flour and add it gradually to the milk and eggs, beating lightly the while. Then pour the whole mixture through, a fine wire strainer into a small pail with cover, in which it can be steamed. This straining is imperative. The cover of the pail should be tight fitting, as the steam getting into the pudding spoils it. Place the pail in a kettle of boiling water, and do not touch or move it until the pudding is done. It takes exactly an hour to cook. If moved or jarred during the cooking, it will be likely to fall. Slip it out of the pail on a hot dish, and serve with cream sauce. A double boiler with tightly fitting cover is excellent for cooking this pudding.

Bread and Fruit Custard.—Soak a cupful of finely grated bread crumbs in a pint of rich milk heated to scalding. Add two thirds of a cup of sugar, and the grated yellow rind of half a lemon. When cool, add two eggs well beaten. Also two cups of canned apricots or peaches drained of juice, or, if preferred, a mixture of one and one half cups of chopped apples, one half cup of raisins, and a little citron. Turn into a pudding dish, and steam in a steamer over a kettle of boiling water for two hours. The amount of sugar necessary will vary somewhat according to the fruit used.

Date Pudding.—Turn a cup of hot milk over two cups of stale bread crumbs, and soak until softened; add one half cup of cream and one cup of chopped and stoned dates. Mix all thoroughly together. Put in a china dish and steam for three hours. Serve hot with lemon sauce.

Rice Balls.—Steam one cup of rice till tender. Wring pudding cloths about ten inches square out of hot water, and spread the rice one third of an inch over the cloth. Put a stoned peach or apricot from which the skin has been removed, in the center, filling the cavity in each half of the fruit with rice. Draw up the cloth until the rice smoothly envelops the fruit, tie, and steam ten or fifteen minutes. Remove the cloth carefully, turn out into saucers, and serve with sauce made from peach of apricot juice. Easy-cooking tart apples may also be used. Steam them thirty minutes, and serve with sugar and cream.

Steamed Bread Custard.—Cut stale bread in slices, removing hard crusts. Oil a deep pudding mold, and sprinkle the bottom and sides with Zante currants; over these place a layer of the slices of bread, sprinkled with currants; add several layers, sprinkling each with the currants in the same manner. Cover with a custard made by beating together three or four eggs, three tablespoonfuls of sugar, and one quart of milk. Put the pudding in a cool place for three hours; at the end of that time, steam one and a quarter hours. Serve with mock cream flavored with vanilla. Apple marmalade may be used to spread between the slices in place of currants, if preferred.

Steamed Fig Pudding.—Moisten two cupfuls of finely grated Graham bread crumbs with half a cup of thin sweet cream. Mix into it a heaping cupful of finely chopped fresh figs, and a quarter of a cup of sugar. Add lastly a cup of sweet milk. Turn all into a pudding dish, and steam about two and one half hours. Serve as soon as done, with a little cream for dressing, or with orange or lemon sauce.

PASTRY AND CAKE.

So much has been said and written about the dietetic evils of these articles that their very names have been almost synonymous with indigestion and dyspepsia. That they are prolific causes of this dire malady cannot be denied, and it is doubtless due to two reasons; first, because they are generally compounded of ingredients which are in themselves unwholesome, and rendered doubly so by their combination; and secondly, because tastes have become so perverted that an excess of these articles is consumed in preference to more simple and nutritious food.

As has been elsewhere remarked, foods containing an excess of fat, as do most pastries and many varieties of cake, are exceedingly difficult of digestion, the fat undergoing in the stomach no changes which answer to the digestion of other elements of food, and its presence interferes with the action of the gastric juice upon other elements. In consequence, digestion proceeds very slowly, if at all, and the delay often occasions fermentative and putrefactive changes in the entire contents of the stomach.

It is the indigestibility of fat, and this property of delaying the digestion of other foods, chiefly that render pastry and cakes so deleterious to health.

We do not wish to be understood as in sympathy with that class of people who maintain that dyspepsia is a disciplinary means of grace, when, after having made the previous statement, we proceed to present recipes for preparing the very articles we have condemned. Pie and cake are not necessarily utterly unwholesome; and if prepared in a simple manner, may be partaken of in moderation by persons with good digestion. Nevertheless, they lack the wholesomeness of more simple foods, and we most fully believe that would women supply their tables with perfectly light, sweet, nutritious bread would cease. However, if pies and cakes must needs be, make them as simple as possible.

General Suggestions for Making Pies.—Always prepare the filling for pies before making the crust, if the filling is to be cooked in the crust. Have all the material for the crust on the table, measured and in readiness, before beginning to put together. Follow some of the simple recipes given in these pages. Have all the material cold, handle the least possible to make it into a mass, and do not knead at all.

When the crust is ready, roll it out quickly to about one half inch in thickness, then fold up like a jelly roll, and cut from the end only sufficient for one crust at a time. Lay this, the flat side upon the board, and roll evenly in every direction, until scarcely more than an eighth of an inch in thickness, and somewhat larger than the baking plate, as it will shrink when lifted from the board.

Turn one edge over the rolling pin, and carefully lift it onto the plate. If there is to be an upper crust, roll that in the same manner, make a cut in the center to allow the steam to escape, fill the pie, slightly rounding it in the center, and lift on the upper crust; press both edges lightly together; then, lifting the pie in the left hand, deftly trim away all overhanging portions of crust with a sharp knife; ornament the edge if desired, and put at once into the oven, which should be in readiness at just the right temperature, a rather moderate oven being best for pies.

The under crust of lemon, pumpkin, custard, and very juicy fruit pies, filled before baking, is apt to become saturated and softened with the liquid mixture, if kept for any length of time after baking. This may be prevented in a measure by glazing the crust, after it is rolled and fitted on the plate, with the beaten white of an egg, and placing in the oven just a moment to harden the egg before filling; or if the pie is one of fruit, sprinkle the crust with a little flour and sugar, brushing the two together with the hand before; adding the filling. During the baking, the flour and melted sugar will adhere together, tending to keep the juice from contact with the crust.

Pies are more wholesome if the crusts are baked separately and filled for use as needed. This is an especially satisfactory way to make pies of juicy fruit, as it does away largely with the saturated under crusts, and the flavor of the fruit can be retained much more perfectly. Pies with one crust can be made by simply fitting the crust to the plate, pricking it lightly with a fork to prevent its blistering while baking, and afterward filling when needed for the table. For pies with two crusts, fit the under crust to the plate, and fill with clean pieces of old white linen laid in lightly to support the upper crust. When baked, slip the pie on a plate, lift off the upper crust, take out the pieces of cloth, and just before serving, fill with fruit, which should be previously prepared.

Canned peaches filled into such a crust make a delicious pie. Strawberries, cherries, gooseberries, and other juicy fruits, that lose so much of their flavor in baking, may be lightly scalded, the juice thickened a little with flour if desired, sweetened to taste, and filled into such a crust. An excellent pie may be made in this manner from apples, stewed carefully so as to keep the slices whole, sweetened to taste, and flavored with lemon, orange, or grated pineapple. One pineapple will be sufficient for four pies. Fresh fruit for filling may be used without cooking, if desired. If desired, several crusts may be baked and put away unfilled. When needed, the crusts may be placed for a few minutes in a hot oven until heated through, then filled with freshly prepared fruit.

In preparing material for custard or pumpkin pies, if the milk used be hot, the pies will be improved and the time of baking be considerably shortened.

Tin or granite-ware plates are preferable to earthen ones for pies, as they bake better on the bottom. The perforated pans are superior in some respects. No greasing is needed; simply rub them well with flour. The time required for baking pies varies from one half to three fourths of an hour. The dampers should be so adjusted as to bake the bottom crust first.

After baking, remove at once to heated earthen plates, or set the tins upon small supports, so that the air can circulate underneath them.

RECIPES.

Paste for Pies.—Sift together equal parts of Graham grits and white flour (Graham flour will do if the grits are not obtainable, but the grits will produce a more crisp and tender crust), and wet with very cold, thin sweet cream. Have the flour also as cold as possible, since the colder the material, the more crisp the paste; mix together very quickly into a rather stiff dough. Do not knead at all, but gather the fragments lightly together, roll out at once, fill and bake quickly, since much of the lightness of the crust depends upon the dispatch with which the pie is gotten into the oven after the materials are thrown together. If for any reason it is necessary to defer the baking, place the crust in the ice-chest till needed.

Corn Meal Crust.—Equal parts of sifted white corn meal and flour, mixed together lightly with rather thin sweet cream which has been set in the ice-chest until very cold, makes a very good crust.

Granola Crust.—For certain pies requiring an under crust only, the prepared granola manufactured by the Sanitarium Food Co. makes a superior crust. To prepare, moisten with thin sweet cream—one half cup of cream for every two thirds cup of granola is about the right proportion, and will make sufficient crust for one pie. Flour the board, and lift the moistened granola onto it, spreading it as much as possible with the hands. Dredge lightly with flour over the top, and roll out gently to the required size without turning. The material, being coarse and granular, will break apart easily, but may be as easily pressed together with the fingers. Change the position of the rolling pin often, in order to shape the crust without moving it. When well roiled, carefully slip a stiff paper under it, first loosening from the board with a knife if necessary, and lift it gently onto the pan. Press together any cracks, trim the edges, fill, and bake at once. Use the least flour possible in preparing this crust, and bake as soon as made, before the moisture has become absorbed. Such a crust is not suited for custard or juicy fruit pies, but filled with prune, peach, or apple marmalade, it makes a most delicious and wholesome pie. A cooked custard may be used in such a crust.

Paste for Tart Shells.—Take one half cup of rather thin sweet cream, which has been placed on ice until very cold;

add to it the stiffly beaten whites of two eggs, and whip all together briskly for ten minutes. Add sufficient white flour to roll. Cut into the required shape, bake quickly, but do not brown. Fill after baking. This paste, rolled thin and cut into shapes with a cookie-cutter, one half of them baked plain for under crusts, the other half ornamented for tops by cutting small holes with a thimble or some fancy mold, put together with a layer of some simple fruit jelly between them, makes a most attractive looking dessert. It is likewise very nice baked in little patty pans, and afterward filled with apple or peach marmalade, or any of the following fillings:—

Cream Filling.—One cup of rich milk (part cream if it can be afforded) heated to boiling. Into this stir one scant tablespoonful of flour previously braided smooth with a little cold milk. Add to this the well-beaten yolk of one egg and one tablespoonful of sugar. Turn this mixture into the hot milk and stir until it thickens. Flavor with a little grated lemon rind, vanilla, or, if preferred, flavor the milk with cocoanut before using. Fill the tart shells, and meringue with the white of the egg beaten stiff with a tablespoonful of sugar.

Grape Tart.—Into one pint of canned or fresh grape juice, when boiling, stir two tablespoonfuls of cornstarch braided with a little water, and cook for five minutes. Sweeten to taste, and fill a baked crust.

Lemon Filling.—Into one cup of boiling water stir one tablespoonful of cornstarch previously braided smooth with the juice of a large lemon. Cook until it thickens, then add one half cup of sugar and a little grated yellow rind of the lemon.

Tapioca Filling.—Soak one tablespoonful of tapioca over night in one cup of water; mash and stir the tapioca, simmer gently until clear and thick, adding enough water to cook it well; add half a cup of white sugar and a tablespoonful each of lemon and orange juice. If desired, a little raspberry or currant juice may be added to make the jelly of a pink color.

Apple Custard Pie.—Stew good dried apples till perfectly tender and there remains but very little juice. Rub through a colander. For each pie use one cup of the sifted apples, one and a half cups of rich milk, two eggs, five tablespoonfuls of sugar, and a little grated lemon rind for flavoring. Bake with under crust only. Stewed fresh apples, beaten smooth or rubbed through a colander, can be used if preferred. The eggs may be omitted, and one half cup more of the sifted apples, with more sugar, may be used instead.

Banana Pie.—For each pie required prepare a custard with one and one half cups of milk, the yolks of two eggs, and two heaping tablespoonfuls of sugar. Mash two large bananas through a colander, strain the custard over them, and beat well together. Bake in an under crust only, and meringue the top with the whites of the eggs beaten to a stiff froth with two tablespoonfuls of sugar.

Bread Pie.—Soak a slice of very light bread in a pint of rich milk. When it is quite soft, rub through a colander and afterward beat well through the milk. Add one well-beaten egg, four tablespoonfuls of sugar, and a little grated lemon rind for flavor. Bake with under crust only, till the custard is set. This is sufficient for one pie.

Carrot Pie.—Boil, drain, and rub the carrots through a colander. For each pie required, use two large tablespoonfuls of carrot thus prepared, two eggs, two cups of milk, a little salt if desired, four tablespoonfuls of sugar, and lemon or vanilla for flavoring. Bake with under crust only.

Cocoanut Pie.—Flavor a pint of milk with two tablespoonfuls of desiccated, or finely grated fresh cocoanut according to directions on page 298; strain, and add enough fresh milk to make a pint in all. Add three tablespoonfuls of sugar, heat, and as the milk comes to a boil, add a tablespoonful of cornstarch rubbed smooth in a little cold milk. Boil for a minute or two till the cornstarch thickens the milk; then remove from the stove. Allow it to get cold, and then stir in one well-beaten egg; bake in an under crust. Tie a tablespoonful of desiccated cocoanut in a clean cloth, and pound it as fine as flour; mix it with a tablespoonful of sugar and the white of an egg beaten to a stiff froth. When the pie is done, spread this over the top, and brown in the oven for a moment only.

Cocoanut Pie No. 2.—Steep one half cup of cocoanut in a pint of milk for one half hour. Strain out the cocoanut and add sufficient fresh milk to make a pint. Allow it to become cold, then add a quarter of a cup of sugar and two well-beaten eggs. Bake with an under crust only. When done, the top may be covered with a meringue the same as in the preceding recipe.

Cream Pie.—For one pie beat together one egg, one half cup of sugar, one tablespoonful of flour, and two cups of rich milk. Bake in one crust.

Cranberry Pie.—Stew a quart of cranberries until broken in a pint of boiling water. Rub through a colander to remove the skins, add two cups of sugar and one half cup of sifted flour. Bake with under crust only.

Dried Apple Pie.—Stew good dried apples till perfectly tender in as small a quantity of water as possible. When done, rub through a colander; they should be about the consistency of fruit jam; if not, a little flour may be added. Sweeten to taste, fill under crusts with the mixture, and bake. If lemon flavor is liked, a few pieces of the yellow rind may be added to the apples a little while before they are tender. If the apples are especially tasteless, lemon juice or some sour apple jelly should be added after rubbing through the colander. The crusts may first be baked, and filled with the mixture when needed; in which case the sauce should be simmered lightly till of the desired consistency. The top may be ornamented with strips or rings of crust, if desired.

Dried Apple Pie with Raisins.—Rub a quart of well-stewed dried apples through a colander, add a cupful of steamed raisins, sugar to sweeten, and bake with two crusts. This is sufficient for two pies.

Dried Apricot Pie.—Stew together one third dried apricots and two thirds dried apples or peaches. When soft, rub through a colander, add sugar to sweeten, and if very juicy, stew again until the juice is mostly evaporated; then beat until light and bake in a granola crust.

Farina Pie.—Cook one fourth cup of farina in a double boiler for an hour in three cups of rich milk. Allow it to become cool, then add one half cup of sugar, the yolks of two eggs, and a little grated lemon rind. Bake with under crust only. Meringue the top with the white of the egg beaten to a stiff froth with one tablespoonful of sugar and a little grated lemon rind for flavoring. The quantity given is sufficient for two small pies.

Fruit Pies.—Apples, peaches, and all small fruits and berries may be made into palatable pies without rich crusts or an excess of sugar, or the addition of unwholesome spices and flavorings. Bake the crust separately, and fill when needed with prepared fruit; or, fill with the fruit, using only sufficient sugar to sweeten; add no spices, and bake quickly. Prepare apples for pies by paring, coring, and dividing in eighths. Peaches are best prepared in a similar manner. Fill crusts in which the fruit is to be baked quite full and slightly heaping in the center. If flavoring is desired, let it be that of some other fruit. For apple pies, a teaspoonful or two of pineapple juice, a little grated lemon or orange peel, or a little strawberry or quince syrup, may be used for flavoring. For pies made of apples, peaches, and fruits which are not very juicy, add a tablespoonful or so of water or fruit juice; but for very juicy fruits and berries, dredge the under crust with a tablespoonful of sugar and a little flour mixed together before filling, or stir a spoonful of flour into the fruit so that each berry or piece may be separately floured.

Grape Jelly Pie.—Cook perfectly ripe, purple grapes; rub them through a colander to remove the seeds and skins. Return the pulp to the fire and thicken with rice flour or cornstarch, to the consistency of thick cream or jelly, and sweeten to taste. Fill an under crust with the mixture, and bake. The top may be ornamented with pastry cut in fancy shapes if desired.

Jelly Custard Pie.—Dissolve three tablespoonfuls of nice, pure fruit jelly in very little warm water, add one and one half cups of milk and two well-beaten eggs, stirring the whites in last. Bake with under crust only. Jellies are usually so sweet that no sugar is needed. Apple, raspberry, currant, strawberry, and quince jellies all make nice pies, prepared in this way.

Lemon Pie.—Take four tablespoonfuls of lemon juice (one large lemon or two small ones will yield about this quantity), the grated yellow portion only of the rind of half a lemon, and two thirds of a cup of sugar. Beat the lemon juice and sugar together. Braid a slightly heaping tablespoonful of cornstarch with as little water as possible, and pour over it, stirring constantly, one half pint of boiling water, to thicken the starch. Add the lemon and sugar to the starch, and let it cool; then stir in the yolks of two eggs and half the white of one, well beaten together. Beat thoroughly, pour into a deep crust, and bake. When done, cover with the remaining whites of the eggs, beaten with one and a half tablespoonfuls of sugar, and brown lightly in the oven.

Lemon Meringue Custard.—Heat two cups of milk to boiling, add a tablespoonful of cornstarch well braided with a little cold milk; let the whole simmer till thickened, stirring constantly. Allow it to cool, add one third of a cup of sugar and the beaten yolks of two eggs. Bake in an under crust, and cover with a meringue made of the whites of the eggs beaten to a stiff froth with two tablespoonfuls of sugar mixed with grated lemon peel. If liked, a spoonful of lemon juice may be added, a few drops at a time, during the beating of the meringue.

One-Crust Peach Pie.—Pare and remove the stones from ripe, nice flavored peaches; stew till soft in the smallest quantity of water possible without burning. Rub through a colander, or beat smooth with a large spoon. Add sugar as required. Bake with one crust. If the peach sauce is evaporated until quite dry, it is very nice baked in a granola crust. When done, meringue with the whites of two eggs whipped stiff with two tablespoonfuls of sugar. The flavor is improved by adding by degrees to the egg while whipping, a tablespoonful of lemon juice. Return to the oven and brown lightly. Serve cold.

Canned peaches or stewed dried peaches may be used in place of the fresh ones. In using the dried peaches, carefully examine and wash; soak them over night in cold water, and stew them in the same water until soft enough to rub through the colander. For each pie, add two tablespoonfuls of sweet cream, and sufficient sugar to sweeten; too much, sugar destroys the flavor of the fruit. Evaporated peaches, soaked over night and stewed carefully until tender, then removed from the syrup, which may be sweetened and boiled until thick and rich and afterward turned over the peaches, makes a delicious pie. Bake in one crust, with or without a meringue.

Orange Pie.—Rub smooth a heaping tablespoonful of cornstarch in three tablespoonfuls of water; pour over it a cup of boiling water, and cook until clear, stirring frequently that no lumps form. Add one cupful of sour orange juice, a little grated rind, and the juice of one lemon, with two eggs. Bake with under crust only. Meringue the top when baked, with the whites of the eggs well beaten with a tablespoonful of sugar, and a very little grated orange peel sprinkled over it.

Peach Custard Pie.—Cover a pie plate with an under crust. Take fresh peaches, pare, halve, and stone them, and place a layer, hollow side up, in the pie. Prepare a custard with one egg, one cup of milk, and three tablespoonfuls of sugar. Pour the custard over the peaches, and bake. If the quantity given will not entirely cover the peaches, a little more must be prepared. Canned peaches which are not broken can be used instead of fresh ones. The pieces should be drained free from juice, and less sugar used.

Prune Pie.—Prepare and cook sweet California prunes as directed for Prune Marmalade. Fill an under crust and bake. The top may be ornamented with strips of crust or pastry leaves; or if desired, may be meringued with the whites of two eggs beaten to a stiff froth with two tablespoonfuls of sugar and a little grated lemon peel. This pie is excellent baked in a granola crust.

Pumpkin Pie.—To prepare the pumpkin, cut into halves, remove the seeds, divide into moderately small pieces, and bake in the oven until thoroughly done. Then scrape from the shell, rub through a colander, and proceed as follows: For one and one third pints of the cooked pumpkin use one quart of hot, rich, sweet milk. Add one half cup of sugar and the well-beaten yolks of three eggs, beat well together, add the whites of the eggs beaten to a stiff froth, and beat thoroughly. Line the tins with a stiff cream paste, fill, and bake in a moderate oven till the pies are barely firm in the center, or till the custard is well set.

Pumpkin Pie No. 2.—For each pie desired, take one half pint of baked pumpkin, a pint of rich milk, one third of a cup of sugar, and two eggs. Mix the sugar and eggs, add the pumpkin, and lastly the milk, which should be hot, and beat all together with an egg beater until very light. Fill the crust, and bake slowly.

Pumpkin Pie without Eggs.—Prepare the pumpkin as previously directed. For two medium-sized pies, heat a pint and a half of milk in a farina kettle, and when scalding, stir into it two scant tablespoonfuls of white flour rubbed smooth in a little cold milk. Cook, stirring often, until it thickens. Add half a cup of sugar, or a little less of syrup, to a pint and a half of the sifted pumpkin, and after beating well together, stir this into the hot milk. Bake in an under crust; or, for three pies, take one quart and a cupful of pumpkin, three fourths of a cup of sugar, two thirds of a cup of best New Orleans molasses, and three pints of hot milk. Beat all together thoroughly. Line deep plates with a cream crust, and bake an hour and a half in a moderate oven.

Simple Custard Pie.—For one pie, take one pint of milk, two well-beaten eggs, one third of a cup of sugar, and a little grated lemon rind for flavor. Bake in an under crust. If eggs are scarce, a very good pie can be made by using only one egg, and a tablespoonful of cornstarch, with the above proportions of milk and sugar; in which case, heat the milk to scalding, stir in the cornstarch, and cook till thickened; cool, and then add the well-beaten egg. If preferred, the crust may be baked before filling, and the custard steamed, meanwhile.

Squash Pie.—Squash prepared as directed for pumpkin, and flavored with rose water, makes an excellent pie. Or, for each pie desired, take one pint of rich milk (part cream if it can be afforded), add one cup of nicely baked mealy squash which has been rubbed through a colander, one third of a cup of sugar, and two well-beaten eggs. Beat all together thoroughly. Bake in a deep pan slowly and carefully until firm.

Squash Pie without Eggs.—Bake the squash in the shell; when done, remove with a spoon and mash through a colander. For one pie, take eight tablespoonfuls of the squash, half a cup of sugar, and one and one third cups of boiling milk. Pour the milk slowly over the squash, beating rapidly meanwhile to make the mixture light. Bake in one crust.

Sweet-apple Custard Pie.—Into one pint of new milk, grate three ripe sweet apples (Golden Sweets are excellent); add two well-beaten eggs, and sugar to taste. Bake with under crust only.

Sweet Potato Pie.—Bake sufficient sweet potatoes to make a pint of pulp when rubbed through a colander; add a pint of rich milk, a scant cup of sugar, salt if desired, the yolks of two eggs, and a little grated lemon rind for flavor. Bake with under crust. When done, meringue with the whites of the eggs beaten up with a tablespoonful of sugar.

CAKE.

General Suggestions.—Always sift the flour for cake before measuring out the amount required. Use the best granulated white sugar. Eggs for use in cake are better to have the yolks and whites beaten separately. Beat the former until they cease to froth and begin to thicken as if mixed with flour. Beat the whites until stiff enough to remain in the bowl if inverted. Have the eggs and dishes cool, and if practicable, beat in a cool room. Use earthen or china bowls to beat eggs in.

If fruit is to be used, it should be washed and dried according to directions given on page 298, and then dusted with flour, a dessertspoonful to the pound of fruit. For use in cup cake or any other cake which requires a quick baking, raisins should be first steamed. If you have no patent steamer, place them in a close covered dish within an ordinary steamer, and cook for an hour over a kettle of boiling water. This should be done the day before they are to be used.

Use an earthen or granite-ware basin for mixing cake. Be very accurate in measuring the materials, and have them all at hand and all utensils ready before beginning to put the cake together. If it is to be baked at once, see that the oven also is at just the right temperature. It should be less hot for cake than for bread. Thin cakes require a hotter oven than those baked in loaves. They require from fifteen to twenty minutes to bake; thicker loaves, from thirty to sixty minutes. For loaf cakes the oven should be at such a temperature that during the first half of the time the cake will have risen to its full height and just begun to brown.

The recipes given require neither baking powder, soda, nor saleratus. Yeast and air can be made to supply the necessary lightness, and their use admits of as great a variety in cakes as will be needed on a hygienic bill of fare.

In making cake with yeast, do not use very thick cream, as a rich, oily batter retards fermentation and makes the cake slow in rising. If the cake browns too quickly, protect it by a covering of paper. If necessary to move a cake in the oven, do it very gently. Do not slam the oven door or in any way jar a cake while baking, lest it fall. Line cake tins with paper to prevent burning the bottom and edges. Oil the paper, not the tins, very lightly. Cake is done when it shrinks from the pan and stops hissing, or when a clean straw run into the thickest part comes up clean.

As soon as possible after baking, remove from the pan, as, if allowed to remain in the pan, it is apt to become too moist.

RECIPES.

Apple Cake.—Scald a cup of thin cream and cool to blood heat, add one and a half cups of sifted white flour, one fourth of a cup of sugar, and a gill of liquid yeast or one half cake of compressed yeast dissolved in a gill of thin cream. Beat well together, set in a warm place, and let it rise till perfectly light. When well risen, add one half cup of sugar mixed with one half cup of warm flour. Beat well and set in a warm place to rise again. When risen a second time, add two eggs, whites and yolks beaten separately, and about one tablespoonful of flour. Turn the whole into three round shallow baking tins, which have been previously oiled and warmed, and place where it will rise again for an hour, or until it is all of a foam. Bake quickly in a moderately hot oven. Make this the day before it is needed, and when ready to use prepare a filling as follows: Beat together the whites of two eggs, one half cup of sugar, the juice of one lemon, and two large tart apples well grated. Heat in a farina kettle until all are hot; cool, and spread between the layers of cake. This should be eaten the day the filling is prepared.

Cocoanut Custard Cake.—Make the cake as directed in the preceding recipe. For the filling, prepare a soft custard by heating just to the boiling point one pint of rich milk previously flavored with cocoanut; into which stir A tablespoonful of cornstarch braided with a little milk, and let it boil until thickened. Beat together an egg and one third of a cup of sugar, and turn the hot mixture slowly over it, stirring constantly till the custard thickens. When cold, spread between the layers of raised cake.

Cream Cake.—Prepare the cake as above. Spread between the layers when cold a cream made as follows: Stir into one half pint of boiling milk two teaspoonfuls of cornstarch rubbed smooth in a little cold milk. Take with two tablespoonfuls of sugar; return to the rest of the custard and cook, stirring constantly until quite thick. Cool and flavor with a teaspoonful of vanilla or rose water.

Delicate Cup Cake.—This cake contains no soda or baking powder, and to make it light requires the incorporation of as much air as possible. In order to accomplish this, it should be put together in the same manner as directed for Batter Breads (page 154). Have all material measured and everything in readiness before beginning to put the cake together, then beat together the yolk of one egg, one cup of sugar, and one cup of very cold sweet cream, until all of a foam; add a little grated lemon rind for flavoring; stir in slowly, beating briskly all the time, two cups of granular white flour (sometimes termed gluten flour) or Graham meal. When all the flour is added, add lastly the beaten whites of two eggs, stirring just enough to mix them well throughout the whole; turn at once into slightly heated gem irons which have been previously oiled, and bake in a moderately quick oven. If made according to directions, this cake will be very light and delicate. It will not puff up much above its first proportions, but will be light throughout.

A nice cake may be prepared in the same manner with Graham meal or even white flour, by the addition of a heaping tablespoonful of cornstarch sifted into the flour, in the way in which baking powder is ordinarily mixed with flour before using.

Fig Layer Cake.—Prepare the cake as directed for Apple Cake. Chop one half pound of figs very fine, add one half cup of sugar, one cup of water and boil in a farina kettle until soft and homogeneous. Cool, and spread between the cakes. Or chop steamed figs very fine, mix with an equal quantity of almondine, and use.

Fruit Jelly Cake.—Prepare the cake as in the foregoing, using fruit jelly between the layers.

Gold and Silver Cake.—Prepare the cake as for Apple Cake. When it has risen the second time, measure out one third of it, and add the yolks of the eggs to that portion with a little grated lemon rind for flavoring; add the whites with some very finely pulverized desiccated cocoanut to the other two thirds. Make two sheets of the white and one of the yellow. Allow them to become perfectly light before baking. When baked, place the yellow portion between the two white sheets, binding them together with a little frosting or white currant jelly.

Icing for Cakes.—Since icing adds to the excess of sugar contained in cakes, it is preferable to use them without it except when especially desired for ornament. An icing without eggs may be prepared by boiling a cup of granulated sugar in five tablespoonfuls of sweet milk for five minutes, then beating until cool enough to spread. One with egg may be easily made of six tablespoonfuls of powdered sugar, the white of one egg, and one teaspoonful of boiling water mixed without beating. A colored icing may be made by using a teaspoonful of boiling cranberry juice or other red fruit juice instead of water. The top of the icing may be ornamented with roasted almonds, bits of colored sugar or frosted fruits, directions for the preparation of all of which have already been given.

Orange Cake.—Prepare the cake as for Apple Cake, and bake in two layers. For the filling, take two good-sized, juicy oranges. Flavor two tablespoonfuls of sugar by rubbing it over the skin of the oranges, then peel, remove the white rind, and cut into small pieces, discarding the seeds and the central pith. Put the orange pulp in a china bowl, and set in a dish of boiling water. When it is hot, stir in a heaping teaspoonful of cornstarch which has been braided smooth in two spoonfuls of water. Stir constantly until the starch has cooked, and the whole becomes thickened. Beat the yolk of one egg to a cream with two tablespoonfuls of sugar. Stir this very gradually, so as not to lump, into the orange mixture, and cook two or three minutes longer. Remove from the fire, and when cool, spread between the cakes. If the oranges are not very tart, a little lemon juice is an improvement. Meringue the top of the cake with the white of the egg beaten up with the two tablespoonfuls of sugar flavored with orange.

Fruit Cake.—Make a sponge of one pint of thin cream which has been scalded and cooled to lukewarm, one gill of liquid yeast or one half cake of compressed yeast dissolved in a gill of cream, one half cup of sugar, and two and one half cups of flour. Beat all together very thoroughly and let rise until light. When light, add another half cup of sugar, one half cup of rather thick cream which has been scalded and cooled, one cup of warm flour, and after beating well together, set away to rise again. When well risen, add one cup of seeded raisins, one fourth cup of citron chopped fine, one half cup of Zante currants, two well-beaten eggs, and about one and one third cups of flour. Turn into a brick loaf bread pan, let it rise until very light, and bake. When done, remove from the pan and set away until at least twenty-four hours old before using.

Loaf Cake.—Scald a cup of rather thin cream, and cool to blood heat. Add one and one half cups of warm flour, one half a cup of sugar, and one fourth cake of compressed yeast dissolved in two tablespoonfuls of thin cream or as much of liquid yeast. Beat well, and let rise until perfectly light; then add one half cup more of sugar mixed with one half cup of warm flour. Beat well, and set away to rise a second time. When again well risen, add the whites of three eggs beaten to a stiff froth, one half cup of warm flour, and a little grated lemon rind, or two teaspoonfuls of rose water to flavor. Turn into a brick loaf bread pan lined with oiled paper, allow it to become perfectly light again, and bake. This cake, like other articles made with yeast, should not be eaten within at least twenty-four hours after baking.

Pineapple Cake.—Prepare as for orange cake, using grated pineapple in place of oranges.

Plain Buns.—These are the simplest of all cakes. Dissolve half a small cake of compressed yeast in a cup of thin cream which has been previously warmed to blood heat, add two cups of warm flour, and beat thoroughly together. Put in a warm place, and let it rise till very light. Add three tablespoonfuls of sugar mixed well with a half cup of warm flour, one half cup of Zante currants, and sufficient flour to make of the consistency of dough. Buns should be kneaded just as soft as possible, and from fifteen to twenty minutes. Shape into biscuits a little larger than an English walnut, place them on tins far enough apart so they will not touch each other when risen. Put in a warm place till they have risen to twice their first size, then bake in a moderately quick oven. If desired, the currants may be omitted and a little grated lemon rind for flavoring added with the sugar, or a bit of citron may be placed in the top of each bun when shaping. When taken from the oven, sprinkle the top of each with moist sugar if desired, or glace by brushing with milk while baking.

Sponge Cake.—For this will be required four eggs, one cup of sugar, one tablespoonful of lemon juice with a little of the grated rind, and one cup of white flour. Success in the making of sponge cake depends almost wholly upon the manner in which it is put together. Beat the yolks of the eggs until very light and thick, then add the sugar little by little, beating it in thoroughly; add the lemon juice and the grated rind. Beat the whites of the eggs until perfectly stiff and firm, and fold or chop them very lightly into the yolk mixture. Sift the flour with a sifter little by little over the mixture and fold it carefully in. On no account stir either the white of the eggs or the flour in, since stirring will drive out the air which has been beaten into the eggs. Do not beat after the flour is added. The cake, when the flour is all in, should be stiff and spongy. If it is liquid in character, it will be apt to be tough and may be considered a failure. Bake in a shallow pan in a rather hot oven fifteen or twenty minutes.

Sugar Crisps.—Make a soft dough of two and one fourth cups of Graham flour, one half cup of granulated white sugar, and one cup of rather thick sweet cream. Knead as little as possible, roll out very thinly, cut in rounds or squares, and bake in a quick oven.

Variety Cake.—Make the same as Gold and Silver Cake, and mix a half cup of Zante currants and chopped raisins with the yellow portion. The white portion may be flavored by adding a very little chopped citron instead of the cocoanut, if preferred.

TABLE TOPICS.

If families could be induced to substitute the apple—sound, ripe, and luscious—for the pies, cakes, candies, and other sweetmeats with which children are too often stuffed, there would be a diminution of doctors' bills, sufficient in a single year to lay up a stock of this delicious fruit for a season's use.—*Prof. Faraday.*

Food for repentance—mince pie eaten late at night.

Young Student—"This cook book says that pie crust needs plenty of shortening. Do you know what that means, pa?"

Father—"It means lard."

"But why is lard called shortening, pa?"

"Because it shortens life."

The health journals and the doctors all agree that the best and most wholesome part of the New England country doughnut is the hole. The larger the hole, they say, the better the doughnut.

An old gentleman who was in the habit of eating a liberal slice of pie or cake just before retiring, came home late one evening after his wife had gone to bed. After an unsuccessful search in the pantry, he called to his wife, "Mary, where is the pie?" His good wife timidly acknowledged that there was no pie in the house. Said her husband, "Then where is the cake?" The poor woman meekly confessed that the supply of cake was also exhausted; at which the disappointed husband cried out in a sharp, censorious tone, "Why, what would you do if somebody should be sick in the night?"

Woman (to tramp)—"I can give you some cold buckwheat cakes and a piece of mince pie." *Tramp*—(frightened) "What ye say?" *Woman*—"Cold buckwheat cakes and mince pie." *Tramp*—(heroically) "Throw in a small bottle of pepsin, Madam, and I'll take the chances."

GRAVIES AND SAUCES

Gravies for vegetables, sauces for desserts, and similar foods thickened with flour or cornstarch, are among the most common of the poorly prepared articles of the *cuisine*, although their proper preparation is a matter of considerable importance, since neither a thin, watery sauce nor a stiff, paste-like mixture is at all palatable. The preparation of gravies and sauces is a very simple matter when governed by that accuracy of measurement and carefulness of detail which should be exercised in the preparation of all foods. In consistency, a properly made sauce should mask the back of the spoon; that is to say, when dipped into the mixture and lifted out, the metal of the spoon should not be visible through it as it runs off. The proportion of material necessary to secure this requisite is one tablespoonful of flour, slightly rounded, for each half pint of water or stock. If the sauce be made of milk or fruit juice, a little less flour will be needed. If cornstarch be used, a scant instead of a full tablespoonful will be required. The flour, or cornstarch should be first braided or rubbed perfectly smooth in a very small amount of the liquid reserved for the purpose (salt or sugar, if any is to be used, being added to the flour before braiding with the liquid), and then carefully added to the remaining liquid, which should be actively boiling. It should then be continuously stirred until it has thickened, when it should be allowed to cook slowly for five or ten minutes until the starch or flour is well done. If through any negligence to observe carefully these simple details, there should be lumps in the sauce, they must be removed before serving by turning the whole through a fine colander or wire strainer.

The double boiler is the best utensil for the preparation of sauces and gravies, since it facilitates even cooking and renders them less liable to become scorched. The inner cup should be placed on the top of the range until the sauce has become thickened, as in the cooking of grains, and afterwards placed in the outer boiler to continue the cooking as long as needed.

Cream gravies for vegetables may be delicately flavored with celery, by steeping a few bits of celery in the milk for a few minutes, and removing with a fork before adding the thickening. Sauces for puddings may be similarly flavored, by steeping cocoanut or bits of orange or lemon rind in the milk.

GRAVIES AND SAUCES FOR VEGETABLES.

RECIPES.

Brown Sauce.—Heat a pint of thin cream, and when boiling, add half a teaspoonful of salt and a tablespoonful of flour browned in the oven as directed on page 274, and rubbed to a smooth paste with a little cold milk. Allow it to boil rapidly, stirring constantly until thickened; then cook more slowly, in a double boiler, for five or ten minutes. If desired, the milk may be flavored with onion before adding the flour. This makes a good dressing for potatoes.

Cream or White Sauce.—Heat a pint of rich milk, part cream if it can be afforded, to boiling, and stir into it one tablespoonful of flour previously rubbed smooth in a little milk. Season with salt, and cook in a double boiler five or ten minutes, stirring frequently that no lumps be formed. If lumps are found in the sauce, turn it quickly through a fine, hot colander into the dish in which it is to be served.

Celery Sauce.—Cut half a dozen stalks of celery into finger-lengths, and simmer in milk for ten or fifteen minutes. Skim out the celery, add a little cream to the milk, salt to taste, and thicken with flour as for white sauce. This is very nice for potatoes and for toast.

Egg Sauce.—Heat a pint of milk to boiling, and stir in a dessertspoonful of flour rubbed smooth in a little milk. Stir constantly until the sauce is well thickened; add the well-beaten yolk of an egg, turning it in very slowly and stirring rapidly so that it shall be well mingled. Boil up once only, add a very little salt, and serve. The egg makes an excellent substitute for cream.

Pease Gravy.—A gravy prepared either of dried or green peas as directed for Lentil Gravy on page 226, makes a suitable dressing for baked potatoes. Lentil gravy is also good for the same purpose. The addition of a little lemon juice to the lentil gravy makes another variety.

Tomato Gravy.—A gravy made of tomatoes as directed on page 261, is excellent to use on baked or boiled sweet potatoes.

Tomato Cream Gravy.—Prepare a gravy as for Cream Sauce, using a slightly heaping measure of flour. When done, add, just before serving, for each quart of the cream sauce, one cup of hot, stewed tomato which has been put through a fine colander to remove all seeds. Beat it thoroughly into the sauce and serve on boiled or baked potato.

SAUCES FOR DESSERTS AND PUDDINGS.

RECIPES.

Almond Sauce.—Heat a pint of rich milk in the inner cup of a double boiler, placed directly upon the stove. When the milk is boiling, stir into it a heaping tablespoonful of flour which has been rubbed to a cream in a little cold milk. Boil rapidly until thickened, stirring constantly; then add three tablespoonfuls of almondine; place in the outer boiler, and cook for five or ten minutes longer.

Caramel Sauce.—Stir a cup of sugar in a saucepan over the fire until melted and lightly browned. Add one cup of boiling water, and simmer ten minutes.

Cocoanut Sauce.—Flavor a pint of new milk with cocoanut, as directed on page 298. Skim out the cocoanut, and add enough fresh milk to make one pint. Heat the milk to boiling, add two tablespoonfuls of sugar, thicken with two even spoonfuls of cornstarch, and proceed in the same manner as for Mock Cream.

Cream Sauce.—Beat together two thirds of a cup of sugar, one tablespoonful of thick, sweet cream, and one egg.

Wet half a teaspoonful of cornstarch with a little milk, and stir in with the mixture; then add five tablespoonfuls of boiling milk, stirring rapidly all the time. Pour into the inner cup of a double boiler; have the water in the outer cup boiling, and cook five minutes. Flavor to taste.

Cranberry Pudding Sauce.—To a quart of boiling water add two cups of sugar, and when well dissolved, one quart of carefully sorted cranberries. Mash the berries as much as possible with a silver spoon, and boil just seven minutes. Turn through a colander to remove skins, cool and serve.

Custard Sauce.—Rub two teaspoonfuls of flour to a smooth paste with half a cup of new milk. Heat two and a half cups of fresh milk in a double boiler to scalding, then stir in the braided flour; heat again, stirring constantly till just to the boiling point, but no longer; remove from the stove and cool a little. Beat together one egg, three tablespoonfuls of sugar, and a little lemon rind for flavoring. Turn the hot milk over this, a little at a time, stirring briskly meanwhile. Return the whole to the double boiler, and cook, stirring frequently, until when a spoon is dipped into the custard a coating remains upon it. Then remove at once from the fire. If the spoon comes out clean, the custard is not sufficiently cooked.

Egg Sauce.—Separate the yolks and whites of three eggs. Beat the whites to a stiff froth, and stir in very gently, so as not to let the air out of the beaten whites, one cup of powdered sugar and a teaspoonful of vanilla or lemon flavoring powder. Lastly, stir in carefully the beaten yolks of the eggs, and serve at once.

Egg Sauce No. 2.—Beat the whites of three eggs to a stiff froth with one half cup of sugar. Add three tablespoonfuls of lemon juice and one of water. Serve at once.

Foamy Sauce.—Beat one egg or the whites of two very thoroughly with one half cup of sugar and a little grated lemon rind. Pour on this very slowly, stirring constantly to make it smooth, one cup of boiling milk, part cream if it can be afforded. If the whites alone are used, they should not be beaten stiff. If preferred, the lemon may be omitted and a tablespoonful or two of currant juice or quince jelly added last as flavoring.

Fruit Cream.—Take the juice pressed from a cupful of fresh strawberries, red raspberries, or black caps, add to it one third of a cup of sugar, and place in the ice chest till chilled. Set a cup of sweet cream also on ice till very cold. When thoroughly cold, whip with an egg beater till the froth begins to rise, then add to it the cold fruit juice and beat again. Have ready the white of one egg beaten to a stiff froth, which add to the fruit cream, and whip till no more froth will rise. This makes a delicious dressing for simple grain molds and blancmanges, but is so rich it should be used rather sparingly. Serve as soon as possible after being prepared. Fruit syrup, in the proportion of two or three tablespoonfuls to the pint of cream, may be used in the same manner when the fresh juice is not available. The juice of orange, quince, and pineapple may also be used in the same manner as that of berries.

Fruit Sauce.—Heat a pint of red raspberry, currant, grape, strawberry, apricot, or any other fruit juice to scalding, and stir in a tablespoonful of cornstarch previously rubbed to a cream with a little cold water. Cook till it thickens; then add sugar according to the acidity of the fruit. Strain and cool before using. If fruit juice is not available, two or three tablespoonfuls of pure fruit jelly may be dissolved in a pint of hot water and used instead of the juice. A mixture of red and black raspberry juice, or currant and raspberry, will be found acceptable for variety.

Fruit Sauce No. 2.—Mash a quart of fresh berries, add one cup of sugar, beat very thoroughly together, and set away until needed. Just before it is wanted for serving, turn into a granite fruit kettle and heat nearly to boiling, stirring constantly to avoid burning. Serve hot with hot or cold puddings, or molded desserts.

Lemon Pudding Sauce.—Heat to boiling, in a double boiler, a pint of water in which are two slices of lemon, and stir into it a dessertspoonful of cornstarch; cook four to five minutes, or until it thickens. Squeeze the juice from one large lemon, and mix it with two thirds of a cup of sugar. Add this to the cornstarch mixture, and allow the whole to boil up once, stirring constantly; then take from the fire. Leave in the double boiler, surrounded by the hot water, for ten minutes. Cool to blood heat before serving.

Mock Cream.—Heat a pint of fresh, unskimmed milk in a double boiler. When the milk is boiling, stir in two tablespoonfuls of sugar, and two even tablespoonfuls of cornstarch which has first been rubbed smooth in a very little cold milk. Bring just to a boil, stirring constantly; then pour the hot mixture, a little at a time, beating thoroughly all the while, over the well-beaten white of one egg. Put again into the double boiler, return to the fire, and stir till it thickens to the consistency of cream.

Molasses Sauce.—To one half cup of molasses, add one half cup of water, and heat to boiling. Thicken with a teaspoonful of flour rubbed to a cream with a little cold water. Serve hot.

Orange Sauce.—Squeeze a cupful of juice from well-flavored, sour oranges. Heat a pint of water, and when boiling, thicken with a tablespoonful of cornstarch. Add the orange juice, strain, and sweeten to taste with sugar that has been flavored by rubbing over the yellow rind of an orange until mixed with the oil in the rind. If a richer sauce is desired, the yolk of an egg may be added lastly, and the sauce allowed to cook until thickened.

Peach Sauce.—Strain the juice from a well-kept can of peaches. Dilute with one half as much water, heat to boiling, and thicken with cornstarch, a scant tablespoonful to the pint of liquid.

Plain Pudding Sauce.—Thicken one and one half cups of water with one tablespoonful of cornstarch; boil a few minutes, then stir in two thirds of a cup of sugar, and one half cup of sweet cream. Take off the stove, and flavor with a little rose, vanilla, or lemon.

Red Sauce.—Pare and slice a large red beet, and simmer gently in three cups of water for twenty minutes, or until the water is rose colored, then add two cups of sugar, the thin yellow rind and juice of one lemon, and boil until the whole is thick syrup. Strain, add a teaspoonful of rose water or vanilla, and serve.

Rose Cream.—Remove the thick cream from the top of a pan of cold milk, taking care not to take up any of the milk. Add sugar to sweeten and a teaspoonful or two of rose water. Beat with an egg beater until the whole mass is thick. Good thick cream, beaten in this manner, makes nearly double its original quantity.

Sago Sauce.—Wash one tablespoonful of sago in two or three waters, then put it into a saucepan with three fourths of a cup of hot water, and some bits of lemon peel. Simmer gently for ten minutes, take out the lemon peel, add half a cup of quince or apricot juice; and if the latter, the strained juice of half a lemon, and sugar to taste. Beat together thoroughly.

Whipped Cream Sauce.—Beat together with an egg beater until of a stiff froth one cup of sweet cream which has been cooled to a temperature of 64° or less, one teaspoonful of vanilla or a little grated lemon rind, and one half cup of powdered white sugar, and the whites of one or two eggs. The sauce may be variously flavored with a little fruit jelly beaten with the egg, before adding to the cream.

TABLE TOPICS.

Whether or not life is worth living, all depends upon the liver.—*Sel.*

Diet cures mair than doctors.—*Scotch Proverb.*

According to the ancient Hindu Scriptures, the proper amount of food is half of what can be conveniently eaten.

Every hour you steal from digestion will be reclaimed by indigestion.—*Oswald.*

"Very few nations in the world," says a sagacious historian, "produce better soldiers than the Russians. They will endure the greatest fatigues and sufferings with patience and calmness. And it is well know that the Russian soldiers are from childhood nourished by simple and coarse vegetable food. The Russian Grenadiers are the finest body of men I ever saw,—not a man is under six feet high. Their allowance consists of eight pounds of black bread, and four pounds of oil per man for eight days."

Colonel Fitzgibbon was, many years ago, colonial agent at London for the Canadian Government, and wholly dependent upon remittances from Canada for his support. On one occasion these remittances failed to arrive, and it being before the day of cables, he was obliged to write to his friends to ascertain the reason of the delay. Meanwhile he had just one sovereign to live upon. He found he could live upon a sixpence a day,—four pennyworth of bread, one pennyworth of milk, and one pennyworth of sugar. When his remittances arrived a month afterward, he had five shillings remaining of his sovereign, and he liked his frugal diet so well that he kept it up for several years.

An hour of exercise to every pound of food.—*Oswald.*

Some eat to live, they loudly cry;
But from the pace they swallow pie
And other food promiscuously,
One would infer they eat to die.—*Sel.*

BEVERAGES

The use of beverages in quantities with food at mealtime is prejudicial to digestion, because they delay the action of the gastric juice upon solid foods. The practice of washing down food by copious draughts of water, tea, or coffee is detrimental, not only because it introduces large quantities of fluid into the stomach, which must be absorbed before digestion can begin, but also because it offers temptation to careless and imperfect mastication, while tea and coffee also serve as a vehicle for an excessive use of sugar, thus becoming a potent cause of indigestion and dyspepsia. It is best to drink but sparingly, if at all, at mealtimes. Consideration should also be given to the nature of the beverage, since many in common use are far from wholesome. Very cold fluids, like iced water, iced tea, and iced milk, are harmful, because they cool the contents of the stomach to a degree at which digestion is checked. If drunk at all, they should be taken only in small sips and retained in the mouth until partly warmed.

Tea is often spoken of as the "cup that cheers but not inebriates." "The cup that may cheer yet does injury" would be nearer the truth, for there is every evidence to prove that this common beverage is exceedingly harmful, and that the evils of its excessive use are second only to those of tobacco and alcohol. Tea contains two harmful substances, theine and tannin,—from three to six per cent of the former and more than one fourth its weight of the latter. Theine is a poison belonging to the same class of poisonous alkaloids, and is closely allied to cocaine. It is a much more powerful poison than alcohol, producing death in less than one hundredth part the deadly dose of alcohol; and when taken in any but the smallest doses, it produces all the symptoms of intoxication. Tannin is an astringent exercising a powerful effect in delaying salivary and stomach digestion, thus becoming one of the most common causes of digestive disorders. It is also a matter of frequent observation that sleeplessness, palpitation of the heart, and various disorders of the nervous system frequently follow the prolonged use of tea. Both theine and tannin are more abundant in green than in black tea.

The dependence of the habitual tea-drinker upon the beverage, and the sense of loss experienced when deprived of it, are among the strongest proofs of its evil effects, and should be warnings against its use. No such physical discomfort is experienced when deprived of any article of ordinary food. The use of tea makes one feel bright and fresh when really exhausted; but, like all other stimulants, it is by exciting vital action above the normal without supplying extra force to support the extra expenditure. The fact that a person feels tired is evidence that the system demands rest, that his body is worn and needs repair; but the relief experienced after a cup of tea is not recuperation. Instead, it indicates that his nerves are paralyzed so that they are insensible to fatigue.

Some people suppose the manner of preparing tea has much to do with its deleterious effects, and that by infusion for two or three minutes only, the evils resulting from the tannin will be greatly lessened. This, however, is a delusion, if the same amount of tea be used proportionate to the water; for tannin in its free state, the condition in which it is found in tea is one of the most readily soluble of substances; and tea infused for two minutes is likely to hold nearly as much tannin in solution as that infused for a longer period.

Tea is not a food, and it can in no wise take the place of food, as so many people attempt to make it, without detriment to health in every respect.

Coffee, cocoa, and chocolate rank in the same category with tea, as beverages which are more or less harmful. Coffee contains caffein, a principle identical with theine and a modified form of tannin, though in less quantity than tea. Cocoa and chocolate contain substances similar to theine and equally harmful, though usually present in much less proportion than in tea.

Custom has made the use of these beverages so common that most people seldom stop to inquire into their nature. Doubtless the question arises in many minds; If these beverages contain such poisons, why do they not more commonly produce fatal results?—Because a tolerance of the poison is established in the system by use, as in the case of tobacco and other narcotics and stimulants; but that the poisons surely though insidiously are doing their work is attested by the prevalence of numerous disorders of the digestive and nervous systems, directly attributable to the use of these beverages.

Both tea and coffee are largely adulterated with other harmful substances, thus adding another reason why their use should be discarded. It is stated on good authority that it is almost impossible to obtain unadulterated ground coffee.

In view of all these facts, it certainly seems wisest if a beverage is considered essential, to make use of one less harmful. Hot milk, hot water, hot lemonade, caramel coffee, or some of the various grain coffees, recipes for which are give in the following pages, are all excellent substitutes for tea and coffee, if a hot drink is desired.

RECIPES.

Beet Coffee.—Wash best beets thoroughly, but do not scrape; slice, and brown in a moderate oven, taking care not to burn. When brown, break in small pieces and steep the same as ordinary coffee.

Caramel Coffee.—Take three quarts best bran, one quart corn meal, three tablespoonfuls of molasses; mix and brown in the oven like ordinary coffee. For every cup of coffee required, use one heaping tablespoonful of the caramel. Pour boiling water over it, and steep, not boil, for fifteen or twenty minutes.

Caramel Coffee No. 2.—Take one cup each of white flour, corn meal, unsifted Graham flour, and molasses. Mix well, and form into cakes half an inch thick and a little larger around than a silver dollar. If the molasses is not thin enough to take up all the dry material, one fourth or one half a cup of cold water may be added for that purpose. Bake the cakes in the oven until very dark brown, allowing them to become slightly scorched. When desired for use, take one cake for each cup of coffee required, pour sufficient water over them, and steep, not boil, twenty minutes.

Caramel Coffee No. 3.—To three and one half quarts of bran and one and one half quarts of corn meal, take one pint of New Orleans molasses and one half pint of boiling water. Put the water and molasses together and pour them over the bran and corn meal which have been previously mixed. Rub all well together, and brown slowly in the oven, stirring often, until a rich dark brown. Use one heaping tablespoonful of coffee to each small cup of boiling water, let it just boil up, then steep on the back of the stove for five or ten minutes.

Caramel Coffee No. 4.—Beat together four eggs and one pint of molasses, and mix thoroughly with four quarts of good wheat bran. Brown in the oven, stirring frequently. Prepare for use the same as the preceding.

Mrs. T's Caramel Coffee.—Make a rather thick batter of Graham grits or Graham meal and milk, spread it in shallow pans and bake in a moderate oven until evenly done throughout. Cut the cake thus prepared into thin strips, which break into small uniform pieces and spread on perforated tins or sheets and brown in the oven. Each piece should be very darkly and evenly browned, but not burned. For each cup of coffee required, steep a small handful in boiling water for ten or fifteen minutes, strain and serve.

Parched Grain Coffee.—Brown in the oven some perfectly sound wheat, sweet corn, barley, or rice, as you would the coffee berry. If desired, a mixture of grains may be used. Pound or grind fine. Mix the white of an egg with three tablespoonfuls of the ground grain, and pour over it a quart of boiling water. Allow it to come just to the boiling point, steep slowly for twelve or fifteen minutes, and serve.

Wheat, Oats and Barley Coffee.—Mix together equal quantities of these grains, brown in the oven like ordinary coffee, and grind. To one quart of boiling water take three tablespoonfuls of the prepared coffee mixed with the white of an egg, and steep in boiling water ten or fifteen minutes.

RECIPES FOR COLD BEVERAGES.

Blackberry Beverage.—Crush a quart of fresh blackberries, and pour over them a quart of cold water; add a slice of lemon and a teaspoonful of orange water, and let it stand three or four hours. Strain through a jelly bag. Sweeten to taste with a syrup prepared by dissolving white sugar in hot water, allowing it to become cold before using. Serve at once with bits of broken ice in the glasses, or place the pitcher on ice until ready to serve.

Fruit Beverage.—A great variety of pleasant, healthful drinks may be made by taking equal quantities of water and the juice of currants, strawberries, raspberries, cherries, or a mixture of two kinds, as raspberries and currants, sweetening to taste, and putting into each glass a small lump of ice. Directions for the preparation of fruit juices will be found on page 209.

Fruit Beverage No. 2.—Mash a pint of red raspberries, add one cup of canned pineapple or half a fresh one chopped fine; pour over all three pints of water. Stir frequently, and let the mixture stand for two hours. Strain, add the juice of six lemons, and sugar or syrup to sweeten.

Another.—Extract the juice from three lemons and as many sour oranges, add a quart of cold water, sugar or syrup to sweeten, half a teaspoonful of rose water, and a cup of pure grape juice; or the rose water and grape juice may be omitted and two tablespoonfuls of strawberry, raspberry, or cherry juice used instead, and the whole poured over half a dozen slices of pineapple, and allowed to stand until well flavored before using.

Fruit Cordial.—Crush a pint of blackberries, raspberries, grapes, currants, or cherries, adding the juice of two sour oranges, and a sliced lemon; pour over all a quart of cold water. Stir the mixture frequently and let it stand for two hours, then strain and add a syrup made by dissolving white sugar in boiling water, sufficient to sweeten. Cool on ice and serve.

Grape Beverage.—Crush two pounds of perfectly ripened purple grapes and strain the juice through a jelly bag. Add to the juice three tablespoonfuls of granulated sugar or syrup, and dilute with cold water to suit the taste.

Lemonade.—Use three large or four medium-sized lemons for each quart of water, and from six to eight tablespoonfuls of sugar. Rub or squeeze the lemons till soft. Cut a slice or two from each, and extract the juice with a lemon drill; strain the juice through a fine wire strainer to remove the seeds and bits of pulp, and pour it over the sugar. Add the slices of lemon, and pour over all a very little boiling water to thoroughly dissolve the sugar; let it stand ten or fifteen minutes, then add the necessary quantity of cold water, and serve. Or rub the sugar over the outside of the lemons to flavor it, and make it into a syrup by adding sufficient boiling water to dissolve it. Extract and strain the lemon juice, add the prepared syrup and the requisite quantity of cold water, and serve.

Mixed Lemonade.—A very pleasant, cooling summer drink is made from the juice of six oranges and six lemons, with sugar to taste; add to this some pounded ice and the juice of a small can of pineapple, and lastly pour over the whole two quarts of water.

Oatmeal Drink.—Boil one fourth of a pound of oatmeal in three quarts of water for half an hour, then add one and one half tablespoonfuls of sugar, strain and cool. It may be flavored with a little lemon or raspberry syrup if desired; or the sugar may be omitted and a quart of milk added. Cool on ice and serve.

Orangeade.—Pare very thin from one orange a few bits of the yellow rind. Slice three well-peeled sour oranges, taking care to remove all the white portion and all seeds. Add the yellow rind and a tablespoonful of sugar; pour over all a quart of boiling water. Cover the dish, and let it remain until the drink is cold. Or, if preferred, the juice of the oranges may be extracted with a lemon drill and strained as for lemonade.

Pineapple Beverage.—Pare and chop quite fine one fresh pineapple; add a slice or two of lemon, and cover with three pints of boiling water. Let it stand for two hours or more, stirring frequently; then strain and add the juice of five lemons, and sugar or syrup to sweeten.

Pineapple Lemonade.—Lemonade made in the usual manner and flavored with a few spoonfuls of canned pineapple juice, is excellent for variety.

Pink Lemonade.—Add to a pint of lemonade prepared in the usual manner half a cup of fresh or canned strawberry, red raspberry, currant, or cranberry juice. It gives a pretty color besides adding a pleasing flavor.

Sherbet.—Mash a quart of red raspberries, currants, or strawberries, add the juice of a lemon, and pour over all three pints of cold water. Stir frequently, and let it stand for two or three hours. Strain through a jelly bag, sweeten to taste, and serve.

Tisane.—This is a favorite French beverage, and is prepared by chopping fine a cupful of dried fruits, such as prunes, figs, or prunelles, and steeping for an hour in a quart of water, afterward straining, sweetening to taste, and cooling on ice before using.

TABLE TOPICS.

The nervousness and peevishness of our times are chiefly attributable to tea and coffee. The digestive organs of confirmed coffee drinkers are in a state of chronic derangement which reacts on the brain, producing fretful and lachrymose moods. The snappish, petulant humor of the Chinese can certainly be ascribed to their immoderate fondness for tea.—*Dr. Bock.*

Dr. Ferguson, an eminent physician who has carefully investigated the influence of tea and coffee upon the health and development of children, says he found that children who were allowed these beverages gained but four pounds a year between the ages of thirteen and sixteen, while those who had been allowed milk instead, gained fifteen pounds in weight during the same period.

Dr. Richardson, the eminent English physician and scientist, asserts that the misery of the women of the poorer classes of the population in England is more than doubled by the use of tea, which only soothes or stimulates to intensify the after-coming depression and languor.

A physician recommended a lady to abandon the use of tea and coffee. "O, but I shall miss it so," said she.

"Very likely," replied her medical adviser, "but you are missing health now, and will soon lose it altogether if you do not."

Dr. Stenhouse, of Liverpool, once made a careful analysis of a sample package of black tea, which was found to contain "some pure Congo tea leaves, also siftings of Pekoe and inferior kinds, weighing together twenty-seven per cent of the whole. The remaining seventy-three per cent was composed of the following substances; Iron, plumbago, chalk, China-clay, sand, Prussian-blue, tumeric, indigo, starch, gypsum, catechu, gum, the leaves of the camelia, sarangna, *Chlorantes officinalis*, elm, oak, willow, poplar, elder, beach, hawthorn, and sloe."

MILK CREAM BUTTER

MILK.

Chemically considered, the constituents of milk are nitrogenous matter (consisting of casein and a small proportion of albumen), fat, sugar of milk, mineral matter, and water, the last constituting from sixty-five to ninety per cent of the whole.

The proportion of these elements varies greatly in the milk of different animals of the same species and of the same animals at different times, so that it is not possible to give an exact analysis.

The analysis of an average specimen of cow's milk, according to Letheby, is:—

Nitrogenous matter	4.1
Fat	3.9
Sugar of milk	5.2
Mineral matter	0.8
Water	86.0

If a drop of milk be examined with a microscope, it will be seen as a clear liquid, holding in suspension a large number of minute globules, which give the milk its opacity or white color. These microscopic globules are composed of fatty matter, each surrounded by an envelope of casein, the principal nitrogenous element found in milk. They are lighter than the surrounding liquid, and when the milk remains at rest, they gradually rise to the top and form cream. Casein, unlike albumen, is not coagulated by heat; hence when milk is cooked, it undergoes no noticeable change, save the coagulation of the very small amount of albumen it contains, which, as it solidifies, rises to the top, carrying with it a small portion of the sugar and saline matter and some of the fat globules, forming a skin-like scum upon the surface. Casein, although not coagulable by heat, is coagulated by the introduction into the milk of acids or extract of rennet. The curd of cheese is coagulated casein. When milk is allowed to stand for some time exposed to warmth and air, a spontaneous coagulation occurs, caused by fermentative changes in the sugar of milk, by which it is converted into lactic acid through the action of germs.

Milk is sometimes adulterated by water, the removal of more or less of the cream, or the addition of some foreign substance to increase its density.

The quality of milk is more or less influenced by the food upon which the animal is fed. Watery milk may be produced by feeding a cow upon sloppy food.

The milk of diseased animals should never be used for food. There is no way by which such milk can invariably be detected, but Prof. Vaughan, of Michigan University, notes the following kinds of milk to be avoided:

1. Milk which becomes sour and curdles within a few hours after it has been drawn, and before any cream forms on its surface. This is known in some sections as 'curdly' milk, and it comes from cows with certain inflammatory affections of the udder, or digestive diseases, or those which have been overdriven or worried.

2. "Bitter-sweet milk" has cream of a bitter taste, is covered with 'blisters,' and frequently with a fine mold. Butter and cheese made from such milk cannot be eaten on account of the disagreeable taste.

3. 'Slimy milk' can be drawn out into fine, ropy fibers. It has an unpleasant taste, which is most marked in the cream. The causes which lead to the secretion of this milk are not known.

4. 'Blue milk' is characterized by the appearance on its surface, eighteen or twenty-four hours after it is drawn, of small, indigo-blue spots, which rapidly enlarge until the whole surface is covered with a blue film. If the milk be allowed to stand a few days, the blue is converted into a greenish or reddish color. This coloration of the milk is due to the growth of microscopic organisms. The butter made from 'blue milk' is dirty-white, gelatinous, and bitter.

5. 'Barnyard milk' is a term used to designate milk taken from unclean animals, or those which have been kept in filthy, unventilated stables. The milk absorbs and carries the odors, which are often plainly perceptible. Such milk may not be poisonous, but it is repulsive.

There is no doubt that milk often serves as the vehicle for the distribution of the germs of various contagious diseases, like scarlet fever, diphtheria, and typhoid fever, from becoming contaminated in some way, either from the hands of milkers or from water used as an adulterant or in cleansing the milk vessels. Recent investigations have also shown that cows are to some extent subject to scarlet fever, the same as human beings, and that milk from infected cows will produce the same disease in the consumer.

Milk should not be kept in brass or copper vessels or in earthen-ware lined with lead glazing; for if the milk becomes acid, it is likely to unite with the metal and form a poisonous compound. Glass and granite ware are better materials in which to keep milk.

Milk should never be allowed to stand uncovered in an occupied room, especially a sitting-room or bedroom, as its dust is likely to contain disease-germs, which falling into the milk, may become a source of serious illness to the consumer. Indeed it is safest to keep milk covered whenever set away, to exclude the germs which are at all times present in the air. A good way is to protect the dishes containing milk with several layers of cheese-cloth, which will permit the air but not the germs to circulate in and out of the pans. Neither should it be allowed to stand where there are strong odors, as it readily takes up by absorption any odors to which it is exposed.

A few years ago Dr. Dougall, of Glasgow, made some very interesting experiments on the absorbent properties of milk. He inclosed in jars a portion of substances giving off emanations, with a uniform quantity of milk, in separate vessels, for a period of eight hours, at the end of which time samples of the milk were drawn off and tested. The result was that milk exposed to the following substances retained odors as described:—

Coal gas, distinct; paraffine oil, strong; turpentine, very strong; onions, very strong; tobacco smoke, very strong; ammonia, moderate; musk, faint; asafetida, distinct; creosote, strong; cheese (stale), distinct; chloroform, moderate; putrid fish, very bad; camphor, moderate; decayed cabbage, distinct.

These facts clearly indicate that if the emanations to which milk is exposed are of a diseased and dangerous quality, it is all but impossible that the milk can remain free from dangerous properties.

Too much pains cannot be taken in the care of milk and vessels containing it. Contact with the smallest quantity of milk which has undergone fermentation will sour the whole; hence the necessity for scrupulous cleanliness of all vessels which have contained milk before they are used again for that purpose.

In washing milk dishes, many persons put them first into scalding water, by which means the albumen in the milk is coagulated; and if there are any crevices or seams in the pans or pails, this coagulated portion is likely to adhere to them like glue, and becoming sour, will form the nucleus for spoiling the next milk put into them. A better way is first to rinse each separately in cold water, not pouring the water from one pan to another, until there is not the slightest milky appearance in the water, then wash in warm suds, or water containing sal-soda, and afterward scald thoroughly; wipe perfectly dry, and place if possible where the sun will have free access to them until they are needed for further use. If sunshine is out of the question, invert the pans or cans over the stove, or place for a few moments in a hot oven.

The treatment of milk varies with its intended use, whether whole or separated from the cream.

Cream rises best when the milk is quite warm or when near the freezing-point. In fact, cream separates more easily from milk at the freezing-point than any other, but it is not thick and never becomes so. An intermediate state seems to be unfavorable to a full rising of the cream.

A temperature of 56° to 60°F. is a good one. Milk to be used whole should be kept at about 45° and stirred frequently.

All milk obtained from city milkmen or any source not certainly known to be free from disease-germs, should be sterilized before using. Indeed, it is safest always to sterilize milk before using, since during the milking or in subsequent handling and transportation it is liable to become infected with germs.

To Sterilize Milk for Immediate Use.—Put the milk as soon as received into the inner dish of a double boiler, the outer vessel of which should be filled with boiling water. Cover and heat the milk rapidly to as near the boiling point as possible. Allow it to remain with the water in the outer boiler actively boiling for half an hour, then remove from the stove and cool very quickly. This may be accomplished by pouring into shallow dishes, and placing these in cold water, changing the water as frequently as it becomes warm, or by using pieces of ice in the water. It is especially important to remember that the temperature of the milk should be raised as rapidly as possible, and when the milk is sufficiently cooked, cooled very quickly. Either very slow heating or slow cooling may prove disastrous, even when every other precaution is taken.

Or, well-cleaned glass fruit cans may be nearly filled with milk, the covers screwed on loosely, then placed in a kettle of cold water, gradually heated to boiling and kept at that temperature for a half hour or longer, then gradually cooled. Or, perfectly clean bottles may be filled with milk to within two inches of the top, the neck tightly closed with a wad of cotton, and the bottles placed in a steam cooker, the water in which should be cold at the start, and steamed for half an hour.

This cooking of milk, while it destroys many of the germs contained in milk, particularly the active disease-germs which are liable to be found in it, thus rendering it more wholesome, and improving its keeping qualities somewhat, does not so completely sterilize the milk that it will not undergo fermentative changes. Under varying conditions some thirty or forty different species of germs are to be found in milk, some of which require to be subjected to a temperature above that of boiling water, in order to destroy them. The keeping quality of the milk may be increased by reboiling it on three successive days for a half hour or longer, and carefully sealing after each boiling.

To Sterilize Milk to Keep.—This is a somewhat more difficult operation, but it may be done by boiling milk sealed in very strong bottles in a saturated solution of salt. The milk used should be perfectly fresh. It is best, when possible, to draw the milk from the cow directly into the bottles. Fill the bottles to within two inches of the top, cork them immediately and wire the corks down firmly and place them in the cold salt solution. Boil fifteen minutes or half an hour. Allow the solution to cool before removing them. If the bottles are removed from the solution while hot, they will almost instantly break. When cold, remove the bottles, and cover the tops with sealing wax. Store in a cool place, shake thoroughly once or twice a week. Milk sterilized in this manner will keep indefinitely.

Condensed Milk.—Condensed milk is made by evaporating milk in a vacuum to one fifth its original volume; it is then canned like any other food by sealing at boiling temperature in air-tight cans. When used, it should be diluted with five times its bulk of warm water.

Condensed milk, when not thoroughly boiled in the process of condensation, is liable to harbor disease-germs the same as any other milk.

CREAM.

Cream varies in composition according to the circumstances under which it rises.

The composition of an average specimen as given by Letherby is:—

Nitrogenous matter	2.7
Fat	26.7
Sugar of milk	2.8
Mineral matter	1.8
Water	66.0

In the process of churning; the membranes of casein which surround each of the little globules constituting the cream are broken, and the fat of which they are composed becomes a compact mass known as butter. The watery looking residue containing casein, sugar of milk, mineral matter, and a small proportion of fat, comprises the buttermilk.

Skim-milk, or milk from which the cream has been removed, and buttermilk are analogous in chemical composition.

The composition of each, according to Dr. Edward Smith, is:—

SKIM-MILK.

Nitrogenous matter	4.0
Sugar	3.8
Fat	1.8

Mineral matter	0.8
Water	88.0

BUTTERMILK.

Nitrogenous matter	4.1
Sugar	3.6
Fat	0.7
Mineral matter	0.8
Water	88.0

Skim-milk and buttermilk, when the butter is made from sweet cream and taken fresh, are both excellent foods, although lacking the fat of new milk.

Cream is more easily digested than butter, and since it contains other elements besides fat, is likewise more nutritious. In cream the fat is held in the form of an emulsion which allows it to mingle freely with water. As previously stated, each atom of fat is surrounded with a film of casein. The gastric juice has no more power to digest casein than it has free fat, and the little particles of fat thus protected are carried to the small intestines, where the pancreatic juice digests them, and on their way they do not interfere with the stomach digestion of other foods, as the presence of butter and other free fats may do.

It is because of its greater wholesomeness that in the directions for the preparation of foods given in this work we have given preference to the use of cream over that of butter and other free fats. The usual objection to its use is its expense, and the difficulty of obtaining it from city dealers. The law of supply and cost generally corresponds with that of demand, and doubtless cream would prove no exception if its use were more general.

Creamery.

Cream may be sterilized and preserved in a pure state for some time, the same as milk.

Milk requires especial care to secure a good quality and quantity of cream. Scrupulous cleanliness, good ventilation, and an unvarying temperature are absolute essentials. The common custom of setting milk in pans is objectionable, not only because of the dust and germs always liable to fall into the milk, but also from the difficulty of keeping milk thus set at the proper temperature for cream-rising. Every family using milk in any quantity ought to have a set of creameries of large or small capacity according to circumstances, in which the milk supply can be kept in a pure, wholesome condition, and so arranged as to facilitate the full rising of the cream if desired. A very simple and satisfactory creamery, with space for ice around the milk, similar to that represented in the accompanying cut, may be constructed by any tinman.

The plan of scalding milk to facilitate the rising of the cream is excellent, as it not only secures a more speedy rising, but serves to destroy the germs found in the milk, thus lessening its tendency to sour. The best way to do this is to heat the milk in a double boiler, or a dish set inside another containing hot water, to a temperature of 150° to 165°F. as indicated by wrinkles upon its surface. The milk must not, however, be allowed to come to a boil. When scalded, it should be cooled at once to a temperature of about 60° F. and kept thus during the rising of the cream.

BUTTER.

Of all foods wholly composed of fat, good fresh butter is the most wholesome. It should, however, be used unmelted and taken in a finely divided state, and only in very moderate quantities. If exposed to great heat, as on hot buttered toast, meats, rich pastry, etc., it is quite indigestible. We do not recommend its use either for the table or for cooking purposes when cream can be obtained, since butter is rarely found in so pure a state that it is not undergoing more or less decomposition, depending upon its age and the amount of casein retained in the butter through the carelessness of the manufacturer.

Casein, on exposure to air in a moist state, rapidly changes into a ferment, which, acting upon the fatty matter of the butter, produces rancidity, rendering the butter more or less unwholesome. Poor, tainted, or rancid butter should not be used as food in any form.

Good butter is pale yellow, uniform throughout the whole mass, and free from rancid taste or odor. White lumps in it are due to the incorporation of sour milk with the cream from which it was produced. A watery, milk-like fluid exuding from the freshly cut surface of butter, is evidence that insufficient care was taken to wash out all the buttermilk, thus increasing its liability to spoil.

The flavor and color of butter vary considerably, according to the breed and food of the animal from which the milk was obtained. An artificial color is often given to butter by the use of a preparation of annatto.

Both salt and saltpeter are employed as preservatives for butter; a large quantity of the former is often used to increase the weight of the butter.

Artificial Butter.—Various fraudulent preparations are sold as butter. Oleomargarine, one of the commonest, is made from tallow or beef-fat, cleaned and ground like sausage, and heated, to separate the oil from the membranes. It is then known as "butter-oil," is salted, cooled, pressed, and churned in milk, colored with annatto, and treated the same as butter. Butterine, another artificial product, is prepared by mixing butter-oil and a similar oil obtained from lard, then churning them with milk.

An eminent analyst gives the following excellent way of distinguishing genuine butter from oleomargarine:—"When true butter is heated over a clear flame, it 'browns' and gives out a pleasant odor,—that of browned butter. In heating there is more or less sputtering, caused by minute particles of water retained in washing the butter. On the bottom of the pan or vessel in which true butter is heated, a yellowish-brown crust is formed, consisting of roasted or toasted casein. When oleomargarine is heated under similar circumstances, it does not 'brown,' but becomes darker by overheating, and when heated to dryness, gives off a grayish steam, smelling of tallow. There is no 'sputtering' when it is being heated, but it boils easily. If a pledget of cotton or a wick saturated with oleomargarine be set on fire and allowed to burn a few moments before being extinguished, it will give out fumes which are very characteristic, smelling strongly of tallow, while true butter behaves very differently."

Butter in Ancient Times.—Two kinds of butter seem to have been known to the ancient Jews, one quite like that of the present day, except that it was boiled after churning, so that it became in that warm climate practically an oil; the other, a sort of curdled milk. The juice of the Jerusalem artichoke was mixed with the milk, when it was churned until a sort of curd was separated. The Oriental method of churning was by putting the milk into a goat-skin and swinging and shaking the bag until the butter came, as illustrated in the accompanying cut.

An article still sold as butter in Athens is made by boiling the milk of goats, allowing it to sour, and then churning in a goat-skin. The result is a thick, white, foamy substance appearing more like cream than butter.

Butter-Making.—The manufacture of good butter is dependent upon good cows and the care given them, as well as most careful treatment of the milk and cream. The milk to be used for butter making, as indeed for all purposes, should be most carefully strained through a wire strainer covered with three or four thicknesses of perfectly clean cheese cloth.

The following points given by an experienced dairyman will be found worthy of consideration by all who have to do with the manufacture of this article:—

"Milk is almost as sensitive to atmospheric changes as mercury itself. It is a question among many as to what depth milk should be set to get the most cream. It does not make so much difference as to the depth as it does the protection of the milk from acid or souring. As soon as the milk begins to sour, the cream ceases to rise.

"With a clear, dry atmosphere the cream will rise clean in the milk; but in that condition of the atmosphere which readily sours the milk, the cream will not rise clean, but seems to hang in the milk, and this even when the milk is protected by being set in water.

"The benefit of setting milk in cold water is that the water protects the milk from becoming acid until the cream has time to rise. For cream to rise readily on milk set in cold water, the atmosphere in the room should be warmer than the water. As much cream will rise on milk set in cold water in one hour as on milk not set in water in twenty-four hours. The milk should be skimmed while sweet, and the cream thoroughly stirred at each skimming.

"Cream skimmed from different milkings, if churned at the same time in one churn, should be mixed eight to ten hours before churning; then the cream will all come alike.

"The keeping qualities of butter depend principally upon two things: First, the buttermilk must be all gotten out; and secondly, the grain of the butter should be kept as perfect as possible. Butter should not be allowed to be churned after it has fairly come, and should not be gathered compactly in the churn in taking out, but the buttermilk should be drained from the butter in the churn, through a hair sieve, letting the butter remain in the churn. Then take water and turn it upon the butter with sufficient force to pass through the butter, and in sufficient quantity to rinse the buttermilk all out of the butter. With this process of washing the butter the grain is not injured or mashed, and is thus far kept perfect. And in working in the salt the ladle or roll or worker, whatever it is, should never be allowed to slip on the butter,—if it does, it will destroy the grain,—but it should go upon the butter in a pressing or rolling motion."

Test the temperature of the cream with a thermometer, and churn it at 60° in summer and 62° in winter. If the butter is soft, it may be hardened by pouring onto it while working a brine made by dissolving a pint of salt in ten quarts of water. The salt used in the butter should be carefully measured, three fourths of an ounce of salt to the pound being the usual allowance.

Butter, like milk, absorbs odors readily, and should never be allowed to remain in occupied rooms or any place exposed to strong or foul odors, but be kept covered in a cold place.

CHEESE.

Cheese is a product of milk prepared by separating the casein, with more or less of the cream, according to the manner in which it has been prepared, from the other ingredients of the milk. It is an article, which, although possessing a large proportion, of nutritive material, is very difficult of digestion, and the use of which is very questionable, not only for this reason, but because it is very liable to contain a poison called tyrotoxicon, capable of producing most violent and indeed fatal results, according to the remarkable researches of Prof. Vaughan of Michigan University. This poison is sometimes found in ice cream and custards, cream-puffs, etc., made from stale milk or cream.

It is much better to use milk in its fresh, natural state than in any of its products. Made into either butter or cheese, we lose some of its essential elements, so that what is left is not a perfect food.

RECIPES.

Hot Milk.—Milk is more easily digested when used hot. This is not due to any marked chemical change in the milk, but to the stimulating effect of heat upon the palate and stomach.

To prepare hot milk, heat it in a double boiler until a wrinkled skin appears upon the surface. In the double boiler it may be kept at the proper temperature for a long time without difficulty, and thus prepared, it forms one of the most healthful of foods.

Milk, either cold or hot, should be taken a few sips only at a time, and not be drank in copious draughts when used in connection with other foods at mealtime. It will then coagulate in the stomach in small flakes much more easily digested than the large mass resulting when a large quantity is swallowed at a time.

Devonshire or Clotted Cream.—This is prepared as follows: Strain the milk as it comes fresh from the cow into a deep pan which will fit tightly over a kettle in which water can be boiled, and set away in a cool well-ventilated place, where it should be allowed to remain undisturbed from eight to twelve hours or longer. Then take the pan up very carefully so as not to disturb the cream, place over a kettle of water, heat to near the boiling point, or until a rim of bubbles half an inch wide forms all around the dish of milk. It must not, however, be allowed to boil, or the cream will be injured. Now lift the pan again with equal care back to a cool place and allow it to stand from twelve to twenty-four hours longer. The cream should be a compact mass of considerable thickness, and may be divided with a knife into squares of convenient size before skimming. It is delicious for use on fruit and grains.

Cottage Cheese.—This dish is usually prepared from milk which has curdled from lack of proper care, or from long standing exposed to the air, and which is thus in some degree decomposing. But the fact that the casein of the milk is coagulated by the use of acids makes it possible to prepare this dish in a more wholesome manner without waiting for decomposition of the milk. Add to each four quarts of milk one cupful of lemon juice; let it stand until coagulated, then heat slowly, but do not boil, until the curd has entirely separated from the whey. Turn the whole into a colander lined with a square of clean cheese cloth, and drain off the whey. Add to the curd a little salt and cream, mix all together with a spoon or the hands, and form into cakes or balls for the table. The use of lemon gives a delicious flavor, which may be intensified, if desired, by using a trifle of the grated yellow rind.

Cottage Cheese from Buttermilk.—Place a pail of fresh buttermilk in a kettle of boiling water, taking care to have sufficient water to come up even with the milk in the pail. Let the buttermilk remain until it is heated throughout to about 140°, which can be determined by keeping a thermometer in the milk and stirring it frequently. When it is sufficiently heated, empty the curd into strong muslin bags and hang up to drain for several hours. If properly scalded and drained, the curd will be quite dry and may be seasoned and served the same as other cottage cheese. If scalded too much, it will be watery.

Cottage Cheese with Sour Milk.—Take a pan of newly-loppered thick sour milk, and place it over a kettle of boiling water until the whey separates from the curd, breaking and cutting the curd as the milk becomes warmed, so as to allow the whey to settle. The milk should be well scalded, but not allowed to boil, as that will render the curd tough and leathery. Have ready a clean piece of cheese cloth spread inside a colander, dip the curd into it, and leave it to drain. If preferred, the corners of the cloth may be tied with a string, thus forming a bag in which the cheese may be hung up to drain. When well drained, remove the dry curd to a dish, rub it fine with the hands, add salt, and season with sweet cream, beating it well through the curd with a silver fork. It may be shaped into balls with the hands or pressed in large cups or bowls.

French Butter.—Fill a large, wide-mouthed glass bottle or jar about half full of thick sweet cream. Cork tightly, and with one end of the bottle in each hand shake it vigorously back and forth until the butter has separated from the milk, which it will generally do in a few minutes. Work out the buttermilk, make into small pats, and place on ice until ready to serve. As a rule this butter is not washed or salted, as it is intended for immediate use.

Shaken Milk.—Fit a conical tin cup closely over a glass of milk and shake it vigorously until all of a foam, after which it should be slowly sipped at once; or a glass of milk may be put into a quart fruit can, the cover tightly screwed on, and then shaken back and forth until the milk is foamy.

Emulsified Butter.—Boil the butter with water for half an hour to destroy any germs it may contain; use plenty of water and add the butter to it while cold. When boiled, remove from the fire and allow it to become nearly cold, when the butter will have risen to the top and may be removed with a skimmer, or it may be separated from the water by turning the whole after cooling into a clean strainer cloth placed inside a colander. The butter may be pressed in the cloth if any water still remains. If hardened, reheat just sufficient to soften, and add to it, while still liquid, but cooled to about blood heat, the yolk of one egg for each tablespoonful of butter, and stir until very thoroughly mingled.

Or, add to each tablespoonful of the liquid butter two level tablespoonfuls of flour, rub together thoroughly, and cook until thickened in a half cupful of boiling water. If cream is not obtainable and butter must be used for seasoning, it is preferable to prepare it in one of the above ways for the purpose, using the quantity given as an equivalent of one cupful of thin cream. It will be evident, however, that these preparations will not only season but thicken whatever they are used in, and that additional liquid should be used on that account.

TABLE TOPICS.

A little six-year-old boy went into the country visiting. About the first thing he got was a bowl of bread and milk. He tasted it, and then hesitated a moment, when his mother asked if he didn't like it; to which he replied, smacking his lips, "Yes, ma'am. I was only wishing that our milkman in town would keep a cow!"

When Horace Greeley was candidate for the presidency, he at one time visited New Orleans, whose old creole residents gave him a dinner; and to make it as fine an affair as possible, each of the many guests was laid under contribution for some of the rarest wines in his cellar. When dinner was announced, and the first course was completed, the waiter appeared at Mr. Greeley's seat with a plate of shrimp. "You can take them away," he said to the waiter, and then added to the horrified French creole gentleman who presided, "I never eat insects of any kind." Later on, soup was served, and at the same time a glass of white wine was placed at Mr. Greeley's right hand. He pushed it quietly away, but not unobserved by the chief host. "Do you not drink wine?" he asked.

"No," answered Mr. Greeley; "I never drink any liquors."

"Is there anything you would like to drink with your soup?" the host then asked, a little disappointed.

"If you've got it," answered Mr. Greeley, "and it isn't any trouble, I'd like a glass of fresh buttermilk."

Said the host afterward in his broken English, "Ze idea of electing to ze presidency a man vot drink buttermilk vis his soup!"

Old friendships are often destroyed by toasted cheese, and hard salted meat has often led to suicide.—*Sydney Smith.*

A German sitting beside a Spanish officer on board a Havana steamer, was munching Limberger cheese with evident satisfaction when it occurred to him that he ought to offer some to his neighbor, who very coolly declined. "You think it unhealthful to eat that?" inquired the German in polite astonishment. "*Unhealthful?*" exclaimed the Hidalgo, with a withering look and a gasp for a more adequate word; "No, sir: I think it an unnatural crime!"—*Oswald.*

Good for Dyspepsia.—"Really, don't you think cheese is good for dyspepsia?" said an advocate of the use of this common article of food. "Why, my uncle had dyspepsia all his life, and he took a bit of cheese at the close of every meal!"

Mattieu Williams tells us, "When common sense and true sentiment supplant mere unreasoning prejudice, vegetables oils and vegetable fats will largely supplant those of animal origin in every element of our dietary."

EGGS

As will be seen from the analysis given below, an egg is particularly rich in nitrogenous elements. It is indeed one of the most highly concentrated forms of nitrogenous food, about one third of its weight being solid nutriment, and for this reason is often found serviceable in cases of sickness where it is desirable to secure a large amount of nourishment in small bulk.

Composition of the white of an ordinary hen's egg.

Nitrogenous matter	20.4
Fatty matter	10.0
Mineral matter	1.6
Water	68.0

Composition of the yolk.

Nitrogenous matter	1.0
Fatty matter	30.7
Mineral matter	1.3
Water	52.0

The white of egg is composed mainly of albumen in a dissolved state, inclosed in layers of thin membrane. When beaten, the membranes are broken, and the liberated albumen, owing to its viscous or glutinous nature, entangles and retains a large amount of air, thus increasing to several times its original bulk.

The yolk contains all the fatty matter, and this, with a modified form of albumen called vitellin, forms a kind of yellow emulsion. It is inclosed in a thin membrane, which separates it from the surrounding white.

The yolk, being lighter than the white, floats to that portion of the egg which is uppermost, but is held in position by two membranous cords, one from each end of the egg. The average weight of an egg is about two ounces, of which ten per cent consists of shell, sixty of white, and thirty of yolk.

How to Choose Eggs.—The quality of eggs varies considerably, according to the food upon which the fowls are fed. Certain foods communicate distinct flavors, and it is quite probable that eggs may be rendered unwholesome through the use of filthy or improper food; hence it is always best, when practicable, to ascertain respecting the diet and care of the fowls before purchasing eggs.

On no account select eggs about the freshness of which there is any reason to doubt. The use of stale eggs may result in serious disturbances of the digestive organs.

An English gentleman who has investigated the subject quite thoroughly, finds upon careful microscopical examination that stale eggs often contain cells of a peculiar fungoid growth, which seems to have developed from that portion of the egg which would have furnished material for the flesh and bones of the chick had the process of development been continued. Experiments with such eggs upon dogs produce poisonous effects.

There are several ways of determining with tolerable accuracy respecting the freshness of an egg. A common test is to place it between the eye and a strong light. If fresh, the white will appear translucent, and the outline of the yolk can be distinctly traced. By keeping, eggs become cloudy, and when decidedly stale, a distinct, dark, cloud-like appearance may be discerned opposite some portion of the shell. Another test is to shake the egg gently at the ear; if a gurgle or thud is heard, the egg is bad. Again, eggs may be tested by dropping into a vessel containing a solution of salt and water, in the proportion of a tablespoonful to a quart. Newly laid eggs will sink; if more than six days old, they will float in the liquid; if bad, they will be so light as to ride on the surface of the brine. The shell of a freshly laid egg is almost full; but owing to the porous character of the shell, with age and exposure to air a portion of the liquid substance of which the egg is composed evaporates, and air accumulates in its place at one of the extremities of the shell. Hence an egg loses in density from day to day, and the longer the egg has been kept, the lighter it becomes, and the higher it will rise in the liquid.

An egg that will float on the surface of the liquid is of too questionable a character to be used without breaking, and is apt to be unfit for use at all.

How to Keep Eggs.—To preserve the interior of an egg in its natural state, it is necessary to seal the pores of the shell air-tight, as the air which finds its way into the egg through the pores of the shell causes gradual decomposition. Various methods are devised to exclude the air and thus preserve the egg. A good way is to dip perfectly fresh eggs into a thick solution of gum-arabic,—equal parts of gum and water,—let the eggs dry and dip them again, taking care that the shells are entirely covered with the solution each time. When dry, wrap separately in paper and pack in a box of sawdust, bran, salt, or powdered charcoal, and cover tightly to keep out the air.

There is a difference of opinion as to which end should be placed down in packing; most authorities recommend the smaller end. However, an experienced poultryman offers the following reasons for packing with the larger end down: "The air-chamber is in the larger end, and if that is placed down, the yolk will not break through and touch the shell and thereby spoil. Another thing: if the air-chamber is down, the egg is not so liable to shrink away."

It would be well for housekeepers to make the test by packing eggs from the same lot each way and noting the result.

Melted wax or suet may be used to coat the shells. Eggs are sometimes immersed and kept in a solution of lime water, a pound of lime to a gallon of cold water, or simply packed in bran or salt, without a previous coating of fat or gum. By any of these methods they will keep for several weeks. Eggs, however, readily absorb flavors from surrounding substances, and for that reason lime water or salt solution are somewhat objectionable. Nothing of a disagreeable odor should be placed near eggs.

Eggs for boiling may be preserved by placing in a deep pan, and pouring scalding water over them. Let them stand half a minute, drain off the water, and repeat the process two or three times. Wipe dry, and when cool, pack in bran.

Eggs should be kept in a cool, not cold, place and handled carefully, as rough treatment may cause the mingling of the yolk and white by rupturing the membrane which separates them; then the egg will spoil quickly.

The time required for the digestion of a perfectly cooked egg varies from three to four hours.

It is generally conceded that eggs lightly cooked are most readily digested. What is generally termed a hard-boiled egg is not easily acted upon by the digestive juices, and any other manner of cooking by which the albumen becomes hardened and solid offers great resistance to digestion.

To Beat Eggs.—This may seem trivial, but no dish requiring eggs can be prepared in perfection, unless theyare properly beaten, even if every other ingredient is the best. An egg-beater or an egg-whip is the most convenient utensil for the purpose; but if either of these is not to be had, a silver fork will do very well, and with this the beating should be done in sharp, quick strokes, dipping the fork in and out in rapid succession, while the egg should grow firmer and stiffer with every stroke. When carelessly beaten, the result will be a coarse and frothy instead of a thick and cream-like mass. Use a bowl in beating eggs with an egg-beater, and a plate when a fork or egg-whip is employed.

If the white and yolk are used separately, break the shells gently about the middle, opening slowly so as to let the white fall into the dish, while retaining the yolk in one half of the shell. If part of the white remains, turn the yolk from the one half to the other till the white has fallen. Beat the yolks until they change from their natural orange color to a much lighter yellow. The whites should be beaten until firm and dry enough not to fall from the bowl if turned upside down. The yolk should always be beaten first, since, if the white is left to stand after being beaten, a portion of the air, which its viscous nature allows it to catch up, escapes and no amount of beating will render it so firm a second time. Eggs which need to be washed before breaking should always be wiped perfectly dry, that no water may become mingled with the egg, as the water may dilute the albumen sufficiently to prevent the white from becoming firm and stiff when beaten.

In cold weather, it is sometimes difficult to beat the whites as stiff as desirable. Albumen is quite susceptible to temperature, and this difficulty may be overcome by setting the dish in which the eggs are beaten into warm water—not hot by any means—during the process of beating. In very hot weather it is often advantageous to leave the eggs in cold or ice water for a short time before beating. When a number of eggs are to be used, always break each by itself into a saucer, so that any chance stale egg may not spoil the whole. If the white or yolk of an egg—is left over, it may be kept for a day or two if put in a cool place, the yolk thoroughly beaten, the white unbeaten.

RECIPES.

Eggs In Shell.—The usual method of preparing eggs for serving in this way is to put them into boiling water, and boil or simmer until they are considered sufficiently cooked. Albumen, of which the white of the egg is composed, is easiest digested when simply coagulated. The yolk, if cooked at all, is easiest digested when dry and mealy. Albumen coagulates at 160°, and when the boiling point is reached, it becomes hardened, tough, and leathery, and very difficult of digestion. If the egg were all albumen, it might be easily and properly cooked by dropping into boiling water, allowing it to remain for a few seconds, and removing it, since the shell of the egg would prevent its becoming sufficiently heated in so short a time as to become hardened; but the time necessary to cook properly the white of the egg would be insufficient for the heat to penetrate to and cook the yolk; and if it is desirable to cook the yolk hard, the cooking process should be carried on at a temperature below the boiling point, subjecting the egg to a less degree of heat, but for a longer time. The most accurate method is to put the eggs into water of a temperature of 160°, allowing them to remain for twenty minutes and not permitting the temperature of the water to go above 165°. Cooked in this way, the white will be of a soft, jelly-like consistency throughout, while the yolks will be hard. If it is desired to have the yolks dry and mealy, the temperature of the water must be less, and the time of cooking lengthened. We have secured the most perfect results with water at a temperature of 150°, and seven hours' cooking. The temperature of the water can be easily tested by keeping in it an ordinary thermometer, and if one possesses a kerosene or gas stove, the heat can be easily regulated to maintain the required temperature.

Another method, although less sure, is to pour boiling water into a saucepan, draw it to one side of the range where it will keep hot, but not boil, put in the eggs, cover, and let stand for twenty minutes. If by either method it is desired to have the yolk soft-cooked, lessen the time to ten minutes or so, according to the hardness desired. Eggs are best served as soon as done, as the white becomes more solid by being kept in a hot shell.

It should be remarked that the time necessary to cook eggs in the shell will vary somewhat with the firmness of the shell, the size of the eggs, and the number cooked together.

Eggs in Sunshine.—Take an earthen-ware dish which will stand heat and also do to use in serving the eggs. Oil it and break therein as many eggs as desired; sprinkle lightly with salt, and put into the oven for two or more minutes till the eggs are set. Have ready some hot tomato sauce prepared as for Tomato Toast; pour the sauce over them, and serve.

Eggs Poached in Tomatoes.—Take a pint of stewed tomatoes, cooked until they are homogeneous or which have been rubbed through a colander; season with salt if desired, and heat. When just beginning to boil, slip in gently a half dozen eggs, the shells of which have been so carefully broken that the yolks are intact. Keep the tomato just below the boiling point until the eggs are cooked. Lift the whites carefully with a fork as they cook, until they are firm, then prick them and let the yellow mix with the tomato and the whites. The whole should be quite soft when done, but showing the red of the tomatoes and the white and yellow of the eggs quite distinctly. Serve on toast. If the flavor is agreeable, a little onion.

Eggs in Cream.—Put a half cupful or more of cream into a shallow earthen dish, and place the dish in a kettle or pan of boiling water. When the cream is hot, break in as many eggs as the bottom of the dish will hold, and cook until well set, basting them occasionally over the top with the hot cream. Or, put a spoonful or two of cream into individual egg or vegetable dishes, break a fresh egg in each, and cook in the oven or in a steamer over a kettle of boiling water until the white of the egg is well set.

Poached or Dropped Eggs.—Break each egg into a saucer by itself. Have a shallow pan half filled with scalding, not boiling, water on the stove. If desired, a little salt and a tablespoonful of lemon juice may be added. Slip the eggs gently from the saucer upon the top of the water, holding the edge of the saucer under water to prevent the eggs from scattering; dip the water over them with a spoon and let them stand five minutes, or until the yolk is covered with a film, and the white is firm but not hardened; keep the water just below the boiling point. Take out the eggs one by one on a skimmer, and serve in egg-saucers, or on slices of nicely browned toast moistened with a little sweet cream, as preferred. If one is especially particular to keep the shape of the eggs, an egg poacher should be used, or a set of muffin-rings may be laid in the bottom of the pan, and the eggs turned into the rings.

Poached Eggs with Cream Sauce.—Poach eggs as in the foregoing, and pour over them a sauce made according to direction on page 351.

Quickly Prepared Eggs.—A good way to cook quickly a large number of eggs, is to use a large-bottomed earthen dish, which will stand the heat and in which the eggs may be served. Oil it well; break the requisite number of eggs separately, and turn each carefully into the dish; sprinkle lightly with salt; set the dish in the oven or in a steamer over a kettle of boiling water for a few minutes until the eggs are set, then serve.

Scrambled Eggs.—Beat four eggs lightly, add a little salt if desired, and half a cup of milk or cream. Have ready a hot, oiled saucepan; turn the eggs in and cook quickly, stirring constantly until firm, but soft.

Steamed Eggs.—Break eggs into egg or vegetable dishes or patty-pans, salt very lightly, and set in a steamer over a kettle of boiling water until the whites are set and a film has formed over the yolk. Serve the same as poached eggs, with or without toast.

Whirled Eggs.—Have a small kettle of water heated almost to boiling, and with a wooden spoon, stir it rapidly round and round in the same direction until a miniature whirlpool is produced. Have ready some eggs broken in separate cups, and drop them carefully one at a time into the whirling water, the stirring of which must be kept up until the egg is a soft round ball. Remove with a skimmer, and serve on cream toast.

OMELETS.

RECIPES.

Plain Omelet.—Beat the yolks of three eggs to a cream and beat the whites to a stiff froth. Add to the yolks three tablespoonfuls of milk or cream, one tablespoonful of finely grated bread crumbs, and season lightly with salt; lastly, fold, not stir, the whites lightly in. An omelet pan is the best utensil for cooking, but if that is not to be had, an earthenware pudding dish which will stand the heat is good; an iron spider will do, but a larger omelet would need to be prepared. A tin saucepan is apt to cook the omelet so rapidly as to burn it in spots. Whatever the utensil used, it should be hot, the fire clear and steady, and all in readiness by the time the eggs are beaten.

Oil the dish well and gently pour in the omelet mixture; cover, and place the pan on the range where the heat will be continuous. Do not stir, but carefully, as the egg sets, lift the omelet occasionally by slipping a broad-bladed knife under it, or with a fork by dipping in here and there. It should cook quickly, but not so quickly as to burn. From three to five minutes will generally be ample time. When the middle of the omelet is set, it may be put into a hot oven to dry the top. As soon as the center is dry, it should be removed immediately, as it will be hard and indigestible if overdone. To dish, loosen from the pan by running a knife under it, lay a hot platter, bottom upward, over the pan, and invert the latter so as to shake out the omelet gently, browned side uppermost; or if preferred, double one part over the other before dishing. Serve at once, or it will fall.

An omelet of three eggs is sufficient for two or three persons; if more is desired, a second omelet of three eggs may be made. Larger ones are not so light nor so easily prepared. The dish used should be reserved for that purpose alone, and should be kept as smooth and dry as possible. It is better to keep it clean by wiping with a coarse towel than by washing; if the omelet comes from the pan perfectly whole and leaving no fragments behind.

Foam Omelet.—Prepare as above, leaving out the white of one egg, which must be beaten to a stiff froth and spread over the top of the omelet after it is well set. Let this white just heat through by the time the omelet is done. Fold the omelet together, and dish. The whites will burst out around the edges like a border of foam.

Fancy Omelets.—Various fancy omelets may be made by adding other ingredients and preparing the same as for plain omelets. Two or three tablespoonfuls of orange juice instead of milk, with a little grated rind for flavor and three tablespoonfuls of sugar, may be combined with the eggs and called an orange omelet.

A little cold cauliflower or cooked asparagus chopped very fine and mixed in when the omelet is ready for the pan, may be denominated a vegetable omelet.

Soft Omelet.—Beat together thoroughly one quart of milk and six eggs. Season with salt. Pour into a shallow earthen pudding dish, and bake in the oven until well set.

TABLE TOPICS.

The candidates for ancient athletic games were dieted on boiled grain, with warm water, cheese, dried figs, but no meat.

An unpleasant reminder.—(Scene, Thanksgiving dinner, everybody commenting on the immense size of the turkey.) An appalling silence fell upon the crowd when Tommy cried out, "Mamma, is that the old sore-headed turkey?"

The eminent Prof. Wilder was reared a vegetarian, having passed his earlier years without even knowing that flesh food was ever eaten by human beings. When six years old, he saw on the table for the first time, a roasted chicken, at which he gazed for some moments in great bewilderment, when he seemed to make a discovery, and in his astonishment burst out with the remark, "I'll bet that's a dead hen!"

A story is told of a minister who was spending the day in the country, and was invited to dine. There was chicken for dinner, much to the grief of a little boy of the household, who had lost his favorite hen to provide for the feast. After dinner, prayer was proposed, and while the preacher was praying, a poor little lonesome chicken came running under the house, crying for its absent mother. The little boy shouted, "Peepy! Peepy! I didn't kill your mother! They killed her for that big preacher's dinner!" The "Amen" was said very suddenly.

MEATS

This is the term usually applied to the flesh and various organs of such animals, poultry, and game as are used for food. This class of foods contains representatives of all nutritive elements, but is especially characterized by as excess of albuminous matter. But in actual nutritive value flesh foods do not exceed various other food materials. A comparison of the food grains with beefsteak and other flesh foods, shows, in fact, that a pound of grain is equivalent in food value to two or three pounds of flesh.

At present time there is much question in the minds of many intelligent, thinking people as to the propriety of using foods of this class, and especially of their frequent use. Besides being in no way superior to vegetable substances, they contain elements of an excrementitious character, which cannot be utilized, and which serve only to clog and impede the vital processes, rendering the blood gross, filling the body with second-hand waste material which was working its way out of the vital domain of the animal when slaughtered. To this waste matter, consisting of unexpelled excretions, are added those produced by the putrefactive processes which so quickly begin in flesh foods exposed to air and warmth.

That flesh foods are stimulating has been shown by many observations and experiments.

Flesh foods are also specially liable to be diseased and to communicate to the consumer the same disease. The prevalence of disease among animals used for food is known to be very great, and their transmission to man is no longer a matter of dispute. It has been abundantly proved that such diseases as the parasitic, tuberculous, erysipelatous, and foot and mouth diseases are most certainly communicable to man by infected flesh. All stall and sty fed animals are more or less diseased. Shut up in the dark, cut off from exercise, the whole fattening process is one of progressive disease. No living creature could long retain good health under such unnatural and unwholesome conditions. Add to this the exhaustion and abuse of animals before slaughtering; the suffering incident to long journeys in close cars, often without sufficient food and water; and long drives over dusty roads under a burning sun to the slaughter house, and it will be apparent to all thoughtful persons that such influences are extremely liable to produce conditions of the system that render the flesh unfit for food.

Thousands of animals are consumed each year which were slaughtered just in time to save them from dying a natural death. It is a common thing for cattle owners, as soon as an animal shows symptoms of decline, to send it to the butcher at once; and when epidemics of cattle diseases are prevalent, there can be no doubt that the meat markets are flooded with diseased flesh.

There are few ways in which we can more effectually imperil our health than in partaking freely of diseased animal food. This is no new theory. The Jews have for ages recognized this danger, and their laws require the most careful examination of all animals to be used as food, both before and after slaughtering. Their sanitary regulations demand that beast or fowl for food must be killed by bleeding through the jugular vein, and not, according to custom, by striking on the head, or in some violent way. Prior to the killing, the animal must be well rested and its respiration normal; after death the most careful dissection and examination of the various parts are made by a competent person, and no flesh is allowed to be used for food which has not been inspected and found to be perfectly sound and healthy. As a result, it is found in many of our large cities that only about one in twenty of the animals slaughtered is accepted as food for a Jew. The rejected animals are sold to the general public, who are less scrupulous about the character of their food, and who are in consequence more subject to disease and shorter-lived than are Jews.

Trichinæ, tapeworms, and various other parasites which infest the flesh of animals, are so common that there is always more or less liability to disease from these sources among consumers of flesh foods.

Meat is by no means necessary for the proper maintenance of life or vigorous health, as is proved by the fact that at least "four tenths of the human race," according to Virey, "subsist exclusively upon a vegetable diet, and as many as seven tenths are practically vegetarians." Some of the finest specimens of physical development and mental vigor are to be found among those who use very little or no animal food. Says St. Pierre, a noted French author, "The people living upon vegetable foods are of all men the handsomest, the most vigorous, the lease exposed to disease and passion; and they are those whose lives last longest."

The use of large quantities of animal food, however free from disease germs, has a tendency to develop the animal propensities to a greater or less degree, especially in the young, whose characters are unformed. Among animals we find the carnivorous the most vicious and destructive, while those which subsist upon vegetable foods are by nature gentle and tractable. There is little doubt that this law holds good among men as well as animals. If we study the character and lives of those who subsist largely upon animal food, we are apt to find them impatient, passionate, fiery in temper, and in other respects greatly under the dominion of their lower natures.

There are many other objections to the use of this class of foods—so many in fact that we believe the human race would be far healthier, better, and happier if flesh foods were wholly discarded. If, however, they are to be used at all, let them be used sparingly and prepared in the simplest and least harmful manner. Let them be cooked and served in their own juices, not soaked in butter or other oils, or disguised by the free use of pepper, mustard, catsup, and other pungent sauces. Salt also should be used only in the smallest possible quantities, as it hardens the fiber, rendering it more difficult of digestion.

We can conceive of no possible stretch of hygienic laws which admits the use of pork; so we shall give it and its products no consideration in our pages.

Such offal as calves' brains, sheep's kidneys, beef livers, and other viscera, is not fit food for any one but a scavenger. The liver and kidneys are depurating organs, and their use as food is not only unwholesome but often exceedingly poisonous.

Meat pies, scallops, sauces, fricassees, *pâtés*, and other fancy dishes composed of a mixture of animal foods, rich pastry, fats, strong condiments, etc., are by no means to be recommended as hygienic, and will receive no notice in these pages.

In comparative nutritive value, beef ranks first among the flesh foods. Mutton, though less nutritive, is more easily digested than beef. This is not appreciable to a healthy person, but one whose digestive powers are weak will often find that mutton taxes the stomach less than beef.

Veal or lamb is neither so nutritious nor so easily digested as beef or mutton. Flesh from different animals, and that from various parts of the same animal, varies in flavor, composition, and digestibility. The mode of life and the food of animals influence in a marked manner the quality of the meat. Turnips give a distinctly recognizable flavor to mutton. The same is true of many fragrant herbs found by cattle feeding in pastures.

The Selection of Meat.—Good beef is of a reddish-brown color and contains no clots of blood. A pale-pink color indicates that the animal was diseased; a dark-purple color that the animal has suffered from some acute febrile affection or was not slaughtered, but died with the blood in its body.

Good beef is firm and elastic to the touch; when pressed with the finger, no impression is left. It should be so dry upon the surface as scarcely to moisten the fingers. Meat that is wet, sodden, and flabby should not be eaten. Good beef is marbled with spots of white fat. The suet should be dry and crumble easily. If the fat has the appearance of wet parchment or is jelly-like, the beef is not good. Yellow fat is an indication of old, lean animals.

Good beef has little or no odor. If any odor is perceptible, it is not disagreeable. Diseased meat has a sickly odor, resembling the breath of feverish persons. When such meat is roasted, it emits a strong, offensive smell. The condition of a piece of beef may be ascertained by dipping a knife in hot water, drying it, and passing it through the meat. Apply to the nose on withdrawal, and if the meat is not good, a disagreeable odor will be quite perceptible.

Good beef will not shrink greatly in cooking. In boiling or stewing, the shrinkage is computed to be about one pound in four; in baking, one and one fourth pounds in four. Beef of a close, firm fiber shrinks less than meat of coarse fiber.

Good veal is slightly reddish or pink, and the fat should be white and clear. Avoid veal without fat, as such is apt to be too young to be wholesome.

Good mutton should be firm and compact, the flesh, fine-grained and bright-red, with an accumulation of very hard and clear white fat along the borders of the muscles.

Meat should not be kept until decomposition sets in, as by the putrefaction of the albuminous elements certain organic poisons are generated, and flesh partaken of in this condition is liable to result in serious illness. Meat containing white specks is probably infested by parasites and should not be used as food.

Preservation of Meat.—The tendency of flesh foods to rapid decomposition has led to the use of various antiseptic agents and other methods for its preservation.

One of the most common methods is that of immersion in a brine made of a solution of common salt to which a small portion of saltpeter has been added. This abstracts the juice from the meat and also lessens the tendency to putrefaction. Salt is used in various other ways for preserving meat. It should be remarked, however, that cured and dried meats are much more difficult to digest than fresh meat, and the nature of the meat itself is so changed by the process as to render its nutritive value much less.

Meat is sometimes packed in salt and afterward dried, either in the sun or in a current of dry air. Both salting and smoking are sometimes employed. By these means the juices are abstracted by the salt, and at the same time the flesh is contracted and hardened by the action of creosote and pyroligneous acid from the smoke.

What is termed "jerked" beef is prepared by drying in a current of warm air at about 140°. This dried meat, when reduced to a powder and packed in air-tight cans, may be preserved for a long time. When mixed with fat, it forms the pemmican used by explorers in Arctic voyages.

Meat is also preserved by cooking and inclosing in air-tight cans after the manner of canning fruit. This process is varied in a number of ways.

The application of cold has great influence in retarding decomposition, and refrigeration and freezing are often employed for the preservation of flesh foods.

All of these methods except the last are open to the objection that while they preserve the meat, they greatly lessen its nutritive value. It should also be understood that the decomposition of its flesh begins almost the moment an animal dies, and continues at a slow rate even when the flesh is kept at a low temperature. The poisons resulting from this decomposition are often deadly, and are always detrimental to health.

The Preparation and Cooking of Meat.—Meat, when brought from the market, should be at once removed from the paper in which it is wrapped, as the paper will absorb the juices of the meat; and if the wrapping is brown paper, the meat is liable to taste of it. Joints of meat should not be hung with the cut surface down, as the juices will be wasted.

Meat kept in a refrigerator should not be placed directly on the ice, but always upon plates or shelves, as the ice will freeze it or else draw out its juices.

If meat is accidentally frozen, it should be thoroughly thawed in cold water before cutting. Meat should not be cleaned by washing with water, as that extracts the nutritive juices, but by thoroughly wiping the outside with a damp cloth. The inside needs no cleaning.

Meat may be cooked by any of the different methods of cookery,—boiling, steaming, stewing, roasting, broiling, baking, etc.,—according as the object is to retain the nutriment wholly within the meat; to draw it all out into the water, as in soups or broths; or to have it partly in the water and partly in the meat, as in stews. Broiling is, however, generally conceded to be the most wholesome method, but something will necessarily depend upon the quality of the meat to be cooked.

Meat which has a tough, hard fiber will be made tenderest by slow, continuous cooking, as stewing. Such pieces as contain a large amount of gelatine—a peculiar substance found in the joints and gristly parts of meat, and which hardens in a dry heat—are better stewed than roasted.

Boiling.—The same principles apply to the boiling of all kinds of meats. The purpose to be attained by this method is to keep the nutritive juices so far as possible intact within the meat; consequently, the piece to be cooked should be left whole, so that only a small amount of surface will be exposed to the action of the water. Since cold water extracts albumen, of which the juices of the meat are largely composed, while hot water coagulates it, meat to be boiled should be plunged into boiling water sufficient to cover it and kept there for five or ten minutes, by which time the albumen over the entire surface will have become hardened, thus forming a coat through which the juices cannot escape. Afterward the kettle, closely covered, may be set aside where the water will retain a temperature of about 180°. A small portion of albumen from the outer surface will escape into the water in the form of scum, and should be removed.

Meat cooked in this way will require a longer time than when the water is kept boiling furiously, but it is superior in every respect and more digestible. Something depends upon the shape of the piece cooked, thin pieces requiring less time than a thick, cubical cut; but approximately, first allowing fifteen or twenty minutes for the heat to penetrate the center of the meat, at which time the real process of cooking begins, it will require from twelve to fifteen minutes for every pound cooked.

Stewing.—While the object in boiling is to preserve the juices within the meat as much as possible, in stewing, the process is largely reversed; the juices are to be partly extracted. Some of the juices exist between the fibers, and some are found within the fibers. The greater the surface exposed, the more easily these juices will be extracted; hence meat for stewing should be cut into small pieces and cooked in a small quantity of water. Since cold water extracts the albuminous juices, while boiling water hardens them into a leathery consistency, water used for stewing should be neither cold nor boiling, but of a temperature which will barely coagulate the albumen and retain it in the meat in as tender a condition as possible; *i.e.,* about 134° to 160°. To supply this temperature for the prolonged process of cooking necessary in stewing, a double boiler of some form is quite necessary. Put the pieces of meat to be stewed in the inner dish, add hot water enough to cover, fill the outer boiler with hot water, and let this outer water simmer very gently until the meat is perfectly tender. The length of time required will be greater than when meat is stewed directly in simmering water, but the result will be much more satisfactory. The juices should be served with the meat.

Steaming.—Meat is sometimes steamed over boiling water until it is made very tender and afterward browned in the oven.

Another method of steaming, sometimes called smothering, is that of cooking meat in a tightly covered jar in a moderate oven for an hour (the moderate heat serves to draw out the juice of the meat), after which the heat is increased, and the meat cooked in its own juices one half hour for each pound.

Roasting.—This method, which consists in placing meat upon a revolving spit and cooking it before an open fire, is much less employed now than formerly, when fireplaces were in general use. What is ordinarily termed roasting is in reality cooking meat it in own juices in a hot oven. In cooking meat by this method it is always desirable to retain the juices entirely within the meat, which can be best accomplished by first placing the clean-cut sides of the meat upon a smoking-hot pan over a quick fire; press the meat close to the pan until well scared and slightly browned, then turn over and sear the opposite side in the same manner. This will form a coating of hardened albumen, through which the interior juices cannot escape. Put at once into the oven, arrange the fire so that the heat will be firm and steady but not too intense, and cook undisturbed until tender.

Basting is not necessary if the roast is carefully seared and the oven kept at proper temperature. When the heat of the oven is just right, the meat will keep up a continuous gentle sputtering in the pan. If no sputtering can be heard, the heat is insufficient. The heat is too great when the drippings burn and smoke.

Broiling.—This is the method employed for cooking thin cuts of meat in their own juices over glowing coals. When properly done, broiled meat contains a larger amount of uncoagulated albumen than can be secured by cooking in any other manner; hence it is the most wholesome. For broiling, a bed of clear, glowing coals without flame is the first essential. Coke, charcoal, or anthracite coal serves best for securing this requisite.

In an ordinary stove, the coals should be nearly to the top of the fire-box, that the meat may be held so as almost to touch the fire. No utensil is better for ordinary purposes than a double wire broiler. First, rub it well with a bit of suet, then put in the meat with the thickest part in the center. Wrap a coarse towel around the hand to protect it from the heat, hold the meat as near the fire as possible, so as to sear one side instantly, slowly count ten, then turn and sear the other side. Continue the process, alternating first one side and then the other, slowly counting ten before each turning, until the meat is sufficiently done. Successful broiling is largely dependent upon frequent turning. The heat, while it at once sears the surface, starts the flow of the juices, and although they cannot escape through the hardened surface, if the meat were entirely cooked on one side before turning, they would soon come to the top, and when it was turned over, would drip into the fire. If the meat is seared on both sides, the juices will be retained within, unless the broiling is too prolonged, when they will ooze out and evaporate, leaving the meat dry and leathery. Salt draws out the juices, and should not be added until the meat is done. As long as meat retains its juices, it will spring up instantly when pressed with a knife; when the juices have begun to evaporate, it will cease to do this. Broiled meats should be served on hot dishes.

BEEF.

Economy and Adaptability in Selection.—While the greatest care should be exercised in the selection of beef as regards its soundness and wholesomeness, it must likewise be selected with reference to economy and adaptability for cooking purposes, pieces from different portions of the animal being suitable for cooking only in certain ways. Ox beef is said to be best. That beef is most juicy and tender which has fine streaks of fat intermingled with the lean. Beef which is coarse-grained and hard to cut is apt to be tough. An economical piece of beef to purchase is the back of the rump. It is a long piece with only a small portion of bone, and weighs about ten pounds. The thickest portion may be cut into steaks, the thin, end with bone may be utilized for soups and stews, while the remainder will furnish a good roast. Only a small portion of choice tender lean meat is to be found in one animal, and these are also the most expensive; but the tougher, cheaper parts, if properly cooked, are nearly as nutritious.

RECIPES.

Broiled Beef.—Beef for broiling should be juicy and have a tender fiber. Steaks cut from three parts of the beef are in request for this purpose,—tenderloin, porterhouse, and round steak. The last-named is the more common and economical, yet it is inferior in juice and tenderness to the other two. Steak should be cut three fourths of an inch or more in thickness. If it is of the right quality, do not pound it; if very tough, beat with a steak-mallet or cut across it several times on both sides with a sharp knife. Wipe, and remove any bone and superfluous fat. Have the fire in readiness, the plates heating, then proceed as directed on page 398.

Cold-Meat Stew.—Cut pieces of cold roast beef into thick slices and put into a stewpan with six or eight potatoes, a good-sized bunch of celery cut into small pieces; and a small carrot cut in dice may be added if the flavor is liked. Cover with hot water, and simmer for three fourths of an hour. Thicken with a little browned flour.

Pan-broiled Steak.—In the absence of the necessary appliances for broiling over coals, the following method may be employed. Heat a clean skillet to blue heat, rub it with a bit of suet, just enough to keep the meat from sticking, but leave no fat in the pan. Lay in the steak, pressing it down to the pan, and sear quickly on one side; turn, and without cutting into the meat, sear upon the other. Keep the skillet hot but do not scorch; cook from five to ten minutes, turning frequently, so as not to allow the juices to escape. Add no salt until done. Serve on hot plates. This method is not frying, and requires the addition of no water, butter, or stock.

Pan-broiled Steak No.2.—Take a smooth pancake-griddle, or in lieu of anything better, a clean stove-griddle may be used; heat very hot and sear each side of the steak upon it. When well seared, lift the steak into a hot granite-ware or sheet-iron pan, cover, and put into a hot oven for two or three minutes, or until sufficiently cooked.

Roast Beef.—The sirloin and rib and rump pieces are the best cuts for roasting. Wipe, trim, and skewer into shape. Sear the cut surfaces and proceed as directed on page 397, cooking twenty minutes to the pound if it is to be rare, less half an hour deducted on account of soaring. The application of salt and water has a tendency to toughen the meat and draw out its juices; so if it is desired to have the meat juicy and tender, it is better to cook without basting. Unless the heat of the oven is allowed to become too great, when meat is cooked after this manner there will be a quantity of rich, jelly-like material in the pan, which with the addition of a little water and flour may be made into a gravy.

Smothered Beef.—Portions from the round, middle, or face of the rump are generally considered best for preparing this dish. Wipe with a clean wet cloth, put into a smoking-hot skillet, and carefully sear all cut surfaces. Put into a kettle, adding for a piece of beef weighing about six pounds, one cup of hot water. Cover closely and cook at a temperature just below boiling, until the meat is tender but not broken. As the water boils away, enough more boiling water may be added to keep the meat from burning. Another method of securing the same results is to cut the beef into small pieces and put into a moderate oven inside a tightly covered jar for an hour. Afterward increase the heat and cook closely covered until the meat is tender. Thicken and season the juice, and serve as a gravy.

Vegetables with Stewed Beef.—Prepare the beef as directed for Stewed Beef, and when nearly tender, add six or eight potatoes. Just before serving, thicken the gravy with a little browned flour braided in cold water, and add a cup of strained, stewed tomato and a teaspoonful of chopped parsley.

Stewed Beef.—The aitch-bone and pieces from the shin, the upper part of the chuck-rib and neck of beef, are the parts most commonly used for stewing. All meat for stews should be carefully dressed and free from blood. Those portions which have bone and fat, as well as lean beef, make much better-flavored stews than pieces which are wholly lean. The bones, however, should not be crushed or splintered, but carefully sawed or broken, and any small pieces removed before cooking. It is generally considered that beef which has been previously browned makes a much more savory stew, and it is quite customary first to brown the meat by frying in hot fat. A much more wholesome method, and one which will have the same effect as to flavor, is to add to the stew the remnants of roasts or steak. It is well when selecting meat for a stew to procure a portion, which, like the aitch-bone, has enough juicy meat upon it to serve the first day as a roast for a small family. Cut the meat for a stew into small pieces suitable for serving, add boiling water, and cook as directed on page 396. Remove all pieces of bone and the fat before serving. If the stew is made of part cooked and part uncooked meat, the cooked meat should not be added until the stew is nearly done. The liquor, if not of the proper consistency when the meat is tender, may be thickened by adding a little flour braided in cold water, cooking these after four or five minutes.

MUTTON.

The strong flavor of mutton is said to be due to the oil from the wool, which penetrates the skin, or is the result, through heedlessness or ignorance of the butcher, in allowing the wool to come in contact with the flesh. There is a quite perceptible difference in the flavor of mutton from a sheep which had been for some time sheared of its woolly coat and that from one having a heavy fleece.

The smallest proportion of both fat and bone to muscle is found in the leg; consequently this is the most valuable portion for food, and is likewise the most economical, being available for many savory dishes. On account of the disagreeable adhesive qualities of its fat when cold, mutton should always be served hot.

RECIPES.

Boiled Leg of Mutton.—Wipe carefully, remove the fat, and put into boiling water. Skim, and cook as directed on page 395, twelve minutes for each pound.

Broiled Chops.—The best-flavored and most tender chops are those from the loins. Remove carefully all the pink skin above the fat, scraping it off if possible without cutting into the lean. Wipe with a wet cloth, and broil in the same manner as beefsteak over hot coals or in a hot skillet, turning frequently until done; five or eight minutes will suffice to cook. Sprinkle salt on each side, drain on paper, and serve hot.

Pot-roast Lamb.—For this purpose a stone jar or pot is best, although iron or granite-ware will do; wipe the meat well and gash with a sharp knife. If crowded closely in the pot, all the better; cover with a lid pressed down firmly with a weight to hold it if it does not fit tightly. No water is needed, and no steam should be allowed to escape during the cooking. Roast four or five hours in a moderate oven.

Roast Mutton.—The best pieces for this purpose are those obtained from the shoulder, and saddle, loin, and haunches. Wipe carefully, sear the cut surfaces, and proceed as directed for roasting beef. Cook slowly without basting, and unless desired rare, allow twenty-five or thirty minutes to the pound. A leg of mutton requires a longer time to roast than a shoulder. When sufficiently roasted, remove from the pan and drain off all the grease.

Stewed Mutton.—Pieces from the neck and shoulder are most suitable for this purpose. Prepare the meat, and stew as directed for beef, although less time is usually required.

Stewed Mutton Chop.—Wipe, trim off the fat, and remove the bone from two or three pounds of chops. Put into the inner dish of a double boiler with just enough hot water to cover; add a minced stalk of celery, a carrot, and a white turnip cut in dice; cover, and cook until the chops are tender. Sliced potato may be added if liked, when the meat is nearly done. Remove the grease and thicken the liquor with a little browned flour braided with thin cream.

Stewed Mutton Chop No. 2.—Prepare the chops as in the preceding. Place a layer of meat in a deep baking dish, and then a layer of sliced potato, sprinkled with a little minced celery. Add two or more layers of meat, alternating with layers of potatoes. Cover with boiling water and bake closely covered in a very moderate oven two and a half hours.

Veal and Lamb.—Both veal and lamb should be thoroughly cooked; otherwise they are not wholesome. They may be prepared for the tale in the same way as beef or mutton, but will require longer time for cooking.

POULTRY AND GAME.

Poultry and game differ from other animal foods in the relative quantity of fat and the quality of their juices. The fat of birds is laid up underneath the skin and in various internal parts of the body, while but a small proportion is mingled with the fibers or the juices of the flesh. The flesh of the chicken, turkey, and guinea-fowl is more delicately flavored, more tender and easy to digest, than that of geese and ducks. Chickens broiled require three hours for digestion; when boiled or roasted, four hours are needed.

The flesh of poultry is less stimulating than beef, and is thus considered better adapted for invalids. The flesh of wild fowl contains less fat than that of poultry; it is also tender and easy of digestion. Different birds and different parts of the same bird, vary considerably in color and taste. The breed, food, and method of fattening, influence the quality of this class of foods. Fowls poorly fed and allowed wide range are far from cleanly in their habits of eating; in fact, they are largely scavengers, and through the food they pick up, often become infested with internal parasites, and affected with tuberculosis and other diseases which are liable to be communicated to those who eat their flesh.

Suggestions for the Selection of Poultry and Game.—The first care in the selection of poultry should be its freedom from disease. Birds deprived of exercise, shut up in close cages, and regularly stuffed with as much corn or soft food as they can swallow, may possess the requisite fatness, but it is of a most unwholesome character. When any living creature ceases to exercise, its excretory organs cease to perform their functions thoroughly, and its body becomes saturated with retained excretions.

A stall-fed fowl may be recognized by the color of its fat, which is pale white, and lies in thick folds beneath the skin along the lower half of the backbone. The entire surface of the body presents a more greasy, uninviting appearance than that of fowls permitted to live under natural conditions.

Never purchase fowls which have been sent to the market undrawn. All animals intended for use as food should be dressed as quickly as possible after killing. Putrefactive changes begin very soon after death, and the liver and other viscera, owing to their soft texture and to the quantity of venous blood they retain, advance rapidly in decomposition. When a fowl or animal is killed, even if the large arteries at the throat are cut, a large quantity of blood remains in and around the intestines, owing to the fact that only through the capillaries of the liver can the blood in the portal system find its way into the large vessels which convey it to the heart, and which at death are cut off from the general circulation at both ends by a capillary system. This leaves the blood-vessels belonging to the portal circulation distended with venous blood, which putrefies very quickly, forming a virulent poison. The contents of the intestines of all creatures are always in a more or less advanced state of putrescence, ready to undergo rapid decomposition as soon as the preservative action of the intestinal fluids ceases. It will readily be seen, then, that the flesh of an undrawn fowl must be to a greater or less degree permeated with the poisonous gases and other products of putrefaction, and is certainly quite unfit for food.

Young fowls have soft, yellow feet, a smooth, moist skin, easily torn with a pin, wings which will spring easily, and a breastbone which will yield to pressure. Pinfeathers are an indication of a young bird; older fowls are apt to have sharp scales, long hairs, long, thin necks, and flesh with a purplish tinge.

Poultry should be entirely free from disagreeable odors. Methods are employed for sweetening fowls which have been kept too long in market, but if they need such attention, bury them decently rather than cook them for the table.

Turkeys should have clear, full eyes, and soft, loose spurs. The legs of young birds are smooth and black; those of older ones, rough and reddish.

Geese and ducks, when freshly killed, have supple feet. If young, the windpipe and beak can be easily broken by pressure of the thumb and forefinger. Young birds also have soft, white fat, tender skin, yellow feet, and legs free from hairs.

The legs of young pigeons are flesh-colored. When in good condition, the breast should be full and plump, and if young, it is of a light reddish color. Old pigeons have dark flesh; squabs always have pinfeathers.

Partridges, when young, have dark bills and yellow legs.

The breast of all birds should be full and plump. Birds which are diseased always fall away on the breast, and the bone feels sharp and protrudes.

To Dress Poultry and Birds.—First strip off the feathers a few at a time, with a quick, jerking motion toward the tail. Remove pinfeathers with a knife.

Fowls should be picked, if possible, while the body retains some warmth, as scalding is apt to spoil the skin and parboil the flesh. When all the feathers but the soft down have been removed, a little hot water may be poured on, when the down can be easily rubbed off with the palm of the hand. Wipe dry, and singe the hairs off by holding the bird by the legs over the flame of a candle, a gas-jet, or a few drops of alcohol poured on a plate and lighted. To dress a bird successfully, one should have some knowledge of its anatomy, and it is well for the amateur first to dress one for some dish in which it is not to be cooked whole, when the bird may be opened, and the position of its internal organs studied.

Remove the head, slip the skin back from the neck, and cut it off close to the body, take out the windpipe and pull out the crop from the end of the neck. Make an incision through the skin a little below the leg-joint, bend the leg at this point and break off the bone. If care has been taken to cut only through the skin, the tendons of the leg may now be easily removed with the fingers.

If the bird is to be cut up, remove the legs and wings at the joints. Then beginning near the vent, cut the membrane down between the breastbone and tail to the backbone on each side, and separate just below the ribs. The internal organs can now been seen and easily removed, and the body of the bird divided at its joints.

If desired to keep the fowl whole, after removing the windpipe and crop, loosen the heart, liver, and lungs by introducing the forefinger at the neck; cut off the oil-sack, make a slit horizontally under the tail, insert the first and middle fingers, and after separating the membranes which lie close to the body, press them along within the body until the heart and liver can be felt. The gall bladder lies directly under the left lobe of the liver, and if the fingers are kept up, and all adhesions loosened before an effort is made to draw the organs out, there will be little danger of breaking it. Remove everything which can be taken out, then hold the, fowl under the faucet and cleanse thoroughly.

To Truss a Fowl or Bird.—Twist the tips of the wings back under the shoulder and bend the legs as far up toward the breast as possible, securing them in that position by putting a skewer through one thigh into the body and out through the opposite thigh. Then bring the legs down and fasten close to the vent.

To Stuff a Fowl.—Begin at the neck, stuff the breast full, draw the neck skin together, double it over on the back and fasten with a darning needle threaded with fine twine. Put the remainder of the stuffing into the body at the other opening.

RECIPES.

Birds Baked in Sweet Potatoes.—Small birds, of which the breast is the only suitable portion for eating, may be baked in the following manner: Cut a sweet potato lengthwise; make a cavity in each half. Place the breast of the bird therein; fit, and tie together carefully; bake until the potato is soft. Serve in the potato.

Boiled Fowl.—After cleaning and dividing the fowl, put into boiling water, and proceed as directed on page 395.

Broiled Birds.—Pluck and wipe clean with a damp cloth. Split down the middle of the back, and carefully draw the bird. Proceed as directed below.

Broiled Fowl.—A young bird well dressed and singed is best for this purpose. Split down the middle of the back, wipe clean with a damp cloth, twist the top of the wings from the second joint; spread out flat, and with a rolling pin break the projecting breastbone so that the bird will lie flat upon the broiler. When ready to cook, place it skin uppermost and sear the under side by pressing it on a hot pan; then broil the same as beefsteak over glowing coals.

Corn and Chicken.—Clean and divide a chicken in joints. Stew in milk or part milk and water until nearly tender; then add the grains and juice from a dozen ears of corn. Cook slowly until the corn is done; season lightly with salt, and serve with dry toast.

Pigeons, Quails, and Partridges may be half baked, then cooked as directed for Smothered Chicken until tender.

Roast Chicken.—Dress carefully, singe, wash, and wipe dry. Put into a pan of the proper size, add a cup of boiling water, and cook very slowly for the first half hour, then increase the heat, baste frequently, turn occasionally so that no portion will brown too fast. Cook from one to two hours according to size and age of the bird. It is usually considered essential to stuff a fowl for roasting, but a dressing compounded of melted fat and crumbs seasoned with herbs and strong condiments is not to be recommended.

If a dressing is considered necessary, it may be made of a quart of crumbs of rather stale whole-wheat bread, moistened with cream, to which add a small handful of powdered and sifted sage leaves which have been dried in the oven until crisp. Add salt as desired, a well-beaten egg, and a little chopped celery.

Roast Turkey.—Pluck, singe, and dress the turkey; wash thoroughly and wipe with a dry cloth. If dressing is to be used, stuff the body full, sew up, and truss. Place in a dripping-pan, add a pint of boiling water, and put in an oven so moderate that the turkey will not brown for the first hour; afterward the heat may be somewhat increased, but at no time should the oven be very hot. After the bird becomes brown, baste it occasionally with the water in the pan, dredging lightly with flour. Cook until the legs will separate from the body; three or four hours will be necessary for a small turkey. One half hour to the pound is the usual rule. When tender, remove the stuffing and serve it hot, placing the turkey on a large hot platter to be carved. It may be garnished with parsley or celery leaves and served with cranberry sauce.

Ducks and geese may be prepared and roasted in the same manner, but less time will suffice for cooking, about one and one third hours for ducks of ordinary size, and about three hours for a young goose.

A stuffing of mashed potato seasoned with onion, sage, and salt is considered preferable for a goose. Equal parts of bread crumbs and chopped apples moistened in a little cream are also used for this purpose.

Smothered Chicken.—Cut two chickens into joints and put in a closely covered kettle with a pint of boiling water. Heat very slowly to boiling, skim, keep covered, and simmer until tender and the water evaporated; add salt, turn the pieces, and brown them in their own juices.

Steamed Chicken.—Prepare the chicken as for roasting, steam until nearly tender, dredge with flour and a little salt; put into a dripping-pan and brown in the oven. Other birds and fowls may be prepared in the same way.

Stewed Chicken.—Divide a chicken into pieces suitable for serving, and stew as directed for beef on page 400. Old fowls left whole and stewed in this manner for a long time and afterward roasted, are much better than when prepared in any other way. If a gravy is desired, prepare as for stewed beef. Other poultry may be stewed likewise.

FISH.

Fish is a less stimulating article of food than other meats. Edible fish are generally divided into two classes, those of white flesh and those more or less red. The red-fleshed fish, of which the salmon is a representative, have their fat distributed throughout the muscular tissues, while in white fish the fat is stored up in the liver; hence the latter class is much easier of digestion, and being less stimulating, is to be recommended as more wholesome. Different kinds of fish have different nutritive values. Their flavor and wholesomeness are greatly influenced by the nature of their food and the condition of the water in which they are caught; those obtained in deep water with strong currents are considered superior to those found in shallow water. Fish are sometimes poisonous, owing no doubt to the food they eat.

Like all animal foods, fish are subject to parasites, some of which take up their abode in the human body when fish infected with them are eaten. An eminent scientist connected with the Smithsonian Institution, contributed an article to *Forest and Stream* a few years ago, in which he stated that in the salmon no less than sixteen kinds of parasitic worms have been discovered, and undoubtedly many others remain unknown; four species were tapeworms, and four, roundworms. The yellow perch is known to be infested with twenty-three species of parasitic worms.

The pike carries with him at least twenty kinds, while many other varieties of fish are equally infested.

Fish have been highly lauded as a food particularly suited to the development of the brain and nervous system. This no doubt has arisen from the fact that fish contain a considerable amount of phosphorus. Phosphorus is also present in the human brain, and for this reason it has been supposed that fish must be excellent nutriment for the brain; but the truth is, there is no such thing as any special brain or nerve food. What is good to build up one part of the body is good for the whole of it; a really good food contains the elements to nourish every organ of the body.

Salted fish, like salted meat, is deprived of most of its nutriment during the curing process, and being rendered much more difficult of digestion, possesses very little value as a food.

Shell-Fish (Oysters, Clams, Scallops, Lobsters, Crabs,etc.).—Although considered a luxury by epicures, shellfish are not possessed of a high nutritive value. The whole class are scavengers by nature and according to recent researches it appears that they are not altogether safe articles of diet. Many cases of severe and extensive sickness have been traced to the use of clams and oysters. Investigations made to ascertain the cause show the poisonous part of the mussel to be the liver. Rabbits and other small animals inoculated with the poison died in one or two minutes. Not all mussels are thus poisonous, but inasmuch as there is an abundance of wholesome food, it would certainly seem the part of wisdom to discard shellfish altogether.

How to Select and Prepare Fish.—The flesh of good, fresh fish is firm and hard, and will respond at once to pressure with the fingers. If the flesh feels soft and flabby, the fish is not fresh. The eyes should be full and bright and the gills of a clear red color.

Fish should be cleaned as soon as possible after being caught. To do this, lay the fish upon a board, and holding it by the tail, scrape off the scales with a dull knife held nearly flat, working from the tail toward the head. Scrape slowly, and rinse the knife frequently in cold water. Cut off the head and fins, make an opening from the gills halfway down the lower part of the body, scrape out the entrails and every particle of blood. Remove the white part that lies along the backbone, then thoroughly rinse and wipe dry.

Keep in a cool place until ready to cook, but do not place directly on ice, as that will have a tendency to soften the flesh. Fresh fish should never be allowed to soak in water. If salt fish is to be used, it should be freshened by placing it skin-side up in cold water, and soaking for several hours, changing the water frequently.

Frozen fish should be placed in cold water to thaw, and when thawed, should be cooked immediately.

Fish is cooked by nearly all methods, but retains more nourishment when broiled or baked. It should be thoroughly cooked, being both indigestible and unpalatable when underdone.

Boiled fish is usually dependent for flavor upon some kind of rich sauce so incompatible with healthy digestion that we do not recommend this method.

RECIPES.

Baked Fish.—Select a perfectly fresh, properly dressed fish. Rinse thoroughly and wipe dry. Fold it together and place in a dripping pan with a cup of boiling water. Cook slowly and steadily until tender. A fish weighing three or four pounds will require at least two hours. If desired, the fish may be lightly dredged with flour, toward the last, as it begins to brown.

Broiled Fish.—Thoroughly clean the fish, and if small, split down the back. Fish of larger size should be cut into inch slices. Use a double wire broiler well oiled with a bit of suet. Lay the fish, with its thickest part next the center of the broiler, skin uppermost, and broil over a bed of clear coals until the flesh-side is of an even brown. The time required will vary, according to the size of the fish, from five to twenty minutes; then turn and brown on the other side. If the fish be very thick, when both sides are browned, put the broiler in the oven over a dripping pan and cook until done.

MEAT SOUP.

Soups made from meat require first the preparation of a special material called *stock*, a liquid foundation upon which to begin the soup.

Beef, veal, mutton, and poultry are all made into stock in the same manner, so that general rules for its preparation will be sufficient for all meat soups.

The principal constituents of meat and bones, the material from which stock is compounded, are fiber, albuminous elements, gelatinous substances, and flavoring matters. The albuminous elements are found only in the flesh. The gelatinous substance found in bones, skin, and tendons, is almost devoid of nutriment. In selecting material for stock, therefore, it is well to remember that the larger the proportion of lean meat used, the more nutritious will be the soup.

But little else than gelatine is obtained from the bones, and although serviceable in giving consistency, a soup made principally from bones is not valuable as a food. The amount of bone used for soup should never exceed the flesh material in weight. The bones, trimmings, and remnants of steaks, chops, and roasts may be advantageously utilized for soups. Bits of roast meat and roast gravies are especially serviceable material, since they are rich in the flavoring elements of meat. It should be remembered, however, that these flavoring matters are chiefly excrementitious or waste substances, derived from the venous blood of the animal.

The greatest care must be observed to keep the scraps perfectly sweet and fresh until needed, as stale meat is exceedingly unwholesome. If the scraps are mostly cooked meats and bones, a small portion of raw, lean meat should be used with them; it need not be of the choicest quality; tough, coarse meat, when fresh and good, can be advantageously used for soup stock.

If fresh material is to be procured, select for beef soups a piece from the shin or lower round; the same choice of pieces may be made of veal; of mutton, pieces from the forequarter and neck are best.

In preparing meat for soup, if it is soiled, scrub the outside thoroughly with a clean cloth wet in cold water, or cut away the soiled portion. Break the bones into as small pieces as convenient; cut the meat into inch dice, remove the marrow from the bones, and put it aside. If added to the stock, it will make it greasy.

Having selected proper material and prepared it for use, the next step is to extract the juices. To do this put it into cold water, bring very gradually to the boiling point,—an hour is not too long for this,—then cook slowly but continuously. In the observation of these simple measures lies the secret of success in stock-making.

The albuminous elements of the meat, which are similar in character to the white of an egg, are readily dissolved in cold or tepid water, but boiling water coagulates them. If the meat is put into boiling water, the albumen coagulates, or hardens, forming a sort of crust on the outside of the meat, which prevents the inner juices from escaping; on the contrary, if the meat is put to cook in cold water, and is gradually raised to the boiling point, the soaking and simmering will easily extract and dissolve the juices.

Salt likewise hinders the extraction of the meat juices, and should not be added to stock during its preparation.

The best utensil for use in the preparation of stock is a soup digester. This is a porcelain-lined kettle, resting on standards, with a cover fitting closely into a groove, so that no steam can escape except through a valve in the top of the cover. In this the meat can be placed and allowed to cook for hours without burning. An ordinary granite-ware kettle with tightly fitting cover set on a stove ring or brick, answers quite well. It should, however, be kept entirely for this purpose. A double boiler is also suitable.

The correct proportion of water is to be used is about one quart to each pound of meat and bones, though this will vary somewhat with the material and the length of time required for cooking. The scum which is thrown to the surface of the water during the cooking process is composed of blood and other impurities, and should be removed as rapidly as it rises. If allowed to remain after the water reaches the boiling point, it will become incorporated into the stock and injure it in flavor and wholesomeness.

If the meat and bones are well cut and broken, the juices ought to be all extracted, with proper cooking, in three or four hours. Longer cooking will render the stock thicker and more gelatinous but not more nutritious, and too long cooking will detract from its flavor. As soon as the meat will fall from the bones, the stock should be removed from the pot and strained at once.

A good way to strain stock is to place a colander over an earthen crock or jar (the colander should fit inside the jar), with a cloth strainer within the colander. Then dip the contents of the stock kettle into the colander, and leave it there to drain for fifteen or twenty minutes. Do not squeeze the cloth, and when well drained, throw the scraps away.

Arrangement for Straining Stock.

French cooks, with their propensity for economy, sometimes select a good quality of beef, cook it so as to retain a portion of the juices in the meat, and make it serve both for preparing the soup and for boiled beef on the bill of fare. The meat is not cut up, but is heated quickly and removed as soon as tender, so that only part of the juices are extracted.

Set the stock where it will become cold. The more rapidly it cools, the more delicate will be its flavor, and the better it will keep. The fat will rise to the surface, and can be easily removed when desired. If the quantity of fat in the material used was considerable, a solid cake will cover the top. This fat, by excluding the air, helps keep the stock sweet, and should not be removed until the stock is needed.

If only a portion is to be used at one time, the remainder with the fat should be reheated and cooled, that a new crust may be formed. In winter, stock may be kept several days, if care is thus taken to reheat it. In summer, unless kept in a very cold place, it will spoil in a few hours.

Soup should never be greasy, and hence, before using the stock, every particle of the fat should be removed. To accomplish this, loosen the cake of fat from the dish with a knife, and if solid, it will sometimes come off whole; if soft, remove all that is possible without cutting into the stock, and afterwards wipe the top of the jellied stock with a cloth wrung out of very hot water, which will readily absorb any lingering portion of fat. If the stock is not jellied, skim off all the fat possible, and then turn the stock through a napkin wrung out of ice water. This will harden the grease, which will adhere to the napkin. It is always better to prepare stock long enough before it is needed to allow it to become perfectly cold; if, however, it is necessary to use the stock very soon after it is prepared, the fat may be quickly hardened by turning the stock into a dripping pan or some other shallow dish, and placing it on ice in a cool place; if there is no time for this, strain several times through a napkin wrung out of ice-cold water, removing the particles of fat each time and wringing the cloth anew before straining again. A little cold water poured into hot stock will also cause the grease to rise so that it can be easily skimmed off; but this method weakens the stock.

Stock may be prepared from one kind of meat only, or from two or more different kinds mixed together. Chicken stock is generally conceded to be better if a small portion of beef is combined with the fowl. Beef and veal are largely used together; but mutton on account of its strong flavor is better used alone.

Stock, when prepared from a single kind of meat, is termed simple stock or broth. When prepared from two or more kinds of flesh cooked together, or when stock prepared separately from different kinds of meat are mixed together, the result is termed compound stock or double broth. With either of these stocks as a foundation, an innumerable variety of soups may be prepared, either by serving them as plain broth or by the addition of some of the various grains and vegetables, the distinctive name of each soup being given it according to its principal solid ingredient.

To Clarify Soup Stock.—Having removed all the fat from the stock, add to it before reheating, the shell of an egg, and the whole of one egg well beaten, with a little cold water, for every three pints of soup. Place the soup over the fire and stir it constantly to keep the egg from setting until it is hot. Simmer for fifteen minutes, removing the scum as it rises, and strain through a flannel cloth or napkin laid in a colander. It is also a good plan to place a fine wire strainer on the napkin to catch the shells and scum. Do not squeeze the cloth or stir the liquid with a spoon to hasten the straining process. If the cloth is clogged so that the stock does not run through well, carefully change it in the colander so that the liquid will run down upon a clean portion. When strained, it may be reheated, seasoned, and served as clear soup.

RECIPES.

Asparagus Soup.—This soup is prepared in every way like the one on page 276, except that while stock made from veal is used instead of milk. Green pea soup, celery soup, green corn soup, and green bean soup may be prepared according to the recipes already given for these soups by substituting for milk the same quantity of the stock of veal or chicken.

Barley, Rice, Sago, or Tapioca Soup.—Any kind of stock may be used in making these soups, though chicken and mutton stock are generally considered preferable. Prepare the grains, the sago, or the tapioca, by steaming or boiling till well cooked, and add to the stock, which should be at boiling temperature. Season and serve.

Caramel for Coloring Soup Brown.—Melt a half pint of sugar and one tablespoonful of water in a saucepan over the fire; stir constantly until it is of a dark brown color; then add a half pint of boiling water, simmer ten minutes, strain, and put into an air-tight can or bottle. When needed, mix such a quantity with the soup as will give the desired degree of color.

Julienne Soup.—Take an equal proportion of carrot, parsnip, turnip, celery, and string beans, cut into thin pieces of inch lengths, sufficient to make one pint. Simmer the vegetables gently in a small quantity of water until tender, but not long enough to destroy their shape. Heat a quart of clear stock to boiling, add vegetables, salt to taste, and serve.

Other vegetables, as peas, asparagus, etc. may be used in the season. Sometimes the vegetables are cut into dice or fancy shapes with a vegetable cutter. It makes little difference about the shape, so that the pieces are small and uniform in size. Such vegetables as potatoes, carrots, or turnips, when used for soups, are easiest cut, after paring in the usual manner, by taking the vegetable in the left hand, holding it on the table or board between thumb and finger, and with the right hand cutting downward in even slices not over one third of an inch wide, to within a quarter of an inch of the bottom. Turn the vegetable and repeat the process, cutting across the first slices. Again lay the vegetable on its side, and make a third series of cuts, which will divide it into cubes. If several kinds of vegetables are used, those which require a longer time for cooking should be cut into smaller pieces.

Tomato Soup.—Into two quarts of boiling beef stock stir a teaspoonful of cornstarch well braided with a little cold water, and a pint of strained, stewed tomatoes. Boil a few minutes, and serve. A teaspoonful of sugar may also be added, if desired.

White Soup.—White soups are made from veal or chicken stock, seasoned with cream, flavored with onion or celery, and thickened with cornstarch or flour.

Vermicelli or Macaroni Soups.—Drop into boiling water and cook the macaroni about one hour, the vermicelli ten minutes. Drain well, dash cold water through them to separate the pieces, which are apt to stick together, and add to boiling stock (beef and veal are preferable) in the proportion of a pint of cooked macaroni or vermicelli to a quart of soup. Salt to taste and serve.

Puree with Chicken.—Take a quart of chicken stock from which the fat has been removed. Add a stalk or two of celery cut into finger-lengths, and a slice of onion, and put to boil. Beat together the mashed yolk of two hard boiled eggs, and a half cup of sweet cream. Chop the white meat of the chicken until fine as meal and beat with the egg mixture. Add slowly a cup and a half of hot milk. Remove the celery and onion from the hot stock, and stir all together. Boil up, salt to taste, and serve. If too thick, a little more stock or milk can be added.

Tapioca Cream Soup.—Soak two tablespoonfuls of tapioca over night. Heat a quart of stock prepared from the white meat of chicken, to boiling, in a saucepan. Then stir the tapioca in gradually. Move the saucepan to the side of the range where it will simmer till the tapioca is transparent. Have ready in a large dish a mixture prepared by beating together very thoroughly the yolks of three eggs and four tablespoonfuls of sweet cream. When the tapioca is clear, remove the stock from the range and pour it very gradually onto the egg mixture, stirring briskly all the time, so that the egg will not curdle. Season with salt if desired. The soup may be returned to the stove and warmed before serving if necessary, but it must not be boiled or allowed to stand a long time.

TABLE TOPICS.

Animal food is one of the greatest means by which the pure sentiment of the race is depressed. *—Alcott.*

An English medical author says, "It is no doubt true that the constant use of animal food disqualifies the mind for literary application. We can scarcely imagine a philosopher living on horse flesh like a Tartar, or on buffalo meat like an Indian; and it is a fact that these tribes appear incapable of civilization until they acquire the habit of using a less stimulating diet, and begin to cultivate the fruits of the earth for their own use. The difference, in the success of Christian missions, between such people and those whose chief sustenance is farinaceous food, is very striking and worthy of especial notice. In the East, and in Polynesia, literature and Christian doctrines are seized upon with avidity. But in vain were the most earnest labors of the best men to introduce reading and writing among the American Indians until they had first been taught to grow corn and to eat bread."

An American gentleman traveling in the East met a Brahmin priest, who refused to shake hands with him for fear of pollution. The reason he assigned was that Americans eat hogs. Said the priest, "Why, I have heard that in America they put hogs' flesh in barrels and eat it after it has been dead six months! Horrible!"

Pork is by no means a favorite food in Scotland. King James is said to have abhorred pork almost as much as he did tobacco. He said, "If I were to give a banquet to the devil, I would provide a loin of pork and a poll of ling, with a pipe of tobacco for digestion!" *—Scott.*

The Hindu would as soon think of becoming a cannibal as of eating swine's flesh. It is stated that the Indian mutiny so frightful in its results originated in a fear among the Sepoys that they would be forced to eat pork. A lady in India had an amusing experience which illustrates the Hindu sentiment on the subject of pig. Arriving late at a grand dinner, she and her husband saw the first course being carried in as they went down the hall. A row of khitmutgars was drawn up, waiting to follow the dish into the dining-room, and serve their respective employers; as a dish of ham was carried by, each man gravely and deliberately spat upon it! Needless to say, Mrs. B. and her lord waited for the second course.

Both the ancient Syrians and Egyptians abstained from flesh-eating out of dread and abhorrence, and when the latter would represent any thing as odious or disagreeable by hieroglyphics,they painted a fish.

Yes, Agassiz does recommend authors to eat fish because the phosphorus in it makes brains. So far you are correct. But I cannot help you to a decision about the amount you need to eat—at least with certainty. If the specimen composition you send is about your fair usual average, I should judge that perhaps a couple of whales would be all you want for the present; not the largest kind, but simply good, middling-sized whales!*—Mark Twain's Letter to a Young Author.*

FOOD FOR THE SICK

There is no branch of the culinary art which requires more skill than that of preparing food for the sick and feeble. The purpose of food at all times is to supply material for repairing—the waste which is constantly be chosen with reference to its nutritive value. But during illness and convalescence, when the waste is often much greater and the vital powers less active, it is of the utmost importance that the food should be of such a character as will supply the proper nutrition. Nor is this all; an article of food may contain all the elements of nutrition in such proportions as to render it a wholesome food for those in health, and not be a proper food for the sick, for the reason that its conversion into blood and tissue lays too great a tax upon the digestive organs. Food for the sick should be palatable, nutritious and easily assimilated. To discriminate as to what food will supply these requisites, one must possess some knowledge of dietetics and physiology, as well as of the nature of the illness with which the patient is suffering; and such a knowledge ought to be part of the education of every woman, no matter to what class of society she belongs.

There are no special dishes suitable alike for all cases. Hot buttered toast, tea, rich jellies, and other dainties so commonly served to the sick, are usually the very worst articles of diet of which they could partake. As a general rule, elaborate dishes are not suitable.

Well-cooked gruel, a nicely broiled steak, a glass of milk, or some refreshing drink often serve far better than foods which combine a greater variety of ingredients, and require more extensive preparation. The simplest foods are always the best, because the most readily assimilated.

Scrupulous neatness and care in all the minute particulars of the cooking and serving of food for invalids, will add much to its palatableness. The clean napkin on the tray, the bright silver, and dainty china plate, with perhaps a sprig of leaves and flowers beside it, thinly sliced bread, toast or cracker, and the light cup partly filled with hot gruel, are far more appetizing to the invalid than coarse ware, thickly cut bread, and an overflowing cup of gruel, though the cooking may be just as perfect. Anything that suggests excess or weight fatigues the sick. The appearance of milk served in a bowl, water in a mug, beef-tea in a saucer, though seemingly a trivial thing, is often sufficient to remove all desire for food.

So far as practicable, the wants of the patient should be anticipated, and the meal served, a surprise. The capricious appetite of an invalid may sometimes be coaxed by arranging his simple food upon a tray so planned that in the napery and service-ware used, some one particular color predominates, and if this color be selected to accord or harmonize as far as possible with the food allowed, the *tout ensemble* presents a pleasing fancy, which will tempt the eye, and through its influence, the appetite of the patient. For example: an invalid whose dietary must consist of fruit and grains, might be served to a "purple" dinner, with bill of fare including a fresh, cool bunch of purple grapes, a glass of unfermented grape juice, a saucer of blackberry mush, a plate of nicely toasted wafers, Graham puffs or zwieback, with stewed prunes, or a slice of prune toast served on dishes decorated with purple. Tie the napkin with a bow of purple ribbon, and place a bunch of purple pansies just within its folds. The monotonous regimen of a poor dyspeptic which poached eggs, beaten biscuit, wheat gluten, eggnog, with, perhaps, stewed peaches or an orange, are served on gilt-band china with a spray of goldenrod, a bunch of marigolds, or a water-lily to give an additional charm.

Foods which are ordered to be served hot, should be *hot,* not merely warm, when they reach the patient. To facilitate this, let the dish in which the food is to be served, stand in hot water for a few moments; take out, wipe dry, turn in the hot food, place on the tray, and serve. An oil stove, alcohol lamp, or a pocket stove is very convenient for warming gruels, broths and other similar foods, as either can be made ready for use in a moment, and will heat the small quantity of food necessary for an invalid in one fourth the time in which it could be accomplished over the range, if necessary to reduce the fire.

In the preparation of food for the sick, a scrupulously clean dish for cooking is of the first importance. It is a good plan in every household to reserve one or two cooking utensils for this purpose, and not be obliged to depend upon those in daily use. Utensils used for the cooking of fruits, vegetables, meat, etc., unless cleaned with the utmost call will sometimes impart a sufficiently unpleasant flavor to the food to render it wholly unpalatable to an invalid whose senses are preternaturally acute.

GRUELS

These simple foods, the base of which is usually some one of the grains, play an important part in the dietary for the sick, if properly prepared; but the sloppy messes sometimes termed gruel, the chief merit of which appears to be that they "are prepared in ten minutes," are scarcely better than nothing at all. Like other dishes prepared from the grains, gruel needs a long, continuous cooking. When done, it should be the very essence of the grain, possessing all its nutritive qualities, but in such form as to be readily assimilated. For the making of gruels, as for the cooking of grains for any other purpose, the double boiler is the best utensil.

Gruel Strainer.

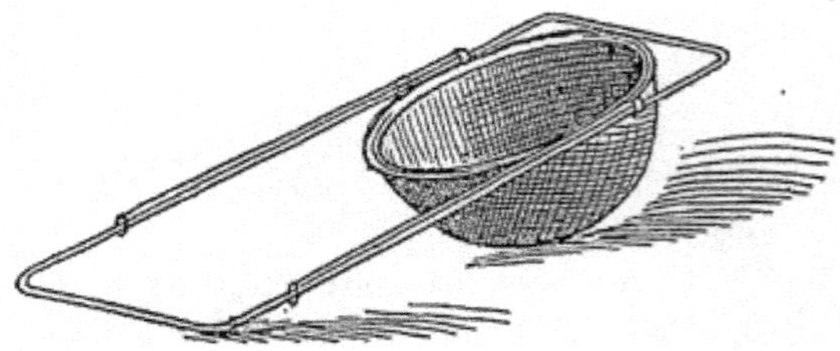

Extension Strainer.

If it is desirable to strain the gruel before serving, have a fine wire strainer of a size to stand conveniently within a large bowl or basin, turn the gruel into this, and rub it through with a wooden or silver spoon, using a second spoon, if necessary, to remove that which hangs beneath the sieve. On no account use the first spoon for the latter operation, as by so doing one is apt to get some of the hulls into the gruel and destroy its smoothness. When as much of the gruel as possible has been rubbed through the sieve, pour the strained liquid into a clean dish, reheat to boiling, and season as desired before serving. An extension strainer which can be fitted over any sized dish is also serviceable for straining gruels.

Gruels, like all other foods, should be retained in the mouth for proper insalivation, and it is well to eat them with wafers or some hard food, when solid food is allowed.

RECIPES.

Arrowroot Gruel.—Rub a dessertspoonful of *pure* arrowroot to a thin paste in two tablespoonfuls of cold water, and stir it into a half pint of boiling water, or, if preferred, a cup and a third of boiling milk, and stir rapidly until thickened and clear. If desired, a little lemon peel for flavoring may be infused in the water or milk, before adding the arrowroot. Sweeten, if allowed, and serve.

Barley Gruel.—Wash three heaping tablespoonfuls of pearl barley, drop it into a pint of boiling water, and parboil five minutes. Pour this water off and add a quart of fresh boiling water. Let it simmer gently for three hours. Strain, season, and serve. A small piece of lemon rind added to the gruel a half hour before it is done, gives it a very agreeable flavor. Equal quantities of milk and barley gruel make a very nourishing drink; the milk, however, should not be added to the gruel until needed, as in a warm atmosphere it undergoes quite rapid change, and is likely to ferment. A little lemon juice, with sugar to sweeten to taste, is sometimes preferred as seasoning for barley gruel.

Egg Gruel.—Heat a cup of milk to boiling, and stir into it one well-beaten egg mixed with one fourth cup of cold milk. Stir constantly for a few minutes till thickened, but do not allow it to boil again. Season with a little salt, or if preferred and allowed, a little loaf sugar.

Egg Gruel No. 2.—Boil the yolks of three eggs until dry and mealy, mash perfectly smooth, then add a cup of boiling milk. Season with salt, and serve.

Farina Gruel.—Moisten two table spoonfuls of farina with a very little cold milk, and stir it into a cupful of boiling water. Boil until it thickens, add a cupful of new milk, turn into a double boiler, and cook again for twenty or thirty minutes. Strain if necessary, season with salt or sugar, and serve.

Flour Gruel.—Rub one heaping tablespoonful of whole-wheat flour to a thin paste with three tablespoonfuls of cold milk, and stir it into a pint of boiling milk. Cook for ten or twelve minutes. Season with salt, strain if necessary, and while hot, stir in the beaten white of one egg. The egg may be omitted if preferred; or the yolk of the egg and a little sugar may be used instead, if the patient's condition will allow it.

Gluten Gruel.—Stir two and one half tablespoonfuls of the wheat gluten prepared by the Sanitarium Food Co., Battle Creek, Mich., into a pint of boiling milk; boil until thickened, when it is ready to serve.

Gluten Gruel No. 2.—Into a pint of boiling water stir three heaping tablespoonfuls of the prepared gluten. Boil until thickened, and add a half cup of thin cream.

Gluten Cream.—Heat a pint of thin cream to boiling, and stir into it three tablespoonfuls of wheat gluten. When thickened, it is ready to serve.

Gluten Meal Gruel.—Into a cup and a half of boiling water stir four tablespoonfuls of gluten meal (prepared by the Sanitarium Food Co.), let it boil for a moment, add six tablespoonfuls of rather thin, sweet cream, and serve.

Graham Gruel.—Heat three cups of water in the inner dish of a double boiler, and when vigorously boiling stir into it carefully, a little at a time, so as not to check the boiling, one scant cup of Graham flour which has been rubbed perfectly smooth in a cup of warm, not hot, water. Stir until thickened, then place in the outer boiler and cook for an hour or longer. When done, strain if necessary, season with salt if desired, and a half cup of sweet cream.

Graham Grits Gruel.—Cook three heaping tablespoonfuls of Graham grits in a quart of boiling water, as directed in the chapter on Grains, for three hours. Turn through a soup strainer to remove any lumps, season with half a cup of cream, and salt if desired. Well cooked Graham grits may be made into gruel by thinning with water or milk, straining and seasoning as above.

Gruel of Prepared Flour.—Knead a pint of flour with water into a ball, and tie firmly in a linen cloth; put it into a granite-ware basin or kettle, cover with boiling water, and boil slowly, replenishing with boiling water as needed, for twelve hours. Put it before the fire to dry. Afterward remove the cloth, and also a thick skin which will have formed over the ball. Dry the interior again. When needed for use, rub a tablespoonful of the prepared flour smooth with three spoonfuls of cold milk, and stir it into a pint of boiling milk. Cook from three to five minutes. Season with salt if desired.

Indian Meal Gruel.—Make a thin paste of one teaspoonful of flour, two tablespoonfuls of best cornmeal, and a little water. Stir this into a quart of boiling water, or milk and water in equal proportions, as preferred. Boil until the meal has set, stirring constantly; then turn into a double boiler and cook for an hour and half or two hours. Season with salt, and strain. If too thick, thin with milk or cream.

Lemon Oatmeal Gruel.—The United States Dispensary recommends the following method of preparing oatmeal gruel for fever patients; "Rub one heaping tablespoonful of fine oatmeal smooth in a little cold water; stir this into three pints of boiling water. Cook until the quantity is reduced to two pints; then strain, and let it cool and settle. When it is quite cold, pour the clear gruel from the sediment, add the juice of a lemon, and sugar to sweeten slightly. If desirable to serve it warm, reheat before adding the lemon juice." Freshly cooked oatmeal may be thinned with boiling water, strained and seasoned in the same manner.

Milk Oatmeal Gruel.—Take a pint of milk and one of water, and heat to boiling. Stir in three heaping table spoonfuls of oatmeal, and cook in a double boiler for two or three hours.

Milk Porridge.—Take one pint of milk and the same quantity of water, and heat to boiling. Stir in two heaping tablespoonfuls of cornmeal or Graham grits, boil, stirring continuously, until the meal has set, then turn into a double boiler and cook for two hours or longer. Season with salt, and a tablespoonful of sweet cream if allowed.

Oatmeal Gruel.—Into one quart of boiling water stir two heaping tablespoonfuls of fine oatmeal; let it boil until it thickens, stirring all the time; then turn into a double boiler and cook for three and a half or four hours. Strain before serving. A little cream may also be added, unless contra-indicated by the patient's condition.

Oatmeal Gruel No. 2.—Pound one half cup of coarse oatmeal until it is mealy. The easiest way to do this is to tie the oatmeal in a coarse cloth and pound it with a wooden mallet. Put it in a pint bowl, and fill the bowl with cold water. Stir briskly for a few moments until the water is white, then allow the meal to settle. Pour off the water, being careful to get none of the sediment. Fill the bowl a second time with cold water, stir thoroughly, let settle, and pour off the water as before. Do this the third time. Boil the liquid one half hour, strain, and serve hot. If very thick, a little cream or milk may be added.

Oatmeal Gruel No, 3.—Add to one cup of well-cooked oatmeal while hot two cups of hot milk, or one cup of hot milk and one of hot water. Beat all thoroughly together, add a little salt if desired, strain, and serve.

Peptonized Gluten Gruel.—Prepare the gruel as directed for Gluten Gruel No. 1. Strain if needed, cook to lukewarm, and turn it into a pitcher, which place in a dish containing hot water even in depth with the gruel in the pitcher; add the peptonizing fluid or powder, stir well, and let it stand in the hot water bath for ten minutes. The temperature must not be allowed to rise over 130°. Put into a clean dish and serve at once, or place on ice till needed. Other well-cooked gruels maybe peptonized in the same way.

Raisin Gruel.—Stone and quarter two dozen raisins and boil them twenty minutes in a small quantity of water. When the water has nearly boiled away, add two cups of new milk. When the milk is boiling, add one heaping tablespoonful of Graham or whole-wheat flour which has been rubbed to a thin paste with a little cold milk. Boil until thickened, stirring all the time; then turn into a double boiler and cook for twenty minutes or half an hour. Season with salt and serve.

Rice Water.—Wash half a cup of rice very thoroughly in several waters. Put it into a saucepan with three cups of cold water and boil for half an hour. Strain off the rice water, season with salt if desired, and serve.

PREPARATIONS OF MILK.

Milk Diet.—An almost exclusive milk diet is sometimes a great advantage in cases of sickness. It is usually necessary to begin the use of the milk in moderate quantities, gradually withdrawing the more solid food and increasing the quantity of milk. In the course of a week, all other food should be withdrawn, and the quantity of milk increased to three or four quarts a day. Milk is easily digested, and hence may be taken at more frequent intervals than other food.

RECIPES.

Albumenized Milk.—Shake together in a well-corked bottle or glass fruit can, a pint of fresh milk and the well-beaten whites of two eggs, until thoroughly mixed. Serve at once.

Hot Milk.—Hot milk is an excellent food for many classes of invalids. The milk should be fresh, and should be heated in a double boiler until the top is wrinkled over the entire surface.

Junket, or Milk Curd.—Heat a cup of fresh milk to 85°, add one teaspoonful of the essence of pepsin, and stir just enough to mix thoroughly. Let it stand until firmly curded, and serve.

Koumiss.—Dissolve one fourth of a two-cent cake of compressed yeast, and two teaspoonfuls of white sugar, in three tablespoonfuls of lukewarm water. Pour this into a quart bottle and add sufficient fresh, sweet milk to nearly fill. Shake well, and place in a room of the temperature of 70° to 80° F., and allow it to ferment about six hours. Cork tightly and tie the cork in. Put in a cool place, act above 60° and let it remain a week, when it will be ready for use. In making koumiss be sure that the milk is pure, the bottle sound, and the yeast fresh. Open the bottle with a champagne tap. If there is any curd or thickening resembling cheese, the fermentation has been prolonged beyond the proper point, and the koumiss should not be used.

Milk and Lime Water.—In cases where milk forms large curds, or sours in the stomach, lime water prepared in the following manner may be added to the milk before using:—

Into a gallon jar of water, put a piece of lime the size of one's fist. Cover the jar and let the lime settle over night. In the morning, draw the water off the top with a syphon, being careful not to move the jar so as to mix again the particles of lime with the water.

Two tablespoonfuls of the lime water is usually sufficient for a pint of milk.

Peptonized Milk for Infants.—One gill of cows' milk, fresh and unskimmed; one gill of pure water; two tablespoonfuls of rich, sweet cream; two hundred grains of milk sugar, one and one fourth grains of *extractum pancreatis*; four grains of sodium bicarbonate. Put the above in a clean nursing bottle, and place the bottle in water so warm that the whole hand cannot be held in it longer for one minute without pain. Keep the milk at this temperature for exactly twenty minutes. Prepare fresh just before using.

BEEF-TEA, BROTHS, ETC.

Beef tea and meat broths are by no means so useful as foods for the sick as is generally supposed. The late Dr. Austin Flint used to say of these foods, that "the valuation by most persons outside of the medical profession, and by many within it, of beef tea or its analogues, the various solutions, most of the extracts, and the expressed juice of meat, is a delusion and a snare which has led to the loss of many lives by starvation.

"The quantity of nutritive material in these preparations is insignificant or nil, and it is vastly important that they should be reckoned as of little or no value, except as indirectly conducive to nutrition by acting as stimulants for the secretion of the digestive fluids, or as vehicles for the introduction of the nutritive substances. Furthermore, it is to be considered that water and pressure not only fail to extract the alimentary principles of meat, but that the excrementitious principles, or the products of destructive assimilation, *are* thereby extracted."

Vegetable broths prepared from grains and legumes possess a much higher nutritive value, while they lack the objectionable features of meat broths.

RECIPES.

Beef Extract.—Take a pound of lean beef, cut it up into small dice, and put into a glass fruit jar. Screw on the cover tightly, put the jar into a vessel filled with cold water to a depth sufficient to come to the top of contents of the jar, and set over a slow fire. As soon as the water boils, set where it will keep just boiling, but no more; and cook for an hour or an hour and a quarter. Then strain, season, and serve. If preferred, a double boiler may be used for the preparation of the extract.

Beef Juice.—Cut a thick slice of round steak, trim off every particle of fat, and broil it over a clear fire just long enough to heat it throughout. Next gash it in many places with a sharp knife, and with the aid of a beef-juice press or lemon squeezer, press out all the juice into a bowl set in hot water, salt but very slightly, remove all globules of fat, and serve. This may also be frozen and given the patient in small lumps, if so ordered.

Beef Tea.—Take a pound of fresh, lean, juicy beef of good flavor,—the top of the round and the back and middle of the rump are the best portions for the purpose,—from which all fat, bones, and sinews have been carefully removed; cut into pieces a quarter of an inch square, or grind in a sausage-cutter. Add a quart of cold water, and put into a clean double boiler. Place over the fire, and heat very slowly, carefully removing all scum as it rises. Allow it to cook gently for two or three hours, or until the water has been reduced one half. Strain, and put away to cool. Before using, remove all fat from the surface, and season. In reheating, a good way is to place a quantity in a cup, and set the cup into hot water until the tea is sufficiently hot. This prevents waste, and if the patient is not ready for the tea, it can be easily kept hot.

Beef Tea and Eggs.—Beat the yolk of an egg thoroughly in a teacup and fill the cup with boiling beef tea, stirring all the while. Season with a little salt if desired.

Beef Broth and Oatmeal.—Rub two tablespoonfuls of oatmeal smooth in an equal quantity of cold water, and stir into a quart of boiling beef broth. Cook in a double broiler for two hours, strain, and season with salt and a little cream if allowed. Or, thin well-cooked oatmeal mush with beef-tea; strain, reheat, season, and serve.

Bottled Beef Tea.—Cut two pounds of round steak into small dice, rejecting all skin and fat. Put it into a glass fruit jar with one cup of cold water. Cover the can sufficiently tight to prevent any water from boiling in, and place it on a wisp of straw or a muffin ring in a kettle of cold water. Heat very gradually, and keep it just below the boiling point for two or more hours; or, place the can in a deep dish of hot water, and cook in a moderate oven for three hours. Allow the meat to cook thus four or five hours, or until it appears white, by which time it will have discharged all its juice. Turn the liquor off, strain through a piece of muslin or cheese cloth laid in a colander, and cool; then if any fat has been left, it will harden on the top, and can be removed. When needed for use, reheat, season, and serve.

Chicken Broth.—Take a well dressed, plump spring chicken, cut it into half-inch pieces, cracking well all the bones; add cold water,—a quart to the pound of meat and bones,—and cook the same as beef-tea. Allow the broth to cool before using, and carefully skim off all particles of fat before reheating. If allowed, a tablespoonful of steamed rice may be added to the broth, or a well-beaten egg may be stirred in while hot just before serving. Heat until the whole becomes thickened, but do not boil.

If preferred, the broth may be prepared by using only the white portion of the chicken in connection with lean beef. This is liked better by some to whom the strong flavor of the chicken is not pleasant. Or, prepare equal quantity of rich milk, season with salt, reheat, and serve. The broth may be flavored with celery if allowed.

Mutton Broth.—Cut a pound of perfectly fresh, lean mutton or lamb—the scrags of neck are best—into small dice. Add a quart of cold water, and simmer gently for two or three hours. Strain, and when cold skim off all fat. Reheat when needed for use.

If preferred, a tablespoonful of rice which has been soaked for an hour in a little warm water, or a tablespoonful of cooked barley, may be simmered in the broth for a half hour before serving. Season with salt as desired.

Vegetable Broth.—Put a cupful of well washed white beans into a quart of cold water in a double boiler, and cook slowly until but a cupful of the liquor remains. Strain off the broth, add salt, and serve hot. If preferred, a few grains of powdered thyme may be added as flavoring.

Vegetable Broth No. 2.—Pick over and wash a cup of dried Scotch peas, and put to cook in a quart of cold water, cook slowly in a double boiler or in a kettle placed on the range where they will just simmer, until but a cupful of liquid remains. Strain off the broth, add salt and one third of a cupful of the liquor, without pulp, from well-stewed tomatoes. Serve hot.

Mixed Vegetable Broths.—Broths may be prepared as directed from both black and white beaus, and combined in the proportion of one third of the former to two thirds of the latter; or a broth of lentils may be used instead of the black bean.

RECIPES FOR PANADA.

Broth Panada.—Use beef or chicken broth in place of water, and proceed the same as in Egg Panada, omitting the egg.

Chicken Panada.—Take a cupful of the white meat of chicken, pounded to a paste in a mortar, and half a cup of whole-wheat crust or zwieback crumbs. Add sufficient chicken broth to make a thick gruel. Season with salt, boil up for a few minutes, and serve hot.

Egg Panada.—Put two ounces of light, whole-wheat crusts into a pint of cold water in a granite-ware stewpan; simmer gently for three quarters of an hour, stirring occasionally. Season with a spoonful of sweet cream and a little salt, then stir in the well-beaten yolk of an egg, and serve.

Milk Panada.—Heat a pint of milk to boiling, then allow it to cool. Add two ounces of nice, light, whole-wheat crusts, and simmer for half an hour, stirring frequently. Season with a little sugar, if allowed. Granola may be used in place of the crusts, if preferred.

Raisin Panada.—Boil a half cup of raisins in a half pint of water. Break a slice of zwieback into fragments in a bowl. Add a well-beaten egg and a teaspoonful of sugar. Pour in the raisins, water and all, and beat very thoroughly.

GRAINS FOR THE SICK.

For invalids able to digest solid food, rice, cracked wheat, Graham grits, oatmeal, barley, farina and other grains may be prepared and cooked as previously directed in the chapter on Grains.

The various cooked preparations of grains—granola, wheatena, avenola, wheat gluten and gluten meal—manufactured by the Sanitarium Food Co., Battle Creek, Mich., form excellent articles of diet for many invalids, when served with hot milk or cream, or prepared in the form of mush. Several recipes for their use have already been given in preceding chapters; the following are a few additional ones:—

RECIPES.

Gluten Mush.—Heat together a cup of thin cream and three cups of water; when boiling, sift in lightly with the fingers, stirring continuously meanwhile, enough wheat gluten to make a mush of the desired consistency. Boil up once and serve. A few blanched or roasted almonds may be stirred in just before serving, if desired.

Tomato Gluten.—Heat a pint of stewed tomato, which has been rubbed through a fine colander to remove the seeds, to boiling, add salt to season, and three tablespoonfuls of gluten meal. Boil together for a moment until thickened, and serve hot.

Tomato Gluten No. 2.—Prepare the same as the preceding, using five tablespoonfuls of the gluten meal, and seasoning with two tablespoonfuls of rather thick, sweet cream.

MEATS FOR THE SICK.

All meats for the sick should be prepared in the very simplest way, served with the plainest possible dressing, and without the use of condiments other than salt.

RECIPES.

Broiled Steak.—Take a half pound of round steak and a slice of tenderloin; wipe well with a clean, wet cloth. Have a clear fire; place the meat in an open wire broiler or on a gridiron over the coals, and cook, turning as often as you can count ten, for four or five minutes, if the slices are about one inch thick; then with a lemon squeezer squeeze the juice from the round steak over the tenderloin, season with a little salt, and serve at once on a hot plate.

Chicken.—For an invalid, the breast of a tender chicken broiled quickly over hot coals is best. For directions for broiling chicken see page 406.

Chicken Jelly.—Dress a small chicken. Disjoint, break or pound the bones, and cut the meat into half-inch pieces. Remove every particle of fat possible. Cover with cold water, heat very slowly, and simmer gently until the meat is in rags, and the liquid reduced about one half. Strain off the liquor, cool, and remove all the fat. To make the broth more clear, add the shell and white of an egg, then reheat slowly, stirring all the time until hot. Strain through a fine cloth laid inside of a colander. Salt and a little lemon may be added as seasoning. Pour into small cups, and cool.

Minced Chicken.—Stew the breast of a young chicken until tender; mince fine with a sharp knife. Thicken the liquor in which it was stewed with a little flour, add salt and a little cream if allowed, then the minced chicken, and serve hot on zwieback, softened with cream as directed in the chapter on Breakfast Dishes.

Mutton Chop.—Select a chop containing a large tenderloin: cut thick, and broil for eight or ten minutes as directed for beef steak. Season lightly with salt, and serve hot.

Minced Steak.—Mince some nice, juicy steak with a chopping knife, or in a sausage-cutter, rejecting as much of the fiber as possible; make into small cakes and broil the same as steak. Salt lightly when done, and for dressing use a little beef juice prepared as directed on page 427. It may be thickened with a little flour as for gravy, if preferred.

Scraped Steak.—Take a small piece of nice, juicy steak, and with a blunt case-knife or tablespoon, scrape off all the pulp, being careful to get none of the fibers. Press the pulp together in the form of patties, and broil quickly over glowing coals. Salt lightly, and serve hot. It is better to be as rare as the patient can take it. Instead of butter, turn a spoonful or two of thick, hot beef juice over the steak, if any dressing other than salt is required.

EGGS FOR THE SICK.

RECIPES.

Floated Egg.—Separate the white from the yolk, and drop the yolk, taking great care not to break it, into boiling, salted water. Cook until hard and mealy. In the meantime, beat the white of the egg until stiff and firm. When the yolk is cooked, remove it from the water with a skimmer. Let the water cease to boil, then dip the beaten white in spoonfuls on the top of the scalding water, allowing it to remain for a second or two until coagulated, but not hardened. Arrange the white in a hot egg saucer, and place the cooked yolk in the center, or serve on toast. This makes a very pretty, as well as appetising dish, if care is taken to keep the yolk intact.

Gluten Meal Custard.—Beat together thoroughly, one pint of rich milk, one egg, and four tablespoonfuls of gluten meal. Add a little salt if desired, and cook with the dish set in another containing boiling water, until the custard has set. Or, turn the custard into cups, which place in a dripping pan partly filled with hot water, and cook in a moderate oven until the custard is set.

Gluten Custard.—Into a quart of boiling milk stir four tablespoonfuls of wheat gluten moistened with a little of the milk, which may be reserved for the purpose. Allow it to cook until thickened. Cool to lukewarm temperature, and add three well-beaten eggs, and a trifle of salt, if desired. Turn into cups, and steam over a kettle of boiling water until the custard is set.

Steamed Eggs.—Break an egg into an egg saucer, sauce-dish, or patty pan, salt very slightly, and steam until the white has just set. In this way, it will retain its shape perfectly, and not be mixed with the few drops of water so annoying to invalids, and so hard to avoid in dishing a poached egg from water.

Soft Custard.—Boil some milk, then cool it to 180°, add three whipped eggs to each quart of milk, and keep at the temperature of 180° for fifteen or twenty minutes. The object is to coagulate the eggs without producing the bad effect of exposure to a high temperature.

Raw Eggs.—Break a fresh egg into a glass, add a tablespoonful of sugar, and heat to a stiff froth; a little cold water may be added if liked.

White Of Egg.—Stir the white of an egg into a glass of cold water, or water as warm as it can be without coagulating the egg, and serve.

White of Egg and Milk.—The white of an egg beaten to a stiff froth and stirred into a glass of milk, forms a nourishing food for persons of weak digestion.

REFRESHING DRINKS AND DELICACIES FOR THE SICK.

In many fevers and acute diseases, but little food is required, and that of a character which merely appeases hunger and quenches thirst, without stimulation and without affording much nourishment.

Preparations from sago, tapioca, and other farinaceous substances are sometimes serviceable for this purpose. Oranges, grapes, and other perfectly ripened and juicy fruits are also most excellent. They are nature's own delicacies, and serve both for food and drink. They should not, however, be kept in the sick room, but preserved in some cool place, and served when needed, as fresh and in as dainty a manner as possible. Like all food provided for the sick, they should be arranged to please the eye as well as the palate. The capricious appetite of an invalid will often refuse luscious fruit from the hand of a nurse, which would have been gladly accepted had it been served on dainty china, with a clean napkin and silver.

The juice of the various small fruits and berries forms a basis from which may be made many refreshing drinks especially acceptable to the dry, parched mouth of a sick person.

Fruit juices can be prepared with but little trouble. For directions see page 209.

Beverages from fruit juices are prepared by using a small quantity of the juice, and sufficient cold water to dilute it to the taste. If it is desirable to use such a drink for a sick person in some household where fruit juices have not been put up for the purpose, the juice may be obtained from a can of strawberries, raspberries, or other small fruit, by turning the whole into a coarse cloth and straining off the juice; or a tablespoonful of currant or other jelly may be dissolved in a tumbler of warm water, and allowed to cool. Either will make a good substitute for the prepared fruit juice, though the flavor will be less delicate. The hot beverages and many of the cold ones given in the chapter on Beverages will be found serviceable for the sick, as will also the following additional ones:—

RECIPES.

Acorn Coffee.—Select plump, round, sweet acorns. Shell, and brown in an oven; then grind in a coffee-mill, and use as ordinary coffee.

Almond Milk—Blanch a quarter of a pound of shelled almonds by pouring over them a quart of boiling water, and when the skins soften, rubbing them off with a coarse towel. Pound the almonds in a mortar, a few at a time, adding four or five drops of milk occasionally, to prevent their oiling. About one tablespoonful of milk in all will be sufficient. When finely pounded, mix the almonds with a pint of milk, two tablespoonfuls of sugar, and a little piece of lemon rind. Place the whole over the fire to simmer for a little time. Strain, if preferred, and serve cold.

Apple Beverage.—Pare and slice very thin a juicy tart apple into a china bowl. Cover with boiling water, put a saucer over the bowl, and allow the water to get cold. Strain and drink. Crab apples may be used in the same way.

Apple Beverage No. 2.—Bake two large, sour apples, and when tender, sprinkle a tablespoonful of sugar over them, and return to the oven until the sugar is slightly browned. Break and mash the apples with a silver spoon, pour over them a pint of boiling water; cover and let stand until cold; then strain and serve.

Apple Toast Water.—Break a slice of zwieback into small pieces, and mix with them two or three well-baked tart apples. Pour over all a quart of boiling water, cover, and let stand until cold, stirring occasionally. When cold, strain, add sugar to sweeten if desired, and serve.

Baked Milk.—Put a quart of new milk in a stone jar, tie a white paper over it, and let it stand in a moderately heated oven eight or ten hours. It becomes of a creamy consistency.

Barley Lemonade.—Put a half cup of pearl barley into a quart of cold water, and simmer gently until the water has become mucilaginous and quite thick. This will take from an hour to an hour and a half. The barley will absorb most of the water, but the quantity given should make a teacupful of good, thick barley water. Add to this two teaspoonfuls of lemon juice and a tablespoonful of sugar. Let it get cold before serving. By returning the barley to the stewpan with another quart of cold water, and simmering for an hour or an hour and a half longer, a second cap of barley water may be obtained, almost as good as the first.

Barley and Fruit Drink.—Prepare a barley water as above, and add to each cupful a tablespoonful or two of cranberry, grape, raspberry, or any tart fruit syrup. The pure juice sweetened will answer just as well; or a little fruit jelly may be dissolved and added.

Barley Milk.—Wash two tablespoonfuls of pearl barley in cold water until the water is clear. Put it to cook in a double boiler, with a quart of milk, and boil till the milk is reduced to a pint. Strain off the milk, and sweeten if desired.

Cranberry Drink.—Mash carefully selected, ripe cranberries thoroughly in an earthen dish, and pour boiling water over them. Let the mixture stand until cold, strain off the water, and sweeten to taste. Barberries prepared in the same manner make a nice drink.

Currantade.—Mash thoroughly a pint of ripe, red currants, and one half the quantity of red raspberries; add sugar to sweeten and two quarts of cold water. Stir, strain, cool on ice, and serve.

Crust Coffee.—Brown slices of Graham bread in a slow oven until very ark in color. Break in pieces and roll fine with a rolling pin. A quantity of this material may be prepared at one time and stored in glass fruit cans for use. When needed, pour a cupful of actively boiling water over a dessertspoonful of the prepared crumbs, let it steep for a few moments, then strain and serve.

Egg Cream.—Beat the white of an egg to a stiff froth, add one tablespoonful of white sugar, then beat again. Next add the yolk, and beat; then a tablespoonful of milk, one of cold water, and one of any fruit juice desired.

Egg Cream No. 2.—Prepare as above, using two tablespoonfuls of water instead of one of water and one of milk, and a teaspoonful of lemon juice in place of other fruit juice.

Egg Cream No. 3.—Beat the yolk of a freshly laid egg with a tablespoonful of sugar until it is light and creamy; add to this, one half cup of hot milk and stir in lightly the stiffly beaten white of the egg. Serve at once.

Egg Lemonade.—Beat the white of an egg to a stiff froth, then mix with it the juice of a small lemon, and one tablespoonful of sugar. Add a half pint of cold water. Or, beat together with an egg beater a tablespoonful of lemon juice, a teaspoonful of sugar, the white of an egg and a cup of cold water, until thoroughly mingled, then serve at once.

Flaxseed Tea.—Take an ounce of whole flaxseed, half an ounce of crushed licorice root, an ounce of refined sugar, and four tablespoonfuls of lemon juice. Pour a quart of boiling water over them; keep near the fire for four hours, and then strain off the liquid. The flaxseed should not be crushed, as the mucilage is in the outer part of the kernel, and if braised, the boiling water will extract the oil of the seed, and render the decoction nauseous. Make fresh daily.

Gum Arabic Water.—Pour a pint of boiling water over an ounce of clean gum arabic. When dissolved, add the juice of one lemon and a teaspoonful of sugar, and strain.

Hot Water.—Put good, fresh water into a perfectly clean granite-ware kettle, already warmed; let it come to a boil very quickly, and use at once. Do not leave it to simmer until it has become insipid through the loss of the air which it contains.

Hot lemonade.—Put in a glass a thin slice of lemon and the juice of half a small lemon, being careful to remove all seeds; mix with it one dessertspoonful of white sugar, and fill the glass with boiling water. Or, remove the peel of a lemon in very thin parings, turn one pint of boiling water over them, letting it stand for a few moments covered. Remove the peel, add the juice of a lemon and one tablespoonful of sugar, and serve.

Irish Moss Lemonade.—Soak one fourth of a cup of Irish moss in cold water until it begins to soften; then work it free from sand and tiny shells likely to be on it, and thoroughly wash. Put it in a granite-ware basin, and pour over it two cups of boiling water. Leave on the back of the range where it will keep hot, but not boil, for half an hour; strain, add the juice of one lemon, and sugar to taste. Drink hot or cold, as preferred.

Orangeade.—Rub lightly two ounces of lump sugar on the rind of two nice, fresh oranges, to extract the flavor; put this sugar into a pitcher, to which add the juice expressed from the oranges, and that from one lemon. Pour over all one pint of cold water, stir thoroughly, and serve.

Plain Lemonade.—For one glass of lemonade squeeze the juice of half a small lemon into the glass; carefully remove all seeds and particles. Add a dessertspoonful of sugar, and fill the glass with cold water.

Slippery Elm Tea.—Pour boiling water over bits of slippery elm bark or slippery elm powder, cool, and strain, if desired, a little lemon juice and sugar may be added to flavor.

Toast Water.—Toast a pint of whole-wheat or Graham bread crusts very brown, but do not burn. Cover with a pint of cold water. Let it stand an hour, strain, and use. Sugar and a little cream may be added if allowed.

Tamarind Water.—Boil four ounces of tamarinds and the same of raisins slowly, in three quarts of water, for fifteen or twenty minutes, or until the water is reduced nearly one fourth; strain while hot into a bowl with a small slice of lemon peel in it. Set away until cold before using.

BREAD.

For invalids who are able to partake of solid foods, the Breakfast Rolls, Whole-wheat Puffs, Beaten Biscuit, Crisps, and other unfermented breads, directions for the preparation of which are given in the chapter on Bread, will be found excellent.

The various crackers, wafers, and invalid foods manufactured by the Sanitarium Food Co., Battle Creek, Mich., are also to be recommended. Zwieback, prepared as directed on page 289, will be found serviceable and wholesome to be used with broths and gruels. It may be prepared so as to look especially tempting by cutting off the crust of the bread, and cutting the slice into fancy shapes with a cookie-cutter before toasting. In cases where their use is allowable, many of the various toasts given under the head of Breakfast Dishes will be relished.

RECIPES.

Diabetic Biscuit.—Make a stiff dough of Graham or entire-wheat flour and water. Knead thoroughly, and let it stand three hours; then place on a sieve under a faucet, turn a stream of water over the dough, and wash out the starch, kneading and working with the hands so that all portions of the dough will be equally washed. When the starch has been all washed out, as will be indicated by the water running off clear, the dough will be a rubber-like, glutinous mass. It may then be cut into long strips, and these divided into equal-sized pieces or cubes. Place the pieces on shallow baking pans in a rather hot oven, which, after a short time, should be allowed to cool to moderate heat, and bake for two hours, when they should be of a dark, rich brown color and light and crisp throughout. If tough, they need rebaking. If the oven is too hot, the pieces will puff up, becoming mere hollow shells; if not sufficiently hot, they will not rise properly.

Diabetic Biscuit No. 2.—Prepare a dough and wash out the starch as in the preceding. Add coarse middlings so that the dough can be rolled into thin cakes, and bake.

Gluten Meal Gems.—Beat together one half cup of ice water, one half cup of thick, sweet cream, and one egg; then add one cup and a tablespoonful of the gluten meal prepared by the Sanitarium Food Co. Turn into slightly heated gem irons, and bake in a moderately hot oven from one half to three fourths of an hour.

JELLIES AND OTHER SIMPLE DESSERTS FOR THE SICK.

Invalids whose digestion will allow of other than the plainest foods will find most of the desserts made with fruits and those with fruits and grains given in the chapter on Desserts, excellent for their use. The following are a few additional recipes of a similar character:—

RECIPES.

Arrowroot Jelly.—Rub two heaping teaspoonfuls of arrowroot smooth in a very little cold water, and stir it into a cupful of boiling water, in which should be dissolved two teaspoonfuls of sugar. Stir until clear, allowing it to boil all the time; lastly, add a teaspoonful of lemon juice. Serve cold, with cream and sugar if allowed.

Arrowroot Blancmange.—Rub two and a half tablespoonfuls of best arrowroot smooth in half a cup of cold milk, and stir slowly into two and one half cups of boiling new milk. When it begins to thicken, add three fourths of a cup of sugar, and cook, stirring constantly for several minutes. Turn into molds and cool. Serve with fruit juice or fruit sauces.

Currant Jelly.—Soak an ounce of Cox's gelatine in half a pint of cold water for fifteen minutes, then pour over it a teacupful of boiling water; strain, and add one pint at currant juice, one tablespoonful of sugar, and set on ice to cool.

Iceland Moss Jelly.—Wash about four ounces of moss very clean in lukewarm water. Boil slowly in a quart of cold water. When quite dissolved, strain it onto a tablespoonful of currant or raspberry jelly, stirring so as to blend the jelly perfectly with the moss. Turn into a mold, and cool.

Iceland Moss Blancmange.—Substitute milk for the water, and proceed as in the foregoing. Flavor with lemon or vanilla. Strain through a muslin cloth, turn into a mold, and let stand till firm and cold.

Orange Whey.—Add the juice of one sour orange to a pint of sweet milk. Heat very slowly until the milk is curded, then strain and cool.

White Custard.—Beat the whites of three eggs to a stiff froth, add a little salt if desired, and two tablespoonfuls of sugar. A bit of grated lemon rind may also be used for flavoring. Add lastly a pint of new milk, little by little, beating thoroughly all the while. Bake in cups set in a pan of hot water. When firm in the center, take out and set in a cool place.

TABLE TOPICS.

Regimen is better than physic.—*Voltaire.*

Many dishes have induced many diseases.—*Seneca.*

Dr. Lyman Beecher tells the following story of his aunt, which well illustrates a popular notion that sick people should be fed with all sorts of dainties, no matter what the nature of the disease. When a boy eight or nine years of age, he was one day suffering in the throes of indigestion, as the result of having swallowed a large amount of indigestible mince pie. His kind-hearted aunt noticed the pale and distressed look on his face, and said to him, with genuine sympathy in her voice, "Lyman, you look sick. You may go into the pantry and help yourself to a nice piece of fruit cake just warm from the oven."

Fix on that course of life which is the most excellent, and custom will render it the most delightful.—*Pythagoras.*

A MERE indigestion can temporarily metamorphose the character. The eel stews of Mohammed II. kept the whole empire in a state of nervous excitement, and one of the meat-pies which King

Philip failed to digest caused the revolt of the Netherlands.—*Oswald.*

Few seem conscious that there is such a thing as physical morality. Man's habitual words and acts imply that they are at liberty to treat their bodies as they please. The fact is, that all breaches of the laws of health are physical sins.—*Herbert Spencer.*

Practical right and good conduct are much more dependent on health of body than on health of mind.—*Prof. Schneider.*

Dr. Abernathy's reply to the Duke of York when consulted about his health was, "Cut off the supplies and the enemy will soon leave the citadel."

FOOD FOR THE AGED AND THE VERY YOUNG.

FOOD FOR THE AGED

One of the first requisites of food for the aged is that it shall be easy of digestion, since with advancing age and decreasing physical energy, digestion and assimilation may be taken with impunity at an earlier period of life, overtax the enfeebled organs and prove highly injurious. The fact that the vital machinery is worn and weakened with age has led to the popular notion that old people require a stimulating diet as a "support" for their declining forces. That this is an error is apparent from the fact that stimulation either by drink or food lessens instead of reinforces vital strength, thus defeating the very purpose desired. Flesh food in quantities is a peculiarly unsuitable diet for the aged, not alone because it is stimulating, but because it produces a tendency to plethora, a condition which is especially inimical to the health of old persons. Eminent authorities on diet also reason that the loss of the teeth at this period, whereby thorough mastication of flesh food is done with difficulty, even with the best artificial aids, should be considered a sign that nature intends such foods to be discarded by the old.

A milk, grain, and fruit diet is undoubtedly the one best suited to the average person in old age. Vegetables and legumes in well-prepared soups may also be used to advantage. Directions for such soups, as also for cooking grains and grain products, will be found in the preceding pages.

The following bills of fare, one for each season of the year, will perhaps serve to illustrate how a varied and appetizing regimen may be provided without the use of flesh foods:—

BREAKFAST	BREAKFAST
Fresh Fruits Graham Grits and Cream Prune Toast Graham Puffs Cream Crisps	Fresh Fruits Rolled Oats and Cream Baked Sweet Apples Macaroni with Cream Sauce Whole-Wheat Puffs Stewed Peaches

Strawberries Caramel Coffee or Hot Milk DINNER Vegetable Broth with Toasted Rolls Baked Potato with Pease Gravy Stewed Asparagus Cracked Wheat and Cream Whole-Wheat Bread Canned Berries Manioca with Fruit Caramel Coffee or Hot Milk	Caramel Coffee or Hot Milk DINNER Lentil Soup Baked Potato with Cream Sauce Escalloped Tomato Green Corn Pulp Browned Rice and Cream Fruit Bread Lemon Apple Sauce Prune Pie Caramel Coffee or Hot Milk
BREAKFAST Fresh Fruits Blackberry Mush and Cream Cream Toast Graham Crusts Blueberries Caramel Coffee or Hot Milk DINNER Green Pea Soup Mashed Potato Macaroni with Tomato Sauce Pearl Barley and Cream Cream Rolls Blackberries Stewed Fruit Pudding Caramel Coffee or Hot Milk	BREAKFAST Fresh Fruits Rolled Wheat and Cream Tomato Toast Corn Bread Graham Gems Stewed Prunes Caramel Coffee or Hot Milk DINNER Vegetable Oyster Soup Baked Sweet Potato Mashed Peas Steamed Rice with Fig Sauce Graham Bread Stewed Dried Fruit Apples Caramel Coffee or Hot Milk

In the selection of a dietary for elderly persons, much must depend upon their physical condition, the daily amount of exercise to which they are accustomed, their habits in earlier life, and a variety of other circumstances.

The quantity as well as quality of food for the aged should receive consideration. Diminished bodily activity and the fact that growth has ceased, render a smaller amount of food necessary to supply needs; and a decrease in the amount taken, in proportion to the age and the activity of the subject, must be made or health will suffer. The system will become clogged, the blood filled with imperfectly elaborated material, and gout, rheumatism, apoplexy, or other diseased conditions will be the inevitable result. The digestion of heavy meals is a tax upon vital powers at any time of life, but particularly so as age advances; and for him who has passed his first half-century, over-feeding is fraught with great danger. Cornaro, an Italian of noble family, contemporary with Titian in the sixteenth century, after reaching his eighty-third year wrote several essays upon diet and regimen for the aged, in one of which he says: "Thereare old lovers of feeding who say that it is necessary that they should eat and drink a great deal to keep up their natural heat, which is constantly diminishing as they advance in years; and that it is therefore their duty to eat heartily and of such things as please their palate, be they hot, cold, or temperate, and that if they were to lead a sober life, it would be a short one. To this I answer; Our kind Mother Nature, in order that old men may live to still greater age, has contrived matters so that they may be able to subsist on little, as I do; for large quantities of food cannot be digested by old and feeble stomachs."

Cornaro lived to be one hundred years old, doubtless owing largely to his simple, frugal habits.

DIET FOR THE YOUNG.

A very large share of the mortality among young children results from dietetic errors which proper knowledge and care on the part of those who have them in charge might commonly avoid. From infancy to the age of twelve or eighteen months, milk is the natural and proper food. Milk contains all the food elements except starch, which cannot be digested by very young children, owing to the insufficient formation of digestive elements of the salivary secretion during the first few months. If the child is deprived of the milk provided by nature, the best artificial food is cow's milk; it, however, requires very careful selection and intelligent preparation. The animal from which the milk comes, should be perfectly healthy and well cared for. The quality of her food should also receive attention, as there is little doubt that disease is often communicated to infants by milk from cows improperly fed and cared for. An eminent medical authority offers the following important points on this subject:—

"The cow selected for providing the food for an infant should be between the ages of four and ten years, of mild disposition, and one which has been giving milk from four to eight weeks. She should be fed on good, clean grain, and hay free from must. Roots, if any are fed, should be of good quality, and she should have plenty of good clean water from a living spring or well. Her pasture should be timothy grass or native grass free from weeds; clover alone is bad. She should be cleaned and cared for like a carriage horse, and milked twice a day by the same person and at the same time. Some cows are unfit by nature for feeding infants."

Milk from the same animal should be used if possible. Changing from one cow's milk to another, or the use of such milk as is usually supplied by city milkmen, often occasions serious results. The extraction of the heat from the milk immediately after milking and before it is used or carried far, especially in hot weather, is essential. While the milk itself should be clean and pure, it should also be perfectly fresh and without any trace of decomposition. To insure all these requisites, besides great care in its selection, it must be sterilized, and if not intended for immediate use, bottled and kept in a cool place until needed. It is not safe to feed young children upon unsterilized milk that has stood a few hours. Even fresh milk from the cleanest cows, unless drawn into bottles and sealed at once, contains many germs. These little organisms, the cause of fermentation and decomposition, multiply very rapidly in milk, and as they increase, dangers from the use of the milk increase.

There is no doubt that cholera infantum and other digestive disturbances common among young children would be greatly lessened by the use of properly sterilized milk. Directions for sterilizing milk, and additional suggestions respecting points to be considered in its selection, are to be found in the chapter on Milk, etc.

Cow's milk differs from human milk in that it contains nearly three times as much casein, but only two thirds as much fat and three fourths as much sugar. Cow's milk is usually slightly acid, while human milk is alkaline. The casein of cow's milk forms large, hard curds, while that of breast milk forms fine, soft curds. These facts make it important that some modification be made in cow's milk to render it acceptable to the feeble stomach of an infant. Cases are rare where it is safe to feed a child under nine months of age on pure, undiluted cow's milk. A common method of preparing cow's milk so as to make it suitable for infant feeding, is to dilute it with pure water, using at first only one third or one fourth milk, the proportion of milk being gradually increased as the child's stomach becomes accustomed to the food and able to bear it, until at the age of four months the child should be taking equal parts of milk and water. When sterilized milk is to be thus diluted, the water should be first boiled or added before sterilizing. A small amount of fine white sugar, or what is better, milk sugar, should be added to the diluted milk. Barley water, and thin, well-boiled, and carefully strained oatmeal gruel thoroughly blended with the milk are also used for this purpose. A food which approximates more nearly the constituents of mother's milk may be prepared as follows:—

Artificial Human Milk No. 1.—Blend one fourth pint of fresh, sweet cream and three fourths of a pint of warm water. Add one half ounce of milk sugar and from two to ten ounces of milk, according to the age of the infant and its digestive capacity.

Artificial Human Milk No. 2.—Meigs's formula: Take two tablespoonfuls of cream of medium quality, one tablespoonful of milk, two of lime water, and three of water to which sugar of milk has been added in the proportion of seventeen and three fourths drams to the pint. This saccharine solution must be prepared fresh every day or two and kept in a cool place. A child may be allowed from half a pint to three pints of this mixture, according to age.

Artificial Human Milk No. 3.—Prepare a barley water by adding one pint boiling water to a pint of best pearl barley. Allow it to cool, and strain. Mix together one third of a pint of this barley water, two thirds of a pint of fresh, pure milk, and a teaspoonful of milk sugar.—*Medical News.*

Peptonized milk, a formula for the preparation of which may be found onpage 426, is also valuable as food for infants, especially for those of weak digestion.

Mucilaginous Food Excellent in Gastro-enteritis.—Wheat, one tablespoonful; oatmeal, one half tablespoonful; barley, one half tablespoonful; water, one quart. Boil to one pint, strain, and sweeten.—*Dietetic Gazette.*

Prepared Foods for Infants.—Of prepared infant foods we can recommend that manufactured by the Sanitarium Food Co., Battle Creek, Mich., as thoroughly reliable. There are hundreds of prepared infant foods in the market, but most of them are practically worthless in point of food value, being often largely composed of starch, a substance which the immature digestive organs of a young child are incapable of digesting. Hundreds of infants are yearly starved to death upon such foods.

All artificial foods require longer time for digestion than the food supplied by nature; and when making use of such, great care should be taken to avoid too frequent feeding. It is absolutely essential for the perfect health of an infant as well as of grown people, that the digestive organs shall enjoy a due interval of rest between the digestion of one meal and the taking of another. As a rule, a new-born infant may be safely fed, when using human milk, not oftener than once in every three or four hours. When fed upon artificial food, once in five or six hours is often enough for feeding. The intervals between meals in either case should be gradually prolonged as the child grows older.

Quantity of Food for Infants.—Dr. J.H. Kellogg gives the following rules and suggestions for the feeding of infants:—

"During the first week of a child's life, the weight of the food given should be 1/100 of the weight of the infant at birth. The daily additional amount of food required for a child amounts to about one fourth of a dram, or about one ounce at the end of each month. A child gains in weight from two thirds of an ounce to one ounce per day during the first five months of its life, and an average of one half as much daily during the balance of the first year.

"From a series of tables which have been prepared, as the result of experiments carefully conducted in large lying-in establishments, we have devised this rule:—

"To find the amount of food required by a child at each feeding during the first year of life, divide the weight of the child at birth by 100 and add to this amount 3/100 of the gain which the child has made since birth. Take, for example, a child which weighs 7-1/2 lbs—at birth, or 120 ounces. Dividing by 100 we have 1.2 oz. Estimating the weight according to the rule above given, the child at the end of nine months will have gained 210 oz. Dividing this by 100 and multiplying by 3, we have 6.3 oz. Adding to this our previous result, 1.3, we have 7.5 oz, as the amount of food required at each feeding at the end of nine months by a child which weighed 7-1/2 lbs. at birth. To save mothers the trouble of making these calculations, we have prepared the following table, which will be found to hold good for the average child weighing 7-1/2 lbs. at birth. This is rather more than the ordinary child weighs, but we have purposely chosen a large child for illustration, as it is better that the child should have a slight excess of food than too little.

AGE OF CHILD.

	1 week	1 month	2 months	3 months	4 months	6 months	9 months	12 months
Amount of each feeding in ounces	1	1½-2	3	4	5	6	7½	9
Number of feedings	10	8	6	6	6	6	5	5
Amount of food daily, in ounces	10	12-16	18	24	30	36	37½	45
Interval between feedings, in hours	2	2½	3	3	3	3	3½	3½

"In the above table the first column represents quantities for the first week, the second for the end of the second month, the third for the end of the third month, etc. It need not be mentioned that the change in quantity should be even more gradual than represented in the table.

"Attention should also be called to the fact that the time mentioned as the interval for feeding at different ages, does not apply to the whole twenty-four hours. Even during the first week, the child is expected to skip two feedings during the night, making the interval four hours instead of two. By the end of the second month, the interval between the feedings at night becomes six hours, and at the end of the ninth month, six and one half hours.

"From personal observation we judge that in many cases children will do equally well if allowed a longer interval between feedings at night. The plan of feeding five times daily instead of six, may be begun at as early an age as six months in many instances."

Manner of Feeding Artificial Foods.—All artificial foods are best fed with a teaspoon, as by this method liability to over-feeding and danger from unclean utensils are likely to be avoided. If a nursing-bottle is used, it should be of clear flint glass so that the slightest foulness may be easily detected, and one simple in construction, which can be completely taken apart for cleaning. Those furnished with conical black rubber caps are the best. Each time after using, such a bottle should have the cap removed, and both bottle and cap should be thoroughly cleansed, first with cold water, and then with warm water in which soda has been dissolved in the proportion of a teaspoonful to a pint of water. They should then be kept immersed in weak soda solution until again needed, when both bottle and cap should be thoroughly rinsed in clean boiled water before they are used. Neglect to observe these precautions is one of the frequent causes of stomach disturbances in young children. It is well to keep two bottles for feeding, using them alternately.

Diet for Older Children.—No solid food or table-feeding of any kind should be given to a child until it has the larger share of its first, or milk teeth. Even then it must not be supposed that because a child has acquired its teeth, it may partake of all kinds of food with impunity. It is quite customary for mothers to permit their little ones to sit at the family table and be treated to bits of everything upon the bill of fare, apparently looking upon them as miniature grown people, with digestive ability equal to persons of mature growth, but simply lacking in, stomach capacity to dispose of as much as older members of the family. The digestive apparatus of a child differs so greatly from that of an adult in its anatomical structure and in the character and amount of the digestive fluids, that it is by no means proper to allow a child to eat all kinds of wholesome foods which a healthy adult stomach can consume with impunity, to say nothing of the rich, highly seasoned viands, sweetmeats, and epicurean dishes which seldom fail to form some part of the bill of fare. It is true that many children are endowed with so much constitutional vigor that they do live and seemingly thrive, notwithstanding dietetic errors; but the integrity of the digestive organs is liable to be so greatly impaired by continued ill-treatment that sooner or later in life disease results. Till the age of three years, sterilized milk, whole-wheat bread in its various forms, such of the grains as contain a large share of gluten, prepared in a variety of palatable ways, milk and fruit toasts, and the easily digested fruits, both raw and cooked, form the best dietary. Strained vegetable soups may be occasionally added for variety. For from three to six years the same simple regimen, with easily digested and simply prepared vegetables, macaroni, and legumes prepared without skins, will be all-sufficient. If desserts are desirable, let them be simple in character and easily digestible. Tea, coffee, hot bread and biscuit, fried foods of all kinds, salted meats, preserves, rich puddings, cake, and pastries should be wholly discarded from the children's bill of fare.

It is especially important that a dietary for children should contain an abundance of nitrogenous material. It is needed not only for repairs, but must be on deposit for the purpose of food. Milk, whole-wheat bread, oatmeal, barley, and preparations of wheat, contain this element in abundance, and should for this reason be given great prominence in the children's dietary.

Flesh foods are in no way necessary for children, since the food elements of which they are composed can be supplied from other and better sources, and many prominent medical authorities unite in the opinion that such foods are decidedly deleterious, and should not be used at all by children under eight or ten years of age. Experiments made by Dr. Camman, of New York, upon the dietary of nearly two hundred young children in an orphan's home, offer conclusive evidence that the death rate among children from gastro-intestinal troubles is greatly lessened by the exclusion of meat from their dietary. Dr. Clouston, of Edinburgh, an eminent medical authority, states that in his experience, those children who show the greatest tendencies to instability of the brain, insanity, and immoral habits are, as a rule, those who use animal food in excess; and that he has seen a change of diet to milk and farinaceous food produce a marked change in their nervous irritability.

Scores of other authorities corroborate. Dr. Clouston's observation, and assert that children fed largely on flesh foods have capricious appetites, suffer more commonly from indigestion in its various forms, possess an unstable nervous system, and have less resisting power in general.

Candy and similar sweets generally given to children as a matter of course, may be excluded from their dietary with positive benefit in every way. It is true, as is often stated in favor of the use of these articles, that sugar is a food element needed by children; but the amount required for the purpose of growth and repair is comparatively small, and is supplied in great abundance in bread, grains, fruits, and other common articles of food. If an additional quantity is taken, it is not utilized by the system, and serves only to derange digestion, impair appetite, and indirectly undermine the health.

Children are not likely to crave candy and other sweets unless a taste for such articles has been developed by indulgence in them; and their use, since they are seldom taken at mealtime, helps greatly to foster that most pernicious habit of childhood—eating between meals. No food, except at their regular mealtimes, should be the universal rule for children from babyhood up; and although during their earliest years they require food at somewhat shorter intervals than adults, their meal hours should be arranged for the same time each day, and no piecing permitted. Parents who follow the too common practice of giving their little ones a cracker or fruit between meals are simply placing them under training for dyspepsia, sooner or later. Uninterrupted digestion proceeds smoothly and harmoniously in a healthy stomach; but interruptions in the shape of food sent down at all times and when the stomach is already at work, are justly resented, and such disturbances, if long continued, are punished by suffering.

The appetite of a child is quite as susceptible of education, in both a right and wrong direction, as are its mental or moral faculties; and parents in whose hands this education mainly rests should give the subject careful consideration, since upon it the future health and usefulness of their children not a little devolve. We should all be rulers of our appetites instead of subject to them; but whether this be so or not, depends greatly upon early dietetic training. Many a loving mother, by thoughtless indulgence of her child, in season and out of season, in dainties and tidbits that simply serve to gratify the palate, is fostering a "love of appetite" which may ruin her child in years to come. There are inherited appetites and tendencies, it is true; but even these may be largely overcome by careful early training in right ways of eating and drinking. It is possible to teach very young children to use such food as is best for them, and to refrain from the eating of things harmful; and it should be one of the first concerns of every mother to start her children on the road to manhood and womanhood, well trained in correct dietetic habits.

TABLE TOPICS.

"The wanton taste no flesh nor fowl can choose,
For which the grape or melon it would lose,
Though all th' inhabitants of earth and air
Be listed in the glutton's bill of fare."—*Cowley.*

Jean Jacques Rousseau holds that intemperate habits are mostly acquired in early boyhood, when blind deference to social precedents is apt to overcome our natural antipathies, and that those who have passed that period in safety, have generally escaped the danger of temptation. The same holds good of other dietetic abuses. If a child's natural aversion to vice has never been wilfully perverted, the time will come when his welfare may be intrusted to the safe-keeping of his protective instincts. You need not fear that he will swerve from the path of health when his simple habits, sanctioned by nature and inclination, have acquired the additional strength of long practice. When the age of blind deference is past, vice is generally too unattractive to be very dangerous.—*Oswald.*

That a child inherits certain likes and dislikes in the matter of food cannot be questioned, and does not in the least forbid the training of the child's taste toward that which is healthful and upbuilding; it merely adds an element to be considered in the training.—*Sel.*

Prevention is better than cure. It is worth a life effort to lift a man from degradation. To prevent his fall is better.—*Gough.*

A cynical French writer of the last century intending a satire upon the principles of vegetarianism adopted by Phillippe Hecquet, puts into the mouth of one of the characters in his book what, in the grossly voluptuous life of that country and time, the author no doubt imagined to be the greatest absurdities conceivable in reference to diet, but which, in the light of present civilization are but the merest hygienic truths. A doctor had been called to a gouty and fever-stricken patient. "Pray what is your ordinary diet?" asked the physician.

"My usual food," replied the patient, "is broth and juicy meat."

"Broth and juicy meat!" cried the doctor, alarmed. "I do not wonder to find you sick; such dishes are poisoned pleasures and snares that luxury spreads for mankind, so as to ruin them the more effectually.... How old are you, pray?"

"I am in my sixty-ninth year," replied the patient.

"Exactly," ... said the physician; "if you had drunk nothing else than pure water all your life, and had been satisfied with simple nourishment,—such as boiled apples for example,—you would not now be tormented with the gout, and all your limbs would perform their functions with ease."

Dr. Horace Bushnell says: "The child is taken when his training begins in a state of naturalness as respects all the bodily tastes and tempers, and the endeavour should be to keep him in that key, to let no stimulation of excess or delicacy disturb the simplicity of nature, and no sensual pleasure in the name of food become a want or expectation of his appetite. Any artificial appetite begun is the beginning of distemper, disease, and a general disturbance of natural proportion. Nine tenths of the intemperate drinking begins, not in grief and destitution, as we so often hear, but in vicious feeding."

Always let the food be simply for nourishment—never more, never less. Never should food be taken for its own sake, but for the sake of promoting bodily and mental activity. Still less should the peculiarities of food, its taste or delicacy ever become an object in themselves, but only a means to make it good, pure, wholesome nourishment; else in both cases the food destroys health.—*Froebel.*

Since what need mortals, save twain things alone,
Crushed grain (heaven's gift), and steaming water-draught?
Food nigh at hand, and Nature's aliment—
Of which no glut contents us.
Pampered taste hunts out device of other eatables.—*Euripides.*

FRAGMENTS & LEFT-OVER FOODS

Economy, one of the cardinal principles of success in the details of housekeeping, as in all other occupations in life, consists not alone in making advantageous use of fresh material, but in carefully preserving and utilizing the "left-over" fragments and bits of food which accrue in every household. Few cooks can make such perfect calculation respecting the desires and needs of their families as to provide just enough and no more, and the improvident waste of the surplus thus prepared, is in many homes fully equal to one half the first cost of the meal. Scarcely anything need ever be wasted—certainly nothing which was at first well cooked. There are ways of utilizing almost every kind of cooked food so that it will be quite as appetizing and nutritious as when first prepared.

All left-over foods, as grains, vegetables, or others of a moist character, should be removed to clean dishes before putting away. Unless this precaution is observed, the thin smears and tiny bits about the edges of the dish, which become sour or moldy much sooner than the larger mass, are apt to spoil the whole. They should also be set on ice or be kept in a cool, dry place until needed. Left-over foods of any kind, to be suitable again for use, must be well preserved. Sour or moldy fragments are not fit for food.

Uses of Stale Bread.—If properly made from wholesome and nutritious material and well preserved, there are few other foods that can be combined into more varied and palatable dishes than left-over bread. To insure the perfect preservation of the fragments, the loaf itself should receive good care. Perfectly sweet, light, well-baked bread has not the same propensity to mold as a poorer loaf; but the best of bread is likely to become musty if its surroundings are not entirely wholesome. The receptacle used for keeping the loaves should be frequently washed, scalded, and well dried. Crumbs and fragments should be kept in a separate receptacle and as thoroughly cared for. It is well in cutting bread not to slice more than will be needed, and to use one loaf before beginning on another. Bread grows stale much faster after being cut.

Whole or half slices of bread which have become too dry to be palatable may be utilized for making zwieback, directions for the use and preparation of which are given on page 289.

Broken pieces of bread not suitable for zwieback, crusts, and trimmings of the loaf make excellent *croutons*, a most palatable accompaniment for soups, gruels, hot milk, etc. To prepare the *croutons* cut the fragments as nearly uniform in size as possible,—half-inch cubes are convenient,—and place them on tins in a warming oven to dry. Let them become crisply dry, and lightly browned, but not scorched. They are preferable to crackers for use in soups, and require so little work to prepare, and are so economical withal, that one who has once tried them will be likely to keep a supply on hand. The crumbs and still smaller fragments may be utilized for thickening soups and for various dressings and puddings, recipes for many of which are given in preceding chapters.

If crumbs and small bits of bread accumulate more rapidly than they can be used, they may be carefully dried, not browned, in a warming oven, after which put them in a mortar and pound them, or spread them upon an old bread board, fold in a clean cloth and roll them with a rolling pin until fine. Prepared thus, stored in glass fruit cans and put away in a dry place, they will keep almost indefinitely, and can be used when needed. For preparing escalloped vegetables of all kinds, these prepared crumbs are excellent; they give a fine, nutty flavor to the dish, which fresh crumbs do not possess.

Left-over Grains.—Left-over grains, if well kept, may be reheated in a double boiler without the addition of water, so as to be quite as palatable as when freshly cooked. Small quantities of left-over grains can be utilized for preparing various kinds of desserts, where the ingredients require previous cooking. Rice, barley, pearl wheat, and other whole grains can be satisfactorily used in soups in which a whole grain is required; oatmeal, rolled oats, corn meal, grits, etc., with the addition of a little milk and cream, may be made into delicious gruels; they may also be used advantageously in the preparation of vegetable soups, many of which are even improved by the addition of a few spoonfuls of well-kept cooked oatmeal or rolled oats. The left-over grains may also be utilized in a variety of breads, directions for the preparation of which are given in the chapter on Bread.

Left-over Vegetables.—Left-over portions of most varieties of vegetables can be best utilized for soups as stated on page 275. Cold mashed potato may be made into potato cakes as directed on page 237 of the chapter on Vegetables, where will also be found many other recipes, suited to the use of these left-over foods.

Left-over Meats.—Most cook books offer numerous recipes for croquettes, hashes, and fried dishes prepared from remnants of meat and fish, which, although they serve the purpose of using up the fragments, are not truly economical, because they are generally far from wholesome. Most fragments of this character are more digestible served cold as a relish, or utilized for soups and stews, than compounded into fancy dishes requiring to be fried and highly seasoned or served with rich sauces.

Left-over Milk.—Small quantities of unsterilized milk or cream left over should always be carefully scalded, then cooled at once to a temperature of 60,° and put in a cool place, in order to keep it sweet and fresh until the next meal.

TABLE TOPICS.

"Care preserves what Industry gains. He who attends to his business diligently, but *not* carefully, throws away with one hand what he gathers with the other."—*Colton.*

"What does cookery mean?"

It means the knowledge of all fruits and herbs and balms and spices—it means carefulness, and inventiveness, and watchfulness, and willingness, and readiness of appliance. It means the economy of your great grandmothers and the science of modern chemists,—it means much tasting and no wasting.—*Ruskin.*

A penny saved is two pence clear
A pin a day's a groat a year.—*Franklin.*

Bad cooking is waste—waste of money and loss of comfort. Whom God has joined in matrimony, ill-cooked joints and ill-boiled potatoes have very often put asunder.—*Smiles.*

Never sacrifice the more precious things—time, health, temper, strength—in attempting to save the less precious—money.—*Sel.*

Learn by how little life may be sustained and how much nature requires. The gifts of Cerea and water are sufficient nourishment for all peoples.—*Pharsalia.*

THE ART OF DINING

Human nature is so susceptible to externals, while good digestion is so dependent upon interior conditions, that all the accessories of pleasant surroundings—neatness, cheeriness, and good breeding—should be brought into requisition for the daily gathering of the family at mealtime. The dining room should be one of the airiest, choicest rooms in the house, with a pleasant outlook, and, if possible, with east windows, that the morning sun may gladden the breakfast hour with its cheering rays. Let plants, flowers, birds, and pictures have a place in its appointments, that the association with things bright and beautiful may help to set the keynote of our own lives in cheerful accord. A dark, gloomy, ill-ventilated room brings depression of spirits, and will make the most elaborate meal unsatisfactory; while the plainest meal may seem almost a feast when served amid attractive surroundings. Neatness is an important essential; any home, however humble, may possess cleanliness and order, and without these, all charms of wealth and art are of little account.

A thorough airing each morning and opening of the windows a few minutes after each meal to remove the odor of food, are important items in the care of the dining room. The furnishing may be simple and inexpensive,—beauty in a home is not dependent upon expense,—but let it be substantial, tasteful, harmonious in color and soft in tone, nothing gaudy or showy. Use no heavy draperies, and have no excess of ornament and bric-a-brac to catch dust and germs. A hard-finished wood floor is far superior to a carpet in point of healthfulness, and quite as economical and easy to keep clean. The general furnishing of the room, besides the dining table and chairs, should include a sideboard, upon which may be arranged the plate and glassware, with drawers for cutlery and table linen; also a side-table for extra dishes needed during the service of a meal.

An open fireplace, when it can be afforded, aids in ventilation as well as increases the cheerful aspect of the room.

A moveable china closet with glass encasements for keeping the daintier china, glass, or silver ware not in common use is often a desirable article of furniture in small homes; or a shallow closet may be built in the wall of the dining-room for this purpose. A good size for such a closet is twelve inches deep and three feet wide. Four shelves, with one or more drawers below, in which may be kept the best table napery, afford ample space in general. The appearance of the whole may be made very pleasing by using doors of glass, and filling in the back and sides of the shelves with velvet paper in dark-brown, dull-red, or any shade suitable for background, harmonizing with the general furnishing of the room. The shelves should be of the same material and have the same finish as the woodwork of the room. The upper side may be covered with felt if desired; and such artistic taste may be displayed in the arrangement of the china as to make the closet ornamental as well as convenient.

Table-Talk.—A sullen, silent meal is a direct promoter of dyspepsia. "Laugh and grow fat" is an ancient adage embodying good hygienic doctrine. It has long been well understood that food digests better when seasoned with agreeable conversation, and it is important that unpleasant topics should be avoided. Mealtime should not be made the occasion to discuss troubles, trials, and misfortunes, which rouse only gloomy thoughts, impair digestion, and leave one at the close of the meal worried and wearied rather than refreshed and strengthened. Let vexatious questions be banished from the family board. Fill the time with bright, sparkling conversation, but do not talk business or discuss neighborhood gossip. Do not let the food upon the table furnish the theme of conversation; neither praise nor apology are in good taste. Parents who make their food thus an especial topic of conversation are instilling into their children's minds a notion that eating is the best part of life, whereas it is only a means to a higher end, and should be so considered. Of all family gatherings the meals should be the most genial and pleasant, and with a little effort they may be made most profitable to all. It is said of Dr. Franklin that he derived his peculiarly practical turn of mind from his father's table talk.

Let themes of conversation be of general interest, in which all may take a part. If there are children, a pleasant custom for the breakfast hour is to have each in turn relate something new and instructive, that he or she has read or learned in the interval since the breakfast hour of the previous day. This stimulates thought and conversational power, while music, history, adventure, politics, and all the arts and sciences offer ample scope for securing interesting items.

Another excellent plan is the selection of a special topic for conversation for each meal or for the meals of a day or a week, a previous announcement of the topic being made, that all, even the youngest, may have time to prepare something to say of it. The benefits from such social intercourse around the board can hardly be over-estimated; and if thus the mealtime is prolonged, and too much appears to be taken out of the busy day, be sure it will add to their years in the end, by increasing health and happiness.

Table Manners.—Good breeding and true refinement are nowhere more apparent than in manners at table. These do not relate alone to the proper use of knife and fork, napkin and spoon, but to habits of punctuality, neatness, quietness, order, and that kind thoughtfulness and courteous attention which spring from the heart—"in honor preferring one another." The purpose of eating should not be merely the appeasement of hunger or the gratification of the palate, but the acquiring of strength for labor or study, that we may be better fitted for usefulness in the world. Consequently, we should eat like responsible beings, and not like the lower orders of animals.

Good table manners cannot be put on for special occasions and laid aside like a garment. Persons not wont to observe the rules of politeness in the every-day life of their own households can never deceive others into thinking them well bred on "company" occasions. Ease and refinement of manners are only acquired by habitual practice, and parents should early accustom their children by both precept and example to observe the requirements of good behavior and politeness at table. Elaborate details are not necessary. We subjoin a few of the more simple rules governing table etiquette:—

1. Eat slowly, never filling the mouth very full and avoiding all appearance of greediness.

2. Masticate thoroughly, keeping the lips closed. Eating and drinking should be noiseless.

3. Never speak with the mouth full, nor interrupt another when talking. Any remark worthy of utterance will keep.

4. Do not express a choice for any particular portion or dish, unless requested to do so; and do not find fault with the food. If by chance anything unpleasant is found in it, do not call the attention of others to the fact by either remark or manner.

5. Sit conveniently near the table, but not crowded up close against it; and keep the hands, when not in use to convey food to the mouth, in the lap, beneath the table, never resting upon the table, toying with knife, fork, or spoon.

6. Do not tilt back your chair, or lean upon the table with the elbow, or drum with the fingers.

7. It is contrary to good breeding to shovel one's food into the mouth with a knife. Everything which can be eaten with a fork should be taken with that utensil alone. If necessary, use the knife for dividing the food, and afterward the fork to convey it to the mouth. Use a spoon for soups and juicy foods.

8. Bread should be broken, not cut. In eating large fruits, like apples or pears, divide with a knife, and take in small portions, holding the knife by the handle rather than the blade.

9. Soup is eaten from the side of the spoon, which is filled without noisily touching the plate.

10. Seeds or stones to be rejected should be taken from the lips with a spoon, never with the fingers. The mouth should not go to the food, but the food to the mouth.

11. Do not crumble food about your plate, nor in any avoidable way soil the table linen.

12. Do not hang the napkin about the neck like a bib, but unfold and lay across the lap in such a manner that it will not slide to the floor. Carefully wipe the mouth before speaking, and as often at other times as may keep the lips perfectly clean of food and drink. At the close of a meal, if at home, fold the napkin neatly and place it in the ring. If at a hotel or away from home, leave the napkin unfolded by your plate.

13. Do not appear impatient to be served, and ordinarily at the home meals wait until all are served before commencing to eat. At a public table where waiters are provided, it is proper to begin eating as soon as the food is served. This is admissible because the wants of other guests are supposed to be similarly looked after.

14. Never reach across a neighbor's plate for anything. If something beyond him is needed, ask to have it passed to you.

15. Do not tilt your plate or scrape it for the last atom of food.

16. Drink very sparingly, if at all, while eating, and then do not pour the liquid down the throat like water turned from a pitcher.

17. Children should not be allowed to use their fingers to aid themselves in eating. If their hands are too small or too awkward to use a fork, a piece of bread or cracker may be held in the left hand to aid in pushing the food upon the fork or spoon.

18. To help one's self to butter or any other food from a common dish with one's own knife or spoon is a gross breach of table etiquette.

19. Never use the handkerchief unnecessarily at the table, and do not cough or sneeze if avoidable.

20. It is not considered proper to pick the teeth at table. If this becomes absolutely necessary, a napkin should be held before the mouth.

21. When a meal or course is finished, lay the knife and fork side by side upon the plate.

22. Except at a hotel or boarding house, it is not proper to leave the table before the rest of the family or guests, without asking the hostess to excuse you.

23. If a guest declines a dish, he need give no reason. "No, I thank you," is quite sufficient. The host or hostess should not insist upon guests' partaking of particular dishes, nor put anything upon their plates which they have declined.

The Table.—None will deny that the appearance of the table affects one's enjoyment of the food upon it. A well-appointed table with its cloth, though coarse in texture, perfectly clean and neatly laid, its glass and china bright and shining, and the silver showing by its glistening surface evidence of frequent polishings, gives far more comfort and enjoyment than one where little attention is given to neatness, order, or taste. In many families, effort is made to secure all these important accessories when guests have been invited; but for common use, anything is considered "good enough for just one's own folks." This ought not to be, and mothers who permit such a course, need not be surprised if their children exhibit a lack of self-respect and genuineness as well as awkwardness and neglect of manners.

The table around which the family meals are taken, ought to be at all times the model of what it should be when surrounded by guests. As a writer has well said, "There is no silent educator in the household that has higher rank than the table. Surrounded each day by the family who are eager for refreshment of body and spirit, its impressions sink deep; and its influences for good or ill form no mean part of the warp and woof of our lives. Its fresh damask, bright silver, glass, and china, give beautiful lessons in neatness, order, and taste; its damask soiled, rumpled, and torn, its silver dingy, its glass cloudy, and china nicked, annoy and vex us at first, and then instill their lessons of carelessness and disorder. An attractive, well-ordered table is an incentive to good manners, and being a place where one is incited to linger, it tends to control the bad habits of fast eating; while, on the contrary, an uninviting, disorderly table gives license to bad manners, and encourages the haste which is proverbial among Americans. The woman, then, who looks after her table in these particulars, is not doing trivial work, for it rests with her to give silently these good or bad lessons in manners and morals to her household as they surround the daily board."

A well-appointed table requires very little time and labor. No pretense or ostentation is necessary; neatness and simplicity are far more pleasing.

Setting the Table.—Lay a piece of double-faced canton flannel underneath the tablecloth. Even coarse napery will present a much better appearance with a sub-cover than if spread directly upon the table. It will likewise lessen noise in changing courses and the likelihood of injury to the table from hot dishes. Spread the tablecloth evenly, without wrinkles, and so that the center fold shall be exactly in the middle, parallel with the sides of the table. Mats, if used, should be placed exactly straight and with regularity. If meat is served, spread a large napkin with points toward the center of the table at the carver's place, to protect the tablecloth. Place the plates upon the table, right side up, at even distances from each other and straight with the cloth and the edge of the table. Lay the napkins directly in front or at the right of each plate. Place the fork at the left, the knife on the right with the edge toward the plate, beyond this the soup spoon and two teaspoons, and at the front of these set the glass, cream glass, and individual butter plate if these are used.

A center piece consisting of a vase of freshly cut flowers, a pot of ferns, a jar of small plants in bloom, a dish of well-polished red apples, peaches, or other seasonable fruit, will add a touch of beauty and attractiveness. If the serving is to be done from the table by members of the family, place large spoons near dishes to be served, also the proper number and kind of separate dishes for the purpose. If fruit is to be served, a finger bowl should be placed for each person. If the service is by course, the extra dishes, knives, forks, and spoons needed, also the finger bowls, water service, and cold foods in reserve for a renewed supply or for other courses, should be made ready and arranged upon the sideboard.

The soup ladle should be placed in front of the lady of the house, who always serves the soup; and if meat is served, the carving knife and fork must, of course, be placed before the carver's place. The necessary dishes for each course should be brought on with the food, those for the first course being placed upon the table just a moment before dinner is announced.

The arrangement of all dishes and foods upon the table should be uniform, regular, and tasteful, so as to give an orderly appearance to the whole. The "dishing up" and arranging of the food are matters of no small importance, as a dull appetite will often be sharpened at the sight of a daintily arranged dish, while the keenest one may have its edge dulled by the appearance of a shapeless mass piled up with no regard to looks. Even the simplest food is capable of looking its best, and the greatest care should be taken to have all dishes served neatly and tastefully.

The table should not be set for breakfast the night before nor kept so from one meal to another, unless carefully covered with a cloth thick enough to prevent the dust from accumulating upon the dishes. The plates and glasses should then be placed bottom-side up and turned just before mealtime. No food of any kind should ever be allowed to remain uncovered upon the table from one meal to another. The cloth for covering the table should be carefully shaken each time before using, and always used the same side up until washed.

Plates and individual meat dishes should be warmed, especially in winter; but the greatest care should be taken that no dish becomes hot, as that not only makes it troublesome to handle, but is ruinous to the dishes.

The Service of Meals.—There are few invariable rules for either table-setting or service. We will offer a few suggestions upon this point, though doubtless other ways are equally good. A capital idea for the ordinary home meal, when no servant is kept, especially if in the family there are older children, is to make different members of the family responsible for the proper service of some dish or course. The fruit, which should be the first course at breakfast, may be prepared and placed upon fruit plates with the proper utensils for eating—napkins and finger bowls at each place before the meal is announced. If apples or bananas are served, a cracker should be placed upon each plate to be eaten in connection with the fruit. Oranges and grapes are, however, to be preferred when obtainable; the former may be prepared as directed on page 180. The hot foods may be dished, and the dishes placed on a side table in a *bain marie*, the hot water in which should be as deep as the food within the dishes. The foods will thus be in readiness, and will keep much better than if placed upon the table at the beginning of the meal. When the fruit is eaten, some member of the family may remove the fruit plates, and bring the hot grains, toasts, and other foods, placing them, together with the necessary individual dishes, before those who have their serving in charge. One member may be selected to pass the bread, another to dish the sauce, etc.; and thus each child, whether boy or girl—even those quite young—may contribute to the service, and none be overburdened, while at the same time it will be a means of teaching a due regard for the comfort and enjoyment of others.

If the meal is dinner, usually consisting of three courses, after the soup has been eaten, it may be the duty of some member of the family to remove the soup plates and place the vegetables, grains, and meats if any are to served, before those chosen to serve them. At the close of this course, another may remove the dishes and food, crumb the cloth, and place the dessert, with the proper dishes for serving, before the lady of the house or her oldest daughter, one of whom usually serves it.

If a servant is employed, the following is an excellent plan of service: The soup plates or bowls should be placed hot upon the table, with the tureen of soup before the lady of the house, and the glasses filled before the dinner is announced.

Grace having been said, the servant removes the cover of the soup tureen, and standing at the left of the lady, takes up with her left hand a soup plate, which she changes to the palm of her right hand and holds at the edge of the soup tureen until the lady has filled it, then carries it, still holding it upon the palm of the hand, and places it before the head of the table. In the same manner all are served to soup. If bowls instead of plates are used, a small silver or lacquered tray may be used on which to carry the bowl. While the soup is being eaten, the servant goes to the kitchen and brings in the hot dishes and foods for the next course, and places them upon the side table. When the soup has been finished, beginning with the one who sits at the head of the table, the servant places before each person in turn a hot dinner plate, at the same time removing his soup plate to the sideboard or pantry. After changing all the plates, she removes the soup tureen, and if meat is to be served, places that before the carver with the individual plates, which, when he has placed a portion thereon, she serves to each in turn; then she takes the potato and other vegetables upon her tray, and serves them, going to the left of each person when passing them a dish, but placing individual dishes at the right; next she passes the bread, refills the glasses, taking each one separately to the sideboard, and then serves the grains.

When every one has finished the course, she begins the clearing of the table by first removing all large dishes of food; after that the plates and all soiled dishes, mats, and all table furniture except the glasses, napkin rings, and center-pieces.

Lastly she removes all crumbs with a brush or napkin. When done, she places in front of each person a plate with a doily and finger bowl upon it, and then brings the dessert and dessert dishes, placing them before the lady of the house, and passes these for her as in the other courses. If the dessert is pudding, a spoon or fork should be placed on the plate at one side of the finger bowl. If the dessert is fruit, a fruit napkin may be used in place of the doily, the real purpose of which is to prevent the bowl from sliding about the plate in moving it. A fork and silver knife, or knife and spoon as the fruit may require, should be served with it.

General Suggestions for Waiters.—In serving a dish from which people are expected to help themselves, always go to the left side.

Soup, food in individual dishes, clean plates, and finger bowls should be set down before people at their right hand.

When removing soiled dishes after a course, always exchange them for clean ones, remembering that the only time when it is allowable to leave the table without plates is when it is being cleared for the dessert.

In serving grains either dish them in small dishes before serving or pass clean saucers at the same time for each to help himself, and in all cases see that each person is served to cream, sugar, and a teaspoon, with grains.

Pass the bread two or three times during each meal, and keep careful watch that all are well supplied.

Pour hot milk and all beverages on the side table; fill only three fourths full, and serve the same as anything else in individual dishes, placing the glass at each person's right hand.

Waiters should be noiseless and prompt, and neatly attired in dress suitable to their occupation.

Suggestions Concerning Dinner Parties.—Much of the success of a dinner party depends upon the guests selected; and the first point for consideration by the lady who decides upon entertaining her friends thus, should be the congeniality of those whom she desires to invite, remembering that after the first greetings the guests see very little of their hostess, and consequently their enjoyment must largely depend upon each other. It is customary to issue invitations in the name of the host and hostess, from five to ten days in advance of the occasion. Printed or written invitations may be used. The following is a proper form:—

Mr. and Mrs. George Brown
request the pleasure
of
Mr. and Mrs. Henry Clark's company
at dinner
December 5th, at four o'clock.
24 Maple Avenue.

If the dinner is given in especial honor to some stranger, a second card is inclosed on which is written:—

To meet

Mrs. Harold Brooks of Philadelphia.

Invitations to a dinner should be promptly accepted or declined, and if accepted, the engagement should on no account be lightly broken.

Unless one has a large establishment, and is very sure of good service, the bill of fare selected should not be an elaborate one, and the choice of dishes should be confined to those which one is used to preparing, and which in cost will not exceed one's means. It is the quality of the dinner which pleases, and not the multiplicity of dishes. Small dinners for not less than six or more than ten guests are always the most pleasant, and for those of moderate means or those unaccustomed to dinner-giving are by far the most suitable.

The arrangement and adornment of the table afford an opportunity for the display of much artistic taste and skill. An expensive outlay is by no means necessary, as highly pleasing effects may be produced by the addition of a few choice, well-arranged flowers or blossoming plants to a table already well laid with spotless linen, bright silver, and clean glass and china ware. A profusion of ornament should be avoided, large pieces of plate, and high, elaborate designs of flowers or fruit should not be used, as they obstruct the intercourse of the guests.

A center piece of flowers, with a small bouquet tied with ribbon for each guest, is quite sufficient. Low dishes filled with violets or pansies; a basket filled with oranges, mingled with orange leaves and blossoms; bowls of ferns and roses; a block of ice wreathed in ferns, with an outer circle of water lilies; dishes of vari-colored grapes resting amid the bright leaves of the foliage plant, are some of many pleasing designs which may be employed for the adornment of the dinner table. The amount of space occupied with decorations must depend upon the style of service employed. If no calculation need be made for placing the different dishes composing the dinner, a strip of colored plush or satin bordered with ivy, smilax, or some trailing vine, is quite frequently used for the decoration of a long table.

A very pleasing custom consists in selecting some especial color for the decorations with which the table napery, dishes, and even the food to be served shall accord; as, for example, a "pink" dinner, with roses as the chief flower, strawberries, pink lemonade, and other pink attractions; or a "yellow" luncheon, served on napery etched with yellow, with vases of goldenrod for center pieces, and dainty bouquets of the same tied with yellow ribbon at each plate, while yellow tapers in golden candlesticks cast a mellow light over all, during the serving of a bill of fare which might include peaches and cream, oranges, pumpkin pie, and other yellow comestibles.

The menu cards afford much opportunity for adding attractiveness to a company dinner. If one possesses artistic skill, a floral decoration or a tiny sketch, with an appropriate quotation, the guest's name, and date of the dinner, make of the cards very pleasing souvenirs. A proper quotation put after each dish is much in vogue as a means of promoting conversation. The quotations are best selected from one author.

There are no absolute rules for the service of company dinners, much depending upon social conditions and established customs. Two modes are in general use,—placing the dishes upon the table to be dished by the host and hostess, and placing all food upon the side table to be dished and served by a waiter. When the latter method is used, it is quite customary to place the plates of soup upon the table before dinner is announced. As many knives, forks, and spoons as will be needed for the courses may be placed beside each plate, or they may be brought in with the course, as preferred. Clean plates are necessary for every course. The manner of serving is essentially like that already described.

Care should be taken to have the dining room at an agreeable temperature, neither too warm nor too cold.

At large dinner parties, each gentleman, as he enters, receives a card upon which is written the name of the lady he is to take in to dinner, to whom the hostess at once presents him. When dinner is announced, the host leads the way with the oldest or most distinguished lady or the one to whom the dinner is given, while the hostess follows last, with the most honored gentleman. The host places the lady whom he escorts on his right. If the number is small, the host indicates the places the guests should occupy as they enter the room; if the party is large, the menu card at each plate bears the name of the guest for whom it is designed. The lady escorted by the host should be the first one served.

Soup is always taken and tasted, whether liked or not; after the first course, it is proper to accept or refuse a dish, as preferred.

No well-bred hostess ever apologizes for the food upon her table or urges anything upon her guests when once declined. No orders should be given to servants during the meal; everything that will contribute to the proper serving of the dinner should be arranged beforehand, and all necessary instructions given.

At the close of the dinner, the hostess gives the sign for retiring.

TABLE TOPICS.

A meal—what is it? Just enough of food
To renovate and well refresh the frame,
So that with spirits lightened, and with strength renewed,
We turn with willingness to work again.—*Sel.*

Do not bring disagreeable things to the table in your conversation any more than you would in your dishes.—*Sel.*

Courtesy in the mistress of the house consists in feeding conversation; never in usurping it. —*Mme. Swetchine*

Good humor and good health follow a good meal; and by a good meal we mean anything, however simple, well dressed in its way.—*Smiles.*

Unquiet meals make ill digestion.—*Shakespeare.*

Eat slowly and do not season your food with care.—*Sel.*

To rise from the table *able* to eat a little more is a proverbially good rule for every one. There is nothing more idiotic than forcing down a few mouthfuls, because they happen to remain on one's plate after hunger is satisfied, and because they may be "wasted" if left. It is the most serious waste to overtax the stomach with even half an ounce more than it can take care of.—*Sel.*

I pray you, O excellent wife! cumber not yourself and me to get a curiously rich dinner for this man and woman who have just alighted at our gate.... These things, if they are desirous of them, they can get for a few shillings at any village inn; but rather let that stranger see, if he will, in your looks, accents, and behavior, your heart and earnestness, your thought and will, that which he cannot buy at any price in any city, and which he may travel miles and dine sparely and sleep hardly to behold.—*Emerson.*

AFTER MEAL TIME

To no other department of domestic work perhaps is so little thought given or so little science applied as to the routine work of clearing the table and washing the dishes after mealtime. Any way to accomplish the object, seems to be the motto in very many households. But even for these prosaic tasks there is a best way, which, if employed, may make of an otherwise irksome service a really pleasurable one.

Clearing the Table.—First of all, put back the chairs, and brush up the crumbs from the floor, then collect all untouched foods and store them away in clean dishes; next gather the silver, place it handles upward in pitchers or other deep dishes, and pour hot water over it. For gathering the silver a compartment tray in which knives, forks, and spoons may be placed separately is important. Many of the scratches and marks on their silver ware, which housekeepers deplore, come from the careless handling together of forks, knives, and spoons. Now in a deep basin upon a tray, collect all the refuse and partly eaten foods, carefully emptying cups, glasses, finger bowls, etc., and scraping all dishes which contained food as clean as possible; for no crumbs or particles of food should be introduced into the dishwater. Pile the dishes as fast as cleaned upon a second tray in readiness for washing. It saves much liability of breakage in transferring from the dining room to the kitchen, if each kind of soiled dishes is packed by itself.

Wipe carefully, if not needing to be washed, and replenish all salts, granola cups, and sugar bowls before putting away. Gather the soiled napkins for the laundry, and put those clean enough to be used again in their proper places. Especial care must be taken, however, so to designate those reserved for future use that each shall receive the same again, as nothing is more disgusting to a sensitive person than to be tendered a napkin which has been used by some one else. Some form of napkin holder should be considered an essential part of the table furnishing. If rings cannotbe afforded, ordinary clothes pins, gilded and decorated with a bit of ribbon, make very pretty substitutes.

Brush the tablecloth, fold in its creases, also the sub-cover of canton flannel, and lay both away until again needed.

Washing the Dishes.—Plenty of hot water and clean towels are the essential requisites for expeditious and thorough dish-washing. A few drops of crude ammonia added to the water will soften it and add to the luster of the silver and china. Soap may be used or not according to circumstances; all greasy dishes require a good strong suds. There should also be provided two dish drainers or trays, unless there is a stationary sink with tray on which to drain the dishes. For washing glassware and fine china, *papier-maché* tubs are preferable to anything else, as they are less liable to occasion breakage of the ware. If many dishes are to be washed, frequent changes of water will be necessary as the first becomes either cold or dirty. Perfectly sweet, clean dishes are not evolved from dirty dishwater. The usual order given for the washing of dishes is, glasses, silver, fine china, cups, saucers, pitchers, plates and other dishes. This is, however, based upon the supposition that cups and saucers are used for beverages, and plates are soiled by the use of various greasy foods; but in families where tea and coffee and animal foods are dispensed with, and saucers are used for grains with cream dressing, the plates are often cleaner than the saucers and should be washed first.

The general rule to be followed is always to wash the dishes least soiled first, and all of one kind together. The latter item is specially important, since much of the nicking of dishes and breaking of handles from cups, covers, and pitchers is the result of piling dishes promiscuously together while washing.

It is quite as easy to finish washing one kind before beginning on another as to do it in any less safe and systematic way, and if wiped in the same order, it does away with the need of sorting when putting the dishes away.

If for any reason the dishes must wait for a time before being washed, the best plan is to pack them carefully into large pans, cover with warm water, and let them soak. When ready to wash them, prepare hot suds and clear water for rinsing in additional pans. Do not use too hot water, as a high temperature will break glass and "check" the enamel of ordinary ware. The law of expansion holds good with both china and glassware, and all glass and glazed wares should be dipped into hot water in such a manner that all its surfaces may receive the heat and expand together.

All dishes used for milk should be first thoroughly rinsed in cold water before being washed in hot water or suds.

Be sure that the inside of all cups and pitchers is thoroughly clean. It is a good plan to have a mop made by fastening finger-lengths of coarse cotton twin to a suitable handle, for washing the inside of pitchers.

In cleaning forks, spoons, or cups, which have been employed in beating or eating eggs, rinse them in cold water before putting them into hot suds, as hot water cooks the egg and causes it to adhere. Common table salt is said to be excellent for removing the egg tarnish from silver. Clean Dover egg beaters by beating a dish of cold water, or by holding under a stream of cold water from the faucet, then carefully rinse and wipe perfectly dry. Do not put the upper part of the beater into hot water, as it will remove the oil from the wheels so that they will not work easily.

Grain-boilers and mush-kettles should be allowed to cool, then filled with cold water and allowed to soak during the meal hour, when they can be easily cleaned.

Tin dishes should be washed with hot suds as soon as possible after using.

Wire Dishcloth

For cleaning; iron pots, use soft water and soap or washing-soda with a wire dishcloth or kettle scraper. If the food adheres to the sides, fill with cold water and soak. Kettles and all dishes placedover a fire should be cleaned on the outside as well as the inside. To remove the soot, rub first with pieces of dry paper and afterward with damp paper; then wash with hot suds and a cloth. Kettles and saucepans burned on the inside may he cleaned by putting a little cold water and ashes in them and allowing them to soak on the range until the water is warm. Porcelain-lined and granite-ware utensils stained from food burning ón, may be cleaned after soaking for a time in a solution of sal-soda, which may be prepared by pouring boiling water over the soda in the proportion of two pints of water to one pound ofsal-soda, and stirring until dissolved. It may be prepared in quantity and stored in a stone jar until needed.

Wash wooden ware and bread boards with cold water and sand soap. In scraping dough from the bread board, always scrape with the grain of the wood and be careful not to roughen the surface.

Steel knives and forks with ivory or wooden handles should not be put into dishwater. Hot water will expand the steel and cause the handles to crack. Wash them thoroughly with the dishcloth, scour with bath brick, and wipe dry.

All tin and iron dishes should be thoroughly dried before putting away, to prevent rusting.

If draining is considered preferable to wiping dishes, a good plan, if one has not a patent dish drainer, is to fold an old tablecloth in several thicknesses and spread upon the table. Wash the dishes carefully and rinse in hot water. Place a cup or bowl bottom upward, lay a plate on each side, then one between and above them, with two more on the outside, and so on, not permitting them to touch more than necessary.

Dishcloths and Towels.—No dishes or utensils can be well cared for without good, clean dishcloths and towels, and plenty of them. An excellent dishcloth may be either knit or crocheted in some solid stitch of coarse cotton yarn. Ten or twelve inches square is a good size. Several thicknesses of cheese-cloth basted together make good dishcloths, as do also pieces of old knitted garments and Turkish toweling. If a dish mop is preferred, it may be made as follows: Cut a groove an inch from the end of a stick about a foot in length and of suitable shape for a handle; cut a ball of coarse twine, into nine-inch lengths, and lay around the stick with the middle of the strands against the groove; wind a fine wire or cord around the twine to fasten it in the groove; then shake down the twine, so it will lie all one way like a mop, and fasten it to the handle by tying a second cord around it on the outside.

Towels for drying dishes should be of three different grades,—fine ones without lint for glass, silver, and fine china; coarser ones for the ordinary table ware, and still another quality for pans, kettles, and other kitchen ware. The right size is a yard in length and half as wide, with the ends hemmed. As to material, fine checked linen is usually employed for glass and silver towels, and crash for ordinary dishes, for iron and tinware towels which have become somewhat worn, or a coarse bag opened and hemmed, may be used. Old, half-worn tablecloths may be cut into excellent dish towels.

It is of the greatest importance that all dishcloths, mops, and towels be kept perfectly sweet and clean. Greasy dishcloths and sour towels are neither neat nor wholesome and are a most fertile source of germs, often breeding disease and death. After each dish washing, the dishcloth, towels, and mops should be thoroughly washed in hot water with plenty of soap, well rinsed and hung up to dry either upon a line out of doors or a rack made for the purpose near the kitchen range. If care is always taken to clean the dishes as much as possible before washing and to change the suds as often as they become dirty, the towels will not be hard to keep clean and sweet-smelling. Those used during the week should go into the wash as regularly as other household articles. Dish towels are also much better for being ironed. It gives them a "surface" which facilitates the drying operation.

The Care of Silver, Glass, Etc.—If silver is well washed in hot water containing a few drops of ammonia, and carefully dried with a fine, soft towel, it will keep bright for a long time without other cleaning. If special cleaning is necessary, try the following: Place the silver in a pan of hot water, then with a soft cloth, soaped and sprinkled with powdered borax, scour the silver well; afterward rinse in clear cold water, and dry with a clean cloth. If a more thorough cleaning is needed, apply moistened Spanish whiting with a silver brush and soft flannel, afterward polishing with dry whiting and chamois skin. Frequent scouring should be avoided by careful washing, as too much rubbing wears out plated ware and dulls the best of silver. Silver ware and plate which is not in ordinary use can be kept from tarnishing by varnishing with collodion, a solution of gun-cotton in ether. The articles should be carefully brushed in this colorless varnish with an elastic brush, taking care that the entire surface is covered. The film of collodion will protect the underlying metal from the action of the sulphurous vapors to which is due the blackening of silver.

Tinware which has become blackened may be made to look bright and shining again by rubbing with a damp cloth dipped in sal-soda. Afterward wipe dry. Sand soap or sapolio may be used for the same purpose.

Cut-glass ware which has become in any way blurred or tarnished can be restored by polishing it with a soft piece of newspaper. First rub well with a piece slightly moistened and afterward repeat the process with dry paper. Rubbing with a soft brush dipped in fine, soft whiting is another method often employed for the same purpose. Cut-glass water-bottles dim or stained on the inside are best cleaned by rinsing with dilute muriatic acid, then carefully rinsing several times in clear cold water to remove all trace of the acid, which is a poison.

All fine china should be handled carefully in washing and drying. There will be less danger of breakage if the china is gradually heated by allowing it to stand in a pan of warm water before being put into hot water. The same is true of all table ware, and is of especial importance in cold weather.

Brass faucets and other brass or copper articles may be cleaned by rubbing with whiting wet with aqua ammonia.

Yellowed ivory handles may be restored to their original whiteness by rubbing with sandpaper and emery; mineral soap or pumice stone may be used for the same purpose. Nice table cutlery packed away for a season may be kept from rusting by covering the metal portion with a thin coating of paraffine. Rust may be removed from steel by scouring with emery and oil; but if there is much corrosion, some weak muriatic acid will be needed. This, however, will take some of the metal with the rust, and must be washed off quickly.

Trays and japanned goods should never have boiling water poured over them, as it will make the varnish crack and peel. If a tray is badly soiled, wet with a sponge moistened in warm water and soap, and rub with a dry cloth; if it looks smeary, dust on a little flour and rub again. Marks and scratches may sometimes be removed by rubbing with a flannel cloth dipped in sweet oil.

Care of the Table Linen.—Much of the attractiveness of the table depends upon the linen used; if this is not well cared for, the finest table ware cannot make up for the defect.

Stains upon table linen made by acids and vinegar may be removed by simply washing in clear water; berry stains are easily taken out by pouring boiling water over them; peach stains are best removed by soaking for some time in cold water and then washing with soap before allowing warm water to touch them. Chlorine water or a solution of chloride of lime will remove fruit stains, and vegetable colors. Coffee stains rubbed with a mixture of warm water and the yolk of egg, are said to disappear when the mixture is washed off with clean warm water. Sour buttermilk well rubbed into the material, dried in, and afterward washed out in several waters, is said to be effectual in removing tea stains. All stains should be removed as soon as possible after being made, and always before putting the linen into the wash.

In washing table linen, housekeepers should remember that hard rubbing is the worst wear which it can receive. If soaked over night, a gentle squeezing will usually be quite sufficient to remove all soil, or if a little borax (a handful to ten gallons of water) or household ammonia in the proportion of two tablespoonfuls to a pail of water be added, two or three hours' soaking will suffice. Care should also be taken in hanging and fastening properly upon the line. Fold the cloth over the line six or eight inches at least, and in such a manner as to keep the thread straight, and fasten with three or more clothes pins. Table linen is often sadly frayed at the corners by being pinned so that all strain comes upon the corners, and if left to whip in the wind, is soon ruined. Napkins in summer are much nicer if dried upon the grass. Only the merest trifle of starch, if any, should be used for table linen.

Table linen should be taken from the line while still damp, folded evenly lengthwise with the selvage together, then folded lengthwise again, rolled tight, and wrapped in damp towels so that the outside will not become dry, and ironed the same day. The irons should be heavy and as hot as possible without danger of scorching, and the board should be well padded with several thicknesses of flannel. Iron the linen in single folds, keeping a damp cloth over portions which will not be immediately reached. When the entire surface has been ironed, fold evenly lengthwise and with the selvage edges toward the ironer, again go over the entire upper side; then fold with the just completed portion inside, iron again, and so continue until the whole is ironed and folded. Both napkins and tablecloths are ironed in this way. They should be thoroughly dried with the iron and well aired before being laid away, in order to bring out the patterns well and to give them the desirable glossy finish.

Colored table linen should be washed in tepid water containing a little powdered borax, which serves to set the color.

Very little, if any, soap should be used. Rinse in tepid water containing a small quantity of boiled starch; dry in the shade, and iron while yet damp.

Table linen should be carefully darned at once when it begins to wear and become thin, and may thus be preserved for a long time. When new, it should be washed before being made up, and the threads raveled or drawn, so as to make the ends exactly straight. Napkins should be washed before being cut apart. When not required for regular use, the linen should be folded loosely, and laid away without ironing in some place where it will not be subjected to pressure. When needed, it can be quickly dampened and ironed.

The Garbage.—What to do with the waste accumulating from preparation of foods is a question of no small importance. The too frequent disposition of such material is to dump it into a waste-barrel or garbage box near the back door, to await the rounds of the scavenger. Unless more than ordinary precautions in regard to cleanliness are observed, such a proceeding is fraught with great danger. The bits of moist food, scraps of meat, vegetables, and other refuse, very quickly set up a fermentative process, which, under the sun's rays, soon breeds miasm and germs; especially is this true if the receptacle into which the garbage is thrown is not carefully cleaned after each emptying.

A foul-smelling waste-barrel ought never to be permitted under any circumstances. The best plan is to burn all leavings and table refuse as fast as made, which may be done without smell or smoke by opening all the back drafts of the kitchen range, and placing them on the hot coals to dry and burn. Some housekeepers keep in one end of the sink a wire dish drainer into which all fruit and vegetable parings are put. If wet, the water quickly drains from them, and they are ready to be put into the stove, where a very little fire soon reduces them to ashes. All waste products which cannot well be burned, may be buried at a distance from the house, but not too much in one spot, and the earth should be carefully covered over afterward. Under no circumstances should it be scattered about on the surface of the ground near the back door, as heedless people are apt to do.

If the table refuse must be saved and fed to animals, it should be carefully sorted, kept free from all dishwater, sour milk, etc., and used as promptly as possible. It is a good plan to have two tightly covered waste pails of heavy tin to be used on alternate days. When one is emptied, it may be thoroughly cleansed and left to purify in the air and sunshine while the other is in use. Any receptacle for waste should be entirely emptied and thoroughly disinfected each day with boiling suds and an old broom. This is especially imperative if the refuse is to be used as food for cows, since the quality of the milk is more or less affected by that of the food.

CPSIA information can be obtained
at www.ICGtesting.com
Printed in the USA
LVHW061947191222
735554LV00011B/394

9 781805 470847